W9-AJT-206

The Complete Guide
to
GARDEN FLOWERS

An Encyclopedia of Garden Planning

Board of Advisory Editors

The
COMPLETE GUIDE
to
GARDEN FLOWERS

An Encyclopedia of Garden Planning

EDITED BY
HERBERT ASKWITH

ASSISTED BY
CATHERINE E. MEIKLE

And an Advisory Board of
Six Eminent Horticulturists
(See List on Opposite Page)

A. S. BARNES AND CO.
New York

Library of Congress Catalog Card Number: 61–13912

A. S. BARNES AND CO., INC.
11 East 36th Street
New York 16, N. Y.

THOMAS YOSELOFF, LTD.
123 New Bond Street
London W. 1, England

PRINTED IN THE UNITED STATES OF AMERICA

Typography and Illustrations by

J. HORACE MCFARLAND COMPANY
Mount Pleasant Press
Harrisburg, Pa.

How to Use This Book

1. Look up the flower (or plant, shrub, ornamental tree) that interests you, under its *popular* name, in its proper alphabetical place. If not there, look in the INDEX (pages 13–16).

2. If the botanical or Latin name is more familiar to you, look first in the INDEX.

3. In addition to the detailed description of each flower, etc., there are 24 general articles scattered through the book—in their alphabetical place, according to the first word of the subject title—dealing with every essential phase of garden planning and development. A list of these articles appears in the CONTENTS (page 9). Together these articles comprise a helpful guide to success in your gardening efforts. Sooner or later you should read them all.

4. A special effort is made in this book to avoid using horticultural or botanical terms that may not be immediately understood by beginning gardeners. A few such words, however, are practically unavoidable—and you are urged, therefore, to read through the brief GLOSSARY (page 8), so you will be familiar with the exact meaning of these terms when you come across them.

5. When botanical or Latin names are mentioned, especially under "Varieties," the object is to help you understand these names when you find them in flower catalogs, and make it easier for you to order and obtain the exact variety you want.

6. Check the maps on pages 10 and 11, to find out when the last frost is likely to occur in the spring in your area—and when the first frost is to be expected in the fall. With this knowledge to guide you, you will be able to "play safe" in choosing the proper time to plant, in accord with the instructions given in this book.

7. Sooner or later you are likely to be "bitten by the bug" of a specialty. You will develop a keen interest in some particular flowers—roses, peonies, iris, camellias, or what have you. The list of garden books "For Further Reading" on page 12 will help you to satisfy your hunger for more knowledge about these flowers, and thus add a very satisfying hobby to your pleasures.

ACKNOWLEDGMENTS

The courtesy of the following firms in making possible the use of many of the plates in this book is gratefully acknowledged.

Armstrong Nurseries, Ontario, Calif.
Bobbink Nurseries, Inc., East Rutherford, N. J.
Bodger Seeds, Ltd., El Monte, Calif.
F. W. Bolgiano & Co., Inc., Washington, D. C.
Bongarzone Nursery, Inc., New Shrewsbury, N. J.
The Bosley Nurseries, Inc., Mentor, Ohio
Bristol Nurseries, Bristol, Conn.
Burnett Bros., Inc., New York, N. Y.
W. Atlee Burpee Co., Philadelphia, Pa.
Carroll Gardens, Westminster, Md.
Colonial Nursery, Inc., Harrisburg, Pa.
Commercial Nursery Co., Decherd, Tenn.
The Conard-Pyle Co., West Grove, Pa.
DeKalb Nurseries, Inc., Norristown, Pa.
The Denholm Seed Co., Los Angeles, Calif.
Farr Nursery Co., Womelsdorf, Pa.
Ferry-Morse Seed Co., Mountain View, Calif.
James I. George & Son, Fairport, N. Y.
Germain's, Inc., Los Angeles, Calif.
H. G. German, Smethport, Pa.
Glen Saint Mary Nurseries Co., Glen Saint Mary, Fla.
Greenbrier Farms, Inc., Norfolk, Va.
Green Valley Nursery, Inc., Hawthorne, N. Y.
Gulf Stream Nursery, Inc., Wachapreague, Va.
H. G. Hastings Co., Atlanta, Ga.
Holmes Nurseries, Tampa, Fla.
Howard & Smith, Montebello, Calif.
Jackson & Perkins Co., Newark, N. Y.
The Lehman Gardens, Faribault, Minn.
McArdle's Seed Co., Greenwich, Conn.
The Meyer Seed Co., Baltimore, Md.
Oregon Bulb Farms, Gresham, Ore.
Pan-American Seeds, Inc., Paonia, Colo.
Paramount Rose Co., West Grove, Pa.
Peterson & Dering, Scappoose, Ore.
Pitzonka's Pansy Farm and Nursery, Bristol, Pa.
Reuter Seed Co., Inc., New Orleans, La.
Julius Roehrs Co., Rutherford, N. J.
Rosedale Nurseries, Inc., Hawthorne, N. Y.
Russell Gardens, Spring, Tex.
Walter S. Schell, Inc., Harrisburg, Pa.
Max Schling Seedsmen, Inc., New York, N. Y.
Semmes Nurseries, Semmes, Ala.
The Siebenthaler Co., Dayton, Ohio
Stark Bro's Nurseries, Louisiana, Mo.
Stassen Floral Gardens, Inc., Roslyn Heights, N. Y.
C. W. Stuart & Co., Newark, N. Y.
Geo. Tait & Sons, Inc., Norfolk, Va.
Thomasville Nurseries, Inc., Thomasville, Ga.
Tinari Greenhouses, Bethayres, Pa.
Waller Flowerseed Co., Guadalupe, Calif.
Wayside Gardens, Mentor, Ohio
Weeks Wholesale Rose Grower, Ontario, Calif.
Wight Nurseries, Cairo, Ga.
Winter Garden Ornamental Nursery, Inc., Winter Garden, Fla.
Melvin E. Wyant, Mentor, Ohio

FOREWORD

Garden books in opulent variety, on virtually every phase of the subject, have poured forth from our presses year after year, and many of them (see, for example, the recommended list on page 12) are richly rewarding. But among them all, no single volume has ever attempted what the present book aims to accomplish:

(1) to set forth in simple English (and in compact, quickly accessible form) what the amateur gardener wants to know about the flowers and plants that are ready to add beauty to his garden—what they are like, where they will look best, when and how to plant them, how much they will cost, how to protect them, how good they are for home decoration; —and

(2) to show in true photographic color what all of these desirable and available flowers and plants will look like when they come to life in his garden.

Many garden books and many nursery catalogs have illustrations in color, but none have ever attempted to show EVERY wanted flower and plant, available to the garden lover, in their true colors. How can you do full justice to a flower by showing it in a black-and-white photograph? The home gardener who strives for beauty and color harmony in his garden should be able to "sample" the exact color of a flower or plant before he makes his choice. This is the first book which has attempted to fill this need. Obviously not every variety can be shown, nor the rarer and more exotic plants which would be unobtainable anyway from the average nurseryman. But all the desirable and wanted flowers and ornamental plants which the larger sources of supply are likely to have, throughout the United States and Canada, are here described and illustrated in full color for the first time within the covers of a single volume. The newer prized and prize-winning varieties of many popular flowers, such as roses, iris, tulips, etc., are given preference in the color illustrations, but the older varieties which have held their own against the newcomers are given full recognition.

For making this accomplishment possible, the editor and publisher—and everyone using this book—owe a debt of gratitude to the J. Horace McFarland Company, which for over half a century has devoted itself to amassing the largest and finest collection of color photographs known to horticultural experts. The cooperation of the McFarland Company in making these plates available, together with the courteous consent of the nurserymen and seedsmen (named on another page) who shared in their production, is gratefully acknowledged.

In furtherance of the first objective stated above—namely, to make this book easy to use, and its information instantly accessible—all of the flowers and plants are described in alphabetical order under their popular or common names—not, as is usually done, under their Latin or botanical names. For the benefit of those advanced gardeners who are more familiar with the latter designations, genus names are all listed in the Index. Many of the specific varieties, of course, are identified only by Latin or other "foreign" or trade names in nursery catalogs, and these are always given, under the "Varieties" heading, to enable the gardener to order the exact kind that will suit his purpose. Throughout the book, however, the horticultural jargon and technical terms that so often confuse the seeker after information in many "garden guides" are rigidly avoided. The few horticultural terms which must be used now and then (and which should really become a part of the vocabulary of every gardener) are explained in the Glossary on page 8.

The special chapters or articles on various gardening topics, listed separately on the Contents page, are intended to provide a complete "course" for the amateur gardener. Aside from their reference value, they might well be read and pondered as a helpful guide to successful garden planning.

The dividends which a successful gardener reaps from his efforts are beyond price. If this book helps in any measure to make these dividends come more easily and with less "trial and error," we will all be sharing the happiness which this must bring. As one turns the pages of this book, one cannot help being overwhelmed by the panoply of color and beauty which Nature has put so generously within our reach. With the magic wand of his own right arm, any garden lover can bring this color and beauty to life in his own garden. And others besides gardeners can profit too. The artist and the designer can draw endless inspiration for their creative art from the breath-taking variety of shape and color and texture displayed in this pageantry of flowers.

While the paramount aim of this book has been to "popularize" the horticultural knowledge distilled in it, there has been no lack of regard for scientific accuracy. Every portion of the text has been checked by one or more of the eminent horticulturists who have so generously served as our Board of Advisory Editors (see page 2). For their patient and gracious assistance, and their many highly valued suggestions from which the book has benefited, our warmest appreciation is extended.

It is difficult to express adequately the indebtedness that I feel toward my collaborator and editorial assistant, Catherine E. Meikle, for the untiring labors and expert knowledge she has given to this project. Its accomplishment has been made easier and pleasanter by her devotion to the task. To other members also of the J. Horace McFarland Company staff, and especially to P. M. Parthemore, I am grateful for intelligent and unfailing teamwork in bringing this book to completion.

HERBERT ASKWITH

Larchmont, New York

GLOSSARY of Horticultural Terms

accent plant. One that contrasts with its surroundings in shape, color, height or some other characteristic.

acid soil. Having little or no lime available.

alkaline soil. Having available lime.

All-America Selections. Winners of this award are new varieties that have been tested all over the United States and judged by experts to be superior.

annual. A plant that lives only one season. See also page 24.

anther. The tip of the flower stamen (which see), which bears the pollen.

B&B. Balled and burlapped, in reference to the nurseryman's method of keeping a ball of soil around the roots of plants being moved, and wrapping the ball in burlap for protection.

bedding. A planting for mass effect, primarily for show outdoors rather than for cutting.

biennial. A plant that requires two growing seasons to mature.

broadcast. To sow at random.

broad-leaved evergreen. An evergreen like holly, with flat leaves rather than needles.

bulb. A fleshy underground bud containing miniature flower parts and food for one growing cycle. See also page 52.

calyx. The outer covering from which a flower bud grows.

coldframe. A garden box with a base of soil and a cover of glass or plastic, so located that it catches the sun in order to warm the soil for early planting.

complete fertilizer. Plant food containing all the most important elements to promote growth.

compost. Fertilizer made from decaying plant debris combined with manure, lime, etc.

corm. An underground stem or solid bulb with scale-like leaves, such as gladiolus.

crown. Central part of a plant from which the stems grow.

cultivate. To scratch or loosen the soil.

cutting. Flowers recommended for cutting are those that are appropriate for bouquets. The word also refers to any part of a plant from which roots will grow.

damping-off. A disease affecting young plants, causing them to rot at ground level.

deciduous. Losing its leaves in autumn.

dormant. Asleep or inactive, as a plant or bulb that is resting.

double. With many petals.

edging plant. A low grower suitable for use at the edge of a path, border or flower bed.

evergreen. A plant with leaves that remain more or less green all year round and do not drop all at one time.

everlastings. Flowers that remain attractive when dried and are used for winter decoration indoors.

exotic. A plant brought in from another country.

flat. A shallow box or other container in which seeds are sown or young plants started.

floret. One of the numerous small flowers that make up a cluster.

forcing. Bringing a plant into bloom earlier than its usual time.

foundation planting. A group of plants arranged around the foundation of a building, to improve its appearance.

ground cover. A low-growing plant able to establish and maintain itself without much care, especially where grass is difficult to grow. See also page 125.

hardy. Able to live through severe winter temperatures.

heel in. To cover roots temporarily with soil, to prevent them from drying out before the plant is set in its intended location.

humus. Soil formed through the decaying of plant and animal matter. It is essential for keeping plants in good growth.

hybrid. A plant produced by cross-breeding —transferring the pollen of one flower to another of a different species.

leaf mold. Decayed leaves.

leggy. With stems that have lost their lower leaves.

loam. Soil that is a combination of sand, clay and usually humus. It is neither heavy like clay nor loose like sand.

massing. Planting in close formation, to give a showy over-all effect.

mulch. A covering of leaves, straw, pine needles or similar material spread on the ground to protect plant roots, conserve moisture and reduce weeds.

naturalize. To plant in an informal mass, to create the effect of a wild or natural growth.

needled evergreen. An evergreen like yew, with needles rather than flat leaves.

ornamental. Grown chiefly for decorative purposes.

peat moss. Partly decayed plant material, valuable because it is able to hold moisture well.

perennial. A plant that lives several seasons. See also page 181.

pinching. Removing the tips of young growth on a plant, to encourage bushiness.

rhizome. An underground stem, sometimes thick and starchy, such as iris.

rosette. A thick, circular cushion of leaves growing close to the ground.

screen. A row of plants set close together, to act as a shield or barrier.

self-sow. To drop seeds naturally to the ground, where they sprout easily without help from the gardener.

sepal. One segment of a calyx (which see).

shrub. A woody plant with several stems. See also page 221.

specimen. A plant standing alone, for special effect.

spike. A tall stem with flowers growing close together along it.

stamen. The central part of a flower, bearing pollen.

tamp. To press down hard, in order to make the soil firm.

tender. Unable to stand low temperatures.

trumpet. The central tube of a flower, such as a daffodil.

tuber. An enlarged underground stem, such as a dahlia.

vine. A climbing plant that cannot grow upright without support. See also page 247.

winterkilled. Damaged by low temperatures, winter sun or winds.

CONTENTS

MAP Showing When the Last Frost Occurs in the Spring

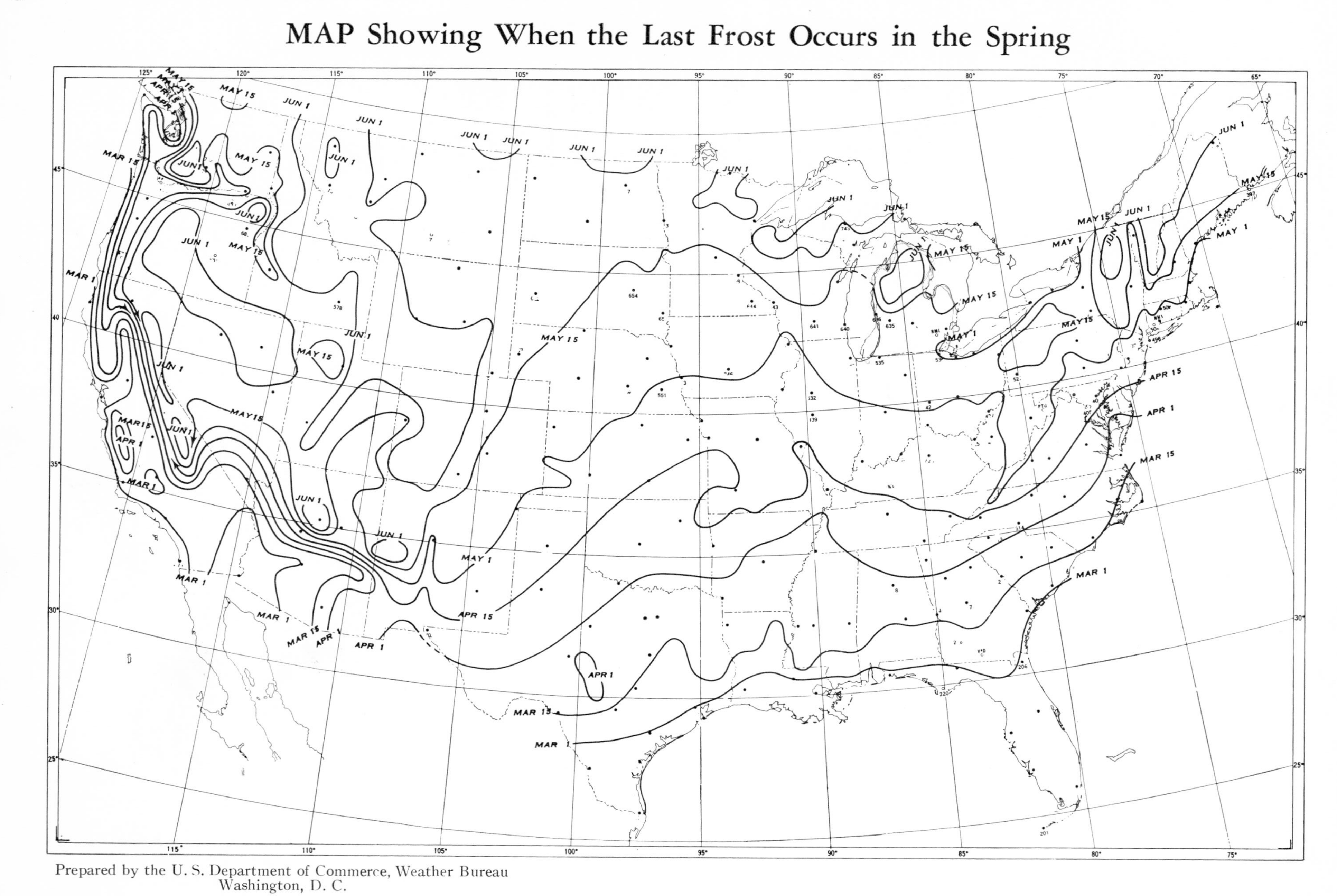

Prepared by the U. S. Department of Commerce, Weather Bureau
Washington, D. C.

MAP Showing When the First Frost Occurs in the Fall

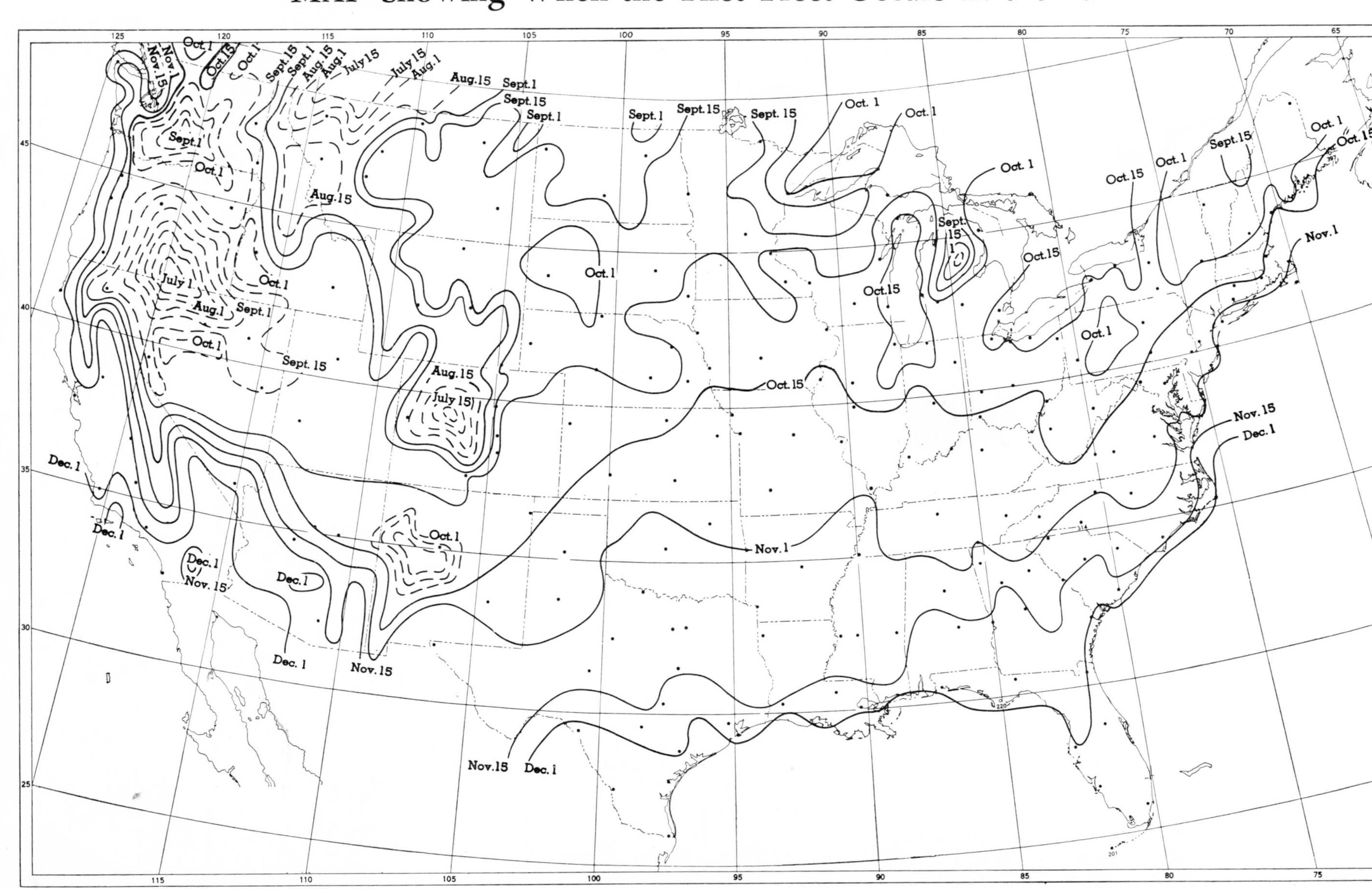

Prepared by the U. S. Department of Commerce, Weather Bureau
Washington, D. C.

For Further Reading

THE fascination of gardening is certain to tempt you to devote more and more time and study to it, and maybe even to adopt some special flower as a hobby. In that case you will want to delve into some of the many alluring books that deal with particular flowers and with various branches of gardening. The list below is just an "appetizer." Look them up, as well as other gardening books, in your public library or your favorite bookstore. They will open up by-paths that you will be eager to explore.

*Books thus marked are by members of our Board of Advisory Editors (see page 2), and will be found especially rewarding.

GENERAL

**The Arnold Arboretum Garden Book*, by Donald Wyman

Aristocrats of the Garden, by Ernest H. Wilson

Color in My Garden, by Louise B. Wilder

The How and Why of Better Gardening, by Laurence Manning

Complete Book of Garden Magic, by Roy E. Biles

PLANNING AND LANDSCAPING

Landscaping Your Own Home, by Alice L. Dustan

Landscaping the Home Grounds, by L. W. Ramsey

Budget Landscaping, by Carlton B. Lees

ANNUALS AND PERENNIALS

**Annuals for Your Garden*, by Daniel J. Foley

Contemporary Perennials, by R. W. Cumming & R. E. Lee

The New Perennials Preferred, by Helen Van Pelt Wilson

How to Grow Annuals, by Ann R. Robbins

Annuals for Every Garden, by Dorothy H. Jenkins

BULBS

**Garden Bulbs in Color*, by McFarland, Hatton & Foley

The Complete Book of Bulbs, by Rockwell & Grayson

Bulb Magic in Your Window, by Ruth M. Peters

Daffodils, Outdoors and In, by Carey E. Quinn

The Amaryllis Manual, by Hamilton P. Traub

The Complete Book of the Gladiolus, by Lee M. Fairchild

The New Book of Lilies, by Jan de Graaff

ROSES

**Roses for Every Garden*, by R. C. Allen

How to Grow Roses, by J. Horace McFarland & Robert Pyle

Anyone Can Grow Roses, by Cynthia Westcott

Climbing Roses, by Helen Van Pelt Wilson

OTHER FLOWERS

**Peonies, Outdoors and In*, by Arno & Irene Nehrling

Iris for Every Garden, by Sydney B. Mitchell

The Complete Book of Chrysanthemums, by Cornelius Ackerson

Dahlias for Every Garden, by Marian C. Walker

All About Begonias, by Bernice Brilmayer

Home Orchid Growing, by Rebecca T. Northen

Geraniums for Home & Garden, by Helen K. Krauss

The Complete Book of African Violets, by Helen Van Pelt Wilson

A Book of Wild Flowers, by Elsa Felsko

GROUND COVERS

**Ground Cover Plants*, by Donald Wyman

**Ground Covers for Easier Gardening*, by Daniel J. Foley

TREES, SHRUBS, VINES

**Trees for American Gardens*, by Donald Wyman

The Home Book of Trees and Shrubs, by J. J. Levison

**Shrubs and Vines for American Gardens*, by Donald Wyman

**Camellias in America*, by H. Harold Hume

**Azaleas, Kinds and Culture*, by H. Harold Hume

**Hollies*, by H. Harold Hume

**Camellias, Kinds and Culture*, by H. Harold Hume

Camellias for Everyone, by Claude Chidamian

Trees and Shrubs for Landscape Effects, by Marian C. Coffin

Landscaping with Vines, by Frances Howard

INDOOR GARDENING

**An Easy Guide to House Plants*, by Arno & Irene Nehrling

The Indoor Gardener, by Daisy T. Abbott

The Picture Primer of Indoor Gardening, by M. O. Goldsmith

House Plants for Every Window, by D. H. Jenkins & H. V. P. Wilson

FLOWER ARRANGEMENT

**Gardening, Forcing, Conditioning and Drying for Flower Arrangements*, by Arno & Irene Nehrling

The Art of Flower & Foliage Arrangement, by Anna H. Rutt

Design in Flower Arrangement, by John T. Arms & Dorothy Arms

Design with Flowers—Unlimited, by Patricia Kroh

Simplified Flower Arrangement, by Patricia E. Roberts

Styling Corsages with Garden Flowers, by Mary H. Drummond

OTHER SPECIAL TOPICS

**Gardening in the Lower South*, by H. Harold Hume

Your Lawn: How to Make It and Keep It, by R. M. Carleton

The Lawn Book, by Robert W. Schery

Songbirds in Your Garden, by John K. Terres

The Scented Garden, by Eleanor S. Rohde

The Wild Garden, by Margaret McKenny

Greenhouse Gardening Around the Year, by Marion Dulles

Window-Box Gardening, by Henry Teuscher

Gardening: A New World for Children, by Sally Wright

Designs for Outdoor Living, by J. B. Brimer

Gardens in Winter, by Elizabeth Lawrence

Greenhouse Gardening as a Hobby, by James U. Crockett

Your Garden in Town, by Ruth M. Peters

INDEX

Individual variety names are not indexed

The Complete Guide to Garden Flowers

ABELIA

GLOSSY leaves and dainty arbutus-like flowers make abelia (ab-beel'ee-uh) a useful and popular shrub in the areas where it can be grown. As far north as New York City it survives most winters, and in mild climates the foliage remains on the plant almost all year round. In autumn the leaves turn a bronze color. Clusters of bell-shaped, pinkish white flowers come in midsummer or earlier and continue over a long period.

Abelia grows 5 or 6 ft. tall if not clipped, but it stands shearing well and for this reason is excellent as a hedge. In shrub borders and as a specimen beside steps or at a doorway it is attractive. Well-drained soil and either complete sun or very light shade will suit it.

Varieties. *Glossy* abelia is the kind commonly offered, at about $2.50 for the 18 to 24-in. size. It blooms from July to fall. *Edward Goucher*, slightly higher in cost, has deeper pink flowers and is almost evergreen.

How and When to Plant. Set out the shrub in spring or early fall. Dig a generous hole, larger than needed for the roots, and in the bottom of it mix some peat moss or leaf mold (obtainable at garden supply stores). Set the plant in position and pack good soil around the roots. When the hole is half filled, water well, then finish filling it with soil.

Care and Protection. If the plant dies back to the ground after a hard winter, prune it severely, and if the roots are still alive it will flower that summer. To keep the plant low, branches that bloomed the year before should be cut back in early spring.

(*Right*) Glossy abelia is a practically evergreen shrub in mild parts of the country, blooming for weeks. Here it is used as a specimen plant.

(*Above*) A close-up of abelia flowers, showing their resemblance to wild trailing arbutus.

(*Left*) Adam's needle claims attention because of its very bold flower spikes and stiff foliage. It likes a sunny location and, in fact, can resist dry growing conditions. Its sword-shaped leaves, ending in a needle-like point, have given it this name.

ADAM'S NEEDLE

NOT only in large borders with other perennials but also among shrubs this extremely picturesque plant may be used for contrast. Usually one is enough, for it makes a very big cluster of stiff evergreen leaves as much as 2½ ft. long, each shaped like a sword and carrying a sharp spine at the tip. Creamy white, bell-shaped flowers, fragrant at night, are borne on an immense stalk in July and August. This is not a plant for a small garden where every foot of space is valuable, but it has its place in large plantings as a distinctive accent. It likes well-drained, light sandy soil and full sun.

Varieties. *Yucca filamentosa* is the hardiest kind, grown over a wide area of the United States. A plant costs about $1.00. *Aloifolia*, also called Spanish bayonet, and *Gloriosa* (Spanish dagger) are good in desert regions and especially at the seashore in the

South. They resist drought well. The Joshua tree, native from California to Utah, is also a member of this family.

How and When to Plant. Set out the plant in either spring or fall, allowing it 3 ft. of space.

Care and Protection. Cut off the flower stalk when the blooms have faded.

AFRICAN DAISY

LIKE cape marigold, this annual comes from South Africa. The dark-centered, daisy-shaped flowers, 2½ to 3 in. in diameter, are carried on good cutting stems 18 in. long or more. Foliage is grayish green. In full sun the plant will bloom all summer and fall, until frost cuts it down. It likes sandy soil and complete drainage. At the front of a border it makes a nice showing when planted in a mass.

Varieties. *Blue-eyed* African daisy (botanically, *Arctotis*) is a vigorous grower 2 ft. tall. The white flowers with mauve center and underside close late in the afternoon. Lower growing *Hybrids* are also offered in shades of cream, yellow, bronze and red.

How and When to Plant. Sow the seed outdoors in spring, and thin or transplant to 12 in. apart.

Care and Protection. Cut the flowers freely for use in bouquets and to keep the plants blooming.

African daisies will give plenty of flowers for bouquets if faded blooms are removed promptly. Give the plants a sunny spot.

AFRICAN VIOLETS

THE queen of flowering house plants has risen to this high position in a short time, for its introduction from Africa occurred only in the 1890's. The plant is not related to violets, but rather to gloxinias. Its almost everblooming habit, exquisite blooms and soft hairy leaves recommend it as a most decorative plant, and the vogue for growing it has become so widespread that hundreds of varieties are now on sale. Colors range through purple, lavender, orchid, blue, cerise, pink, wine-red and white.

Books, magazine articles, catalogs of specialists, and literature of the African violet societies are full of advice on how to grow these plants. Indeed, the challenge presented by conflicting statements seems to increase the interest of growers. For some, the plants are temperamental, while for others they are reliable bloomers practically every month of the year.

One of the most important considerations in growing African violets is the matter of light. They need sunlight but not the full heat of direct sun. Often a north window furnishes the right amount of light, but experimentation is needed to find the exposure that suits them. Where a house has not enough light, they will bloom under fluorescent lighting properly controlled.

African violets need moderate moisture in the soil, supplied from either the top or the bottom of the pot. Soil should never be allowed to become either dry or soggy. The air, too, needs to be humid. This condition may be maintained by setting the pots on a tray of pebbles kept moist always. Room temperature should not go below 60 degrees.

New plants are easily started from a mature leaf with a 2-in. portion of stem attached. The stem is inserted in damp sand or peat moss and kept in a warm, humid room. The new little plant that grows from the stem is potted when well rooted. Instead of sand or peat moss, a glass of water may be used. The stem and base of the leaf should be put into the water.

Varieties. Specialists list so many varieties that it would be impossible to choose a representative list. A plant of a novelty may cost $3.00 or more, but older kinds may be bought for $1.00 to $1.50. Ruffled, bronzy or marbleized foliage and fringed and bicolor flowers in new shades are being offered.

How and When to Plant. It is important to use a pot with good drainage, filled with rich but not heavy, sterilized soil. Wik-fed pots give good results. These and special potting soil, as well as sprays and food, are easily available at garden stores.

Care and Protection. Occasionally spray the leaves with warm water, and give the plants some fertilizer. Spraying with an insecticide about once a month is good insurance against trouble. The plants do not need to be put outdoors in summer, but it is well to give them less fertilizer and water then so that they will have a rest.

If clay pots are used, don't let the leaves rest on the rims. The salts that collect there are injurious. Check the soil daily to be sure it is moist enough, but do not overwater.

When the plant grows so large that it divides into new plants, take it out of the pot in late winter, gently pull it apart, and replant these crowns in separate pots.

Specialists in African violets have their own favorites, and the varieties pictured here are merely a suggestion of the delightful colors and forms it is possible to buy. The foliage as well as the flowers is extremely ornamental. New kinds are continually appearing—many of them the result of amateur rather than professional work. (*Left*) Clementine. (*Right*) Double Pink Dresden. (*Below*) Black Fringe.

Fairy Pink ageratum, a distinct change from the more common blue varieties. The plants begin to bloom when very small and are solid and compact in growth.

Hardy ageratum is a wiry plant about 18 in. tall, blooming from late summer into fall.

AGERATUM

THIS fluffy-headed little annual, also called floss flower, is fine as an edging and for porch boxes and planters, where it blooms from summer through fall. There are white and pinkish kinds of ageratum (aj-er-ray'tum) as well as the more usual blue. Some grow only a few inches tall, others up to 15 or 18 in. This is a neat, compact grower that likes a rather rich soil and plenty of water. It cannot stand a hot, dry location.

There is another plant (*Eupatorium coelestinum* or mist flower) that is familiarly known as hardy ageratum. Growing 18 in. tall, it stays a soft blue color for a long time in late summer. This is a good filler plant under shrubs if given a moist spot in ordinary soil. It spreads rapidly, once established. Part shade is no handicap.

Varieties. *Blue Mink*, 6 in. tall, with large powder-blue flowers, *Blue Perfection*, 12 to 14 in. high, a rich blue, *Midget Blue*, 3 in. high, and 6-in., salmon-pink *Fairy Pink* are among the annual kinds most often grown.

How and When to Plant. Dwarfer kinds should be set 6 to 8 in. apart to form a nice edging, taller sorts 10 to 12 in. apart. Plants are easy to buy at nurseries and garden stores for a small sum. Don't put them outdoors until the danger of frost has passed.

Care and Protection. Keep plants well watered, and see that dead flowers are cut off immediately.

ALLAMANDA

(*Illustration on next page*)

IN southern Florida this tender plant is easily grown outdoors, where it quickly takes hold and blooms over a long season. In other regions allamanda (al-lam-mand'uh) is raised only indoors. It is an evergreen scrambling shrub with bright green leaves and golden yellow, trumpet-shaped flowers. In ordinary soil and full sun or light shade it will develop long shoots that clamber up a wall or fence to a considerable height.

Varieties. *Cathartica* grows to 30 or 40 ft. if allowed to go its own way. It has large, dense, dark green leaves and large golden flowers. In *Williamsi* the blooms have a reddish brown throat. *Neriifolia* is a shrub generally only 3 to 5 ft. tall, with smaller, deep yellow flowers. Plants are available at about 75c.

How and When to Plant. In the far South these plants may be set out at any season, close to the support they are to climb.

Care and Protection. To train allamanda as a shrub rather than a climber, cut back the long shoots in summer.

(*Above*) Blue Mink ageratum is shown here as an edging plant in combination with Spun Gold marigold.

(*Right*) Free-flowering Midget Blue ageratum carries its blooms in dense tufts that practically blanket the plant.

Allamanda Cathartica (described on the preceding page) is an upright-growing evergreen shrub or climber for the South.

ALYSSUM

FOR the impatient gardener who wants to see quick results, alyssum (al-liss'um) is a good annual to choose. Because of its fragrance it is called sweet alyssum. The spreading plant, 4 to 10 in. tall, blooms in six weeks after seed is sown outdoors, and keeps flowering until frost. Nobody could ask for more.

Alyssum is largely used for edgings along walks and beds and for window boxes. The light, dainty flowers, in white, pink and violet tones, set off practically anything they are combined with. Ageratum and dwarf marigolds are good companions.

The hardy form (known as basket of gold or golden tuft) is just as popular in early spring rock gardens, where its big billowy masses of bright or lighter yellow are very prominent. All alyssum is easy to grow in poor to average soil.

Varieties. *Rosie O'Day* is a new variety that adds deep rose color to this family. *Pink Heather* (heather-pink) and *Violet Queen* (rich violet) make attractive masses of bloom, and *Royal Carpet* is still darker. Older white varieties include 3-in.-high *Carpet of Snow* and 6-in. *Little Gem.* The perennial type is listed as *Alyssum saxatile.*

How and When to Plant. Seed may be sown outdoors in very early spring, for alyssum is quite hardy, or plants may be bought inexpensively. Set annual kinds 6 in. apart and perennial ones 12 in. apart, in full sun.

Care and Protection. When plants become straggly in the middle of the summer, cut them back to within a few inches of the ground and dig in some fertilizer. They will grow up again and bloom until frost.

Pink Heather alyssum is likely to be darker in color in cool weather. It blooms until late September.

Alyssum Saxatile is an excellent rock plant for spring gardens. It grows about 10 to 12 in. tall.

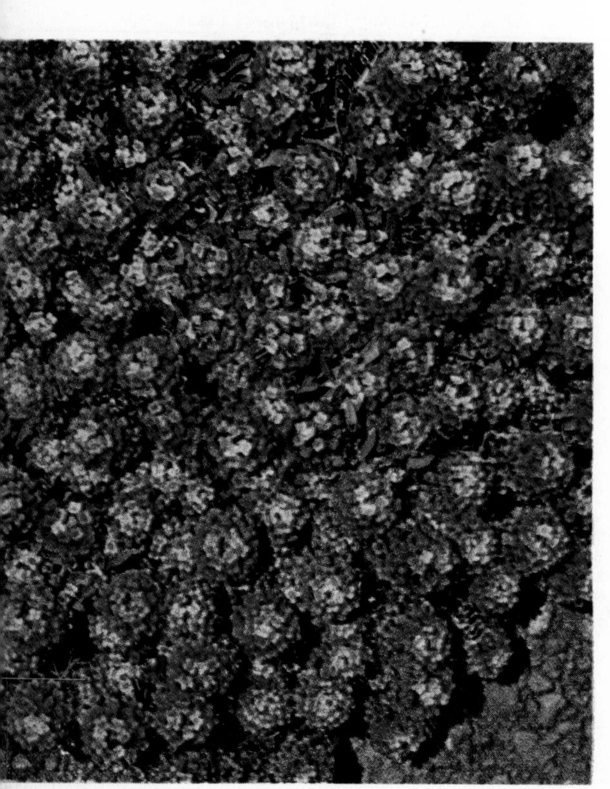

(*Left*) Fragrant Rosie O'Day is an All-America alyssum, adaptable for edgings and rock and wall gardens.

(*Right*) Here Little Gem alyssum has purple verbenas for company. Many pleasing combinations are possible in every garden.

AMARYLLIS

(*Illustrations on opposite page*)

THE huge trumpets of the amaryllis (am-ar-rill'iss) appear in February or March when this bulb is grown as an indoor pot plant. In the South it may be planted in light shade in the open ground, where it flowers between March and May. (See also *Hardy Amaryllis.*) The thick spike carries three or four bright flowers of pink, brick-red, orange, salmon or white; sometimes they are striped. Occasionally a bulb will produce a second flower spike. Usually the long, strap-shaped leaves do not appear until the flower bud is well advanced. Amaryllis is not at all difficult to bring into bloom, and just to watch the fast progress of the bud from day to day is a most interesting experience.

Varieties. Bulbs may be bought in specified colors or mixed, at 60c to 75c each. Newer hybrids with even more gigantic flowers cost about $3.00 to $6.00.

How and When to Plant. In early winter, plant the bulb in good potting soil. This should contain enough sand so that it will drain quickly and never become soggy. Pebbles in the bottom of the pot will also help to insure perfect drainage. The pot should not be more than 3 in. wider than the bulb. Take care to set the bulb so that its neck and top third are left uncovered. Place in a sunny window, watering it only a little until it starts to grow. Then keep well watered. Turn the pot every day so that the flower spike will grow straight.

Care and Protection. When the flowers fade, continue to water the plant so that the leaves will keep on growing. A little liquid fertilizer is recommended at this time. When warm weather comes, put the plant outdoors. Either leave it in the pot and sink the pot in the ground, or plant the bulb in the ground. Before cold weather comes, bring it indoors and let it rest in a dark place, giving it only a little water about once a month. When the neck of the bulb gets green again, new growth is about to start. It is not necessary to repot the bulb every year.

The newest amaryllis hybrids are truly spectacular. Many of them come from Holland. They bring color into window gardens year after year when the bulbs are properly handled.

An amaryllis plant producing two flower spikes at one time is a bonanza for the flower lover.

Brick-red is one of the most common colors to be found among mixed amaryllis bulbs.

(*Above*) Amaryllis bulbs may readily be brought into bloom and are certain to buoy your flagging spirits in late winter.

(*Right*) An amaryllis bulb started in a pot makes a fine gift for an invalid, especially when it turns out to have as beautiful a flower as this one.

ANCHUSA

(*Illustrations on next page*)

THIS is one of the bluest of all blue flowers. The 12-in.-high perennial kind (*A. myosotidiflora*, or *Brunnera macrophylla*) looks like a forget-me-not and is an extremely hardy plant blooming with the daffodils and tulips in April and May. Full grown, it has big heart-shaped leaves on 15-in. stems. It makes a splendid ground cover in either sun or shade, and is useful also in rock gardens. Plants of anchusa (an-kew'suh) cost about 60c each. Bugloss and alkanet are other names for this flower.

Anchusa Italica Dropmore offers rich blue flowers on a tall plant in late summer.

(*Left*) Hardy anchusa, with its broad leaves and graceful clusters of sky-blue flowers, seeds itself and forms a compact ground cover.

An annual form blooms over a longer period if the flowers are cut off as they fade.

Varieties. In addition to the perennial kind mentioned above, *Italica Dropmore* is a long-time favorite. It reaches 4 ft. in height and blooms in late summer. *Blue Bird*, a compact annual variety 18 in. tall, has rich indigo-blue flowers that are especially good with yellow calendulas.

How and When to Plant. Set out the plants in early spring or fall, in sun or light shade. Tallest kinds require 15 in. of space between them. A rich moist soil, well drained, gives best results.

Care and Protection. Be sure the soil is well drained; otherwise plants may not survive the winter.

ANEMONE

EACH flower season has its anemone (an-nem'on-ee)—spring, summer and fall. The varieties are quite different from each other, but all are considered to be very choice perennials even though not all are hardy in the North.

Various parts of a garden may be beautified with these delicate flowers. In spring the kind called pasque flower is a fine addition to a rock garden. Its large purple blooms become fluffy, silvery seed pods later in the season; the foliage is like a carrot top. Wood anemones bloom early in spring, too. These low growers enjoy a shady spot in a rock garden or under trees.

Japanese kinds, blooming from September on, are used as small groups in a border. The single and semi-double, waxy white, pink and red flowers are prized for cutting. They have long slender stems and grow to 3 ft. in height.

Poppy anemones are the ones raised in quantities by florists and admired so much at flower shows. The poppy-like blooms of white, purple, red and blue, up to 2½ in. in diameter, appear in May and June when grown outdoors. These are extremely tender and need winter protection north of Washington, D. C., although they grow easily in the West without any protection. They are very often used in floral arrangements, and they keep well.

Perfect drainage and a good soil well supplied with leaf mold are necessary for all anemones. Pasque flowers like the sun and can stand some lime in the soil. The Japanese type does best with some shade and in a situation protected from the wind. A dark background like an evergreen hedge or a wall will give them this shelter and also help to show off the lovely flowers.

Varieties. Pasque flowers are sold as *Anemone pulsatilla*. Fall-blooming Japanese anemones are offered in several varieties, such as rose-pink *Alice*, pink *Queen Charlotte*, silvery pink and rose *September Charm*, and white *Whirlwind*. Plants cost 75c to 90c each. *St. Brigid* and *De Caen* are popular strains of poppy anemone. They have large, saucer-shaped flowers in many rich colors. Tubers are inexpensive—6 for about 70c.

How and When to Plant. Plant wood anemones in early fall, 2 in. deep. The Japanese kinds may be planted in the fall in mild climates, but spring planting is safer in the North. They should be placed 18 to 24 in. apart, to develop vigorous clumps. Plant the poppy anemone tubers in late fall, 3 in. deep and 5 in. apart.

Care and Protection. Keep Japanese anemones well watered during the heat of summer, and cover them with leaves over winter in the North. It is better not to try to move these plants once they are growing well. Poppy anemones, too, need a heavy winter covering, preferably of strawy manure.

September Charm is a Japanese anemone growing 2 to 2½ ft. tall. The artistic grace of the plant is clearly shown here. (A close-up of the blossom appears in the upper right on the page opposite.)

Other varieties of anemone are shown in the illustrations on the facing page.

(*Left*) St. Brigid, a strain of poppy anemone that comes in a wide range of brilliant colors. The large blooms last well when cut.

(*Right*) Fall-blooming Japanese anemones—Geante Blanche with large, pure white blooms, and delicate pink September Charm.

(*Above*) The poppy anemones are grown from tubers planted in the fall. They are not hardy in the North.

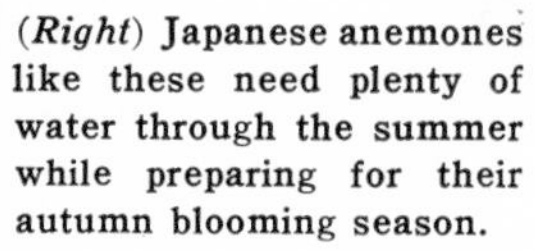

(*Right*) Japanese anemones like these need plenty of water through the summer while preparing for their autumn blooming season.

In the glorious bower of color provided by annuals, any home is a showplace. The scarlet sage, zinnias and marigolds in this mass planting are making good use of the full sun they receive by bursting into a dazzling array of colors.

ANNUALS

UNLIKE your annual club dues, garden annuals do not keep coming back year after year. They are not annual in the sense that they recur. Instead, it is the gardener who must annually do something about it if he wants to have annual plants blooming around him, because the life span of a garden annual is only one growing season. The seed is sown, the plant grows and blooms, and drops its seed and dies, all between spring and frost.

An annual is bent on producing seed that will result in the next generation. Some annuals need such a long warm season in which to accomplish their mission that they must be started indoors before the ground outside is ready to be planted. Others, more rough and ready, can be sown directly outdoors just as early as the soil is workable. Still others cannot safely be planted until warm settled weather comes in spring. Some are such easy growers that when their seeds fall to the ground they stay there and come up the next year without any effort at all on the part of the gardener. This is called self-sowing. It is a desirable trait, provided the plant is one you wanted in the first place.

Why grow annuals if you have to bother with them every year? There are many reasons. For one thing, they give plenty of color in a hurry. Around new homes and summer cottages, for example, where temporary plants are adequate, this is important. Annuals are adaptable to many places in a garden, they furnish armloads of flowers for cutting, and they are inexpensive in comparison to the satisfaction they give. The cost of either seed or plants is very low. Tall kinds can be the backdrop for lower ones; low-growing kinds can be edgers for walks and borders and driveways. Many are ideal for window and porch boxes. Some are useful to fill in where spring bulbs have finished their display of bloom, or to cover almost any temporarily embarrassed spot where some other plant failed. (Detailed descriptions of the important and most desirable annuals will be found in their alphabetical place in this book.)

Annuals should not be depended on year after year to be the backbone of your planting. Pull up the plants when frost has ruined them, and what do you have there all winter? Nothing but a bare spot. Every garden worth the name needs to have permanent shrubs, trees and perennials as its foundation, with annuals as the trimming.

Picking Your Favorites. The three leading annuals, planted coast to coast every season, are petunias, marigolds and zinnias. Exciting new varieties of these big three, as well as other annuals, are put on sale and nationally advertised from time to time. The flowers may be larger or smaller than existing kinds, or in new colors or color combinations, or the plant may have a different growing habit, or it may be healthier or bloom earlier or later than older types—at any rate, the novelties aim to satisfy the desire to have a new package for an old product. This keeps even experienced gardeners interested in trying new things.

Annuals like sweet peas and stock must be grown in cool weather, while others like sunflowers, zinnias and Mexican tulip poppies thrive in the heat of midsummer. Those that need a long growing season are easy to buy as young plants from nurserymen who raise them in a greenhouse in late winter. These are to be had in pots or from flats. Many stores offer containers already planted with seeds of an annual, waiting only for water and warmth to start them growing.

Hints for Care. Practically all annuals require sunshine most of the day, or at least half of the day—morning or afternoon. Some will bloom in light shade but are likely then to be spindly. All need to have dead flowers cut off promptly. This serves two purposes: it keeps the plant always looking its best and it prevents the plant from going to seed. Once you let the flower heads progress to the seed stage, you will have fewer and fewer and finally no blooms. Cutting the flowers for bouquets is the best way to keep your annuals blooming. So cut, cut, cut—every day.

Two other necessary jobs are to keep out the weeds and to water as often as needed. The soil, not the leaves, should get the water. Instead of sprinkling every evening, thoroughly soak the ground once a week. If you wish to save yourself the work of both weeding and watering, try spreading a layer of peat moss, buckwheat hulls or dried grass clippings on top of the soil around your annuals. This is called mulching. It helps to smother the weeds and to keep the soil moist and cool.

Tall-growing annuals in exposed locations should be staked up before wind and rain ruin them. Stakes should be as inconspicuous as possible. Vines like morning glories need string or wire or something else to cling to. This support should be provided while the plants are still small.

In the long run it pays to buy good seed. Even the best is inexpensive. If there is a choice, be sure to get disease-resistant strains. Don't try to save your own seed from one year to the next. That is seldom worthwhile. If you have part of a package left over from the year before, test a few of the seeds on some damp blotting-paper to see whether they will sprout before you sow them.

Growing from Seed. Many kinds of kits containing soil, pots and trays as well as seeds offer an easy means of starting annuals early indoors. If you want to buy your own seed packets, you will need a wooden flat or small clay pots as well. Drainage is important (holes in the bottom, or gravel). Potting soil is easy to buy at a garden supply store; be sure it is sterilized. No fertilizer is necessary. Fill the container to within an inch of the top and make the soil fine, smooth and firm. Scatter the seed thinly, and just barely cover it with soil. Water with a fine spray, and put the container in a sunny window. Don't let it dry out, but don't overwater it either. As soon as the first pair of leaves can be seen, you will need to move each tiny plant to a bigger pot where it will have room to grow until it can be set out in the garden. Peat pots are good for this purpose. They can be placed right in the ground, with the plant. When the plants start to stretch out, nip off the tips of the main stems to make them grow bushier.

Annuals like larkspur and calendulas may be sown directly in the ground just as early in spring as you can work the soil. (You should be able to crumble it in your hand.) First, the soil needs to be dug and raked fine, with some good general fertilizer mixed into it. Get a complete fertilizer and use it at the rate specified on the package, no stronger. Work it well into the ground. Make shallow drills for the seed, and sow it sparingly. Fine seeds like petunia should be mixed with dry sand and pressed into the ground carefully; larger ones like nasturtiums can be covered about three times their own diameter.

When the little plants are big enough to handle, move them to the place where you want them to bloom in the garden. A damp, cloudy day is best. Or if they are like poppies and don't like to be moved, you must thin them out where they stand. You will dislike throwing away these promising youngsters, but it must be done if you want the remaining ones to have a chance. Crowding is fatal. Sowing seed outdoors in the fall is successful with some annuals such as bachelor's button and calliopsis. This produces very early bloom the next spring.

A light application of fertilizer a few weeks after the young plants are set outdoors will be appreciated by many annuals. Some that bloom early will also produce a later crop if the plants are sheared back. Sprays are readily available to combat occasional attacks by insects and diseases. Often the best way to prevent the spread of trouble is simply to pull up and burn the infected plant.

Year in and year out, petunias make a firm bid for first place in the popularity poll of annuals.

Rocket snapdragons, among many other new strains of annuals, whet the interest of gardeners who want the latest.

Artemisia Silver Mound here shows its frosted, silvery foliage among hardy asters and chrysanthemums.

ARTEMISIA

THE naturally dry localities where this perennial grows wild are a clue to the type of soil it prefers in home gardens. The sagebrush of the West belongs to this large group of plants. Most of them are grown primarily for their frosty or silvery foliage. As a contrast in borders their distinctive leaves are very decorative. They are also used for cutting and as dried material for winter bouquets. Light, well-drained soil and full sun are needed for artemisia (art-em-miz'ee-uh).

Varieties. *Silver Mound,* a compact plant only 6 in. tall and about 12 in. broad, has fernlike foliage of bright silvery gray. It is hardy anywhere in a rock garden or as an accent plant, and will come back year after year. *Silver King,* with misty gray foliage, is taller (about 3 ft.). Another tall grower for the rear of the border is *Lactiflora,* with fine-cut, dark green foliage and creamy white flowers in late summer. Silvery-leaved *Dusty Miller* does especially well at the seashore. Plants of artemisia cost about 65c each.

How and When to Plant. Set out the plants in early spring or early fall, 8 to 10 in. apart, in a warm, sunny place. Water well.

Care and Protection. When the clump grows too large, it may be dug up in spring or fall, separated into smaller parts, and replanted.

ASTERS

THERE are two distinct kinds of asters, both very highly regarded—the annuals called China asters and the perennial ones known as Michaelmas daisies. They are among the flowers most closely associated with the fall season, and the lovely range of colors they provide is widely admired. The perennial kinds, which are very hardy and multiply rapidly, are useful in hardy borders, especially with chrysanthemums, while China asters are popular with both florists and home gardeners as extra fine cut flowers. Some of the terms used to describe these showy annuals are ostrich feather, peony flowered, pompon, and chrysanthemum flowered—all of which suggest different shapes. China asters grow 1½ to 3 ft. high and bloom between July and October.

Some hardy asters are low enough to be grown in rock gardens, but many are big bushy plants for mixed borders. They grow in full sun (taller plants will take part shade) and average garden soil; while some kinds are not especially recommended for cutting, they all bloom very freely. September and October see them at their height.

Varieties. China asters have been favorite cut flowers for so long that a great many types and strains have been developed, in many shades of blue, lavender, pink, crimson, rose and peach. Earliest to bloom are the *Queen of the Market,* with medium-sized flowers about 20 in. tall. *Super Giants* and the older *Giants of California* bear 4½-in. flowers with long curly petals from late summer to frost. Other favorites are *Crego* with large, shaggy-petaled blooms on 2½-ft. plants, *Early Beauty, American Branching, Royal,* and *American Beauty. Princess* asters are a newer kind with a high crested center surrounded by several rows of petals. Blooming in late August, they are lovely for cutting. Another

(*Above*) Giants of California is one of the older strains of China aster, in a wide range of colors. The long-stemmed flowers are nice for cutting.

Illustrations here and on pages 27 and 28 show China asters. Hardy asters are pictured on pages 29 and 30.

(*Right*) Crego asters, with long twisted petals, bloom about mid-August. The robust, 2½-ft. plants are well branched.

(*Above*) The compact plants of Princess asters furnish 3-in., long-stemmed flowers in many shades. Space the plants 9 in. apart.

(*Above*) Early Royal asters are among the earliest blooming. They grow 2 to 2½ ft. tall.

(*Above*) Delightfully different are the California Sunshine asters, with their quilled yellow center and single row of colored petals.

The bright, rich color of Rose Marie, a variety of California Sunshine aster, is pleasing both outdoors and for home decoration.

(*Left*) The entire plant of a Bouquet aster may be cut as one big spray, if you wish. It grows very upright, to about 2 ft. in height.

Powderpuffs asters often have as many as twenty long-stemmed flowers on a plant. The colors include rose, crimson, pink, blue and white.

new type is *Bouquet,* with quilled flowers on an upright, 2-ft. plant. They come very early, and a plant in bloom gives the appearance of a whole bouquet. *Powderpuffs,* of the Bouquet type, comes in a good color range. Single asters like *California Sunshine* lend still further diversity to this fine family. *Duchesse* has pure yellow, globe-shaped flowers like a chrysanthemum.

Among the most popular hardy asters or Michaelmas daisies are *Lilac Time, Pink Bouquet,* and white *Niobe,* about 12 in. tall. Violet-blue *Eventide,* rosy lavender *Peace,* and *Harrington's Pink* are sturdy growers reaching 3 to 4 ft. in height. *Mt. Everest* and *Mt. Rainier* (both white) and lavender-blue *Skylands Queen* are also tall growers. Plants average 75c each. *Frikarti* or *Wonder of Staefa* bears lavender-blue flowers from July to October, which are excellent for cutting. In the North it requires protection in winter.

How and When to Plant. Seed of China asters is sown indoors in April or outdoors in May. Tall-growing varieties need to be spaced 15 in. apart in the row, but lower kinds can do with less room. Nurseries and garden stores sell the plants, too. These asters need rich sandy soil, and it is best not to plant them two years in the same place. See that they have plenty of water always, especially during dry spells.

(*Left*) Super Giant asters are sometimes known as Ostrich Feather because of their gracefully curled petals. The large flowers come on 3-ft. plants.

Hardy aster plants are best set out in the spring, 2 ft. apart (or more for the tallest).

Care and Protection. Always buy seed of China asters which has been bred for wilt resistance. Dust or spray the plants frequently with an insecticide containing nicotine (DDT, malathion and lindane are good).

Hardy asters also should be sprayed with a good fungicide during their growing season. The taller varieties will be bushier and stronger stemmed if pinched back several times from late spring to early summer. Every spring, or not quite that often, the clumps should be divided and replanted.

(*Above*) Ballet Queen, an extremely double and early-flowering variety of Queen of the Market type, does especially well in the South.

Skylands Queen is a hardy aster with 2-in. flowers that form a large spray. It is effective from late August on.

The lively color of Harrington's Pink hardy aster makes a bold display in early fall. (*Additional varieties of hardy asters are shown on the following page.*)

The name Sunset Glow is descriptive of the soft rich tones of this 3½-ft. hardy aster.

Aster Frikarti has a long blooming season, from midsummer to October. It looks well when planted near early yellow chrysanthemums. The flowers last up to two weeks when cut.

Free-flowering Blue Jacket has a sturdy plant 3 to 4 ft. tall.

Three more varieties of hardy aster or Michaelmas daisy, described on the preceding pages.

Clean white flowers distinguish Mt. Rainier, another of the tall-growing hardy asters.

The vibrant Red Cloud can be relied on for non-fading color.

The feathery spike of Fanal astilbe appears to be dusted with little frosty crystals.

ASTILBE

PROVIDED it gets plenty of water, this is a first-rate perennial for a sunny or lightly shaded place in a border. Hardy and long lived, astilbe (ass-till'bee) is a fine accent among Shasta daisies and other plants of medium height, and it does well beside water. The feathery flower spikes of white and shades of pink to garnet stand up above the mass of clean, neat foliage in midsummer.

Occasionally this plant is called spirea, which is only confusing because that name belongs to an entirely different family. Potted plants are often forced by florists in late winter; these may later be set outdoors. Rich moist soil is very necessary for astilbe. The shallow roots dry out quickly and must be supplied with water in hot spells.

Varieties. *Deutschland* and *Gladstone* are good white varieties, *Peachblossom* a clear light pink, *Rhineland* crimson, *Granat* crimson-pink, and *Fanal* garnet-red with reddish green foliage. *Simplicifolia Rosea* is dwarfer, with pink flowers, suitable for a rock garden. Plants cost 85c to $1.00.

How and When to Plant. Set out in spring or fall, in soil to which some leaf mold has been added. Press the soil firmly around the roots, and water well.

Care and Protection. Keep well watered during dry weather. About every third year the clump may be dug up in spring, the center part thrown away, and the remaining pieces replanted. In very cold areas some winter protection is advisable.

Granat astilbe sends out a handsome 3-ft. bloom spike in midsummer.

AZALEAS

AN azalea bush in bloom is one of the most lavish displays of spring. All along the Gulf Coast, up the Atlantic seaboard to Long Island, and on parts of the West Coast, some kind of azalea helps to brighten the new season with its riotous profusion of color. These long-lived shrubs have been developed into many forms by plant breeders, and in all cases they are extremely decorative plants that add permanent value to any garden. Many of the most noted estates of the South feature azaleas, and the glorious spring display, especially in Alabama, Florida, South Carolina and Georgia, annually attracts thousands of visitors.

Azaleas are closely associated with rhododendrons (which see). Some kinds grow wild in the eastern United States; they lose their leaves in autumn and show up best against a background of evergreens. Among them are the hardiest azaleas known, with flowers in a wide color range and usually fragrant. From these native kinds have been developed several strains, such as Ghent and Kaempfer hybrids, that are very free flowering, vigorous and resistant to cold.

From eastern Asia, plant explorers have brought evergreen azaleas to add to American gardens. These are not so hardy as our own native ones and can be grown outdoors only in the South and West. Hybridizers have worked with these kinds too, and among the most important evergreen strains they have produced are the Indian and Kurume azaleas. The Indian may be grown outdoors from Virginia to Florida and all along the Gulf Coast. Kurumes also grow outdoors in this same area, but in addition they thrive as far north as Long Island and in some parts of the West Coast.

No one group is adapted to every locality, and it is therefore important to choose the right type for your climate. Some azaleas can stand low winter temperatures; others can stand high summer temperatures. All of them like a humid atmosphere and will perish when subjected to hot dry winds. They must

Mollis hybrid azaleas provide a color range extending through yellow, orange and salmon—different from the more usual strong reds and pinks. Here they are grouped with tall-growing scillas.

A hedge or border of taller evergreen shrubs is a most effective and pleasing way of showing off the colors of an azalea planting.

(*Left*) **This Mucronulata azalea has its roots wrapped in burlap (balled and burlapped). Evergreens and larger shrubs and trees are prepared for moving in this manner.**

(*Above*) **Flame azalea, which grows wild from northern Georgia to Pennsylvania, is adapted to many cold areas. It rates very high among native plants.**

have acid soil with adequate moisture but not of such a nature that it holds too much water or becomes heavy and sticky. A gently sloping location where the plants receive practically full sun, is ideal. Light shade from other plants nearby is desirable, particularly in the sunny South. They can stand some wind but not salt spray.

For garden use, azaleas are of primary importance in borders and foundation plantings with other broad-leaved evergreens that have similar soil and cultural requirements. Both as specimen plants and in combinations with spring-flowering bulbs and trees, they play a leading role in creating exciting beauty in the home grounds.

Azaleas are valuable also for potting and forcing. Plants received from florists should be kept in the sun and moved to larger pots when they have finished blooming. After frost is past, they are moved outdoors and brought in again in the fall.

Varieties. Among the hardy azaleas that lose their leaves in autumn is the *Flame* azalea, one of the very best of all native plants. In May and June this 10-ft. shrub has salmon to scarlet flowers. Lilac-colored *Mucronulata*, blooming earlier, is a pleasant companion for forsythia. *Pinxterbloom* bears very fragrant, light pink flowers in April and May on a 6 to 7-ft. plant. *Pinkshell*, 10 to 15 ft. tall, has shell-pink blooms in May. Semi-evergreen *Poukhanensis* is a low grower with early, lavender-pink flowers. The extra hardy *Mollis* furnishes mainly yellow, salmon and orange colors.

Kurume azaleas are good both as landscape material and as potted plants. They are hardier than Indian azaleas but require winter protection in cold climates. Popular varieties are profuse-blooming pink *Coral Bells*, fiery red *Hinodegiri*, and white *Snow*, among many others.

The tender Indian group bears masses of large flowers outdoors in warm regions. These kinds also are forced by florists. Widely

A massed planting of azaleas in subtly blending colors is more likely to give a pleasing effect than the sharply hued single specimens sometimes used as highlights in mixed plantings.

grown are *Fielder's White*, purplish pink *Formosa*, light pink *Elegans*, and salmon *Lawsal*.

American and European breeders have produced various other groups adapted to certain areas and uses—for example, Belgian and Pericat azaleas for forcing, Gable hybrids for cold regions, and evergreen Glenn Dale hybrids for outdoor planting in the Washington, D. C., area. Azalea plants cost around $2.50 up, depending on size.

How and When to Plant. Planting is best done in the spring in the North. In the lower South winter is preferable. To good garden soil add peat moss, a little cottonseed meal and special azalea fertilizer, well dug in. Set the plant at the same depth at which it previously grew. Water well and syringe the tops from time to time until the plant is established.

Care and Protection. Instead of cultivating around the shallow roots, keep the ground covered with a 2 to 3-in. layer of oak leaves, pine needles, peat moss or sawdust. Always supply plenty of water, especially during the blooming season, when new shoots are growing, and just before freezing weather sets in. Give the plants some fertilizer in early spring and again about the end of June. To encourage more bloom, pinch off the tips of vigorous shoots immediately after the flowering period. To make lower, denser plants, cut back hard just before new growth starts in spring. To combat red spider, the most troublesome insect pest, use a sulphur dust or syringe the plants frequently with water.

(*Above*) The very hardy Pinkshell azalea does well both in damp locations near water and in drier soil. Its native home is the mountains of North Carolina.

Additional illustrations of several types of azalea are shown on the next two pages.

A close-up of a Mollis azalea in soft lemon to apricot tones. Some of these hybrids have survived the rugged winters of New England.

Another Mollis azalea—this one in warm salmon to pinkish colors. All these glowing tones merge beautifully in a planting of azaleas.

(*Left*) A fine flower cluster of a Mollis azalea. (*See other illustrations of Mollis azaleas on preceding page.*) Other varieties of azalea are shown on this and the facing page.

(*Right*) Ghent hybrids include pink, crimson, scarlet and mauve varieties, as well as yellow, orange and copper ones. They are good garden shrubs, and they also force well.

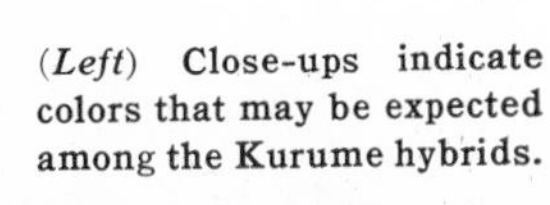

(*Left*) Close-ups indicate colors that may be expected among the Kurume hybrids.

(*Below*) Coral Bells, a low-growing pink Kurume hybrid that is a favorite with both florists and home gardeners.

(*Right*) Soft pink Hinomayo, another widely distributed Kurume hybrid.

(*Lower Right*) The densely branched Hinodegiri, an extremely popular Kurume hybrid, grows broader than tall and is covered with a mass of bright bloom.

(*Right*) Coccinea Major, an Indian azalea like all the others on this page, is an early bloomer and tall grower.

(*Left*) Yodogawa, with double rosy purple flowers, is open and spreading in growth.

Pure white Indica Alba is a pleasant foil for the bright colors of many other azaleas, like those shown in a row to the right.

Criterion, with large, very late flowers.

Elegans, early blooming and fast growing.

Pride of Mobile, or Elegans Superba.

(*Right*) The variegated flower of the George Lindley Taber azalea. This is a midseason bloomer.

(*Left*) The Formosa azalea has plentiful large flowers on a strong plant. It blooms early and is easy to grow.

(*Above*) **Aztec lilies may be grown either in pots or outdoors. The delicately shaped flowers will delight you.**

Baby's breath produces a mass of small, airy blooms especially appreciated in bouquets of mixed flowers.

AZTEC LILY

THIS graceful, velvety crimson flower is not hard to grow. It belongs to the amaryllis family, and is also known as Jacobean lily or St. James lily. Blooming in early summer, this tender bulb may be grown in a pot or in the open ground. It takes full sun and well-drained soil.

Varieties. The botanical name is *Sprekelia formosissima.* A bulb costs about 75c.

How and When to Plant. Bulbs are planted in pots in early spring and are kept watered and fertilized all during the summer. Or they may be planted outdoors as soon as warm weather arrives. Planting depth is 5 to 6 in.

Care and Protection. Potted bulbs are gradually given less water when the leaves begin to die. Keep them dry and cool all winter. They need not be repotted every year. In the South bulbs may be left in the ground over winter, but in colder regions they must be taken up and stored in a frost-free place.

BABY'S BREATH

FEW flowers are better mixers than baby's breath. In a garden its dainty white or pink flower sprays have a softening effect on bolder things such as gaillardia, and it is in demand as a filler for bouquets. Every gardener who delights in making flower arrangements will want to grow baby's breath for its blending and lightening effect on heavy plant material.

These light and graceful sprays come in great quantities, starting about June. Full sun is needed, and a well-drained, sweet soil. Perennial kinds have long thick roots, and for them the soil should be well prepared before planting. Annual baby's breath, 12 in. high, blooms quickly from seed sown in any non-acid garden soil. There is also a trailing kind, fine for use in rock gardens and in wall plantings. It takes full sun and well-drained, sandy soil.

Varieties. *Bristol Fairy,* with double snow-white flowers in masses, needs plenty of space, for it grows 2½ to 3 ft. high and wide. Double pink *Rosy Veil* is good for the front of a border, since it is lower growing. It starts blooming earlier than Bristol Fairy and is very hardy. *Oldhamiana* produces its light pink flowers later in the season. *Repens* is the trailing rock-garden type blooming in early summer. Plants may be had for 85c to $1.25 each.

Covent Garden and *London Market* are popular strains of annual baby's breath.

How and When to Plant. Potted plants and spring planting are to be preferred. Mix a little lime into the soil beforehand. Set the plant 1 to 2 in. below soil level. Bristol Fairy needs 3 to 4 ft. of space, but 8 in. is enough for Repens.

Seed of the annual kinds is sown outdoors in spring, and the little plants are thinned to stand 6 to 9 in. apart.

Care and Protection. Don't try to move plants of baby's breath. They don't like to be disturbed. Keep clipping off the dead flowers to encourage later bloom. Some winter covering is good insurance in coldest sections.

BACHELOR'S BUTTONS

THIS very hardy annual is a mainstay of the garden, so sturdy and easily pleased that anyone can grow it anywhere. Other names for it are cornflower, ragged robin and blue bottle. Most familiar is the rich blue color, but there are also white, red and rose varieties used for borders and for cutting.

Tall kinds grow 3 ft. high and dwarfer ones to about a foot. They like ordinary soil and will thrive in either full sun or part shade. Bachelor's buttons bloom in such profusion that some of the flowers inevitably go to seed. The seed drops to the ground and sprouts the

(*Above*) **Bachelor's buttons come in white and rosy shades, as well as the more common blue. (Uncle Sam might well wear this combination!)**

(*Left*) **Jubilee Gem, a bachelor's button that makes a fine showing as an edging plant.**

(*Left*) **New Alpine balloon flower blooms over a long period and is effective in rock gardens.**

(*Right*) **Double balloon flowers have a second bell set inside the first one. They are popular in midsummer gardens.**

next year, with the result that once you plant these flowers you are sure to have their children and grandchildren too.

Varieties. *Jubilee Gem*, a 12-in. bushy plant with double, dark blue flowers, is especially good for edging. Taller kinds are described by such names as *Pinkie, Rosie, Red Boy, Blue Boy* and *Snowman*.

How and When to Plant. Sow the seed outdoors at almost any season and you can hardly go wrong. It grows quickly and easily. If sown outdoors in October and given a light cover of leaves over winter, the seed will come up in early spring and bloom for Memorial Day. Sown about March, it will flower in midsummer; or make a planting in late June for autumn bloom. Thin out the plants so that they stand 9 in. apart.

Care and Protection. To keep the plants blooming as long as possible, it is necessary to keep dead flowers picked off.

BALLOON FLOWER

THE buds, not the flowers, of this long-lived hardy perennial account for its name. They not only look like balloons but they pop like balloons when pressed between your fingers. Blooming at the height of summer, this 2½ to 3-ft. plant is an excellent candidate for a spot in the middle area of a border. The blue, lavender and white, open bell-shaped flowers, now joined by a pink variety, are especially good with pinks and yellows. Double-flowered kinds are also available, as well as dwarf ones for rock gardens and the front of a border.

Balloon flower is a slow starter. Usually it takes two or three years before a clump is doing its best, and in spring too the plant is slow to put in its appearance. But it blooms even in hot dry locations, and the plants stay where they belong without spreading out of bounds. They prefer light, well-drained soil and either full sun or a little shade.

Varieties. A dollar or less will buy a plant of *White, Blue* or *Shell-Pink* balloon flower (or *Platycodon*). Deep blue *New Alpine*, 18 in. tall, and violet-blue *Mariesi*, 6 to 10 in. tall, are good in rock gardens.

How and When to Plant. Spring or fall is the time to plant. Do not set the crown much below ground level. Water thoroughly.

Care and Protection. Cut off the flowers as they fade. Don't move or disturb the plant, and be careful not to dig around and injure it before it comes up in the spring.

BALSAM

THIS prim little plant, so neat and quaint, has a Victorian air. It is a tender annual easily grown from seed, blooming all summer in shades of pink, rose, salmon and white. Balsam is good for planting in masses. The taller (2½-ft.) kind known as lady slipper has double flowers packed tightly all along the stalk, tucked in among the leaves, but the

(*Above*) **Camellia-flowered balsam, with double flowers crowding on the stalk, grows easily from seed.**

(*Left*) **Tom Thumb bush balsam is an extra dwarf grower for summer beds.**

somewhat lower bush balsam bears its flowers at the top of the stem above the foliage.

Varieties. Lady slippers are sold as *Rose flowered* or *Camellia-flowered*, while bush balsam (such as *Tom Thumb*) may be had in separate or mixed colors.

How and When to Plant. Seed sown outdoors after all frost is over will grow quickly into flowering plants. Allow 10 to 12 in. between them. They like a rich, fairly moist soil, and although they will give some blooms in light shade they do better in the sun.

Care and Protection. Do not pinch back these young plants.

BAMBOO

THESE graceful plants come from many parts of the earth, but it is mainly in the Orient that they are cultivated and used as sources of food and as material for clothing, furniture, and building of many kinds. Actually they are giant grasses.

In the lower South many types are fine garden subjects where a quick effect is wanted. They make thick windbreaks, screens and hedges. Some are such fast growers that they overrun a large area in a short time; these are best omitted from mixed plantings. Clump bamboos are a better choice, although they too need plenty of space. They can stand a great deal of wind.

Bamboos have roots that make a dense mass. Their stems, called canes or culms, are generally hollow; the foliage is green, yellowish or striped and is evergreen in the South. Some varieties can be grown as far north as New York or Boston. In northern gardens the chief advantage of bamboo is its novelty. Low temperatures kill it back, but usually it sprouts again. As with many plants, experimentation shows bamboo to be a possibility for areas formerly thought to be unsuitable.

Varieties. The kinds most often grown in this country are varieties of *Arundinaria* (a fast spreader), *Bambusa* (with canes making a dense tuft) and *Phyllostachys* (with decorative foliage). Clumps are priced according to size.

A flourishing plant of Bambusa, one of the clump bamboos, and close-ups showing the canes and foliage of several of its varieties.

How and When to Plant. In the South, bamboo may be planted in either summer or winter, in moderately rich soil where it receives full sun or a little shade from nearby trees. It needs plenty of water; a location beside a stream or lake is ideal. In the North, planting is best done in the spring.

Care and Protection. Keep bamboo within bounds by cutting some of the oldest canes to the ground in early spring.

BARBERRY

THIS is one of the most commonly grown of all garden shrubs because it is so hardy, makes such a dense thorny hedge, and needs only ordinary soil. There are some evergreen kinds, but they are not winter-hardy. Jap-

(*Above*) This Japanese barberry hedge is being grown naturally, with little or no shearing.

(*Left*) Crimson Pygmy, a dwarf barberry to use as a specimen plant or as an edger. It grows about 10 in. tall and 15 to 24 in. in width. Plants with colorful foliage are decorative and pleasing when carefully placed in relation to their neighbors.

anese barberry, with its thickly branched, spiny plants full of red berries all winter, is a familiar hedge.

Individual plants may also be mixed with other shrubs in foundation plantings. Lower growing types are good edgers for taller shrubs. As hedges, barberries stand trimming well, but they may be grown naturally, with no pruning. They take full sun, average soil, and are extremely easy to grow. Ten plants of Japanese barberry for a hedge may be purchased for about $2.50 or $3.00; newer kinds cost more.

Varieties. *Japanese* and *Red-leaf Japanese* are most widely planted. Both are hardy and have little red berries that hang on most of the winter, making the plant colorful even after the leaves have dropped. Foliage of the Japanese barberry turns bright red before it falls; the Red-leaf variety is purplish red in spring and summer, becoming scarlet in autumn. In the North, *Mentor* barberry stays green through half the winter. It has no berries but is a fine hardy, thorny shrub that stands hot, dry city conditions well, and needs little pruning. *Crimson Pygmy* is a new dwarf kind with red leaves. A slow grower, it makes a good low edging plant. *Truehedge Columnberry* is a barberry of stiff, upright growth.

How and When to Plant. Set out the plants in fall or spring, in a sunny location, in ordinary garden soil. For a hedge, dig a trench 10 to 12 in. deep and the width of a spade, and set the plants 15 to 18 in. apart. Half-fill the trench with soil, tamp it down well and water thoroughly. Let the water settle, and then fill in the remaining soil. Trim back the plants to about 6 in.

Care and Protection. Pruning of the hedge should be done after the flowers fade. It should be kept somewhat wider at the base, so that the lower branches will get plenty of sun and air. If the hedge gets too large, it may be cut back to 6 in. in early spring and allowed to grow again.

Here barrenwort (Niveum and Pinnatum Elegans are shown) is obviously pleased with its home among the rocks where its roots are growing in cool damp earth.

BARRENWORT

BARRENWORT belongs to the select group of plants recommended as ground covers for shady places. It will flower also if planted in the sun. The important point is that its roots be anchored in cool moist soil containing leaf mold or peat moss. This hardy perennial increases rapidly when used as a ground cover in a moist area, and is invaluable in rock and wall gardens where the same growing conditions can be provided. Reaching 9 to 12 in. in height and width, it blooms with early spring bulbs, and continues for several weeks.

Besides the delicately modeled flowers of yellow and white, rose and violet, there is equally good, almost evergreen foliage that is attractive after the flowers have gone. The heart-shaped leaves have rosy bronze tints in spring which become purplish or darker red and remain even into winter. Both flowers and leaves are nice for cutting.

Varieties. *Epimedium alpinum*, with red and yellow flowers, makes a good ground cover. *Niveum* has charming white flowers; *Pinnatum Elegans* is bright yellow. A plant costs around 75c.

How and When to Plant. Set out the plants in spring or early fall, 8 in. apart if wanted in a mass. Often potted plants are available. Be sure the soil has plenty of peat moss or leaf mold.

Care and Protection. Leave the plants alone as long as they do well. After several years they may have to be dug up in spring, separated into smaller pieces and replanted. Old leaves should be left on the plant as protection over winter.

BEARBERRY

ON rocky slopes and sandy banks with poor soil, especially at the seashore, this little creeping evergreen plant is a useful ground cover. It makes a low mat with long trailing stems and small leathery leaves that turn bronzy in autumn. The pinkish white flowers appearing in May are not so noticeable as the red berries that ripen by September and are enjoyed by the birds. This is a native from eastern North America to the Pacific Coast, and grows quickly in sun or part shade in light, well-drained soil.

Varieties. Another name is kinnikinnick. Small potted plants may be had for about $1.00 each.

How and When to Plant. Set out the plants in spring or early fall, a foot apart if a quick ground covering is wanted.

Care and Protection. Keep lime away from these plants. If they spread too far, cut them back in spring.

(*Above*) Bearberry actually prefers thin, acid soil. Perfect as a ground cover, it forms a creeping mat covered in the fall with these red berries.

BEARD TONGUE
(Penstemon)

MANY varieties of this perennial do better in the West than in the eastern part of the United States where the summer weather

(*Right*) Garnet, a variety of beard tongue with large bells on stems 12 to 18 in. tall.

Spikes of Sensation, a form of beard tongue with large flowers in many colors on long stems.

(*Left*) Firebird, another variety of beard tongue, can usually be depended on to bloom until fall. Its richly colored, 2-ft. flower spikes are excellent for cutting.

is not so agreeable to them. It is a big family, with many members growing wild, mostly in the Rocky Mountain region and farther west. Some are dwarf growers only a few inches high, suitable for rock-garden use, while taller ones are grown in perennial borders or as summer annuals. May is the blooming season for some, but others flower on into late summer. The tubular flowers, hanging like bells on slender stems, are very nice to cut. Plar[illegible] look best in groups, for they are sometin[illegible] ungainly and need to be staked.

Complete drainage is absolutely necessa[illegible] if beard tongue is to survive the winter [illegible] the North. In summer it takes plenty of water. It grows in the sun or a little shade, in a sandy soil that is not too rich.

Varieties. *Firebird* has beautiful large, ruby-crimson flowers on long spikes. It blooms most of the [illegible] *Ruby King* and *Rose Elf* are good [illegible] [illegible]cation. They grow 18 to 24 in. ta[illegible] [illegible]*rnet* is 12 to 18 in. high. Some [illegible] are being introduced which pro[illegible] especially useful in the Midwest. Pl[illegible] beard tongue cost 65c to $1.00. *Sensation*, with large tubular blooms from white to crimson, is grown from seed.

How and When to Plant. Spring planting is preferable. Set the plants about a foot ap[illegible]t. Make sure they will have good [illegible]age.

Care and Protection. Don't let the flowers go to seed; cut them off promptly when they fade. Light winter protection is needed in the North, and every other spring the plants should be dug up, pulled apart and replanted. Tall kinds may require summer staking.

BEAUTY BERRY

I[illegible]S beautiful violet-colored berries, produced in tight clusters close to the branches, [illegible]ve this upright shrub its name and are the [illegible]son for growing it. The pinkish [illegible]at appear in summer are rather insignificant, but the autumn fruits form a colorful spot in shrub borders until the birds find them. Foliage turns yellow before it falls.

Give beauty berry (*Callicarpa*) a sheltered place if possible, and a location in full sun. It likes light, well-drained soil and is hardy from Missouri northeast to southern New England.

Varieties. *Chinese* or *Purple* is a graceful dwarf shrub reaching about 4 ft. in height.

Beauty berry is a shrub to plant if you would like to attract the birds. A hard winter may damage the plant temporarily, but recovery usually follows.

American is a native of southeastern United States, where the berries attract hosts of birds. The well-branched plant has bluish flowers. An 18 to 24-in. bush costs $1.50 to $2.50.

How and When to Plant. Planting is done in early spring or fall, in a hole big enough to hold the roots without crowding. Pack good soil firmly about the roots, and water well.

Care and Protection. To improve the shape of the bush, prune away the old branches in winter or very early spring. If the plant dies back following a severe winter, cut it all the way back to the ground in spring. The new shoots that grow out will probably bloom later that summer.

Beauty bush contributes a glorious fountain of pink to early summer gardens, when iris is in bloom.

BEAUTY BUSH

CHINA is the original home of this graceful and free-blooming shrub, but like many other plants from the Orient beauty bush is perfectly adapted to growing conditions in most of the United States. This is a fast-growing, vigorous shrub with myriads of bell-shaped, lightly perfumed, pink flowers in clusters on the arching stems in late spring. Growth is dense, with the outer branches drooping over toward the ground. It makes a handsome specimen 8 to 10 ft. tall and is hardy as far north as the Great Lakes.

With its profusion of bloom and fine-textured foliage, beauty bush contributes a great deal to any garden. It grows in almost any soil but appreciates a fairly rich one. A neglected corner of the lot might be a good place for it, provided it gets the sun.

Varieties. Only one kind is grown; its scientific name is *Kolkwitzia amabilis.* A 2 to 3-ft. bush costs only $1.50 to $2.00.

How and When to Plant. Spring or fall is the time to plant. After digging a hole large enough to hold the roots comfortably, mix some leaf mold in the bottom of it. Set the plant in position, pack soil around the roots, and water well. Finish filling the hole with soil.

Care and Protection. Beauty bush grows so vigorously that it is likely to get unkempt and straggly, taking up too much space. If that happens, cut some of the older stems down to the ground to encourage new shoots to grow. Do this pruning just after the flowers have faded in late spring.

BEE BALM

THE mint-like fragrance of the leaves of this husky perennial attracts bees and hummingbirds. This is a big coarse plant (*Monarda* is the botanical name) found along rivers and in the woods from Michigan southward. It is very hardy and easy to grow in gardens, in the sun or semi-shade, if it has fairly good, moist soil. If grown in strong sun, it should not be in dry soil. It has a shallow root system that soon spreads to form a large clump, and for this reason it should never be placed near fragile plants.

In midsummer borders the striking flower heads, 2 to 3 ft. tall, make a brilliant display with such perennials as phlox and Shasta daisies. It does well in wild gardens, especially near water, and the flowers are good for cutting. Besides the original red, they may be had in white, pink, mahogany and purplish colors.

Varieties. Bright *Cambridge Scarlet,* blooming from June to August, and rosy *Croftway Pink* are popular sorts that may be purchased

Croftway Pink is a free-flowering variety of bee balm growing 2 to 3 ft. tall. This is a very strong grower that blooms all summer. It enjoys a moist location.

for an average of 75c. *Snow Queen* is new; *Granite Pink* is more compact than most.

How and When to Plant. Set out the plants in fall or spring, 15 in. apart.

Care and Protection. Every second or third autumn, dig up the clump, discard the center portion, and replant sections from around the edge. Otherwise, bee balm will grow to be a weed. Keep the seed heads removed to prolong the blooming period.

(*Left*) **Rex begonias are grown for their large, fancifully marked and colored leaves. Be careful not to spray the leaves when watering the plant.**

BEGONIAS

SOME begonias are grown for their flowers but others for their large, beautifully marked and colored leaves. This is a very big family of plants, none of them hardy but all extremely useful for summer bedding or as house plants and porch-box material. Tuberous begonias have blooms so perfect as to look unreal, wax begonias are perhaps the most dependable of all pot plants for winter bloom indoors, and Rex begonias are long-time favorites for their ornamental leaves. They share a liking for rich but light, well-drained soil and a moist atmosphere, with protection from strong sun.

Tuberous kinds, in pink, scarlet, yellow, salmon and white, have flowers of various forms—camellia, carnation, rose, crested or frilled. In sections of the country where summer temperatures are not high, they make a spectacular showing. They are grown in pots, hanging baskets, and beds in the open. A shaded location on the north side of a building is good. The soil must be rich, moist and not compacted. Both flowers and leaves die down in the fall.

Wax begonias, with little single or double flowers, are a standby easily grown outdoors and especially appreciated for almost year-round bloom production in the house. They have glossy evergreen leaves and pink, red or white flowers. The Christmas begonia is an important florists' plant with round, light green leaves and profuse pink flowers.

(*Right*) **Luminosa is a most attractive wax begonia that devotes all its energies to bloom production. It may be raised in a pot or in the open ground in summer.**

(*Below*) **Begonias of the Hanging-Basket Type are beautiful on a protected porch. Line a wire basket with moss, fill it with rich potting soil, and plant tubers in it which have already been started indoors. Keep well watered.**

Rex begonias have leaves about 6 in. across, sometimes hairy, with a metallic sheen and rich purple and red tones mingled with greens.

Varieties. The tuberous kinds are sold by color and are designated by their flower form: *Carnation-flowered*, *Rose-form*, *Camellia-flowered*, *Single Frilled*, *Crested*, *Picotee* and *Hanging-Basket Type*. A tuber costs about 50c.

Christmas Cheer is a crimson wax begonia. *Calla-lily* has white young leaves shaped like a calla lily. *Luminosa* has bronzy foliage and red blooms. Plants may be had for 50c up, depending on size.

How and When to Plant. In March or April plant tuberous begonias indoors in a shallow pot. Peat moss and sand make a good starting mixture. Barely cover the tubers, but keep them damp. When they start growing, move each to a pot filled with rich potting soil to which a little bonemeal has been added, or plant them in the open ground, 12 in. apart, when settled warm weather has arrived.

A north, west or east window is good for wax begonias, so they will get air and light but not direct sunshine. Keep them potted

(*Left*) A tuberous begonia of the Camellia-flowered type, rich salmon-orange in color. Other colors available are shades of pink and yellow, apricot, crimson and rose.

(*Above*) It is easy to see how the Carnation-flowered type received its name. This is a popular form for summer beds.

all year, or plant in the open when the weather gets warm. They need water in moderation, and water spray for the leaves too.

Care and Protection. See that begonias always have moist air, shade, and not too much heat. Tuberous kinds are taken up after frost nips them, dried out, and stored in dry soil or sand over winter. Gradually dry off potted wax begonias after their big burst of bloom and let them rest until late fall, when they should be repotted. New plants of Rex and Christmas begonias may be started from a leaf laid on sand, with the underside down.

(*Left*) Another Camellia-flowered tuberous begonia of very pleasing double form, with heavy petals carefully arranged.

(*Left*) The Rosebud type is a variation of the Camellia-flowered tuberous begonia. The blooms are exquisite in every detail.

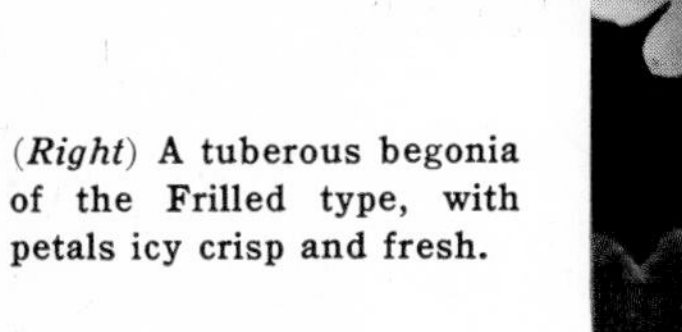

(*Right*) A tuberous begonia of the Frilled type, with petals icy crisp and fresh.

The Cup-and-Saucer Canterbury bells, shown here in several colors, are of always interesting form, like a little handleless teacup set in a neat saucer. They are sold in mixed colors and are very good tall perennials for midsummer borders.

BELLFLOWER

As in most large clans, members of the bellflower family show great variation in size and form. There are dwarf growers only a few inches tall, and some that reach up to 3½ or 4 ft. Some have flowers like open cups, some have "saucers" under the cups, some are more star shaped, some are upward-facing bells, some are quite double. These interestingly formed flowers are pink, white and various shades of blue and purple.

The lower kinds are valuable in rock gardens and the taller ones in borders with such standbys as foxglove, columbine, iris and sweet william. They bloom freely over a long season, and in rock gardens are good to follow the very early bloomers like alyssum. Some varieties are fine cut flowers, and all are healthy.

Bellflowers like well-drained, average garden soil and a spot in sun or partial shade. Rock-garden kinds flourish where their roots can be in moist soil.

Varieties. *Campanula garganica*, with starry light blue flowers in June, is a gem for rock and wall pockets. *Carpatica*, called the Carpathian harebell, has open, clear blue or white flowers on 6 to 10-in. stems over a long season—from June to October. *White Star* is among the newest of this type. *Blue Carpet* and *White Carpet* are especially dwarf, compact varieties, fine for edgings.

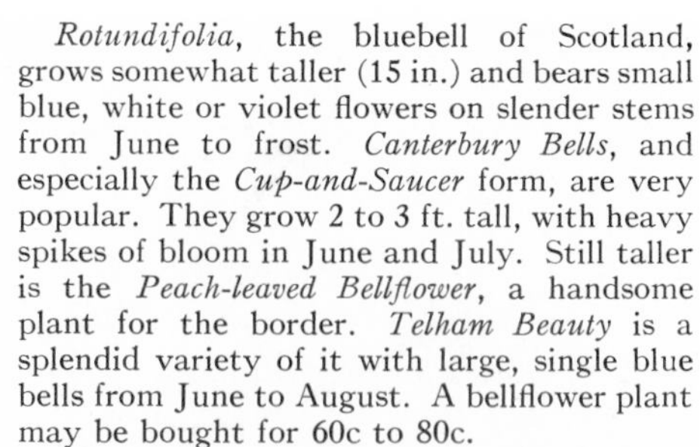

Rotundifolia, the bluebell of Scotland, grows somewhat taller (15 in.) and bears small blue, white or violet flowers on slender stems from June to frost. *Canterbury Bells*, and especially the *Cup-and-Saucer* form, are very popular. They grow 2 to 3 ft. tall, with heavy spikes of bloom in June and July. Still taller is the *Peach-leaved Bellflower*, a handsome plant for the border. *Telham Beauty* is a splendid variety of it with large, single blue bells from June to August. A bellflower plant may be bought for 60c to 80c.

A trailing member of the family, fine as a house plant, is known as *Star of Bethlehem*. It likes some sun. (Not to be confused with the hardy bulb of the same name. See *Star of Bethlehem*.)

How and When to Plant. Early spring or early fall is the time to plant. Dwarf

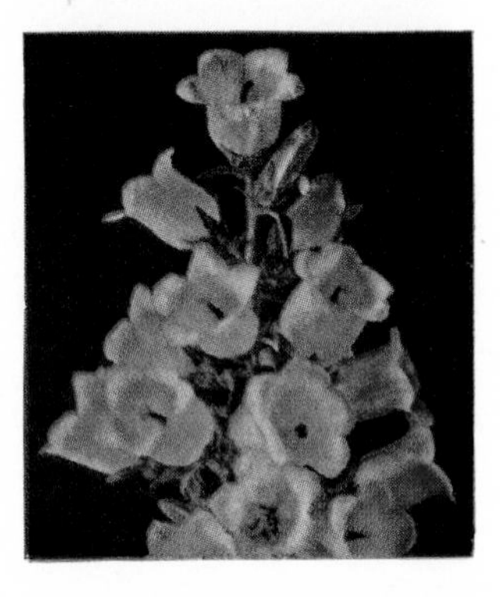

(*Right*) Old-time Canterbury bells, in pink, blue and white, with their upturned cupped flowers, are favorites in perennial borders where they look well with other fairly tall growers.

(*Above*) White Star, a wide-spreading bellflower, has masses of 2-in. white flowers from June onward through the summer. It is very hardy.

(*Right*) Blue Carpet bellflower blooms as freely as anyone could wish. The good rich blue color is an asset.

Peach-leaved bellflowers grow to about 3 ft. in height. Who cares whether the leaves are peach-like when the flowers are as pretty as these?

growers can be 8 to 10 in. apart, but tall ones need up to 15 in. or so. Canterbury bells will have to be replaced each year because they are not perennial.

Care and Protection. Stakes should be provided for Canterbury bells. Divide and replant perennial kinds about every third year. Be faithful about keeping seed pods removed.

BELLS OF IRELAND

THIS all-green annual has decided novelty value for the flower arranger. Although it is not a new plant, it has come into style again in recent years, mainly because its light apple-green, 2-in. flowers are so charming either alone or in a mixed bouquet. They grow close together on the 2-ft., gracefully branching stems and are often dried for winter decoration.

Varieties. No decision to make about what variety to get, but you may enjoy knowing the botanical name: *Molucella laevis*. The green "shells" hold their color well.

How and When to Plant. It is easy to grow these plants. Buy a packet of seed and sow them outdoors when the ground has warmed up. They do not transplant easily. Seedlings can be thinned to stand 12 in. apart.

To Dry the Flowers. When the bell-shaped flowers are fully open, cut them and strip the foliage off the stem. Hang the flowers upside down in a warm, dark, dry place until they are cured.

BIRCH

WHITE clump birch is a hardy tree, small and graceful, with several trunks that share one root system. After a year or two the bark turns white with black patches, and it is this decorative bark and the delicate green foliage that make this tree such a valuable lawn specimen. It offers a pleasing contrast to the predominant green which characterizes most of our home grounds. The trunk stays white the year round, and in autumn the leaves turn yellow before falling. The flowers, like little tassels, are one of the first signs of spring.

Often an entire row of suburban homes—especially when flowers are not much in evidence—will show only an unrelieved mass of green. The home gardener who is wise enough to plant a clump birch in a well-chosen spot on his front lawn will give distinction and added beauty to his home every season of the year.

Grass, as well as other plants, will grow underneath these trees, for the shade they cast is light. Spring-flowering bulbs and shrubs make a happy combination planting near them, and against a background of evergreens clump birch shows to fine effect. These trees are often bent over by storms, but they recover well because the trunks are pliable. They grow in poor soil and can also stand quite a lot of moisture. They are not trees for the South.

Varieties. *White Clump* birch, often called gray birch, is a fast grower and eventually reaches 30 to 35 ft. in height. The 4 to 5-ft. size may be bought for about $4.50. The *Cut-leaf Weeping* form of the European birch, also popular as an ornamental, costs about $3.50 for the same size. It takes a moist location in the sun, and its drooping form is lovely even in winter when the fine-cut leaves are gone.

How and When to Plant. Although these trees may be planted in the fall, the best time is very early spring. Dig a hole wide enough to hold the roots well spread out, without crowding, and deep enough so that the tree will be at the same depth as in the nursery. (A dark mark around the base of the trunk will show what that depth was.) Be careful to avoid exposing the roots to sun or air while planting is going on. After setting the tree in place, pack good soil around the roots, being particular not to leave any empty spots. Fill the hole half full of soil, and then fill it to the top with water. When the water has drained away, finish filling the hole with soil, leaving the surface raked fine. Water frequently until the tree gets a good start.

Care and Protection. Keep the trunks wrapped in burlap for a season or two, as protection. If you ever want to cut off a branch, do it in the summer or fall. Pruning in early spring is to be avoided.

(*Above*) A clump birch is an attractive small tree for any lawn. Fortunately, grass can grow right up to the trunk, for the shade is light and dappled.

(*Left*) Here bells of Ireland are used as an all-green arrangement, but they also are extremely pleasing when combined with brightly colored flowers.

BIRDS IN THE GARDEN

BIRDS not only bring song, color and activity to a garden but are vitally needed by plants as an essential link in the balance of nature. The occasional corn patch or fruit tree raided by birds is small payment for the millions of insects and weed seeds that they destroy every year. Even in winter many birds forage for insect eggs in leaves and bark.

To encourage birds to nest and feed around your home, you must offer them food, water and shelter. You can provide the food not only by maintaining feeding stations but by planting wild fruits and berry-bearing shrubs that are attractive to birds. Sunflower seed is popular with juncos, cardinals, chickadees, nuthatches and downy woodpeckers. Mixed grains attract many seed eaters, and suet tied to a tree trunk is taken by insect eaters. Kitchen scraps such as bread crumbs, apple slices and lettuce leaves, as well as raisins and peanuts, are easy to provide. Peanut butter is a great favorite. Many types of feeding stations and shelves are available for serving these foods to the birds. In every case the food shelter should have a slanting top, to keep squirrels away.

A Wide Choice of Bird Lures. There are many shrubs and trees that have "what it takes" to entice birds. Planting some of them is one of the best means of keeping birds away from the family's fruit trees. A mulberry tree is among the most valuable of these distractions. Others are chokeberry, wild grapes and cherries, elderberries, crabapple, dogwood, hawthorn, cotoneaster, viburnum and wild roses. Some of these will bear in summer and others not until later, but their fruits will be welcomed by the birds at any time. And most of them are nice to have in a garden planting for their other merits as well.

A detailed description of the ornamental shrubs and trees mentioned above will be found in their proper alphabetical place elsewhere in this book.

(*Above*) The gorgeously hued Baltimore oriole gets part of his living from the insects he finds in apple trees.

(*Left*) Firethorn berries add a bright note to your garden, and birds love them. Avoid heavy pruning of the bush, so that plenty of berries can develop.

You can buy or build bird houses of many types and sizes to lure the particular birds you prefer. Evergreen and other trees will also furnish nesting sites. Bird houses should be so placed that they face away from the wind. At nesting time it is helpful to put such materials as yarn, string and shavings in a place where they will be easily found by the birds, which will make good use of them.

Water is appreciated by birds the year round and never fails to bring them to a garden. A metal or concrete bath for both bathing and drinking purposes should have sloping sides. It must be shallow and rather broad. If possible, set it about 2 ft. above ground; if lower, place it in the open where cats cannot lie concealed.

Such undesirable birds as starlings and English sparrows may be scared away only after consulting the local authorities about lawful means of fighting them. Paper and cloth streamers are helpful in warding off birds from seedling plants, and netting can be used for the same purpose.

BITTERSWEET

ALL over the northeastern part of North America and down to North Carolina and New Mexico this attractive vine grows wild. A favorite for home decoration, its clusters of orange and red berries are often gathered for fall bouquets, for they are profusely produced and are very gay. This is a twining vine that is extremely hardy and vigorous, though it does not reach a height of more than about 20 ft. It twists tightly around any support and should not be grown on valued trees or shrubs, for it can strangle them. However, as a rampant climber on a retaining wall, on a trellis or as a cover for rocks and old stumps, bittersweet gives fast and easy results in any soil. (See also *Evergreen Bittersweet.*)

Varieties. Besides the native *American* bittersweet, nurserymen offer the *Oriental,* a native of China and Japan with somewhat smaller berry clusters. Both are very showy. Plants cost $1.25 to $1.50.

How and When to Plant. Set out the plants in fall or spring. To secure berries, it is necessary to have both a male and a female plant in close proximity in order that the flowers may be fertilized. Ask your nurseryman to specify the sex of the plants when he fills your order, if you want to make certain that you have berries.

Care and Protection. Pruning in early spring may be needed every third or fourth year if the vine takes too much space. If necessary, it can be cut back hard without being harmed.

When the yellow outer coating of bittersweet berries bursts open, it shows the orange-scarlet soft center.

BLEEDING HEART

EVERYONE responds to the charm of bleeding heart. This is an old-time hardy perennial that is as much a part of spring gardens as robins hopping on the grass. The slim stems seem to bend with the weight of their necklaces of pink hearts. The plant is very easy to grow, reaching 2 ft. in height and breadth, and blooming at the peak of spring. Old-fashioned bleeding heart has light green leaves that die down and disappear in summer. It will bloom in full sun but part shade is better, in soil that is moist in summer but will not have water standing on it in winter.

Varieties. *Dicentra spectabilis* is the old-fashioned pink variety, growing to 2 ft. A plant may be bought for about a dollar. *Sweetheart,* a lovely pure white variety only 12 to 15 in. tall, blooms from spring to fall and is especially good in a rock or wall garden. The lacy foliage of *Fringed* lasts all summer, along with the deep pink flowers. It too likes conditions in a rock garden. (See the illustration of Fringed bleeding heart on the following page.) *Bountiful* has rich garnet-red hearts. It makes an 18-in. clump, and blooms from May to July.

How and When to Plant. Add leaf mold or peat moss to the soil before planting. Set out in very early spring or early fall.

Care and Protection. Clumps may be left without dividing for several years.

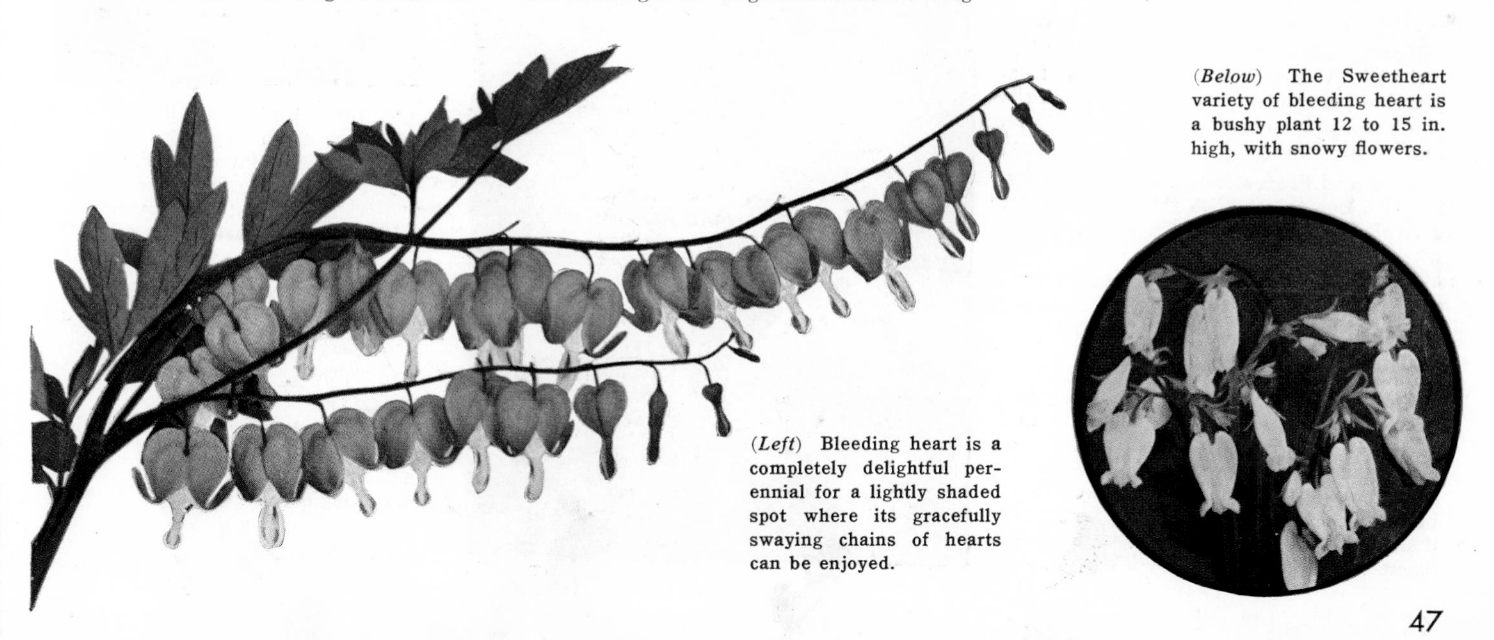

(*Left*) Bleeding heart is a completely delightful perennial for a lightly shaded spot where its gracefully swaying chains of hearts can be enjoyed.

(*Below*) The Sweetheart variety of bleeding heart is a bushy plant 12 to 15 in. high, with snowy flowers.

Fringed bleeding heart (described on the preceding page) has the double advantage of fern-like foliage and flowers that bloom from April to fall.

BLUEBELLS

YOU may know this plant as Virginia cowslip. In eastern United States it grows wild in damp shady woodlands, and where its natural habitat can be approximated it makes a lovely subject for gardens. Blooming at daffodil time, it is a beautiful companion for these and other spring bulbs and wild flowers. Clusters of pink buds become nodding, clear blue bells, 15 to 24 in. tall, above the large, light green leaves. By summer the foliage has disappeared.

Without a cool moist shady spot and soil well enriched with peat moss and leaf mold, it is useless to plant bluebells. But in woodsy places and damp shady parts of a border, mass plantings are successful.

Varieties. *Mertensia virginica* is the botanical name of this hardy perennial. There are white and pink forms, as well as blue. A plant costs about 60c.

How and When to Plant. Mix extra leaf mold with the soil. Best results come from planting between August and frost. Set the plants about 2 in. deep and 6 to 8 in. apart, in a broad mass.

Care and Protection. Bluebells are best if left alone to establish themselves. After several years plants may be divided and reset when the foliage has died down.

BLUE LACE FLOWER

NOT very important, as plants go, but this miniature edition of the wild Queen Anne's lace is so decorative when cut that it is worth growing for that purpose. In the garden the soft lavender-blue color is too delicate to be outstanding. Flowers have been called little lace umbrellas, for that is their shape and texture. About 2½ in. in diameter and 2 ft. high, they last exceptionally well when cut. They take rich soil and full sun, and grow best in cool sections.

Varieties. Soft blue *Didiscus caerulea* blooms from midsummer to frost. *Lace Veil* is a white form, early and free flowering.

How and When to Plant. Sow seed in spring where the plants are to stand, and thin to 9 in. apart.

Care and Protection. Pinch out the tips of young plants to make them branch more.

BLUE MIST SHRUB

THIS neat, low-growing shrub bearing blue flowers in the fall fills a special need. Only 2 to 3 ft. tall, it is suitable for planting in front of other shrubs, and the blue color looks well with late-blooming perennials and annuals in orange and yellow tones. The fringed flowers come in clusters from late August to frost; foliage is silvery green.

In the South and West this shrub does well, but it is not completely hardy north of New Jersey. A protected spot is advisable, in a well-drained, sunny location. Flowers are borne on the new shoots that grow each spring. Blue spirea and bluebeard are other names used.

Varieties. Simply blue mist shrub (botanically, *Caryopteris*) designates it, and $1.25 buys a plant.

How and When to Plant. Spring planting is recommended. Dig a hole large enough to hold the roots without crowding, and in the bottom of it mix some peat moss. Set the plant in place, pack good soil firmly around the roots, and water thoroughly.

Care and Protection. In cold winters this shrub is likely to die to the ground. In that case, cut it all the way back. Even if it is not winterkilled, hard spring pruning will help to keep the plant compact and more free flowering. New shoots will grow in a few weeks.

Blue mist shrub is especially useful because it blooms late in the season when there are plenty of yellow, orange and gold-colored flowers like marigolds and chrysanthemums to bloom nearby.

(*Above*) Blue lace flowers bear these lacy, soft blue parasols from summer to frost. They are grown chiefly for cutting because they are so lasting and are nice mixers with other annuals.

(*Left*) Bluebells need a woodsy spot where the soil is moist and cool. They are beautiful with spring bulbs.

BORDERS

A suburbanite rolls out the red carpet of welcome by planting floribunda roses up his front walk.

YESTERDAY'S prim flower bed in the middle of the front lawn has today become a border. Bordering what? It may run along the back of your building lot, it may separate your lawn from your neighbor's, or it may edge a walk. Usually it combines bulbs, perennials, annuals, shrubs and ornamental trees. In other words, it is a glorious sampling of the whole flowering world, brought together to make a beautiful blended picture.

By combining different types of plants, you can have flowers of some kind for many months. Bulbs such as daffodils and trees like flowering crab bloom while most perennials are just struggling back to life. Annuals will replace the early bulbs and furnish plenty of flowers for cutting, while shrubs and perennials contribute their share of color—each plant in its season. Summer-flowering bulbs like lilies are also valuable in the border. What is most important is not to undertake too much at a time, and not to expect perfection the first season.

In picking the place for a border, you may not have much choice. The only possibility may be along the driveway, or across the end of the backyard. Or it may have to be quite a small planting in the front dooryard. Use whatever space you have. If there is a choice, aim for a background of some kind. When tall shrubs and flowering trees are part of the border, they form the backdrop for lower growing plants. A hedge, fence or wall will also help to show off the flowers and to protect them from crippling winds. It must be an open, mostly sunny area, with at least average garden soil where water does not accumulate. The edge may be either straight or irregularly curved.

If the border is only 2 or 3 ft. wide, it is best not to plant anything very tall. When plants can be seen from both sides, the tallest ones belong down the center, with lower ones on the sides. Against a background, the tallest go at the back, the medium-height next, and the lowest at the edge. However, this needs some variation so that the effect will not be too precise. Plants should not be set close against a hedge or wall. Good air circulation is important, as well as easy access for the gardener to do jobs like staking and cutting.

Points to Remember. Even in a small border, single plants of different varieties should not be used. This gives a jumbled look. It is far better to grow fewer varieties, and about three to five plants of each kind. Do not set in precise rows but in groups, as they might grow in nature. Allow enough space for each group to grow comfortably. Decide which flowers you like best, and let these be the basis of your planting. Place them in several spots, if you like, down the length of the border, but don't overdo any one plant.

The longer your border has some flowers in bloom, the more you will enjoy it. So besides the height of the plants and the color of the flowers, consider the months when each plant will be at its best. Some plants practically disappear when their blooming season is over (such as Oriental poppies and bleeding heart), but others stay presentable even when not in flower. Don't confine yourself to material that blooms all at one time. Aim for a steady succession of color. Colors that might be quarrelsome as neighbors can often be chosen if separated by white. Near patios, white is especially good because it shows up well in the evening when patios are likely to be most in use. Don't put too many flowers of similar form together; mingle the daisy-shaped ones, for example, with some spires. And don't

This handsome midsummer border relies on phlox and daylilies for much of its color. Because they demand so little attention and bloom so steadily through the warm summer months, these two hardy plants are regarded as the hub of the perennial wheel.

The green of the grass and of the sheltering hedge and trees makes this spring shrub border all the more attractive. Azaleas are featured here.

overlook the colors and textures of the foliage. Plants with leaves that stay attractive all summer are best used at the border edge.

Ground for a new border should be spaded in the autumn, when possible, at least 15 in. deep. Leave it rough over winter, and in early spring break it up fine and rake it smooth. Mix some peat moss or leaf mold with the soil, as well as some complete fertilizer and a little bonemeal. Follow the instructions on the container about the amount of fertilizer needed for the space you are planting. It pays to do a good job in getting the ground ready. If any particular plant needs lime or extra leaf mold, that can be added to the spot it is to occupy.

In the long run it pays to buy from a reliable nursery or garden store. Plant material bought at cut-throat prices is seldom satisfactory. Be a good citizen and don't dig up plants in the woods and bring them home to set out. This rarely works.

How and When to Plant. Planting will be easiest if you have made a little layout on paper showing where each plant is to go. Be sure to keep the roots moist and protected from wind and sun while you are planting. Fall and early spring are the main planting seasons, although plants in pots or containers may be set out at almost any time they are available. When the job is done in the fall, it is advisable to give some protection over winter. Holes for the roots should be large enough to hold them without squeezing. Most plants should be set even with the top of the ground, although there are exceptions to this general rule. Always the soil should be pressed tight to the roots, and the watering that follows should be done slowly and thoroughly.

To keep a border looking its prettiest, see that plant stakes are provided for heavy or tall flowers. Dead flowers and dead leaves should be cut off immediately and disposed of. In dry spells, give the border a good soaking as needed, but never just a light sprinkling. It is better not to water when leaves will have to stay wet overnight.

A covering of some material like peat moss, buckwheat hulls, or dried grass clippings laid on the ground around the plants will help to hold down the weeds and also to keep the soil moist and cool. If this is not done, weeds should be pulled out by hand as soon as they appear. A light feeding of fertilizer in early summer, followed by watering, is helpful, and an all-purpose dust or spray used about every other week is good health insurance. There are dozens of pests that may attack your garden, just as there are many illnesses that may attack you, but in either case the risk isn't too great. The best protection is to keep your plants growing vigorously.

After heavy frost has visited your border, pull up and burn the annuals and cut off the old dead stems of the perennials. Where winters are severe, some covering is advisable for many plants.

BOTTLE BRUSH

IN California and all through Florida this tender evergreen shrub may be grown for its curious flower spikes. Set with long, bright red or yellow stamens, they look exactly like a bottle brush. They are produced from March to early summer against narrow, dark, leathery foliage. A dark background shows off the plant effectively, and it may well be grown as an unpruned flowering hedge. It likes full sun and ordinary garden soil.

Varieties. *Callistemon rigidus* is a stocky plant with dense red flower spikes, followed by clusters of flat seed pods which hang on for several years. Light crimson *Lanceolatus* grows fast and can stand rather wet soil.

How and When to Plant. Potted plants, at about a dollar each, are the best to use. They may be set out at any season.

Care and Protection. Don't try to move well-established plants. Do any necessary pruning as soon as the flowers fade.

BOUGAINVILLEA

THROUGH southern California and lower Florida this tropical vine is a spectacular grower and bloomer. It is a big shrubby plant sometimes reaching 40 or 50 ft. in height. Growth is very dense and heavy, with spines on the stems. Bright flowers are borne over an extended season. Actually it is the bract surrounding the flower that furnishes the brilliant color.

Bottle brush blooms best when planted in full sun. This is a tender shrub for California and the South.

(*Left*) **Barbara Karst bougainvillea is a bushy grower good to plant where space is rather limited. The big, bright crimson flowers are striking.**

(*Below*) **Dwarf boxwood forms a neat edging for a bed of roses. It is extremely slow in growth and does not require frequent pruning.**

Bougainvillea (boog-in-vill'ee-uh) can stand both drought and heavy trimming. It flourishes in any soil if given full sun. It may be allowed to scramble over an arbor or a wall or on a porch, or if pruned it may be grown as an informal flowering hedge. In the North it is sometimes seen in greenhouses.

Varieties. Purplish-flowered *Glabra Sanderiana* is widely grown in the far South. It is extremely vigorous and makes a good hedge. *Crimson Lake* and *Barbara Karst* are striking crimson varieties. *Afterglow* comes in varying shades of yellow, orange and salmon. A potted plant costs about $1.50.

How and When to Plant. In warm climates plants may be set out at almost any season of the year.

Care and Protection. To train in shrub form, cut back the shoots in summer.

BOXWOOD

IN early colonial times southern ladies had boxwood planted in their gardens as a reminder of their homes in England. All through the South and Southeast this aristocratic evergreen was featured both as a handsome specimen plant and as a low hedge. Often it was clipped into formal shapes of various kinds and was used to make a quaint garden of its own. In Virginia and other parts of the South many of these plants are still growing. The pungent odor of the leaves and the neat, dense growth are distinctive.

Boxwood stands shearing well but requires little pruning because it is so compact and slow growing. The small dark leaves are beautiful the year round. As an edger for shrubs like azaleas there is nothing more permanent and attractive. Either acid or sweet soil and sun or partial shade is satisfactory.

Varieties. *Common* boxwood, with slender glossy leaves, grows to 15 ft. or more in height and makes a fine specimen tree. *Dwarf* or *Edging* (sometimes called *Old English*) has long been used as an edger. It is very slow growing and may easily be kept to a height of only a few inches. There are a number of variations.

Hardier, however, are the types that originally came from Japan. *Korean*, the hardiest kind, is practical for use as far north as New York. It stays green all winter as a specimen or hedge and grows no more than 2½ or 3 ft. tall, even after many years. Small plants for hedges may be bought for 75c up; specimens are more expensive.

How and When to Plant. Set out the plants in spring or very early fall, 6 to 8 in. apart for a hedge.

Care and Protection. A layer of leaf mold or peat moss is desirable underneath boxwood. Keep the plants well watered through dry weather. In cold regions protect them from winter sun and wind by erecting a screen around them, of burlap or evergreen branches. Any necessary clipping is best done in April or May.

BRIDAL WREATH

(*Illustration on following page*)

TWO of the spirea family are known as bridal wreath. One of them, Vanhoutte, is said to be the most commonly grown shrub in America; fortunately, it is also a very graceful ornamental. The other, the true bridal wreath, has foliage that turns bronzy in the fall. (See also *Spirea.*)

The pure white flowers are borne in little clusters all along the arching branches. Any reasonably good garden soil is suitable, and either a sunny or a lightly shaded location.

Varieties. *Vanhoutte* blooms in late May. The dense plant is quick growing, making a fine specimen or screen. *Prunifolia*, the true bridal wreath, blooms a little earlier. An 18 to 24-in. bush costs a dollar or less.

How and When to Plant. Spring or fall is the time to plant, in any kind of soil, preferably in full sun. Vanhoutte makes a long-lasting hedge if plants are set 2 to 3 ft. apart and allowed to grow naturally.

(*Left*) The gracefully curving stems of bridal wreath (or Van-houtte spirea) are laden with tiny white flowers in late spring.

(*Below*) Pink Spires bugle is vigorous and free blooming. It is used as a ground cover and rock-garden plant.

Care and Protection. Any dead branches should be cut away in early spring. If the plants start to get too large, trim them after they bloom. Try to retain the natural shape of the plant, and to allow new shoots to grow up to replace the older ones.

BUGLE

PRIMARILY for ground covering, this low-growing perennial serves a useful purpose. In difficult places that always look neglected it will spread quickly, making a thick mat that keeps out the weeds. In the no man's land under shrubs and even under trees where there is little light and sun, bugle forms a good cover, green most of the winter. Flowers are carried on little spikes that rise above the foliage in early summer. Growing 6 to 12 in. high, this is also a good choice for either a sunny or a shady spot in a rock garden, where it will be satisfied with the most ordinary soil.

Varieties. The most densely spreading kind is *Ajuga reptans*, 3 to 4 in. high, with deep purplish blue flowers on 8-in. spikes in May and June. *Metallica Crispa* has reddish purple leaves and blue flowers. It is a fast grower, 4 to 5 in. in height. *Genevensis*, with light green foliage and dense blue spikes, makes a nice ground cover with small bulbs. *Pink Spires* is a pleasant change from blue. Bugle plants cost about 75c.

How and When to Plant. Set out the plants in spring or fall, 6 in. apart for quick coverage of the ground.

Care and Protection. Unless you want it to spread at will, frequent division of the plants is necessary. Runners may be taken up and transplanted where wanted.

BULBS

BULBS of many kinds make gardening a delight and an assured success even if you are a rank novice. From the snowdrops of late winter to the tulips of spring, and from the gladiolus of summer to the dahlias of early autumn, you have a bountiful choice of bulbs easy to grow and eager to bloom for your pleasure. (All are described separately in this book, in alphabetical order.) If the shrubs and trees are slow getting started around your new home, you will get plenty of consolation from even a few bulbs. Garden stores, nurseries, bulb specialists, and even super-markets and department stores make it easy to buy them. And even if you are in rented quarters, inexpensive bulbs, blooming quickly, will be eminently worth your while. They are superb for cutting, for indoor decoration, and as gifts for friends.

Because they can be moved so easily from year to year, bulbs are a good way to change the looks of a garden. It is quite simple to experiment with different combinations. You can't very well move trees and shrubs to suit a whim for change, but with bulbs it is different. So watch for new spots where a few of them will give a fresh look.

The smallest bulbs blooming very early outdoors—the heralds of spring—come so soon after the days begin to lengthen that they quite often take even the most experienced gardeners by surprise. (See *Checkered Lily*, *Crocus*, *Glory of the Snow*, *Grape Hyacinths*, *Scilla*, *Snowdrop*, and *Star of Bethlehem*.) Planted where you pass them often or can see them easily from the house, they will be a special joy. Be generous in using these little gems. Scatter them with a free hand, and in a few years you will have many fine clusters.

Tuck some daffodil bulbs in the ground in the fall, and they will reward you with heart-warming color for many springs.

To give your garden a face lifting, experiment with the countless different ways of combining bulbs. Here daffodils are bending over grape hyacinths nestling at their feet.

The hosts of spring-blooming trees and shrubs such as flowering crab, magnolia and forsythia, and early flowers like candytuft, pansies and primroses, are agreeable and indispensable companions for spring bulbs. An evergreen hedge shows off their delicate beauty perfectly. At the edge of a hardy border bulbs are charming. Tiny ones are happy in rock gardens, and some can be massed at random in half-wild areas where the grass is not regularly mowed. Sometimes a small bed close to a doorway, along a driveway or in a sunny corner, will be exactly the right touch.

The Inner Secret of a Bulb. A bulb is actually a fleshy bud underground, containing the beginnings of the next leaves and flower that will be produced by it. The bulb carries within itself the food that will nourish it until its next flowering season. Cutting a daffodil bulb from top to bottom will reveal the sleeping flower parts. This fact points out the need to buy good bulbs in the first place. If the potential flower and the necessary food for it are not present when the bulb is bought and planted, no amount of care will produce a flower from it. And if the foliage evolved by the bulb is not permitted to grow its full term until it dies of its own accord, that bulb will not have within it the embryo flower and food for its next cycle of bloom. The leaves are the manufacturing system for the coming season of growth. Strictly speaking, many so-called bulbs are variations known as corms (gladiolus, crocus), tubers (dahlia, begonia), or rhizomes (iris). Corms are solid; as the plant grows, the corm shrinks and a new one is formed in its place. Potatoes are tubers, with points known as eyes from which growth sprouts. Rhizomes are thickened stems growing underground, producing both leaves and roots.

To Keep Bulbs Happy. Extra rich soil is not necessary for spring-flowering bulbs, but good drainage is. A little bonemeal is recommended as a fertilizer because it is so long lasting. Set your bulbs in clusters and see how much better they look than in thin, stiff rows. And whatever you do, don't cut off the foliage until it has completely died.

Whether to take up the bulbs and replant them in the fall is a puzzling question for beginners. The answer is that you need not move them until the flowers get smaller and fewer. However, tender bulbs like gladiolus, dahlias and tuberous begonias that are planted in the spring must be dug up after they bloom and brought indoors for the winter. Dust them with DDT and a fungicide as a safety measure, and store in a temperature of 40 to 50 degrees.

Bulbs forced into bloom indoors cannot be forced a second time, but if garden space is available they may be planted outdoors for eventual rebloom. Roman hyacinths and paper-white narcissus may as well be discarded at once.

(*Above*) **Tulips set any spring garden aglow. Several bulbs of one variety planted together in a group, as shown above, are more arresting than scrambled colors.**

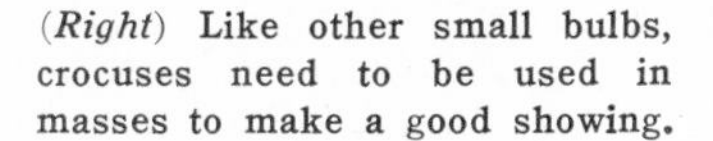

(*Right*) **Like other small bulbs, crocuses need to be used in masses to make a good showing.**

(*Above*) **Dwarf burning bush is valued mainly for its compact habit, slow growth and bright autumn foliage.**

BURNING BUSH

AMONG the hardiest of dense-growing shrubs is this one, which may safely be planted all over the United States and southeastern Canada. It forms a compact bush that grows without difficulty in ordinary soil, in part shade as well as full sun. Its yellow flowers of May and June become red berries by late summer. Foliage is green until fa l, when it turns coppery red before dropping. During winter the unusual corky wings along the stems are especially noticeable. The fiery autumn foliage and the bright berries make it outstanding wherever used. (For others of the same family, see *Euonymus* and *Evergreen Bittersweet.*)

Burning bush reaches 8 to 10 ft. in height, but there is a dwarf form very popular for hedge planting because of its slow growth and neat habit. As a specimen and in a shrub border it is attractive and dependable.

Varieties. *Dwarf* burning bush, growing 4 to 5 ft. high and 4 ft. across, may be purchased for $2.00 to $2.50 (in the 18 to 24-in. size). The taller form may be somewhat lower in cost.

How and When to Plant. Spring or fall planting is successful. For hedge use, buy small plants and set them about 18 to 20 in. apart. Pack the soil well about the roots, and water thoroughly. Trim back the tops to about 6 in.

Care and Protection. Almost no pruning is required. When used as a hedge, dwarf burning bush may need trimming about every second spring.

BUTTERFLY BUSH

THIS pleasing summer-flowering shrub earned its name through its attraction for butterflies. It is sometimes called summer lilac because of its long wands of bloom. Valued for its graceful appearance in the garden, it also provides sweetly fragrant spikes for cutting. Colors include purple, lavender, reddish, blue, pink and white.

The medium tall plant, 5 to 8 ft. high and as much in breadth, is a very vigorous,

Empire Blue butterfly bush comes nearest to real blue. It grows 4 to 6 ft. tall.

(*Above*) **The lavender-pink trusses of Charming butterfly bush are freely produced by this rapid-growing shrub.**

(*Right*) **For a profuse showing in autumn, pinch off the first flowers of butterfly bush as they appear in July. This will help side branches to develop which will bloom in September and October.**

healthy grower and blooms profusely from July through late September. Although it is slow to sprout in the spring, it grows fast once started. It will make an informal hedge and blend well with perennials and other shrubs. A plant may be had for $1.00 to $1.75.

Varieties. *Fascinating* is a nice soft orchid, and *Empire Blue* the nearest to true blue. Lavender-pink *Charming*, wine-red *Dubonnet*, and violet-purple *Ile de France* are popular. *White Profusion*, only 3 ft. tall, is especially good in front of taller shrubs.

How and When to Plant. Set out the plants in early spring or fall, in well-drained soil. They stand full sun or light shade. For a hedge, plant them 3 to 5 ft. apart.

Care and Protection. In hard winters the butterfly bush is likely to die back, perhaps all the way to the ground. This is not usually fatal. Simply cut back to green wood as soon as the plant shows life in spring. It will put out new growth that will bloom later that summer.

(*Above*) Like others of the cactus family, Christmas cactus must have good drainage. If it becomes soggy at the roots, the flower buds may drop off without opening.

(*Left*) Butterfly weed needs very little attention. Its heads of dazzling orange flowers are followed by seed pods like those of milkweed.

BUTTERFLY WEED

THIS is a relative of the common milkweed, but don't let that prevent you from planting it if you have a hot dry place in need of summer color. It is a wild plant requiring no attention in a garden, excellent for providing a big mass of bright orange from July to September. The "weed" in the name suggests that it is a rampant spreader, but that is not true. The 2 to 3-ft. clumps grow slowly in a border. They stand both hard winters and summer drought, and do well in sand at the seashore.

Any light, well-drained soil, especially a dry one, will grow butterfly weed. All-day sun is best. The flowers last well when cut, and their orange color is especially good with blues and purples.

Varieties. *Asclepias tuberosa* is the botanical listing for this fine plant. It has flat umbels of coppery yellow and costs up to 75c.

How and When to Plant. Plant in spring or fall, singly or in a group of three spaced 10 to 15 in. apart.

Care and Protection. This plant is a late starter in spring. Don't dig it up accidentally, and don't try to move it.

CACTUS

PERHAPS no plant name conjures up the desert more than cactus. This is a general term applied to over 2000 species of plants native mostly to the western hemisphere. Often the flowers are extremely showy, but sometimes they are tiny. Some kinds only a few inches high creep along the ground, while others are imposing sentinels of the desert country. Generally they are spiny, often bristly or hairy, with branches and stems in such an assortment of weird shapes that there seems no limit to the forms they can assume. They may be flattened or globular, jointed or furrowed, cylindrical or stringy.

Most varieties of cactus bloom in the summer and do not grow much in the winter. The plant tissues can store up water for a long period. When grown outdoors in hot dry regions or in containers indoors, they need all the sun possible and loose, open-textured soil that does not hold dampness. During their growing season they need moisture, but the pot should not stand in water. Smaller kinds of cactus are practical for dish gardens because they are slow growing and need the warm dry atmosphere found in most homes. It is possible to have a collection in quite a limited space.

Christmas cactus is a popular house plant with jointed stems and scarlet flowers from about November to January. These are carried at the very tips of the branches. Plants become large specimens and live for many years.

Varieties. Among the many small varieties suitable for dish gardens are *Hedgehog Cactus*, *Bishop's Cap*, *Pincushion Cactus*, and *Rabbit Ears*. Plants are readily available at very low cost.

How and When to Plant. Give cactus a sunny spot, outdoors or in, with good drainage. The plants can take more water in summer than in winter.

The showy Scarlet Pimpernelle caladium (described on the following page) has leaves of contrasting red and yellowish green.

(*Left*) **The huge leaves of Mrs. F. Sanders caladium are a combination of deep rose, dark green and chartreuse.**

(*Below*) **The tender caladium boasts flamboyant foliage that makes it perfect for summer beds in light shade. (A third variety of caladium is shown on the preceding page.)**

Care and Protection. To start a new plant, cut off a section of a stem and let it dry in the open air for several days before inserting it in sand.

Christmas cactus should be left in the pot and put outdoors in the shade during the summer. Water and liquid fertilizer should be given it from time to time. Bring in the plant before cold weather, and let it stay rather dry for a month to six weeks before its winter blooming time. Give it plenty of water while it is coming into bloom.

CALADIUM

INTEREST in this tropical foliage plant has increased greatly in the last several years. Although the flowers are not worth mentioning, the large, flat, paper-thin leaves of caladium (kal-lay′dee-um) are so richly colored that nothing else is needed to make it desirable as a bedding or pot plant. It may be grown in the house, in a porch or window box, or in a shady place in the garden. The conditions enjoyed by tuberous begonias also suit fancy-leaved caladiums—rich moist soil and light shade. Even under trees or shrubs they furnish interesting color if the soil has plenty of damp leaf mold in it. A humid atmosphere is good for them.

As pot plants they are extremely decorative all through the summer. Whether in pots or the open ground, the leaves die down in late summer, and the tubers then need a rest until the next spring. Pots may be moved as desired from house to terrace or porch, provided they are kept out of strong winds.

Varieties. Many named varieties are to be had, among them the popular green-ribbed white *Candidum*, pink and green *Mrs. W. B. Haldeman*, *Red Flare* (scarlet blotched green) and *Scarlet Pimpernelle* (red edged light green). Tubers cost about 50c.

How and When to Plant. To grow them in pots, plant the tubers first in a box of peat moss in early spring and keep them in a warm place until they have started to grow. Then transfer each tuber to a pot of its own (not too large), filled with rich potting soil, well watered, and out of the sun.

In cold areas they may be started in this way and moved to the open ground instead of pots as soon as the weather is warm. In warm climates tubers may be planted directly in the ground, 2 in. deep and 8 to 10 in. apart.

Care and Protection. When leaves start to droop in the fall, gradually stop watering. Then put the potful away in a dry, warm place until the next spring. If the plants are growing in outdoor beds, dig up the tubers and store them where they will not dry out completely over winter.

CALENDULAS

SHADES of lemon, gold and orange characterize these easily grown, hardy annuals. Some have flowers shaped like small chrysanthemums; others have petals rolled at the edges to make a quill. They grow 18 to 24 in. tall and are carried on strong stems. Average, well-drained soil and full sun meet their needs.

As cut flowers calendulas (kal-lend′yew-luh) are very desirable and long lasting. They look especially well in pottery bowls. Florists force them for winter use, but they are also widely grown in borders. Blue petunias are good companions for them. They bloom all summer in cool climates, but do not do so well in the heat of midsummer. Often they make their best showing late in the season, with fall flowers like asters and chrysanthemums. Pot marigold is an old English name for calendula.

Varieties. The *Pacific Beauty* strain, a recent development, has been bred to withstand summer heat. The large, well-formed flowers come in clear tones of cream, apricot and lemon. *Orange Quills*, 18 in. tall, has 3-in. blooms. Buttercup-yellow *Chrysantha* and bright orange *Campfire* (*Sensation*) are fine for cutting purposes.

How and When to Plant. Seed may be sown outdoors very early in the spring, and again at the end of June. The little plants are easy to move. Space them 12 in. apart.

Care and Protection. Keep the dead flower heads cut off. In case plant lice attack the plants in hot weather, spray with a good insecticide.

(*Above*) **Calendulas range through orange, gold and yellow tones. They are excellent for cutting.**

(*Left*) **Pacific Beauty calendulas are especially resistant to hot weather. Colors are brilliant and stems long.**

(*Left*) **California poppies are carefree annuals that bloom profusely in light, dry soil. They are a good choice for a child's first efforts at flower growing.**

CALIFORNIA POPPIES

DRIFTS of this gay annual look well near the front of a border where full sun will reach the flowers. The bushy, 12 to 15-in. plant has fine-cut, gray-green foliage that gives a light and airy effect. Individual flowers, single and also double, are short lived but are produced steadily and profusely all summer. Colors run through scarlet, pink, orange, yellow and white.

This plant needs space to spread. It is easy to grow in a hot dry spot in loose, well-drained soil. Seed can be scattered on the ground around spring-flowering bulbs, to provide color after the bulbs are gone. Often it will self-sow.

Varieties. Usually seed is sold in mixture, but separate colors are also available, such as *Carmine King*, *Dazzler* (scarlet), *Gloaming* (coral), and *Golden West*.

How and When to Plant. Scatter the seed in late fall or early spring where it is to grow. Thin out the young plants to about 8 in. apart.

Care and Protection. Don't try to transplant California poppy, and don't let it go to seed if you want bloom to continue.

CALLA LILY

OF simple classic form, the calla lily has a kind of spiritual beauty. Especially at Easter and on through summer, florists use it in quantity. In the very mildest climates it may be raised outdoors, but generally it is regarded as a pot plant. Yellow and pink kinds are available, and even a black one, in addition to white. The flowers bloom in the spring and are long lasting. White ones come a few weeks before the others. The arrow-shaped leaves, some kinds spotted or flecked, white or yellow, are beautiful as they unfurl. Rich moist soil is a necessity.

Varieties. Tubers are bought by color, at 50c to 75c each.

How and When to Plant. In early fall plant the tuber an inch deep in a 6-in. pot filled with potting soil. Give it liquid fertilizer and some water. When growth starts, water more often and place the pot in a warm, sunny window.

Care and Protection. Keep well watered while blooming and until the leaves turn yellow. When all danger of frost is over, take the tuber out of the pot and plant it outdoors. In the fall dig it up, let it dry for six weeks at least, and then pot it up again. Or it may be left in the pot, taken outdoors until the leaves turn yellow, and then allowed to dry out and rest until time to repot.

CAMASSIA

WESTERN North America is the home of this hardy bulb, but camassia (kam-mass'ee-uh) may be grown almost anywhere provided it has a damp location. Along streams and naturalized in half-shaded wild gardens, it bears tall spikes of star-shaped flowers. Groups may also be planted in a border of perennials. Individual flowers are somewhat like those of scilla, but they appear in May or June on 2 to 3-ft. stalks.

Varieties. *Blue Esculenta* or *Quamash*, lavender-blue *Leichtlini*, and light blue *Cusicki* are offered. Bulbs are priced at 60c to $1.00 per dozen.

How and When to Plant. Plant the bulbs in the fall, 4 in. deep and the same distance apart.

Care and Protection. Do not disturb these bulbs; they are long lived and do not need to be moved.

(*Above*) **A sunny or slightly shaded location in moist soil meets the requirements of camassia.**

(*Left*) **Exquisite calla lilies need not be left to the florist to raise. Plant some yourself and thrill to the sight of the unfurling leaves and flowers.**

Two of the important newer camellias—recent All-America Winners that are proving popular and adaptable.

(*Left*) **Sparkling Burgundy, of ruby-rose, often overlaid with a lavender sheen, is a healthy, vigorous sasanqua hybrid.**

(*Right*) **The beautiful Bonnie Marie flowers freely over a long season.**

CAMELLIAS

THROUGH the areas where camellias (kam-mell'ee-uh) can be grown, interest runs high in this noble evergreen shrub. As with so many other ornamentals, its native home is the Orient, where it is found from Indo-China to Korea. Centuries ago Buddhist missionaries in China and Japan planted it around their temples, and in the 1700's a captain of the British East India Company brought it to England. By 1800 it had reached New York, and fifty years later was being tried in California. The name commemorates a Jesuit missionary, George Joseph Kamel, but in the South the plant is familiarly known as japonica.

Camellias are commonly grown outdoors from southeastern Virginia along the Atlantic into Florida, along the Gulf Coast, and from California north to British Columbia. Ardent gardeners raise them in the vicinity of New York City, and they are a favorite of both amateurs and florists for growing in greenhouses. Neither a high nor a very low winter temperature is best for them; the ideal range is 35 to 60 degrees. A high summer temperature is not injurious provided the soil and air are moist. Several show gardens in the South are world-famous for their camellias, and in a number of cities special camellia shows are a yearly feature.

This is a valuable specimen and landscaping plant growing in spring and summer but reaching the height of bloom in February and March. Some kinds start flowering as early as September. It may be used in borders with such shrubs as azaleas and holly, and its glossy dark evergreen foliage makes a rich background for flowering plants of all kinds. Its ability to produce bloom in the shade is a great asset.

Essential for success in growing camellias are fertile, well-drained acid soil and moisture in both soil and air. Plenty of decayed vegetable matter, in such form as peat moss and leaf mold, must be present. Partly shaded locations are better than either complete shade or full sun. To make soil acid, aluminum sulphate and sulphur are useful; half-rotted oak leaves, peat moss and special camellia fertilizer also need to be added to the soil prior to planting. The soil must never be heavy or sticky.

Most widely grown are the japonica camellias, which provide the great bulk of bloom. A great number of varieties are in existence, and there is considerable confusion in names. The sasanquas grow faster and are more winter-hardy. Many are fragrant and bloom earlier than japonicas. Plant breeders at work in Europe and Australia as well as the United States are aiming to produce varieties more vigorous, more tolerant of both heat and cold, and more varied in color and flower form. Colors now run from white through all shades of red, with many blotched and variegated kinds; flowers are single and double, formal and informally ruffled.

Varieties. Nurseries specializing in ca-

Three staple camellias, among many other fine japonica varieties (others are shown on the facing page).

(*Above*) **Mathotiana, one of the handsomest reds.**

(*Left*) **Alba Plena, wax-like, perfectly formed, early blooming.**

(*Right*) **Herme, variegated rose and white.**

mellias can furnish a great number of varieties, costing about $3.00 up for an 18 to 24-in. plant. White *Alba Plena*, one of the earliest japonicas, is still grown; among other old favorites are carmine *Mathotiana*, light pink *Debutante*, and variegated *Herme*. Among good sasanqua varieties are pink *Rosea* and white *Mine-No-Yuki*. Recent winners of the All-America award are light pink *Bonnie Marie*, pale pink *King's Ransom*, and rose-colored *Sparkling Burgundy*.

How and When to Plant. Best time to plant is during the winter, from November to March. The soil must first be well provided with leaf mold or peat moss and camellia fertilizer, well dug in. Small plants are easiest to get established. They may be had in containers, bare rooted or with a ball of earth around the roots. Dig a hole 6 in. deeper and 12 in. wider than necessary to hold the roots, and partly fill it with the enriched soil mixture. Set the plant in the hole so that it will be 2 in. higher than ground level. Pack good soil tightly around the roots, water thoroughly, and syringe the top. Keep well watered and shaded, if necessary, for several days. Put a 2-in. covering of pine needles, peat or oak leaves over the ground.

Care and Protection. Always keep this cover on the ground; do not dig around the roots. Supply water to the soil and also the leaves, by syringing them, especially all

Debutante has peony-form flowers of lovely light pink, 3 to 4 in. in diameter. It is slow growing and early blooming.

(*Above*) Stunning Chang's Temple—a japonica, like all the others on this page—boasts extremely large and glowing flowers.

Margaret Higdon is a fine camellia with 4 to 5-in. flowers on a symmetrical plant.

Augusta Wilson has very full blooms of deep pink. This is a fast grower with large glossy leaves.

Governor Mouton is a very hardy camellia of moderate growth, blooming over a long season. Its blood-red flowers are marbled with white.

(*Above*) Rosea—a sasanqua camellia, like the others shown on this page—has single blooms with prominent golden stamens.

(*Right*) Hiodoshi displays its lavender-pink blooms against the thick, glossy foliage for which camellias are particularly prized.

through the hot weather. Give the plants special camellia fertilizer, at the rate specified on the package, in February and again in June; do not overfeed. When necessary to remove dead twigs or to keep the plants to the size desired, prune just after they bloom. Shade against winter sun, to prevent burning. Plants growing well will be less subject to disease and pests. A spray of white oil emulsion in April will combat scale. New growth that dies back should be cut off and burned. Parathion in winter and sulphur in hot weather will be effective against red spider.

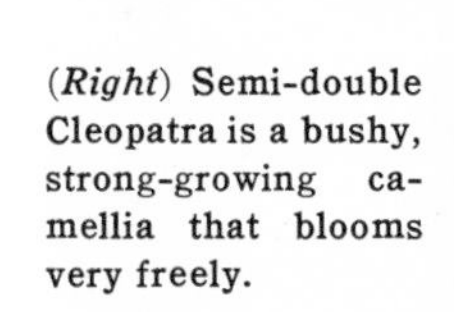

(*Right*) Semi-double Cleopatra is a bushy, strong-growing camellia that blooms very freely.

(*Below*) The showy cupped flowers of Oleifera have creped petals washed with soft rose at the margins, but sometimes they are almost white throughout.

(*Above*) Evergreen candytuft bears a sheet of snowy blooms in spring, which show up well against the dark evergreen leaves.

(*Right*) Annual candytuft comes in mixed colors and is easily grown from seed. Dome-shaped flowers cover the bushy plants.

CANDYTUFT

FOR snow-white masses of bloom to combine with daffodils and tulips in the early spring garden, candytuft is a natural and reliable choice. The little heads of flowers come in profusion at the end of every stem, and they last for about six weeks. This is a very neat, hardy perennial with dark evergreen foliage, almost like a shrub in the way it grows. Undemanding and long lived, it is perfect for low masses at the edge of a border and for white mounds in rock and wall gardens. Usually it is not over 10 in. high, but it spreads to make a 2-ft. cushion. All it asks is full sun and well-drained garden soil.

Annual candytuft offers pink, crimson and blue flowers in addition to white. It does well anywhere, including city gardens, and is nice to cut.

Varieties. *Evergreen* candytuft is the perennial kind most widely grown. It can take a little shade if necessary. A low spreader, it is fine in rock gardens and as a ground cover. *Little Gem* is even more compact in growth. *Snowflake,* 6 to 8 in. tall, has showy pure white flowers in May. Another good dwarf variety is *Purity,* an edger and rock plant with large white flowers and very dark leaves. Plants are 60c to 90c apiece.

How and When to Plant. Either fall or spring planting is successful. Allow 6 in. between plants. Seed of annual candytuft is sown in early spring where it is wanted outdoors. Thin the plants to 8 to 10 in. apart.

Care and Protection. Immediately after they bloom, cut back the plants hard, to make them grow bushy again. Old clumps can be divided in early fall or after they have stopped blooming.

CANNAS

BOLD as a billboard, this plant is nevertheless a tender migrant from the tropics, easily caught by frost. It is so big and formal and the colors so bright that it is widely planted in parks and other public places, where it makes an impressive display through midsummer. It reaches $3\frac{1}{2}$ or 4 ft. in height, with brilliant pink, orange, red or gold flowers, and large green or bronze leaves. (Some of the bronze-foliage varieties may even grow to 6 ft.) A dwarfer strain is also now available, as well as varieties in pastel colors.

Cannas need full sun and plenty of water. The soil should be rich and able to retain moisture.

Varieties. Standard varieties include bright pink *City of Portland,* orange-scarlet *King Humbert,* and gold *King Midas,* among others. Tubers cost 25c to 40c.

How and When to Plant. After all possible danger of frost is past, plant the tubers outdoors, 3 to 4 in. deep and 15 to 20 in. apart. Or start them in pots indoors and move them to the open after the weather has become settled.

Care and Protection. Keep well watered in dry spells. In the fall dig up and store the tubers over winter in a sheltered place.

CAPE MARIGOLD

THIS native of South Africa bears the imposing botanical name *Dimorphotheca.* It also shares the name African daisy with another flower (*Arctotis*). Whatever you want to call it, this is a dainty annual that likes a warm, sunny place where it gets good drainage. Flowers in shades of buff, cream, yellow, salmon and orange are carried on thin wiry 12-in. stems and are inclined to close at night.

A bed of cape marigolds glittering in the sunshine. They bloom most of the summer and fall.

Cannas are bold in color but very susceptible to frost. They require an abundance of water. (*Left to right*) King Humbert (bronze foliage), King Midas, Mrs. Alfred Conard and Wyoming (bronze foliage).

(*Left*) Make cardinal climber your choice when you want a fast-growing vine that will give bright flowers rather than shade.

(*Right*) Hardy garden carnations like white Moon Mist, soft pink Evangeline and rich salmon Old Spice furnish plenty of spicy-scented flowers for cutting. They bloom best in spring and fall.

The plants flower freely from early summer to frost. With other annuals, in rock gardens and for massed effects in borders, they are very useful. Like other daisies, these flowers are nice to cut, especially for mixed bouquets.

Varieties. *Aurantiaca* is a popular kind, with black-centered, bright orange blooms. Varieties of it may be had in assorted colors.

How and When to Plant. Sow seed outdoors in spring where the plants are to grow. Barely cover with soil. Thin out to 6 to 9 in.

Care and Protection. Coming from a hot region, cape marigolds need full sun. They can't stand shade or a heavy soil.

CARDINAL CLIMBER

FOR a quick effect on a trellis or against a wall, this annual climber is very useful. The foliage is too fine-cut to give much shade, but the flowers make a bright display. It grows about 20 ft. in a summer if given average garden soil and a warm, sunny location. The tubular, fiery scarlet flowers, somewhat like little morning glories, are set off by the glossy, rich green foliage. They appear about midsummer and continue until frost.

Varieties. The red-flowered is the only kind (*Quamoclit sloteri*).

How and When to Plant. When frost is over, sow the seed outdoors where it is wanted to grow. Nick the seed with a knife or soak it overnight before planting.

Care and Protection. Do not give this vine any fertilizer.

CARNATIONS

COMMERCIAL growers, especially in Colorado, have vigorously promoted the carnation, and it holds a prominent place in florists' exhibits at flower shows. The spicy scent and clean-cut form have long endeared it for use as a boutonniere, corsage and bouquet flower.

Some carnations may also be raised outdoors where summer temperatures do not go high. Cool air, moist but not heavy, is needed, as well as fully drained soil and complete sun. Soil should be sweet rather than acid, and if

(*Above*) Hot humid summers don't suit carnations. They like a moist but cool atmosphere.

At the large flower shows commercial carnation growers exhibit such exotically colored blooms as these . . . charming as boutonnieres, delightful for home decoration.

leaf mold is added to it the plants have a better chance of surviving hot weather. A little lime should be mixed with most soils.

The plants may be grouped at the edge of a border, provided they are not crowded. There the distinctive gray-green, grassy foliage will be attractive, as well as the early summer-blooming flowers on 10 to 15-in. stems. (For a smaller garden form, see *Pinks.*)

Varieties. *Grenadin,* with half to fully double flowers, is a compact-growing strain. Among the popular varieties are light pink *Evangeline,* white *Moon Mist,* salmon-pink *Old Spice,* wine-colored *Dubonnet,* and crimson-spotted white *Sweet Memory.* Bright rosy scarlet *Kiss of Fire* has especially good cutting stems; *Red Peppermint* is variegated red and white. Plants average 85c each.

How and When to Plant. Spring planting is to be preferred. Set plants about a foot apart.

Care and Protection. Pick the flowers often, and when the blooming season is over cut the plants back lightly. If your winters are severe, a light cover of evergreen branches is recommended.

Care and Protection. When bloom starts to fade in midsummer, cut back the plants. They will need to be dug up, divided and replanted every few years, in spring.

CHASTE TREE

IN spite of its name, this is not a tree but a large bushy shrub of branching habit, making a good clump 6 to 8 ft. tall unless pruned. In late summer it is studded with fragrant lavender flowers in long spikes. The foliage is grayish green. Practically any soil, even a poor one, will grow this shrub, provided it is well drained and in full sun. This is useful at the back of a perennial border where a bushy filler is wanted, or it may be combined with other shrubs. Its late blooming season is an advantage. It is hardy as far north as New York City.

Varieties. *Vitex macrophylla* is listed, or simply ask for chaste tree. A plant may be bought for as little as $1.25 to $1.50.

How and When to Plant. Spring is the best planting time. Be particularly careful not to let the roots dry out while planting. Water well after packing the soil hard.

Care and Protection. Cut the shoots back to within a few inches of the ground every spring. Even if winter has killed the plant back, new shoots will grow quickly and bloom later that same year if the roots are uninjured.

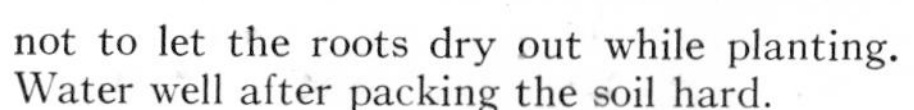

(*Right*) The long, graceful wands of chaste tree are an advantage in any late summer garden. The foliage too is very pleasing.

(*Left*) Light, dry soil and all-day sun will please catmint. Cut off the flowers as they fade, to encourage more bloom.

CATMINT

WITH its silvery gray foliage, catmint is a good contrast plant, ornamental all season. It forms a compact, low spreading mass about 10 to 12 in. high, with lavender flowers rising in little spikes in early summer and continuing off and on until fall. As a low edging, on top of a wall and in the foreground of a perennial border, this hardy plant is extremely pleasing. The restful color combines well with all the gay tones of summer, and the growth never crowds out other plants.

Full sun and light, well-drained soil are needed for catmint. It can stand quite a warm location. Catnip is one of the same family; another variety, known as ground ivy, forms a close mat on the ground.

Varieties. Catalogs list this plant as *Nepeta mussini* and offer it at 60c to 90c.

How and When to Plant. Set out the plants in early spring, 12 in. apart. Avoid a damp, shaded position.

The oddly veined checkered lily is a modest and interesting addition to spring rock gardens.

CHECKERED LILY

ALTHOUGH this bulb is related to the imposing crown imperial, it is easy to grow. As a clump in a rock garden or grouped under a tree where it gets a little shade, it soon becomes established. The nodding, bell-shaped flowers are mostly in bronze and purplish shades, mottled and checkered—which explains why they are sometimes called guinea hen flower. These dainty bells come in April on 10 to 12-in. plants. The light soil of a rock garden suits them.

Varieties. Bulbs are sold in mixture, at 60c to 75c per dozen.

How and When to Plant. Mid-autumn is the time to plant the bulbs, 3 in. deep and 6 in. apart. A small group is needed to make a good effect.

Care and Protection. The bulbs resent being moved, so leave them alone.

CHERRY LAUREL

IN mild climates this sturdy evergreen shrub is especially valued as a windbreak or screen. In the South it becomes tree size if left unclipped. Because it stands severe

(*Left*) **Cherry laurel is a good evergreen shrub that finds many ways to be useful in mild-climate regions.**

(*Above*) **For a child's early attempts at gardening, marigolds have a great deal to offer, for success is practically guaranteed.**

pruning so well, it is very often used as a hedge. The leaves are thick and glossy, and in late winter or early spring there are quantities of fragrant white flowers. Any good garden soil is suitable, and a location in either sun or part shade.

Varieties. Fast-growing *Carolina* cherry laurel, a native of southeastern United States, reaches a height of 40 ft. if not pruned. *European* or *English* grows more broad and compact. Both can be sheared hard. The 2 to 3-ft. size may be purchased for about $4.00 to $5.00.

How and When to Plant. Set out the plant in early spring or early fall, where it will not be crowded. Give it plenty of water until well established.

Care and Protection. Hard pruning should be done in spring, and if desirable a light trimming may also be given later.

CHILDREN'S GARDENS

YOU may never have given very much thought to the pleasant and even wonderful things that could happen if your children took a fancy to gardening. It might well prove the answer to a harried mother's prayer—but above all, it would open up a new world of fun and fascination to the youngsters themselves.

Even a four-year-old will be thrilled by the chance to grow flowers or vegetables in her own special corner. Attach her name to it, so she will know it's her very own, and will watch every flower in it with a keen pride. Help her to get started by picking a sunny spot, with good soil, and prepare the ground well, explaining everything you do so she'll understand how Nature works. Pick plants that are sure to succeed, for any disappointments or failures at this early stage would be a cruel blow. Easy annuals like nasturtiums and marigolds would be a good choice, as well as hardy bulbs like crocuses and daffodils which will create a lot of excitement when they pop out suddenly in early spring. The shouts of joy with which these first flowers will be greeted and announced will repay you for all your trouble.

And once this interest in gardening is off to a good start, it will grow and intensify with very little help from you. You will be amazed at the benefits that will flow from it, both for you and for the youngsters, and in fact the whole family. As they grow older, they will take on bigger and more challenging projects. With a bit of advice or a mere hint from you, Kathy will want to plant her own peony bush, or two or three of them together —and when the gorgeous blooms are cut and proudly displayed in the living-room, be sure to call them "Kathy's peonies" when the family or your guests admire them. Suggest to Johnny that he look into rock gardens as something to sharpen his gardening teeth on, and when he begins to show off the rare beauties cropping out of his domain, be sure to let everybody know that they come from "Johnny's rock garden."

Before you realize what has happened, both Johnny and Kathy will be asking questions about the rules for competing in the garden club's flower show.

Perhaps the easiest way to prevent teen-age headaches long before they might show up is to get your children started on gardening at an early age.

(*Above*) **A handful of tulip bulbs planted in Junior's own garden will delight him when they push out of the ground in March.**

(*Left*) **Your child's enjoyment of his garden will be at least tripled when he picks some of the flowers, such as these nasturtiums, to share with others.**

Three varieties of Chinese forget-me-not, all of them very easy to grow and useful for cutting as well as massing in the garden. (*Left*) Firmament, which forms a compact, leafy plant averaging 15 in. in height. (*Right*) Blue Bird, lighter in color and taller growing. (*Below*) Pink Firmament, nice in combination with the blues.

CHINESE FORGET-ME-NOT

HERE is an annual (botanically, *Cynoglossum*) like a tall forget-me-not, with upright, branching stems of blue flowers making a splendid effect when grown in masses. Pink and white forms are also to be had. For rock gardens and borders with just average soil it is invaluable, particularly since it also furnishes fine cut-flower material for many weeks in summer. The bushy plant grows quickly to a height of 18 to 30 in.

Varieties. Indigo-blue *Firmament,* with a compact, 15-in. plant, does well even in poor dry soil. *Pink Firmament* and *Snowbird* are also good. *Blue Bird,* with sky-blue flowers, grows to 2 ft.

How and When to Plant. Sow seed outdoors in early spring and barely cover it. Thin or move the little plants to allow 8 or 9 in. between them. They will take sun or light shade. Plants may also be purchased in small pots or boxes of a dozen or more from a local grower. They often self-sow.

Care and Protection. None needed!

CHINESE LANTERN PLANT

THE orange-red lanterns hung out by this easy-to-grow, 2-ft. perennial are gay enough to tempt anyone to plant it. But be careful! Although hardy and fast growing, it is not for small gardens, nor for any garden where it will be close to valued plants. The reason is that it spreads like a weed, by means of long creeping underground stems that soon take over any area.

However, the bright seed pods strung along the stems are so decorative and long lasting indoors in winter that if you have plenty of space you might well give up some of it to the Chinese lantern plant. Light soil and full sun are its simple requirements. Wait until the lanterns have turned orange before you cut them. Alone or with other dried everlastings, they stay bright and colorful for weeks, and will add a festive touch to table decorations.

Varieties. Besides the usual *Physalis francheti,* as it is named, there is a dwarf form. A plant costs 50c to 65c.

How and When to Plant. Spring or early fall is the time to plant.

Care and Protection. If it spreads farther than you like, cut out the shoots you don't want. Blooms and lanterns may not be so plentiful if the clump gets overgrown. In that case, dig it up in spring, divide it and reset some of the pieces.

CHOKEBERRY

BIRDS love the bright red berries borne in such profusion by the chokeberry, and anyone who wants to attract birds to a garden should not overlook this native American shrub. Extremely undemanding and easy to grow, it likes any soil at all and either sun or part shade. It can stand a rather low, wet location as well as smoky city conditions and is good for wild plantings. Profuse white flowers come in April or May, followed by big crops of bright red berries

(*Below*) Chinese lantern plant is greedy for space, so think twice before you try it. But if you do, you will have a shower of orange-gold for indoor decorating.

(*Right*) Christmas roses may be cut early in the morning, for use indoors. Plunge the stems in water for two or three hours before arranging them.

(*Below*) The attractive and densely branched chokeberry.

that hang on well until the birds eat them. Autumn foliage is brilliant red. This vigorous, bushy shrub grows wild from Massachusetts west to Minnesota and south to Texas. An 18 to 24-in. plant costs around $1.50.

Varieties. Besides the common 5 to 6-ft. *Red*, there is a *Black* variety that is lower growing and bears shiny black berries. *Brilliant* has red fruits and grows 3 to 5 ft. high. An *Erect* form is also available, recommended for hedge use.

How and When to Plant. Plants may be set out in spring or fall. Pack the soil well around the roots, and water them well.

Care and Protection. If any pruning is needed, do it in early spring.

CHRISTMAS ROSE

LEGEND says this flower sprang from the tears of a little shepherdess who had no gift to take to the Christ Child. It is very choice and desirable, although it has no relationship with roses. The almost unbelievable blooming season—usually December through March—makes it a curiosity, but it is more than that. The flowers are innocent white cups 2 to 4 in. across, becoming pinkish and finally green after many weeks. The handsome evergreen foliage is thick and leathery.

Even cold and snow will do the plant no harm, but a suitable location is very important. It must have a spot sheltered from the wind, with cool moist shade in summer and some sun in winter, where it can be left undisturbed the year round. A good place is under a shrub or tree that loses its leaves in the fall, or near a protecting wall. The soil must be well drained but damp and supplied with woodsy leaf mold. A year or two is often required for a plant to start blooming, but if it is happily located it will in time form a satisfying mass.

Varieties. *Helleborus niger* is the scientific name, but just Christmas rose identifies the plant. It grows a foot tall and costs about $1.50. The Lenten rose, of the same family, produces purplish flowers from late winter to May.

How and When to Plant. Mix leaf mold into the ground before planting. Set out the plants in spring, about an inch below soil level, and 12 in. apart.

Care and Protection. Water thoroughly in dry summers. It is good practice to keep a layer of peat or leaf mold around the plants always, but otherwise leave them alone.

CHRYSANTHEMUMS

Burning Bronze, an All-America winner, provides a good splash of fall color—magnificent tangerine-scarlet-orange.

WHEN tender plants are reeling from the first chill of autumn, chrysanthemums take over the garden. They are, without any doubt, the dominant fall flower. Plant breeders have worked wonders with "mums," with the result that there are now a bewildering number of varieties to choose from, in every color but blue. Many are earlier flowering kinds, which makes it possible to grow them much farther north than previously. By choosing varieties carefully, home growers may have blooms from early August to hard frost. Experiments have shown that a given variety will come into bloom about two days earlier for every hundred miles north that you travel. This is because cool weather and fewer hours of daylight cause the plants to flower sooner.

Besides producing breath-taking outdoor flower shows, mums are wonderful for cutting. It is doubtful whether any cut flower lasts better. Breaking off an inch or two of the stem and changing the water daily makes them last up to two weeks. This renders them doubly valuable to home gardeners anxious

Flair, another All-America winner, is a lively rich lavender that does not tend to fade.

Three more All-America winners, like the two on the preceding page and three on the page following. (*Left*) Mardi Gras, a medley of strong reddish orange hues, becoming bright bronze and yellow. (*Right*) Emperor, a blaze of rich yellow from top to bottom. (*Below*) Headliner, glowing terra-cotta-bronze in the bud, opening to walnut-coral.

to prolong summer and enjoy fresh bouquets as long as possible.

Mums fall into several classes: the decorative with 2 to 5-in. double flowers on 2 to 3-ft. plants, pompons with rounded flowers in sprays on a 2 to 2½-ft. plant, daisy-like singles, cushions that are especially good in the North because the low, mound-like plant blooms so early, spoons that are so charming for flower arrangements, the big commercial or "football" varieties, besides the tiny button and exotic spider kinds. The cushion type is particularly recommended as an edging plant.

Florists find the chrysanthemum to be profitable the year round. With them it is not a flower of autumn but one of the most important items they use for baskets, sprays, and all types of arrangements. Forcing mums into bloom in the greenhouse is a highly developed skill, with many dozens of varieties in use. Their normal flowering time is when the hours of darkness are longer than those of daylight. Forcing them to bloom earlier is therefore done by shading the plants; artificial light, on the other hand, holds off the flowering time until later. In order to have the largest flowers possible, only one bud is allowed to develop on a stem. Temperature, feeding, watering and soil are carefully watched and regulated.

In the garden chrysanthemums deserve a prominent position where they can be enjoyed to the full both by their growers and by those passing by. They need plenty of room for full development and should never be crowded in among annuals where there

The possibilities of a mass planting of hardy garden chrysanthemums are unbounded. For many weeks they can keep your garden alive with color.

Three All-America chrysanthemums (like those on the two preceding pages). (*Left*) Her Majesty, pure white with a cream center. (*Right*) Apricot Sheen, a 15-in. mound covered with dozens of rich apricot flowers. (*Below*) Girl Friend, shell-pink to coral-rose.

will be poor air circulation and the danger of catching disease or insect pests. A convenient feature is the fact that a plant in full bloom may readily be moved from one place in the garden to another if enough soil is taken with it so as not to disturb the roots. In this way mums may fill spots left vacant by earlier blooming plants. Groups may be used at doorways, against evergreens, or as a low divider between different parts of the garden.

Mums are not hard to grow if a few basic conditions are met. They don't like competition from tree or shrub roots and should never be planted close to a hedge. They dislike heavy shade, and like many other plants they don't enjoy standing in water, especially in winter. They do like full sun, good drainage, and a fertile, deep soil.

We are indebted to China for the chrysanthemum. Here it was grown in the time of Confucius, and later found its way to Japan, then to England, and finally to the western hemisphere.

Besides the hardy mums, there are annual kinds raised easily from seed if sown in an open, sunny place and not moved. These are both single and double, dark-centered daisies that grow 9 in. to 2 ft. high. Blooming in late summer, they are fine to cut. Shasta daisies and painted daisies (which see) belong to this same family, as do the northland daisies, which are very hardy but late blooming.

Varieties. So many varieties are available that only an inkling can be given of them here. A number of nurseries specialize in chrysanthemums and offer new ones every year. All-America winners are reliable, and these are well advertised and described in magazines. It pays to watch for them.

Among the recent All-America winners are *Apricot Sheen*, orange-red *Bingo*, creamy-centered white *Her Majesty*, lavender *Flair*, *Pink Cherub*, and *Burning Bronze*.

(*Above*) Mercury, a rugged Korean hybrid with bronze-red to coppery bronze blooms in graceful sprays.

(*Left*) Saladin, another of the Korean mums, has substantial coral-red blooms, 3 in. or more in diameter.

(*Right*) Lilac-pink Venus and softer pink Aphrodite are a good pair of Korean hybrids.

(*Left*) Lavender Lady has retained her laurels through years of competition from newer chrysanthemums. The silvery lavender color is bewitching.

(*Right*) Clara Curtis has daisy-like, salmon-pink flowers on short, well-branched stems. It is very early blooming.

(*Right*) Fred F. Rockwell, vigorous and frostproof, is a brilliant blend of bronze and orange-scarlet.

The Korean Hybrids developed in the early 1930's for extra vigor and hardiness have daisy-like flowers. Yellow *Ceres* and red-bronze *Mercury* are two of many. *Lavender Lady* is a decorative mum that has remained popular. The University of Minnesota has developed a number of varieties for northern conditions, among them creamy white *Prairie Moon*, which has proved reliable. *Bronze Giant* is another dependable early decorative.

Pompons include orange-scarlet to bronze *Fred F. Rockwell*, deep lemon-yellow *Chiquita*, and lavender and rose *Masquerade*. *Clara Curtis*, with salmon-pink flowers in late August, is a fine single mum; alabaster-white *Daisymum* is another. Among the cushion mums, *Minnpink* has made a good showing, as have crimson *Lipstick*, yellow *Bowl o' Gold*, and dark red *Ruby Mound*. Those called azaleamums belong here. All of them are especially good for low edgings in moderate-sized gardens.

The *Bird* series offers early-blooming varieties with 4 to 5-in. flowers. Among the latest additions to the group are bronze and gold *Chestnut Warbler*, pastel *Song Sparrow*, pink *Humming Bird*, and shaggy *Snowy Egret*.

Harvest Giants have been introduced recently. These have very large flowers like florists' mums, on low-growing, hardy plants. They have such pleasing and appropriate names as *Autumn Leaves* (bronze), *September Song* (rose-pink), *Indian Summer* (reddish bronze), and *Full Moon* (creamy white).

(*Above*) Yellow Spoon is a good clear color. The tubular petals flatten out to form a spoon-shaped tip, as do those of Pink Spoon (*at the left*).

(*Right*) September Cloud is a fine white pompon with primrose shading at the heart of the rounded blooms.

(*Left*) **Wood Duck is one of the Bird series of hardy mums. Long stiff stems carry dozens of blooms on each 2½ to 3-ft. plant.**

(*Right*) **Magnolia is creamy pink with soft yellow overtones. It blooms over a long period and does not require staking.**

A standard variety costs 60c to 75c per plant. The newest kinds run from $1.50 to $2.00 each.

How and When to Plant. Set out the plants when settled spring weather has arrived—early May, or even later in northern sections. The ground should be well prepared beforehand, by the addition of some dried manure, bonemeal and peat (available at garden supply stores). Allow the plants 18 in. of space, and press the soil firmly about them. Water well.

Care and Protection. Snip or pinch off the very tip of each shoot when it is 6 in. long, to make the plants bushier. Do it again in a few weeks, but not after the middle of July. Keep plants well watered all through the summer. Tallest ones may need the support of a stake.

Where severe winters occur, cut back the stalks to 5 or 6 in. after hard frost has finally killed them. Then cover the plants with straw or evergreen branches. The purpose is not to protect them from low temperatures but to keep them from alternately freezing and thawing and being heaved up out of the ground. In the spring, remove this cover gradually.

Mum plants should be divided every spring (every second year is often enough for cushion types). Dig up the plant, separate it into smaller pieces, throw away the center and replant the other parts, preferably in a place that did not grow chrysanthemums before.

If leaves get blotched and turn yellow, spray with a good fungicide, following the directions on the label.

(*Above*) **September Song, one of the Harvest Giant mums that have been attracting attention. All of this group bloom continuously until hard frost.**

(*Left*) **Annual chrysanthemums are dark-centered daisies that grow about 10 in. tall and bloom in late summer.**

(*Right*) **Commercial or florists' varieties, like the three shown here, have huge compact flowers brought into bloom under carefully regulated conditions.**

English ivy and yew are two of the best assistants a city gardener can find to keep his surroundings green. Often a lawn must give way to cement or flagstones, especially in small shaded spaces or where table and chairs need a firm foundation.

CITY GARDENING

CITY gardening is beset with many difficulties, but if you are determined to overcome them you can at least achieve a snug, attractive retreat. You may have to give up the rainbow of color you would like to have and settle happily for a haven of greenery in the shape of vines, ground covers and potted foliage plants.

Where the available space is very limited, you must first decide whether to use it mainly as a terrace or patio for rest and perhaps an occasional meal, or whether the garden itself is to be the chief attraction. If table and chairs are to occupy most of the space, you will want a paved area (brick or cement) for a firm base. Plants in tubs, pots and planters can be placed where desired. They can be renewed easily, and moved around at will. Geraniums, petunias and lantanas are easily grown in pots where there is plenty of sun. Begonias and fuchsias will do well in part shade. To screen the area, a wall, a hedge or tall shrubs will do the trick.

A small garden in the city can be very pleasing if the center is left open and the sides planted in more or less formal style. The center is more apt to be a gravel path or flagstones or brick than a lawn. A bench or love seat of wood or iron, a wall fountain or a stone bird bath makes a good focal point.

If the ground is fairly good, it can be improved by digging leaf mold, peat moss and other organic material into the top layer. This will put it in condition to receive plant roots and water and will aerate the soil. Usually soil that has been neglected can stand a light application of lime occasionally. This should not be given every year nor at the same time that fertilizer is added. Allow an interval of a week or ten days between the lime and the fertilizer applications. Lime should not be used near broad-leaved evergreens like holly and rhododendron.

Which Plants to Choose. Once the soil is brought up to par, you can decide which plants to try. English ivy is favored as a ground or wall cover, and does well in the shade. Pachysandra and myrtle are other dependable ground covers. Also preferred for shady places are plantain lily and lily of the valley.

Even in a small city garden there is room for an ornamental tree if the soil is deep enough and if some sun reaches it. Among the possibilities are magnolia, flowering crab and cherry, dogwood and hawthorn. Thornless honey locusts are excellent small trees casting a light shade. Yews are more successful in cities than most evergreen trees.

The protection of a wall, fence or screen of some kind is especially needed to make a haven of a city garden. Morning glory vines will add to the charm—provided there is some sun. Other vines doing well under city conditions are Dutchman's pipe, evergreen bittersweet, trumpet vine, some varieties of clematis, and silver lace vine.

Valuable for backgrounds and for bloom are some of the reliable shrubs grown in practically every city across the country. These include the lilac and mock orange, forsythia and bush honeysuckle, weigela, snowball, hydrangea and spirea. Viburnums are excellent for autumn color, and rose of Sharon resists smoke well. Privet is very good as either a hedge or a specimen shrub. Barberry adapts itself to a city without difficulty. Rhododendrons and hollies, firethorn and leucothoe are among the best broad-leaved evergreens for cities. (Look up the details concerning all of these under their respective headings.)

For color in light shade, caladiums are extremely attractive and cool looking. Spring bulbs are a good choice even if they do have to be replaced almost every year. A precise little bed of hyacinths is lovely in a small garden. Iris and peonies, violas and low chrysanthemums are other possibilities. For dry sunny spots, stonecrop is useful.

A city garden needs watering often, and the foliage also requires frequent cleaning. Regular spraying with a reliable fungicide will help to keep plants healthy. Dead leaves and flowers must be disposed of at once, not only for appearance's sake but to prevent insects and diseases from finding a lodging place. A feeding of plant food in the spring, and a

(Above) **Hicks yew is a pyramidal grower, in contrast to the dwarf form shown at the top of the page. Many types of yew have their place in city gardens.**

(Right) **A few floribunda roses in a spot begging for life and color are as much appreciated as the most elaborate garden in the land.**

(*Left*) **Although castor beans can hardly be recommended as choice garden plants, they do provide foliage quickly where a temporary screen is wanted. They need full sun and 3 or 4 ft. of space each way.**

(*Right*) **Clarkia makes a brilliant show in beds and borders, where it blooms profusely in average garden soil.**

covering of peat moss or buckwheat hulls on the ground in the summer, will prove beneficial. This summer mulch will help to keep the soil moist, cool and weed-free.

Roof gardening is still more exacting, and it is unwise even to try it if you cannot give daily care to the plants. Planters, tubs and window boxes are largely used. The soil in them must be at least 18 in. deep to avoid freezing in the winter and baking in the summer. The tubs should be raised slightly for drainage, and roofing felt should be placed under them as protection against leaks. Such planters require daily watering.

The list of plants that can stand the strong sun and wind on a roof is understandably limited. Privet, Russian olive and dwarf yews are recommended, and English ivy again proves almost indispensable. Geraniums are dependable, as well as petunias, coleus and dwarf zinnias and marigolds. Even hardy bulbs have been grown in roof gardens. Large-leaved castor beans, too rampant for most gardens, prove useful because they grow quickly into a big shrubby plant giving a tropical effect. In a roof garden it is necessary to use pruning shears often, to keep growth under control.

CLARKIA

WELL over a century ago this annual was discovered in the Rocky Mountain area by members of the Lewis and Clark Expedition. It has been found to be a very free bloomer from July to frost, and easy to grow in practically any kind of soil. The dainty rose-like flowers in many colors, borne along wiry stems about 2 ft. tall, are excellent to cut. For this, they should be taken in the bud stage. They like a little shade but not long spells of either rainy or hot weather.

Varieties. *Elegans Double Mixed* has been developed in colors ranging from white through many bright tones. Seed of separate colors may also be bought.

How and When to Plant. Sow the seed outdoors in early spring and thin the plants to stand a foot apart.

Care and Protection. Pinch out the tips of the shoots to make the plants bushier.

CLEMATIS

A SPECIAL favorite of many flower lovers, this hardy ornamental vine is admired for its stunningly beautiful flowers and its habit of growth. A long list of large-flowered hybrids is available. The attractive blooms are of various forms, such as bell or urn, saucer and star shape. Their size ranges from 1 to 10 in., and their colors from wine-red to pure white. Blue and violet tones are most usual, although there are also yellow and pink kinds.

The vines reach a height of 5 to 50 ft., depending on the variety. They cling by twisting their tendrils about a support. Some bloom in late spring and early summer, while others wait until late summer and early fall. Their fruits are often borne in feathery masses. The most vigorous growers are useful for screen planting on porches, arbors and fences, but the large-flowered hybrids of more loose, open habit are better displayed on a trellis or post. Cut blooms last up to ten days in the house and are very desirable material for flower arrangements. Various species are known as virgin's bower, old man's beard and traveler's joy.

Clematis (klem′at-iss) likes a well-drained, rich light loam. Sand and peat moss are useful for loosening a soil that is heavy, and lime should be added to one that is inclined to be

(*Above*) **Montana Undulata, a soft mauve-pink clematis that is effective against a stone wall.**

(*Left*) **Paniculata is a luxuriant-growing vine with decorative foliage and quantities of tiny white fragrant flowers in early fall.**

Crispa is a native of southern swamps, but it grows also in ordinary, well-limed garden soil and survives the winters of northern New York. It blooms from July to September.

Duchess of Edinburgh is especially nice in a shady spot where the double white flowers will be a highlight. The only pruning it needs is removal of dead wood in early spring.

Named for its native state, Texensis has interesting urn-shaped, reddish rose and buff flowers and long-haired seed clusters. Spreading over a stone wall, it is most distinctive.

acid. A sunny location is needed but partial shade is ideal at the base of the plant, for the roots cannot stand a hot, dry condition.

Varieties. *Paniculata,* the most easily grown, bears fragrant white flowers in late August and September, followed by fluffy seed masses. It grows to 30 ft. in height and makes a good screen. *Jackmani* is another familiar kind, with a profusion of velvety violet-purple flowers in midsummer. *Texensis* bears little urn-shaped, reddish blooms in July and grows about 6 ft. tall. Among the dozens of exotic-appearing hybrids are azure-blue *Prins Hendrik,* velvety red *Mme. Edouard Andre,* and lavender-blue *Ramona,* all blooming in midsummer. Red-striped mauve *Nelly*

(*Above*) The lightly ruffled, azure-blue flowers of Prins Hendrik are sometimes 7 in. in diameter. June to September is their blooming season.

(*Above*) Duchess of Albany bears beautiful trumpet-like, pink flowers on slender but strong stems. Plant it where it can be seen easily.

(*Left and Below*) Sparkling bright red Crimson Star is another clematis hybrid of huge size—6 in. or more. It grows 6 to 8 ft. tall and blooms from June to September.

(*Above*) Velvety plum-colored Lord Neville lends a luxurious note to a garden. It is of average height and blooms over a long season.

The silvery lavender to pale mauve flowers of Belle of Woking are borne on year-old wood. Pruning should, therefore, be limited to cutting away dead wood in early spring.

(*Above*) Mme. Edouard Andre is a heavy producer of velvety red flowers with a purplish cast. It grows to about 7 ft. in height. With an evergreen background it makes a stunning picture.

(*Above*) The pointed, reddish violet petals of The President have a lighter bar down the center. This clematis grows 10 to 12 ft. high and blooms freely from June to October.

Moser is very early, and double pale mauve *Belle of Woking* blooms in June. Their usual price is about $1.75 each.

How and When to Plant. In coldest areas spring planting is most successful, but where winters are not severe planting may also be done in the fall. Set the collar of the plant 2 to 3 in. below the surface of the ground, and carefully guide the new stems with string until they reach the wall or trellis on which they will climb.

Care and Protection. Water well in very dry summers. To make sure the ground is damp and cool, keep it covered always with a 2-in. layer of peat moss or plant a ground cover such as ivy. A thicker covering of peat moss is also good protection from winter injury and should be provided in northern states. A handful of fertilizer in early spring and another in midsummer will promote strong growth. Varieties that bloom in spring need little pruning; if any is done, it should be after the blooming season. Those that flower in summer and autumn should be cut back rather severely in early spring.

(*Above*) Tangutica Obtusiuscula seems not to be handicapped by its name, for it has proved to be the best yellow clematis.

(*Above*) Lawsoniana has large blue flowers flushed mauve, with overlapping petals. It is a strong grower and persistent bloomer.

The lilac-rose flowers of Mme. Baron Veillard are darker in cool weather. They are of only medium size but are very freely produced.

Vigorous-growing Ramona blooms well all through the summer. Its short pointed buds open to round-petaled flowers of lavender-blue.

Wine-red Crimson King bears its showy, 6 to 7-in. blooms from June to September. It attains a height of 6 to 8 ft.

In warm climates clock vine grows fast on trellises and porches, producing its lavender-blue flowers in clusters.

CLOCK VINE

IN the far South this rapid-growing vine scrambles to a considerable height on porches and arbors. It is a tender twining climber that grows wild in the tropics of Asia and Africa and does well southward from central Florida. The leaves, pointed at the tip, grow as much as 6 or 8 in. long. Pale lavender-blue flowers about 3 in. long are carried usually in drooping clusters.

Varieties. Besides the blue-flowered kind (*Thunbergia grandiflora*), there is an orange or yellow-flowered variety with dark center, known as black-eyed Susan (not to be confused with the wild flower mentioned under *Coneflower*).

How and When to Plant. Plants grown in containers (about $2.50, depending on size) may be set out at almost any season in light, rich soil.

Care and Protection. Water well in periods of dry weather.

COCKSCOMB

TWO quite different forms of this old-fashioned plant (*Celosia*) are commonly grown—the crested and the feathered cockscomb. Both are extremely showy, with big heads of bloom on both tall and dwarf plants. Reds and golds are the basic colors, although improved kinds now extend the color range. Red varieties look well with some sturdy white flowers nearby. They bloom through summer and autumn, doing best in full sun and a fairly rich soil. They join bells of Ireland and the strawflowers in being easily dried for winter decorations.

Crested cockscomb grows 6 to 24 in. tall. The crinkled heads are like great roosters' combs made of plush. Feathered cockscomb has flowers in a pyramidal-shaped plume at the top of the 1 to 3-ft. plant.

Varieties. *Toreador*, a crested type, bears huge, bright red combs on a 20-in. plant with light green foliage. Ruby-red *Royal Velvet* is about 2 ft. tall. *Empress*, 10 in. tall, with bronzy foliage and velvety crimson-purple combs, is especially nice for cutting. *Gilbert*, an improved strain with pastel tints as well as the more usual colors, is popular for drying.

Among the feathered kinds are *Golden Fleece* with big tawny plumes on a 3-ft. plant, dazzling orange-scarlet *Forest Fire*, and *Pampas Plume* with well-formed, fleecy heads in bright colors. *Fire Feather* and *Golden Feather* are dwarf plumed varieties.

How and When to Plant. Seed may be sown outdoors in early spring where the plants are to grow. Thin to a foot or more apart. Many growers offer plants in flats or boxes. They need an early start, often under glass, in New England and other areas where fall frosts come early.

To Dry the Flowers. Cut the flower heads before they are fully developed. Strip off the leaves and hang the blooms upside down in a warm, dark, dry room for two or three weeks.

(*Above*) Golden Fleece is a feathered or plumed cockscomb with huge plumes on long stems. (*Right*) Royal Velvet, an early-blooming crested cockscomb, has a large center head surrounded by smaller combs.

COLEUS

YOU may have heard this familiar foliage plant called "coley." The vari-colored leaves with fancy markings are so beautiful that they take the place of flowers. The tender plant will reach about 20 in. in height, but it is better kept low and bushy. It is readily pleased in any soil outdoors, in full sun or half shade. Under trees, in window boxes, as an edging, and as a house plant for a sunny window, coleus (koh'lee-us) has become an old household favorite.

Varieties. Seeds of mixed colors are not hard to grow, and small plants may be bought at low cost. Choose the foliage markings that you like best.

How and When to Plant. Use a general potting mixture for growing coleus in pots. Pinch back the tips of the shoots now and then, to make them bushier. It is a very simple matter, also, to root your own cuttings. Take 2 in. from the end of a branch and put the cutting in either sand or water, transferring to a pot when roots have formed.

Care and Protection. Watch out for mealybugs (cottony white insects) on potted plants. If they appear, get rid of the plant, unless you are able to kill them with an aerosol spray or a cotton-wrapped toothpick dipped in alcohol.

(*Left*) The countless rich and brilliant variegations in coleus are always of interest. These plants are decorative in porch and window boxes, in pots and borders.

In spring Nature surpasses herself as every root, seed and bulb lying dormant in the soil bursts into activity. Everything from humble forget-me-nots to bloom-laden trees joins in a soul-lifting pageant of glorious color. Gardeners have a wealth of material to work with at this season.

COLOR IN THE GARDEN

THE home gardener not satisfied with growing merely a collection of plants will plan his plantings for their pictorial values. Color makes a more lasting impression than form or any other element. The psychological effects of the various colors have long been recognized, and gardeners can apply this knowledge just as artists do. Red, being an exciting and deeply moving color, should be used sparingly; blue is restful, yellow delicate and ethereal. White emphasizes bright colors; it separates but does not blend them.

Varying light continually changes outdoor colors, so that no planting remains static. The time of day and the season of the year are contributing factors. Background tones furnished by trees, large shrubs, buildings and fences must be considered, as well as the flowers themselves. It is only by experimenting that the most pleasing combinations of color are discovered.

Careful choosing and grouping of plants is the secret of a colorful garden. A wide variety of plant material means more work in the way of maintenance. The beginning gardener will concentrate on hardy plants adaptable to his region and will combine different varieties of the same family. It is easier to have an all-phlox or an all-iris planting composed of harmoniously blended colors than to keep iris, peonies, phlox and delphinium in top condition in the same border. From a simple beginning you can go on to a more complicated plan.

The lovely colors of Dutch iris may be blended in a garden as an artist uses his paints to achieve the effect he desires. This is true of many plants that come in a wide range of colors. An all-iris border is easier to take care of than a mixture of plants.

Another way of obtaining a color picture without a great deal of labor is to group two or three plants of contrasting color, and then to repeat that group several times down the length of the border. Blue delphinium and yellow daylilies, for instance, are good companions. At least three of each are needed to make a showing.

One-color gardens are not seen so often, but they are a specialized form of color planting for the person with plenty of space and time at his disposal. Blue gardens, white gardens, and even green ones are occasionally seen. Here the emphasis is upon the blending of tones; variety comes from the form, height and texture of the plants used.

Spring Color. Countless combinations will be suggested by considering what plants bloom at the same time. In spring, tulips and bleeding heart look well together, as do

(*Right*) Summer finds annuals like zinnias and marigolds working overtime to mature and drop their seeds before frost catches them. Dahlias and other summer-flowering bulbs such as lilies and hardy amaryllis are especially welcome in spots left vacant by early-blooming perennials and bulbs.

(*Below*) Autumn gardens rely on hardy chrysanthemums for much of their color. Many kinds have softly muted tones that may be skillfully fused into a picture of great charm and distinction.

(*Right*) **Crimson Star is a very pleasing columbine. The vigorous, 2-ft. plant is well branched, and the crimson and white flowers are borne in profusion.**

(*Left*) **Mrs. Scott Elliott's Strain of long-spurred columbines has been a standard for years. It offers a wonderful array of shades. Some flowers are bicolored and others are solid colors.**

daffodils with scilla, grape hyacinths or pansies. Iris, peonies and Oriental poppies come later. Light-colored crocuses show up well against dwarf evergreens. Forget-me-nots and violas are useful ground covers in spring.

Summer Color. Blue delphinium and pink climbing roses make a classic picture, and so do delphinium and lilies. Other plants for the taller part of the border are bellflowers and foxglove, with phlox and daylilies furnishing additional bulk and color. Avoid a stiff, tiered effect. Annuals supply color in late summer and help to replace early-flowering perennials. Ground covers like portulaca will hide the bare spots left by spring-blooming bulbs. Summer bulbs such as montbretia, gladiolus and Peruvian daffodils add a great deal to the total picture.

Autumn Color. Asters in their many tones of blue, and chrysanthemums in the yellow, bronze and pink range, are the main sources of color in the autumn flower garden. Annuals like marigolds reach their peak as summer wanes, and when shrubs lose their fresh green leaves many of them display colored berries. Magnificent autumn foliage brings riotous color to many landscapes.

Winter Color. The many tones of green supplied by evergreen shrubs and trees, and the bright twigs and fruits of other woody plants, are welcome notes all winter. Snow on the ground, so long as it remains white, helps to bring out the varied charm of the evergreens and the berries that may still be in evidence.

COLUMBINE

THE gracefully poised flowers and lacy foliage of columbine are a boon to hardy borders in early summer. Tones of yellow, blue, lavender, red and white are blended in beautiful array, and the intriguing form of the spurred flowers adds to their charm.

A partly shaded spot in the perennial border is ideal for columbine, and there are dwarf species for rock gardens. The dainty, wiry-stemmed flowers are good for cutting, and combine well with roses and many other blooms. A moist but well-drained, rather rich soil is needed. In some regions columbine is incorrectly called honeysuckle (botanically speaking, it is *Aquilegia*).

Varieties. *McKana Hybrids*, with very long-spurred flowers in a bold range of color, are extra good for cutting. They grow 2½ to 3 ft. tall. *Crimson Star* is a striking crimson and white variety; *Silver Queen* is pure white, and *Rose Queen* shades of pink and rose. *Chrysantha* bears yellow flowers on 2½-ft. plants. *Clematiflora*, 18 to 24 in. tall, has blooms somewhat like large-flowered clematis. Yellow *Longissima* has particularly long spurs. *Mrs. Scott Elliott's Strain*, in many mixed colors, is a garden favorite of long standing; and dwarf *Alpina*, blue and white, is fine for rock gardens. Columbine plants may be purchased for about 75c each.

How and When to Plant. Set out the plants early in either spring or fall, about 12

(*Above*) **Longissima columbine is well named, for its spurs are usually 4 in. or more in length.**

(*Left*) **Clematiflora columbine is quite different in appearance from others of its family. Flowers resembling a clematis bloom are mostly in pastel pinks and blues.**

in. apart, in ground previously improved with leaf mold or peat moss. Plants are also easily raised from seed sown in spring, but they do not bloom until the following year.

Care and Protection. To prolong the flowering period, cut off all wilted flowers promptly.

CONEFLOWER

THIS big, coarse-leaved plant, extremely sturdy and easy to get started in ordinary garden soil, is good for furnishing color in late summer. It reaches about 3 ft. in height and is perfectly hardy. In fact, some of the family grow wild, including black-eyed and brown-eyed Susan.

Coneflower may be used singly or in a group toward the back of a border, or wherever its vigorous growth will not crowd less rampant plants. One of its most valuable features is that it stands drought conditions well, blooming in full sun through the heat of late summer. Individual flowers last a long time, and the blooming season continues for two months or more. Flowers are good to use as heavy material in a mixed bouquet.

Annual kinds also may be grown in hot, dry locations. They are about 2 ft. tall and demand no care.

Varieties. *Kelvedon Star,* yellow with mahogany zone and brown cone, is a long-lasting annual.

Perennial coneflowers include *The King,* with a dozen or more flower stems on the 3 to 3½-ft. plant in August. The color is crimson-red with copper cone. A fine companion is *White Lustre,* which blooms freely from late June on. *Goldsturm* has rich yellow, 3 to 4-in. flowers with black cone. *Gold Quelle* is an improved form of the old-time golden glow. It has double flowers and grows 3 ft. high. Coneflower plants cost 75c to $1.00. A new development is gloriosa daisy (which see).

How and When to Plant. Set out the plants in fall or early spring, about 18 in. apart. Sow seed of the annual varieties outdoors in spring, and thin out the plants to 6 in. apart.

Care and Protection. Cut the flowers freely and don't let them go to seed. Every third spring the clump should be dug up, divided into sections and replanted. Spraying for plant lice may sometimes be necessary.

(*Above*) Both the coppery-coned flowers and the foliage of The King coneflower are attractive. Blooms are about 3 in. across. (*Right*) White Lustre has big mahogany-colored cones. The bushy, 3-ft. plant is completely hardy.

CORAL BELLS

THIN wiry stems 15 to 30 in. tall hold these delicate bells. They may be scarlet, rose, pink or white, as well as coral. Outdoors and in, they provide a lovely mist of color, graceful and light in feeling. They last well when cut, and are good filler material in bouquets of mixed flowers.

In gardens it is the foliage as well as the flowers that makes coral bells so desirable. The bronzy green, heart-shaped leaves, often veined, are produced in a low compact tuft that looks well all season. In a clump at the edge of a border where it gets the sun or a little light shade, coral bells easily adapts itself. Well-drained, moist, fairly rich soil is its preference, but it is not fussy. It blooms from late May through most of the summer. Dwarf kinds are popular in rock gardens.

Varieties. Bright crimson *Heuchera sanguinea,* a native of the Southwest, is hardy in New England. *Rosamundi* has long-lasting, coral-pink flowers on 2-ft. stems. Graceful *Pluie de Feu* bears brilliant red bells on slender, 12-in. stems all summer. It is good in borders, edgings and rock gardens. Both the large, deep pink flowers of *Garnet* and the tiny coral-colored ones of *Coral Mist* are charming. Plants may be bought for 75c to $1.00.

How and When to Plant. Plant in fall or early spring, preferably the latter, and place the crown of the plant slightly below soil level. In the border, set the plants 10 in. apart, in groups of at least three.

Care and Protection. Provide water in very dry spells, and cut off dead flowers before they go to seed. Every third or fourth spring is often enough to dig up and divide the clumps. A light winter covering is safest in very cold regions. If the plants get heaved out by frost, push them back firmly into the ground.

(*Above*) Pluie de Feu is a cherry-red variety of coral bells with fine large, graceful spikes of bloom through the summer.

(*Left*) The dainty blooms of coral bells, in white and shades of pink and red, come on slender stems well above the foliage. They are very nice for cutting.

(*Right*) **Coral vine is a very free grower in warm regions, where it makes a thick screen. Coming from Mexico, it needs plenty of warmth.**

(*Below*) **Coralberry is a shrub that will grow in the shade and in the poorest kind of soil. Its berries are a treat for the birds.**

CORALBERRY

PLANT this low-growing shrub at the edge of a border where you can admire the colorful berries before they are devoured by the birds. The purplish red fruits, coming in little bunches the whole length of the branch, last from September to spring if the birds don't find them. Small, yellowish white flowers precede them in July.

This very hardy shrub, 3 to 5 ft. high, grows wild from New Jersey to Georgia and Texas, but adapts itself easily to growing conditions over all of the United States and up into Canada. It will grow in poor soil and even in deep shade, although berry production is better if it is given a place in the sun. Coralberry is good for holding the soil on a slope. (See also the related *Snowberry*.)

Varieties. Another name for coralberry is Indian currant. *Chenault*, an improved form growing 3 ft. tall, with pink flowers and pinkish red berries, is especially fine as an ornamental. Plants are not expensive—about $1.00 for the 18 to 24-in. size.

How and When to Plant. Set out the bush in spring or fall, in a hole large enough to accommodate the roots easily. Pack soil tightly around them, and water well.

Care and Protection. Little if any pruning is needed. Every few years the older branches may be thinned out in very early spring.

CORAL VINE

FROM Mexico comes this tender vine for the South. It grows luxuriantly in warm climates, without demanding more than full sun and ordinary soil. It easily forms a dense screen on a fence or wall to which it can fasten its tendrils. Both the bright pink flowers and the good-sized leaves are heart shaped. The small, profuse flowers are borne in long drooping clusters almost continuously in southern Florida.

Varieties. *Antigonon leptopus* is the botanical name of this showy climber; it is also familiarly known as confederate vine. It grows 30 ft. tall or more. Roots are low priced —about 50c.

How and When to Plant. Planting is done at any time in the lower South. Be sure the support for this vine is close enough so that the tendrils can reach it easily.

Care and Protection. Do not provide any fertilizer. Rich soil promotes leaves at the expense of flowers.

COREOPSIS

BOTH the perennial coreopsis (koh-ree-op′siss) and its annual cousin calliopsis (kal-lee-op′siss) are most dependable bloomers over a long period from early summer to frost. For the border and for masses of cut flowers it is hard to find anything more gay than these yellow, orange and reddish brown daisies. The annual kind often has a band of contrasting color on the single or semi-double flowers. They grow 9 in. to 2½ ft. tall and need a spot in full sunshine. Ordinary soil is good enough; in fact, they can endure a rather hot, dry place.

Coreopsis forms a 2 to 3-ft., spreading plant for the central part of a perennial border. Its ability to stand drought and some neglect

(*Above*) **Mayfield Giant is a variety of the perennial coreopsis with a tall, vigorous plant and broad-petaled, golden flowers.**

(*Right*) **Calliopsis, the annual form of coreopsis, has daisy-like blooms in many tones of gold, mahogany and brown. They bloom from early summer to frost.**

Corn lilies come from South Africa. In warm climates they grow readily outdoors, but in the North they are generally potted and raised indoors.

endears it to busy gardeners. In return for a sunny location it gives long-stemmed, yellow or golden flowers in profusion.

Varieties. *Crimson King* and *Golden Sovereign* are two low annual calliopsis varieties good for the front of the border. *Golden Crown*, 2 ft. high, is yellow with maroon center. *Mayfield Giant* and *Double Sunburst* are perennial kinds with large, golden yellow blooms. Plants of these latter two may be bought for about 50c each.

How and When to Plant. Calliopsis and bachelor's buttons may be grown in the same way—sown either in October or in early spring. Simply scatter the seed and rake in lightly. It usually sows itself, once started. Coreopsis, if sown early outdoors, will bloom later that summer; or plants may be purchased and set 12 to 18 in. apart.

Care and Protection. Don't fail to cut the flowers freely.

CORN LILY

WHERE the weather is mild, corn lily is not hard to grow. It spreads quickly in full sun, and flowers freely in early summer. Graceful spikes 12 to 18 in. tall carry yellow, orange, pink and red flowers like little six-petaled stars, each with a tiny center of a different color. Corn lily may be planted outdoors about as far north as New York if given a sheltered spot and protected over winter, but is more often raised as an indoor plant in the North.

Varieties. Bulbs (*Ixia*, botanically speaking) are usually sold in mixture, at 40c to 75c per dozen.

How and When to Plant. In warm regions, plant the bulbs outdoors in late fall, 3 in. deep and the same distance apart. Cover lightly over winter. Farther north they should be planted not later than October and given a warm covering.

For growing indoors, plant five or six bulbs an inch deep in a 6-in. pot in early fall. Keep the pot moist and cool until roots have developed. Blooms should appear by January.

Care and Protection. Always protect well over the winter outdoors. Bulbs grown indoors may be dried after they bloom and planted again the next fall.

COSMOS

FOR a fast-growing, graceful background plant to make an effect while more permanent things are getting a start, cosmos is tops. It is best in a mass, preferably against an evergreen or shrub border. Along a fence or in a corner its feathery foliage and big daisy flowers also look well. This is among the

(*Above*) The Sensation strain of cosmos has large, long-lasting flowers of crimson, pink and white. For top performance, the plants should be spaced at least 2 ft. apart. This is an early-flowering strain.

(*Above*) Of novelty value is Fiesta, a gaily striped cosmos of bushy habit, growing quickly to a height of 2½ ft. It often self-sows.

(*Above*) Orange Flare is a free-blooming cosmos of bright color, with flowers carried on long stems. Foliage is very lacy.

(*Left*) Double Crested cosmos offers a differently shaped flower with very full center. It grows about 2½ ft. high.

Cotoneasters are not particular about soil or location. Both the scarlet berries and the interesting habit of growth make them valuable garden shrubs.

basic annuals, requiring scant care and giving a lot for a little. Blooms come from July through fall if dead flowers are kept cut. Usual colors are pink, red and white, but yellow and orange are also seen. Cosmos grows about 2½ to 5 ft. high and makes a fine cut flower.

Varieties. The *Sensation* strain, in crimson, pink and white, with fluted petals, has 4 to 6-in. flowers on 5-ft. plants. Coming into bloom ten weeks after seed is sown, it is especially desirable for areas having short summers. *Mandarin* is a new double, golden yellow variety, while *Fiesta* is a novelty with striped orange and scarlet petals. *Double Crested* has a fully double center surrounded by a flat row of petals.

How and When to Plant. Seed is sown outdoors in May in a sunny place, and plants are thinned to 18 or 20 in. apart. Any soil, even quite poor, will do. Cosmos often will self-sow and appear here and there the next year. Pink, white and crimson forms transplant easily; yellow and orange types require careful handling, with soil around the roots.

Care and Protection. Tallest kinds may need staking. Any spindly plants may be pinched back to encourage bushiness. If plant lice appear, spray with nicotine or malathion.

COTONEASTER

THE large cotoneaster (kot-toh-nee-ass'ter) family includes evergreen or almost evergreen shrubs that have proved valuable more for their interesting growing habits and bright fruits than for their flowers. Some kinds lose their leaves in the fall, and these are likely to be hardy farther north than the evergreen varieties. Areas on the borderline will find many varieties that keep their glossy leaves well into winter. Some kinds turn reddish in autumn, with orange-scarlet berries.

This easy-to-grow shrub has many uses in any garden. Taller kinds add to the interest of a shrubbery border, some may go in a foundation planting, and others on banks and in rock gardens. They need well-drained soil and full sun, and they can stand growing conditions at the seashore.

Varieties. *Spreading* is the variety most widely planted. Hardy from Missouri northeast to Massachusetts, it has fine-cut, glossy foliage that turns dull red in the fall. Red berries follow the pinkish flowers. It grows 3 to 4 ft. tall, with arching branches. An 18 to 24-in. plant costs $2.00 to $3.00. *Rock* is lower growing, with tiny boxwood-like foliage, reddish in autumn, and bright red fruit. Its flat, horizontal branches are especially good in a rock garden and on low banks where they can spread out. Less hardy and much taller is *Franchet*, an 8 to 9-ft. shrub of gracefully spreading habit with pink flowers, silvery foliage, and scarlet berries. In the Northwest *Acutifolia* has proved to be a good hedge plant. The dense, 4 to 5-ft. plant has dark glossy leaves.

How and When to Plant. Set out the plant in fall or spring. Dig a generous hole for it, and in the bottom mix some peat moss with the soil. Press the soil firmly about the roots, and water thoroughly.

Care and Protection. This shrub has an interesting manner of growing, and it should be allowed to go its own way. If it gets too thick, overlapping branches may be cut out in winter.

CRAPE MYRTLE

SOUTHERNERS have adopted the crape myrtle, although this vigorous and impressive shrub is really Chinese in origin. All across the South its large heads of crinkled and fringed, pink, white, lavender or red flowers put on a show from early summer through September. It is so easily grown in either shrub or tree form that it is sometimes called the lilac of the South.

It cannot be depended on to survive the winter much north of Maryland, but if given a sheltered location it is worth trying in colder parts. It makes a large lawn specimen, and may be combined with other shrubs in hedges and borders if given enough room. Full sun produces the best flowers, and ordinary garden soil, well drained, is adequate. Crape myrtle stands pruning well, and severe pruning in spring results in larger trusses of flowers.

(*Above*) A close view of Watermelon-Red crape myrtle, which bears huge, showy heads of bloom.

(*Right*) If the wavy-petaled flowers of crape myrtle are clipped off just as they fade, the plant will keep blooming until frost.

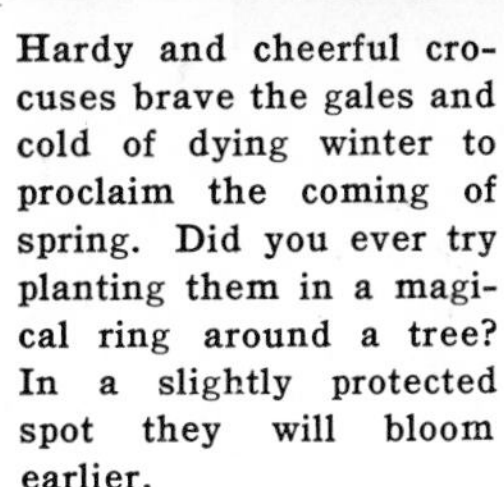

Hardy and cheerful crocuses brave the gales and cold of dying winter to proclaim the coming of spring. Did you ever try planting them in a magical ring around a tree? In a slightly protected spot they will bloom earlier.

Varieties. *Pure White*, *Pink*, *Lavender* and *Rose* are among the colors offered. *Watermelon-Red* is admired for its fine large pyramidal flower clusters. Red *William Toovey* is a more compact and low-spreading variety, especially good for hedges and low screens. Bare-root plants cost around $1.50 for the 2 to 3-ft. size.

How and When to Plant. Set out the plant in late fall or early spring, at the same depth as in the nursery. It is easily transplanted with bare roots, but do not let the roots dry out while planting. Pack good soil around them, and water well.

Care and Protection. Cut off the flowers as soon as they wither, to prolong the blooming season. In the South, prune in late winter, to encourage new flowering shoots to grow. If the plant dies to the ground in a northern winter, it should be cut back and allowed to grow up again from the base. Blooms will come on this new growth.

CROCUS

EVEN the smallest doorstep planting has space for a cluster of crocuses, and no flower of the entire garden year is more appreciated. This hardy little bulb blooms in March, or possibly earlier if given a sheltered spot. It needs full sunshine and well-drained, fairly good garden soil. Flowers are white, gold, and shades of blue and purple.

Crocuses are sometimes scattered in lawns, but this is not very practical because generally the grass needs to be mowed before the bulb foliage is ready to be cut. It is wiser to place them on the edge of a flower border, under shrubs and trees, or in rock gardens. They need to be in groups to make a nice showing. Perennials such as primroses are good replacements after the crocuses have bloomed and disappeared.

Autumn-flowering varieties are desirable also. These flowers come in October after the leaves have gone, and they need other foliage plants as a background.

Varieties. White *Snowstorm*, dark blue *Remembrance*, white and deep mauve *Striped Beauty*, and deep purple *Baron von Brunow* are representative spring-flowering varieties. Autumn-flowering kinds include *Sativus*, purple with orange anthers; *Speciosus*, lilac-blue; and *Zonatus*, rosy lilac. Bulbs cost 60c to 95c per dozen.

How and When to Plant. Spring-blooming crocuses are planted in September, 2 to 3 in. deep and the same distance apart. A dozen of a color planted in a group show up well. Autumn-flowering kinds are planted in late July.

Care and Protection. Don't cut off the foliage until it has completely died down. The bulbs may be left undisturbed for years.

CROWN IMPERIAL

A NATIVE of Persia, crown imperial was introduced into England in the days of Elizabeth I. It is a showy, 2½ or 3-ft. plant with yellow, orange or red flowers in mid-spring. The large head of strong-scented, bell-shaped flowers is crowned by leaves at the top of the stalk. This is a bulb similar to a tulip, but it is not absolutely hardy north of New York. It needs warm, rich soil and is best grown in groups in a sheltered spot in a border. However, nearby plants should not be permitted to crowd it, for crown imperial is not easy to get started, and does not increase rapidly into a large clump. (See also the related *Checkered Lily*.)

Varieties. *Fritillaria imperialis* is the botanical name. A bulb costs around $1.00.

How and When to Plant. To assure good root growth during the autumn, plant the bulbs in late August or early September, 6 in. deep and 8 in. apart.

Care and Protection. Light winter protection is advisable in northern regions. Let the foliage grow without being cut, and do not disturb the bulbs.

(*Above*) Cup and saucer vine (described on the following page) is a fast-growing annual climber that provides plentiful foliage and these bell-shaped flowers.

(*Left*) Crown imperial is a member of the lily family. Bulbs planted in very early autumn produce bloom the following spring.

(*Left*) **Cup flower (Purple Robe is pictured) is covered with lovely violet-colored, cup-shaped blooms from June to frost.**

(*Right*) **Cupid's dart is an attractive perennial that is very good as a cut flower, either fresh or dried like strawflowers. It takes full sun and well-drained soil.**

CUP AND SAUCER VINE

(*Illustration on preceding page*)

CATHEDRAL bells is another name for this rapid-growing annual climber from the tropics. Its bell-shaped flowers rest in a green "saucer" and are very freely produced; they are followed by plum-shaped fruits. Wherever you want a mass of foliage in a hurry, plus flowers, to cover a trellis or wall, this is a vine to consider. It grows as much as 20 ft. until frost cuts it down. Ordinary soil and either full sun or light shade are its requirements. A southern exposure is best.

Varieties. *Cobaea scandens* is the scientific name of the purple-flowered kind. There is also a white one.

How and When to Plant. Sow the seeds indoors about March, placing them on edge and covering very lightly with soil. Move the little plants to small flower pots, and pinch them back to make them bushier when they are 6 in. high. They may also be bought in pots. Set them in the open ground in May, where they have a fence or other support. They put out tendrils at each leaf cluster with which they cling.

Care and Protection. Seeds may rot if sown in too wet soil. Planting them in a slanting position, slightly protruding from the soil, helps to avoid rotting.

CUP FLOWER

SMALL but mighty useful is this neat, free-blooming annual. It makes a compact mound 6 in. tall and 10 in. in diameter, with needle-fine foliage and covered with 1-in., cup-shaped, blue flowers over a long season. They are carried one to a stem. Use it as an edger, in low borders with verbena, in the rock garden and in window boxes. It likes

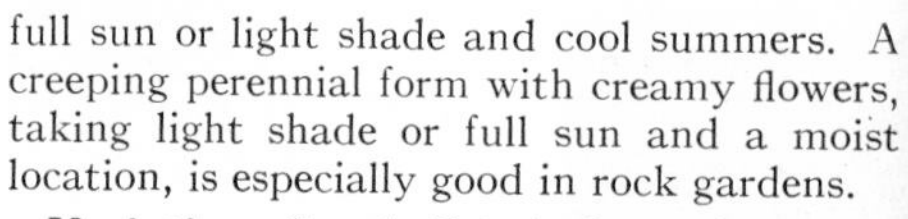

full sun or light shade and cool summers. A creeping perennial form with creamy flowers, taking light shade or full sun and a moist location, is especially good in rock gardens.

Varieties. *Purple Robe* is the variety most used. (*Nierembergia* is the botanical name.) It has deep violet-blue flowers.

How and When to Plant. Since it takes four months for the plants to bloom after the seed is sown, it is advisable to buy plants (about 25c each). Give them good soil and space them 6 in. apart.

Care and Protection. The perennial form needs a light cover in winter. In mild climates the annual variety pictured here may also live over winter if protected.

CUPID'S DART

THE intense blue of this easy-to-grow hardy perennial makes it desirable in both flower gardens and indoor arrangements. Also it can be dried, like strawflowers. Plants grow 1½ ft. tall and bloom freely from June to late August. The chaff-like flowers are borne on wiry stems above the rosette of narrow, grayish foliage. Full sun and ordinary, well-drained garden soil are quite sufficient.

Varieties. The dainty, deep blue *Catananche caerulea* blooms in the latter half of summer. Plants cost 50c to 80c. *Blue Giant* is excellent for cutting.

How and When to Plant. Fall or early spring is the time to set out the plants, 1 ft. apart, in groups of three to six.

Care and Protection. Dig up, divide and replant every year or two, in spring.

CYCLAMEN

DURING the winter months the florists' cyclamen (sik′lam-en) furnishes exquisite blooms with petals turned sharply back as if wind-blown. In white and shades of pink, they rise above interesting heart-shaped leaves covered with silvery white marks.

A plant fresh from the florist will languish quickly if placed in a warm room. It needs to be kept in a temperature of not over 60 to 65 degrees, where it receives light but not strong sunshine. The soil should never be

(*Below*) **Cyclamen plants in full bloom are a mass of delicate, butterfly-like flowers that appear ready to take flight. Careful attention to their needs will prolong their bloom for weeks.**

(*Above*) **Cypress vine (described on the next page) has fern-like foliage and starry flowers. Grow it on a fence or trellis in light soil.**

allowed to become dry; on the other hand, the pot should not stand continuously in water. It is best to water always from below. To maintain the moist air needed by the plant, the pot may be kept on a tray of pebbles. Keep water among the pebbles but never cover completely.

Hardy cyclamen for the garden are lovely, rather uncommon plants that grow from tuberous roots. They like a well-drained, partly shaded spot.

Varieties. Florists' cyclamen plants may be purchased in bloom from Christmas to early spring, at $2.00 up.

Fragrant, crimson-rose *Europaeum*, with bright green leaves marbled silvery white, is a hardy kind blooming from July to September; rosy pink *Neapolitanum* comes a little later. *Repandum*, with crimson flowers, is an early spring bloomer. Tubers cost 75c to $1.00 each.

How and When to Plant. Plant hardy cyclamen outdoors in July or August (a month later is early enough for Repandum). Set the tubers an inch deep, except Neapolitanum, which should be a little deeper.

Care and Protection. After a florists' cyclamen has bloomed, gradually stop watering it. Leave the tuber in the pot over summer, in a cool place either indoors or out. About August it should be repotted in fresh potting soil. Do not cover the tuber more than half. Water from below, and keep the pot in a cool room.

CYPRESS VINE

(*Illustrated on the opposite page*)

THIS graceful, fast-growing annual vine is related to the morning glory and to cardinal climber. Its dark green, feathery foliage produces a very dainty display on a trellis or other support. Star-like, scarlet or white flowers are borne all summer. They look their best early in the morning and in the evening, and it is for the flowers that this vine is grown rather than for shade. It will grow 15 or 20 ft. tall in ordinary garden soil.

Varieties. A packet of mixed seed will give both scarlet and white flowers.

How and When to Plant. Sow the seed outdoors when all frost danger is over. Soak it overnight before planting.

Care and Protection. No fertilizer is necessary.

DAFFODILS (Narcissus)

DANCING yellow daffodils catch the very color and spirit of spring. From late March through April these hardy bulbs provide an impressive show, and with tulips they comprise the largest group of spring-flowering bulbs. Originally they came from Europe, parts of Asia and North African countries bordering the Mediterranean, and they have been grown and admired from very early times. They have been studied, classified and hybridized to a great extent, particularly by the English. New varieties continue to be produced annually by Dutch and American breeders, as well as English.

With florists, daffodils are important for forcing in pots and for cutting. In home gardens they are indispensable, for they demand very little culture and live for many years. Any reasonably good garden soil with adequate drainage will grow them, and the bulbs may be left undisturbed for years at a time. In broad masses associated with spring-flowering shrubs and trees, with other bulbs and perennials, in groups against evergreens, and naturalized in half-wild areas, their many forms are adaptable and always charming. Small kinds are cherished in rock gardens.

All daffodils are known botanically as *Narcissus*. Those with small, very fragrant blooms in clusters and with tubular foliage are called jonquils. The petals are known as the perianth, and the center of the flower is

"I wandered lonely as a cloud
That floats on high o'er vales and hills,
When all at once I saw a crowd,
A host of golden daffodils,
Beside the lake, beneath the trees
Fluttering and dancing in the breeze."

—Wordsworth, "The Daffodils"

(*Left*) **Blue and gold is a pleasing color combination easy to achieve with daffodils and grape hyacinths. These are trumpet daffodils, like all the others pictured on this page.**

(*Right*) **A potful of daffodils that you have grown yourself and brought into glowing beauty will please everyone who sees it . . . And why not have some extras, to use as gifts?**

called a trumpet, a cup, a crown or an eye, depending on its size. Flowers are classified as trumpet, large cupped, small cupped, double (with many short petals in the center), jonquilla (the jonquils), tazetta or poetaz (bunch-flowered, with either single or double flowers), poeticus (with tiny flat eye). Miniature kinds include the triandrus, cyclamineus, and wild daffodils that are especially fine in rock gardens.

Daffodils bloom early enough to be replaced by annuals, which may be set out between the bulbs. The one essential is that the bulb foliage be allowed to grow and die down naturally without being cut. This may mean an untidy-looking place for a time, but if the bulbs are expected to bloom the following year the growth must be permitted to run its course. Tying the leaves in bunches makes them look neater as they are drooping and yellowing.

Where there is a grassy bank not mowed, or an open space under trees where plenty of sunshine filters through, daffodils may be naturalized—that is, planted in great masses at random and allowed to take over the space completely. Poeticus and triandrus varieties are good for this purpose. The bulbs are scattered broadcast and planted where they fall, but no closer than 6 in.

To grow daffodils in pots indoors it is necessary to use good garden soil to which leaf mold and sand have been added. Several bulbs can go in a pot. They are covered with soil, watered and placed outdoors in autumn. They need to be buried in a 6-in. layer of sand or peat moss for six or seven weeks, when they are uncovered and left in a cool, protected place for a time before being brought gradually into a warm room. After the bulbs bloom they may be planted outdoors. (See also *Paper-White Narcissus.*)

(*Above*) **The handsome King Alfred has uniform rich golden yellow flowers.**

(*Below*) **The dainty blooms of W. P. Milner are white in both trumpet and perianth.**

(*Above*) **Spring Glory is a bicolored trumpet variety that is a free bloomer.**

(*Left*) **An extra long trumpet and smooth, snowy white, overlapping petals make Beersheba outstanding. This is a strong grower that increases rapidly into a good-sized clump.**

(*Right*) **The large, expanded trumpet of all-yellow Unsurpassable, evenly flanged and with a notched edge.**

(*Left*) Red Cross, a large cupped daffodil—like all the others on this page—is excellent both in the garden and for cutting. The deep orange cup is densely frilled.

(*Right*) Large, well-formed John Evelyn has a lemon-yellow cup that is fluted or shirred to the base. It is a favorite in its class.

Varieties. As with other very popular garden flowers, there are hundreds of varieties on the market. Only a sampling of those widely sold and grown may be mentioned here. *King Alfred* is said to be the most popular daffodil in the world. It is an all-yellow trumpet variety, as is the very large *Unsurpassable. Queen of Bicolors* has an ivory-white perianth and golden yellow trumpet. *Beersheba* and *Mount Hood* are beautiful all-white trumpet varieties.

Large cupped daffodils are represented by soft yellow *Carlton* and deep lemon-yellow *Fortune*, which has a soft orange cup. *Dick Wellband* (white with coppery orange cup) and *John Evelyn* (white with lemon-yellow cup) are others of the large cupped class. *Mrs. R. O. Backhouse*, the first "pink" variety, has been joined by a great many others with cups in varying shades of apricot, salmon and shell-pink. *Firetail*, white with scarlet cup, is a good small cupped variety, while *Texas* and *Twink* are showy doubles with orange centers.

Among the tazetta or poetaz varieties are creamy white, double-flowered *Cheerfulness* and orange-cupped *Geranium*. These have about three flowers on a stem and bloom a little later than larger-flowered kinds. *Actaea* is one of the largest of the poeticus group. It has snowy petals and an eye margined with dark red. Miniatures include *Bulbocodium* or *Hoop Petticoat*, only a few inches high and blooming extra early; *Triandrus Albus* and *Thalia*, small and dainty, as well as *February Gold*, another very early and choice variety for rock gardens (*see top of page 89*).

Connoisseurs are offered new daffodil va-

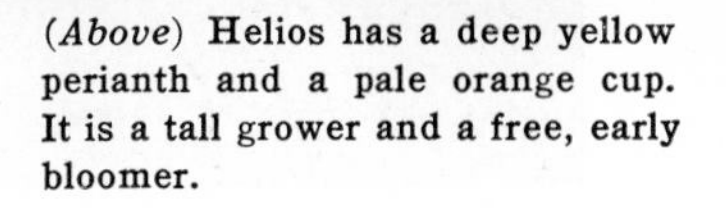

(*Above*) Helios has a deep yellow perianth and a pale orange cup. It is a tall grower and a free, early bloomer.

(*Left*) New "pink" daffodils are offered every year, with cups in many charming tints. Mrs. R. O. Backhouse, pictured here, was the first of these. Although no longer in the novelty class, it is still in great demand.

(*Below*) Fortune is another fine large cupped daffodil. It has an orange-yellow cup, slightly crinkled. This is one of the first to bloom.

(*Above*) The rounded petals of Croesus are pale sulphur-yellow and the cup deeper yellow with a deep orange frill.

(*Above*) Silvery white Her Grace has a delicate sulphur-yellow cup, deeply frilled at the mouth, which passes to pure white.

(*Left*) Bernardino has blooms of firm, waxy texture, with a large, prettily fluted cup that is edged orange-apricot.

(*Right*) The wide cup of Francisca Drake is golden yellow at the base and flame-orange at the frilly edge.

(*Left*) Firetail, one of the best of the small cupped daffodils, has a brilliant red cup flushed orange. This is a long-lasting, medium late variety.

(*Above and Right*) Three additional small cupped daffodils: Bath's Flame (yellow with gold and orange cup), Red Beacon (ivory-white with scarlet cup), and Diana Kasner (snow-white with larger yellow cup edged red).

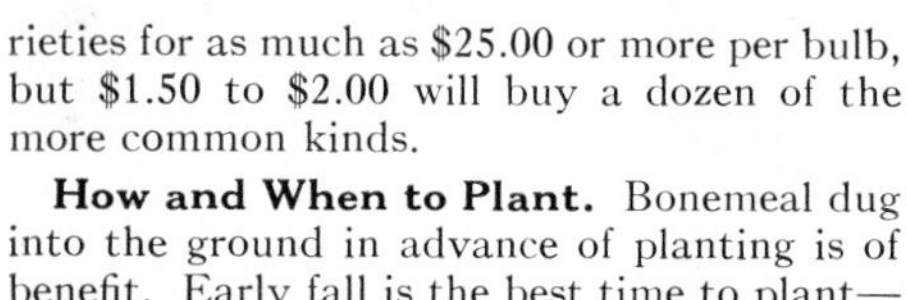

rieties for as much as $25.00 or more per bulb, but $1.50 to $2.00 will buy a dozen of the more common kinds.

How and When to Plant. Bonemeal dug into the ground in advance of planting is of benefit. Early fall is the best time to plant—not later than September, if possible. In the South, bulbs may be planted as late as November. Set large bulbs 4 to 5 in. deep and about that distance apart; smaller ones only 2 to 4 in.

Care and Protection. Always allow the foliage to grow until it matures and dies of its own accord. Leave the bulbs in the ground until the flowers get fewer and smaller (about four or five years). Then dig them up in early July, and replant them at once, spacing them 4 to 5 in. apart.

(*Left*) The touseled double center of Twink is yellow and orange.

(*Below*) Argent is another double daffodil with large, star-shaped flowers of creamy white with a yellow center.

(*Above*) Actaea stands out in the poeticus group. The large, beautifully formed flower is pure white and the eye is orange edged with red.

(*Above and Right*) Three varieties of the poetaz class: white-petaled Laurens Koster with orange center; white Early Perfection with lighter yellow center; and creamy white, double Cheerfulness.

(*Right*) Jonquils have small, very fragrant blooms in clusters. The foliage is tubular rather than flat.

DAFFODILS! Yes, all are of the bewitching miniature type, so perfect for rock gardens and intimate nooks. (*Left to Right*) Triandrus Albus, Bulbocodium or Hoop Petticoat, Thalia and February Gold. (*Described on page 87.*)

DAHLIAS

STATELY and proud, the dahlia is a prized garden flower in late summer. The amazing blooms may be over 10 in. in diameter, carried on 5-ft. plants, and displaying every color except a true blue. Many are warm blends and bicolors. With chrysanthemums, asters, and the late-flowering annuals, dahlias help to ring down the curtain on the flowering season. They may be used in perennial or shrub plantings provided there is free air circulation and good, well-drained soil.

Those who make a hobby of growing dahlias have a chance to enter them in special shows set up by the dahlia societies, local and national. So many flower forms exist that about a dozen categories are necessary to describe them, such as decorative (formal and informal), cactus (straight, semi and incurved), pompon, ball, collarette, orchid-flowered, peony, anemone and single. Biggest flowers are produced by limiting one bloom to a stem. They last best when cut in late afternoon or early morning, and held for several hours in water in a cool dark place before being brought into a room.

For those with smaller gardens and particularly those who want flowers for home decoration, there are miniatures that are extremely popular. Where they are desired primarily for show in the garden, the tips of the shoots are pinched back to produce more bloom. Dahlias are grown both from tubers and from seed. They are killed by frost, and the roots must then be brought indoors and stored over winter.

Plenty of moisture is required, and soil that is rich and deep. Leaf mold, peat moss and bonemeal should be mixed in before

Both formal and informal types of decorative dahlias are represented in this group of five. (*Left*) Fairy, a miniature formal decorative of lavender-pink, balanced on the right by Rapture, a miniature informal decorative of pink and gold. (*Below*) Jersey's Beauty, a pink formal decorative; Jane Cowl, a bronzy gold informal decorative; and Jersey's Beacon, a scarlet formal decorative with buff reflex. See how beautifully these colors would blend in a group planting? (More of the decorative type are shown on the next page.)

(*Left*) The rich scarlet and yellow petals of Forest Fire, an informal decorative dahlia, do indeed suggest leaping flames. The plant is a sturdy grower.

(*Right*) Lord of Autumn, another informal decorative, has clear yellow blooms with unusually shaggy, twisting petals. It too is a good grower.

planting. Coarse ashes put in the planting hole will help make drainage certain. A little shade will do no harm. In the South, dahlias will bloom in the fall if the tubers are held in cold storage and planted in August.

Varieties. A great number of varieties are for sale, and dahlia specialists offer new ones every year, in all the different types. Just a few examples of names might include *Croydon Masterpiece*, an orange-colored decorative; *Pride of Holland*, a rose-pink cactus; *Ike*, a blood-red miniature; and *Atom*, a fiery red pompon. Started plants are especially good to buy where summers are short; they average $1.00 to $2.00 in price. Fanciers pay up to $15.00 or more for a tuber of a new variety, but good standard older sorts may be bought for 75c up.

(*Above*) Anemone-flowered dahlias have tubular petals in the center of the flowers, which give them quite a novel appearance.

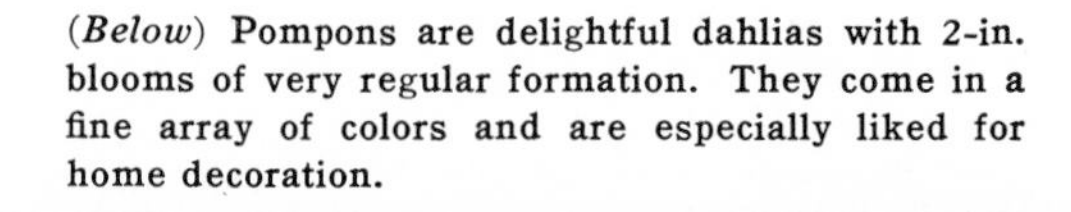

(*Below*) Pompons are delightful dahlias with 2-in. blooms of very regular formation. They come in a fine array of colors and are especially liked for home decoration.

(*Left*) Carol Francis is a cactus dahlia of lovely soft lavender-rose shaded pastel mauve. It is an early-blooming variety and a vigorous grower.

(*Left*) Mignon dahlias produce single flowers on dwarf plants. This is another kind very useful in flower arrangements.

(*Right*) A mixed group of miniature dahlias, showing some of the variations in size, form and color. All of these smaller kinds are excellent for cutting.

Among the annual strains raised from seed are *Coltness Hybrids* with single flowers, 18 to 24 in. tall, and *Unwin's Hybrids*, of the same height but with semi-double flowers. They bloom from late June to fall.

How and When to Plant. When settled warm weather comes, dig a hole 5 in. deep in well-enriched soil. Beside the hole drive a sturdy stake (4 or 5 ft. long for tallest varieties, shorter for low growers). Lay the tuber flat in the hole, being careful not to break off the sprout, and cover it with 2 or 3 in. of soil. As it grows, gradually fill up the hole. Tie the plant to the stake with soft string. Started plants should be taken out of the container and set 2 or 3 in. lower than ground level. Allow 2 ft. between plants.

If using seed, start it indoors in March and set out the young plants 18 in. apart after the soil is warm.

Care and Protection. Never let the ground dry out. A 2-in. layer of straw around the plants will help to keep the soil moist. After the first killing frost, cut off the stalks just above ground and carefully dig up the

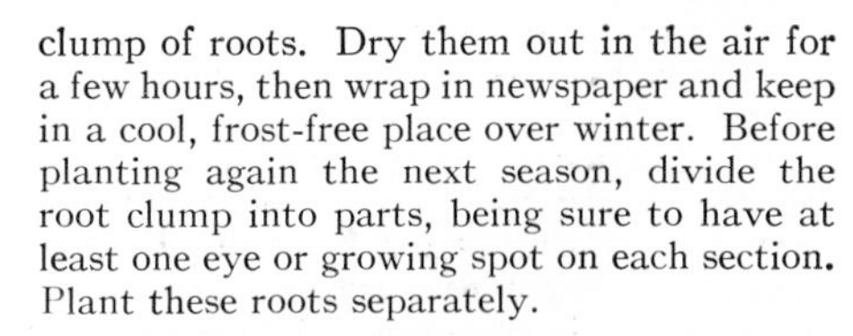

clump of roots. Dry them out in the air for a few hours, then wrap in newspaper and keep in a cool, frost-free place over winter. Before planting again the next season, divide the root clump into parts, being sure to have at least one eye or growing spot on each section. Plant these roots separately.

(*Above and Right*) Coltness Hybrids are grown from seed. The pleasing flowers, about 3 in. across, appear in many showy colors on 18 to 24-in. plants.

(*Left*) Full-centered pink Little Jewel and scarlet Bishop of Llandaff are among the miniature dahlias that may be planted even in small gardens. Both are free blooming and most attractive.

Three varieties of the lovely daphne. (*Left*) Cneorum, or rose daphne, a slow grower with glossy evergreen foliage and fragrant, rose-pink flower clusters. (*Above*) Genkwa, which looks like a small lilac bush when it blooms in very early spring. (*Right*) Somerset, bearing richly perfumed, blush-pink flowers in 6-in. clusters in late spring.

DAPHNE

MOST varieties of this low shrub have fragrant flowers—an added point in their favor. Some hold their leaves all winter, but others do not. In shrub borders they provide bloom early in the season, and they are especially good in foundation plantings when seen against a background of dark evergreens. The lowest growing kinds are very much at home in rock gardens where they can have full sun but a cool moist spot for their roots.

Daphne (daff'nee) must have rich soil and good drainage. It will not do well under hot, dry conditions. Sometimes plants are hard to get started, and small sizes are the best to use. Some kinds are hardy about as far north as New York and Boston.

Varieties. *Cneorum*, also called rose daphne or garland flower, makes a 10-in. evergreen mat in rock gardens or as an edger where its bright pink flower clusters are lovely in May and often again in the fall. It is one of the hardiest kinds, as is the lilac daphne, *Genkwa*, which bears pale lilac flowers in early spring before the leaves appear. This one reaches 2½ to 3 ft. in height. Small plants cost $2.00 to $3.00. Blush-pink *Somerset* stays green most of the winter in Ohio without protection.

How and When to Plant. Set out small plants in fall or early spring, in soil to which some leaf mold or peat moss has been added. Pack the soil firmly around the roots, and water well.

Care and Protection. To help hold moisture in the soil during hot summers, a layer of peat moss may be spread around the plants. Straw or a light covering of evergreen branches will give protection from wind and sun in winter.

DAYLILIES

IF there is a place where this durable perennial will not grow, it hasn't yet been found. Through the untiring work of a number of plant breeders, the familiar old lemon lily of grandma's day has blossomed out into a contender, with phlox, for the title "mainstay of the summer garden." It is planted as enthusiastically in the far South and in difficult areas of the Midwest as it is in the East and North, and to hail the daylily as the All-American perennial would not be an exaggeration.

In foundation plantings, beside steps, in front of a hedge, on a terrace, even under shade trees, as well as in perennial and shrub borders, these persistent plants grow and bloom. They seem especially appropriate beside a pool or a brook, where their graceful foliage and gay trumpets are reflected in the water. Foliage is narrow and arching—some-

(*Above*) Hyperion's long stalk holds the flower well above the foliage.

(*Left*) Daylilies are good pool-side plants. They bend gracefully over the water to admire their own reflection, and the plants spread to comfortable proportions.

(*Left*) Painted Lady is a very large daylily with ruffled blooms up to 8 in. in diameter. In color it is deep yellow overcast with cinnamon and veined darker, with a still darker eye zone. It grows about 3 ft. tall.

(*Right*) Fulva Kwanso bears double flowers on a very sturdy, easy - to - grow plant.

times evergreen—and makes a good background for lower plants.

Colors now extend through many shades and combinations of red, copper, brown and pink besides the original yellows and oranges. The blooms are carried on stems with many branches. Even though an individual flower lasts only a day, that is no drawback because it simply folds up and is replaced next morning by another opening bud. There are some kinds that open in the evening and last into the next day; some are fragrant.

Earliest varieties start blooming with iris in spring. Each kind blooms for several weeks. Others come along later in the season, and by keeping their flowering time in mind when choosing varieties you can have them until September. Heights vary from 18 in. to 4 ft. The flowers tend to face in the direction of the light.

Daylilies are useful in informal bouquets for the house if a stem is cut when the buds are just starting to open. Each morning pinch off the flowers of the previous day.

Practically any growing conditions are acceptable. In complete sun daylilies bloom freely, and in part shade as well. They resist drought but have no objection to a moist location. Moderately good soil produces larger flowers, but if too rich it promotes leaf growth rather than blooms.

(*Right*) High Noon is rich cadmium-yellow, with ruffled petals of good substance. It reaches 3 ft. in height. This is a very popular daylily in all sections of the country.

(*Left*) Its long blooming season helps to make Colonial Dame valuable. The large, light apricot flowers are banded with pale rosy tan, and the crepy petals are ruffled along the edge.

(*Right*) Rich orange Mikado is a large, bold flower prominently marked deep mahogany-red. It blooms in June and July, and often even later. Canary-yellow Hyperion, as much as 7 in. in diameter, is unusually fragrant. July and August find it at its height.

(*Above*) Mrs. John J. Tigert daylily, developed at the University of Florida, has proved excellent in southern gardens and is adaptable to other areas as well.

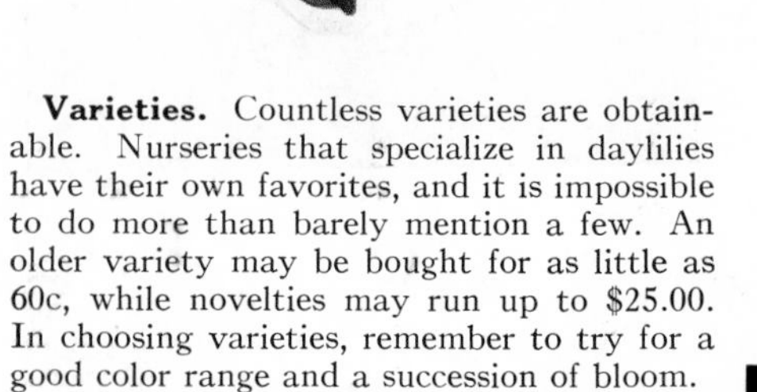

Varieties. Countless varieties are obtainable. Nurseries that specialize in daylilies have their own favorites, and it is impossible to do more than barely mention a few. An older variety may be bought for as little as 60c, while novelties may run up to $25.00. In choosing varieties, remember to try for a good color range and a succession of bloom.

From *Flava*, the old lemon lily, to delicate yellow *Fairy Wings*, recent winner of the Stout Medal (highest daylily award), is a big step. Pale yellow *Hyperion* and cinnamon-flushed yellow *Painted Lady* are fine varieties. Melon-pink *Multnomah* and oxblood *War Eagle* are other popular kinds. Among those especially recommended for Florida are orange-yellow *Emily Hume*, cardinal-red *Kanapaha*, and Brazil-red *Mrs. John J. Tigert*.

How and When to Plant. Plants are set out in spring or early fall, with an allowance of at least 3 ft. of space. Don't plant too deep.

Care and Protection. Daylilies enjoy a deep soaking in extra dry spells. They can be left for years without any special care. When eventually a clump gets too big, dig it up in early spring or late summer and separate it into smaller pieces. Cut off part of the roots and also the leaves before replanting the divisions.

(*Left*) The blooms of Boutonniere are small but are produced in great numbers on freely branching, slender stems. Petals are gracefully recurved.

(*Below*) August Pioneer, orange flushed red, blooms late in the season. Its medium-sized flowers, on strong stems, rise well above the foliage.

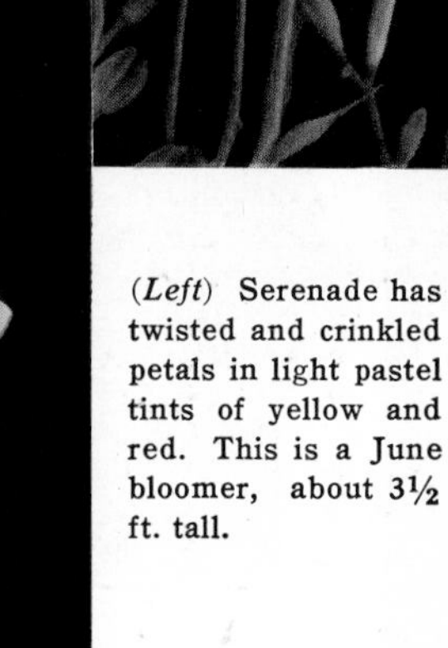

(*Left*) Serenade has twisted and crinkled petals in light pastel tints of yellow and red. This is a June bloomer, about 3½ ft. tall.

(*Right*) The Giant Pacific Hybrid strain of delphinium is widely grown and loved for its long strong spikes of bloom. Summer Skies, King Arthur, Guinevere and Blue Jay series are shown.

(*Below*) Still another of the many colors to be expected from the Giant Pacific Hybrids. The wonderful show that delphiniums put on in a garden is reason enough to give them the extra care they need.

DELPHINIUM

IN June and July the queenly delphinium (del-fin'ee-um) rules any planting where it is established. This is not the easiest perennial to grow, especially where summers are hot and humid, but it puts on such a magnificent show that many gardeners consider it worth the extra care it demands. It doesn't live on for many years, as a peony does. In fact, in the South new plants are set out every season. (For annual delphinium, see *Larkspur*.)

Blue is the color most associated with this flower, but that covers a wide range of tones from purple through lavender and mauve to light blue. Pink and white are also popular. The immense spikes, as much as 4 to 6 ft. tall, make the stateliest accents imaginable in a border, where they lend distinction to any associated plants. They must not, however, be crowded among other plants, for they must always have good air circulation. Lower growing forms with flowers more loosely placed on the spike are especially graceful for cutting purposes, as well as for massing in the garden.

Delphinium needs full sunshine and above all a well-drained location; otherwise it is subject to rotting in winter. Soil should be rich and deep and slightly on the sweet side, rather than acid. A little lime worked into the ground before planting is recommended. If the flower spikes are cut back part way after the main blooming period in early summer, a second crop of bloom can be expected later on. Fertilizer lightly applied around the plant will help new growth. When the

(*Left*) Lamartine delphinium bears its deep rich indigo-blue, white-eyed flowers in loose spikes that are especially good for cutting and combining with other summer flowers.

(*Below*) Cliveden Beauty is a pleasing blue with white center. The spires grow 3 to 4 ft. tall.

(*Above*) Pink forms of delphinium are a beautiful accompaniment for the many shades of blue for which this family is noted. Partial cutting back of the flower stems as they fade will promote a new crop of bloom later in the summer. As new stems grow, the dying ones should be cut back all the way to the ground.

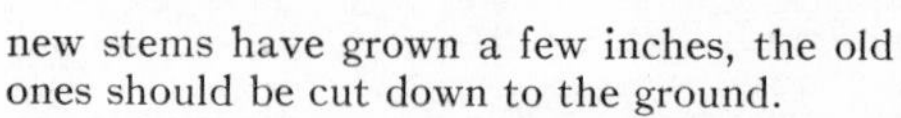

new stems have grown a few inches, the old ones should be cut down to the ground.

Varieties. *Giant Pacific Hybrids* produce large individual flowers on long sturdy spikes. These are sold mixed and also as separate colors known as the Round Table series. The *Astolat* strain introduces many flowers in pink shades. *Cliveden Beauty*, light blue, and *Lamartine*, dark blue, bear airy spikes in early summer which are repeated at intervals. Growing 3 to 4 ft. high, they are fine for cutting. *Blue Mirror* and *Cambridge Blue*, lower growing, bloom all summer if not permitted to go to seed. *Blackmore & Langdon* is an English strain with clear bright colors. A delphinium plant costs 60c to 90c.

How and When to Plant. Before planting, mix a little lime, some bonemeal and complete fertilizer into the soil. Set out the plants in spring or early fall, allowing each one 2 ft. of space. Be careful not to set the crown of the plant deep into the ground, lest it rot, and do not pinch back the tips of the stems to make the plant bushier.

Care and Protection. Water well during dry weather, and provide inconspicuous stakes for the tallest kinds. In the spring, sprinkle a little complete fertilizer on the soil and work it in very gently. Only the shallowest digging is safe, or you will injure the roots. In autumn cover the crown of the plant with an inch or two of coal ashes or sand, and after the ground freezes add some straw for winter protection.

(*Right*) The Round Table series of the Giant Pacific Hybrids resulted from hundreds of crosses. They are valuable for show purposes and will prove a highlight in any garden.

Three varieties of deutzia: (*Above*) Slender deutzia, with its arching branches forming a billowy fountain of white (with detail of blossoms shown in close-up at upper left); Pride of Rochester, with its pink-tinged double flowers (shown in close-up at left); and Pink deutzia, a low bushy shrub pictured at the right, with a closer view of its deeper pink blossoms shown below.

DEUTZIA

BLOOMING with the mock oranges and lilacs, deutzia (dewt'see-uh) contributes its share of spanking white to the spring garden. It is a very familiar, bushy shrub, more or less hardy over the greater part of the United States. Long sprays of bloom are carried on the dense plant in such quantities that the leaves are hidden. When the flowers have disappeared, the bush is of no special interest, and it is therefore important to choose a place for it where the spring bloom may be seen and enjoyed, either alone or with other shrubs. In northern sections it is safest to choose a protected location. Full sun and good soil, well drained but not dry, are essential. Plants cost $1.25 to $2.00 for the 18 to 24-in. size.

Varieties. *Slender* deutzia is named for its slender, arching branches that make a dazzling white fountain of the plant in late May. It does well in the shade, and although its natural height is 4 to 5 ft. it can be kept pruned as a low hedge. One of the hardiest is *Lemoine*, with masses of large white flowers on a spreading, 3 to 4-ft. shrub. The large double flowers of *Pride of Rochester* are tinged pink on the outside. This is an upright grower to 6 or 8 ft. *Pink* deutzia has even deeper colored blooms. Low and bushy, this one does well in either shade or sun and makes a fine edger.

How and When to Plant. Early spring or fall planting brings good results. Dig a hole plenty big enough to hold the roots; pack soil well around them, and give the plant a deep watering.

Care and Protection. As soon as the flowers have faded, cut back some of the flowering stems at the base to encourage new shoots to grow and replace them.

A group of dogwood trees flowering at the edge of a woodland transforms even an ordinary back lot into a scene of unparalleled beauty. A blending of the white and pink forms, as shown here, presents a thrilling picture that can be enjoyed on a smaller scale on your own grounds.

DOGWOOD

THE dogwoods of eastern United States make the spring woods a fairyland of beauty. A hillside where their snowy blooms stand out from the darkness of big sheltering trees not yet in leaf is a picture to keep for a lifetime. From New England down through the Appalachians they are glorious.

Naturally, since they are rapid growing and long lived as well as handsome, dogwoods are planted on a large scale as ornamentals. Those at Valley Forge (in Pennsylvania) make such a fine showing that thousands of motorists visit them every spring. The state of Virginia has selected dogwood as its official tree, and the miles of dogwood trails being planted at Knoxville, Tennessee, are leading this city to proclaim itself the Dogwood Capital.

Every feature of dogwood is remarkably good. These hardy shrubs and small trees are ornamental in flower, foliage, fruit and even branch. The largest grow to about 30 ft. or more in height, while some are shrubby in character. Besides the spring flowers, there are colorful autumn berries; many kinds have foliage that turns beautiful shades before it falls, or branches that show color all winter.

Dogwoods are widely planted in home grounds as lawn specimens and additions to shrub borders. They look best in association with larger trees, as they grow in the wild. An evergreen background provides a beautiful setting. They are especially appropriate to combine with spring-flowering shrubs and bulbs. Specimens cost around $4.00 for the 3-ft. size.

(*Right*) Blooms of the white dogwood express the beauty of simplicity. They make a lacy pattern on horizontal branches that give the tree a distinctive outline.

Varieties. Best known is undoubtedly *White Flowering* dogwood, to 30 ft. high, blooming in May. The white flowers with a small greenish center are carried on branches that grow in a distinctive horizontal manner. Fruit and autumn foliage are scarlet. The *Pink-flowered* form is a lovely companion for it. *Red-Osier*, a shrub type growing to 6 ft. or more, is good for holding the soil on stream banks, for its natural habitat is swamplands. It has small white flowers in flat-topped clusters, blue-white fruits, and red branches in winter.

Japanese dogwood, with snowy flowers and scarlet berries, does best in the shade. The bright green leaves turn scarlet also. *Tatarian* dogwood, a 6 to 10-ft. shrub, has blood-red branches and creamy white flowers and fruit. Another valuable shrub is the 15-ft. *Cornelian Cherry*. The bright yellow flowers of very early spring become large red fruits relished by the birds. Fall foliage is reddish.

(*Above*) This form of the Tatarian dogwood has leaves variegated with yellow. The branches are reddish all winter.

(*Left*) A pink dogwood in its full splendor, with a close-up of the dainty flowers (*above*). Dogwoods outlive most other flowering trees, and where they grow wild there are veterans of many years to be seen.

Yellow-twig dogwood is very decorative. A new variety is *Cherokee Chief*, with ruby-red flowers,* bright red growth in spring, and scarlet leaves in fall.

How and When to Plant. Early spring is the best time to plant, although fall is also a possibility. Balled and burlapped trees have the best chance. Ordinary garden soil, slightly acid, is adequate, and a location in light shade is preferable. A hole wide and deep enough to accommodate the ball of earth without crowding is dug, the soil filled in gradually, and water added. Wrapping the trunk in burlap will protect it.

Care and Protection. Dogwoods are very healthy and hardy, and therefore require little care. Cut out any dead or broken branches in late summer rather than spring.

(*Above*) Yellow-twig dogwood has branches that make a striking contrast with the Red-Osier (*right*), which does well in moist soil and is useful for preventing erosion on steep slopes.

DUTCHMAN'S PIPE

THE small, brownish flowers, like a curved pipe, have given the name to this hardy vine but they are not much in evidence because the broad, heart-shaped leaves hide them. For quick dense shade on a porch or for a screen on a trellis this is a useful twining vine eventually reaching a height of 25 or 30 ft. It likes either full sun or some shade and is not particular about soil, but is such a rampant grower that it should not be used where it will crowd choicer plants.

Varieties. *Aristolochia durior* is the botanical name. A plant averages $2.50 in price.

How and When to Plant. Set out in spring or early fall, where it can twine around some support such as a post or lattice.

Care and Protection. Pruning to keep this very vigorous grower within the space desired should be done in early spring. Some of the shoots should be cut out.

ELAEAGNUS

(*Illustration on following page*)

IN the South elaeagnus (el-ee-ag'nus) is a widely planted evergreen shrub, vigorous, healthy and not particular about location. It does well even in poor, dry soil. There are a number of kinds with margined or variegated leaves, silvery on the underside. The fragrant, drooping flowers, which are also silvery, do not appear until fall. They are followed by scaly, brownish berries.

Varieties. *Pungens* is popular throughout the South, making a strong, 15-ft. shrub with

(*Left*) Cherokee Chief dogwood flowers remain ruby-red throughout their duration. New twigs in spring and early summer are red also. This makes an excellent small specimen for a lawn.

(*Right*) Dutchman's pipe is a very vigorous-growing vine that will quickly shade a porch. It is hardy as far north as New England.

Fruitlandi elaeagnus is a fine shrub for a corner or border planting. It has dark green foliage that is silvery underneath, and rather inconspicuous but fragrant flowers (*at right*).

silvery-backed, dark green leaves all year. Fast-growing *Fruitlandi* stands dust and smoke well, and makes a fine hedge or screen. *Simoni* has leaves marked yellowish. An 18 to 24-in. plant costs around $3.00 to $4.00. (See also *Russian Olive*.)

How and When to Plant. Winter is the best planting time in the South. Dig a hole wider and deeper than necessary to hold the roots, and place the shrub at the same depth as in the nursery. Pack the soil tightly around it, and water well.

Care and Protection. No fertilizer is needed. To keep the plant compact and bushy, cut back the long shoots in summer.

ENGLISH DAISY

FOR massing at the front of a spring border and as an underplanting for early-blooming shrubs, English daisies are colorful and intimate little plants. In small gardens they are very adaptable, finding pansies and spring bulbs particularly good companions. They need moist, well-drained garden soil, for they wilt quickly if subjected to hot dry conditions. Early spring to July is their blooming season.

Varieties. *Monstrosa* is the common garden kind, in pink, red and white. Plants are easy to buy at garden stores and nurseries at a low price.

How and When to Plant. Set out the plants in early spring, 6 in. apart. Rather than try to hold them over for another year, it is wiser to discard them after they finish blooming and get fresh plants the next spring.

Care and Protection. Keep the plants watered and the dead flowers picked off.

ENKIANTHUS

AS a partner for azaleas and rhododendrons, there is nothing better than enkianthus (en-kee-anth'us). It is much less often seen, but it is a neat and handsome bush that furnishes contrast with the dark heavy foliage of the rhododendron. In both late spring and fall it is of particular interest—when the dainty bell-shaped flowers hang in clusters from the branches, and again when the leaves turn bright red and orange before they drop.

Enkianthus, like an azalea, needs well-drained, acid soil. Plant it in full sun or part shade, as a specimen or with other flowering shrubs and evergreens in a foundation planting. An especially appropriate location might be a spot on sloping ground or a terrace where you can look up at the plant and get a better view of the drooping flowers. This is a slow grower, fairly hardy as far as the Great Lakes. In eastern United States it grows to 6 to 8 ft. in height, but in the South it is sometimes tree-like. In the North a rather sheltered location is safest.

Varieties. *Redvein*, with pinkish yellow flowers on an upright, columnar plant, may be bought for about $3.00 (18 to 24-in. size).

How and When to Plant. Spring or fall is the time to plant. Dig a hole of good size and in the bottom mix a generous amount of peat moss or leaf mold. Special fertilizer for

(*Left*) English daisies give a nice touch of color to spring gardens and they are especially adapted for massing with early bulbs. They need moist soil.

(*Above*) Like other broad-leaved evergreen shrubs, enkianthus requires well-drained, acid soil. This is a beautiful partner for azaleas and rhododendrons.

Winter Gem euonymus is a trim evergreen shrub, neat and useful in landscaping.

acid-loving plants (obtainable at garden supply stores) may also be mixed with the soil before planting. Press the soil firmly about the roots, and water well.

Care and Protection. Never use lime around this shrub, and do not try to move it once it is established.

EUONYMUS

BESIDES the colorful burning bush and the hardy evergreen bittersweet (listed separately), the euonymus (yew-on'im-us) tribe includes other very useful shrubs. The flowers are not so important as the strong growth and good foliage. Almost all are hardy in the northern states. They are vigorous in habit and not at all demanding in soil requirements. Some are evergreen, while others lose their leaves in autumn. Bright berries add to their appeal in the fall. All are easy to grow.

Varieties. In the South, *Evergreen* euonymus is popular as a hedge and specimen plant. It grows to about 15 ft. unless pruned. There are many varieties of it with leaves edged or variegated with silver or gold. *Spindle Tree* also grows to about 15 ft., but its leaves drop late in the fall after turning reddish. The fruit is pink at first, later becoming orange. *Spreading* euonymus is a compact shrub with coral-red berries in autumn. It is very hardy and is especially valuable because it does so well in the shade. One of the easiest growing of evergreen or semi-evergreen shrubs, it makes a fine low hedge. Low-growing *Emerald Cushion*, columnar *Emerald Charm*, and bushier *Emerald Leader* and *Emerald Pride* are newer evergreen varieties for landscape use. A 2 to 3-ft. specimen costs about $2.00 (more for newest kinds).

How and When to Plant. Set out the plants in fall or spring, in any reasonably good garden soil. For a hedge, space them 8 to 10 in. apart. Dig generous holes for the roots, pack the soil hard, and water well.

Care and Protection. Where desirable to keep these shrubs trimmed, snip them in early summer. All are susceptible to scale, which requires spraying both in early spring and in summer.

EVENING PRIMROSE

MOST members of this large family grow wild in different parts of North and South America. Some have flowers that do not open until late in the afternoon and then last only until noon of the next day. Others are day blooming. The lowest growing are good in rock gardens, while others show up well at the edge of a sunny border, where their clusters of bright clear yellow, cup shaped flowers are most attractive. They are rampant growers.

Plants are best in groups in full sun. There they bloom continuously most of the summer. Soil should be light and well drained. Heavy, damp clay is not to their liking.

Varieties. A fine rock plant is *Oenothera missouriensis*, with 4-in. yellow cups on a 12-in. plant. *Illumination* has bright lemon-yellow flowers above large, shiny leaves from June to August. It grows to 2 ft. Plants cost 50c to $1.00.

How and When to Plant. Set out the plants in spring or fall, 8 in. apart.

(*Above and Below*) Berries of the evergreen bittersweet (described on the following page) help to make this a valued vine. In the North it is more reliably hardy than English ivy as a wall covering.

(*Above*) Illumination, a compact-growing evening primrose of vivid yellow which bursts into bloom in early summer and continues to flower for many weeks.

(*Left*) Fruticosa Youngi, a 2-ft. evening primrose, is a showy light yellow. Plants are most effective in a mass.

(*Left*) **Fairy lily is a summer - flowering bulb that blooms freely when grown like gladiolus. In the North the bulbs must be stored indoors over winter.**

(*Right*) **Rosy Spire, a variety of false dragonhead with compact flower spikes, is colorful in mid-September. Practically any soil, either wet or dry, will grow this hardy perennial.**

Care and Protection. Keep seed pods removed, to prolong flowering. About every second year, in early spring or fall, the plants should be dug up, divided and replanted.

EVERGREEN BITTERSWEET

(*Illustrations on preceding page*)

THIS excellent vine is valued both for its leathery, rounded, evergreen leaves and for the quantities of yellow and red berries that it produces in late autumn. Hardy into New England, it is more to be relied on than English ivy as a wall cover in northern parts of the United States. It clings to brick and stone and does not mind growing conditions in cities. On walls and rocks, on banks and tree trunks, the rootlets catch hold easily. Average soil and either sun or part shade are suitable. If pruned, it can be kept in shrub form. Wintercreeper is another common name for this part of the euonymus family. (See also *Euonymus* and *Burning Bush*.)

Varieties. Besides evergreen bittersweet (priced at $1.25 to $1.50), other fine wintercreepers are *Coloratus* with leaves that are purplish all winter, and the dainty-leaved *Kewensis* that is such a good evergreen creeper in shady rock gardens.

How and When to Plant. Fall or spring planting is successful. A wall with a northern or eastern exposure is the best choice.

Care and Protection. Any necessary trimming should be done in early spring, which is also the time to prevent scale by adequate spraying.

FAIRY LILY

ALTHOUGH not on a par with gladiolus in popularity, this summer-flowering bulb is grown in much the same way outdoors. It needs light, well-drained soil and complete sun. This is a profuse bloomer with grass-like leaves and showy pink, yellow or white flowers on 8 to 10-in. stems. Another name for it is zephyr lily (botanically, *Zephyranthes*). Where a cool room is available, it can also be grown in a pot indoors.

Varieties. Bulbs are sold in separate colors or mixed, at about 15c to 20c each.

How and When to Plant. Plant outdoors in the spring after all danger of frost is past. Set the bulbs about 2 or 3 in. deep and 3 to 4 in. apart. In warm regions planting may be done in early fall.

Care and Protection. Where winters are mild, bulbs may be left in the ground. In the North, dig them up after frost and store in sand in a cool, frostproof place.

FALSE DRAGONHEAD

THICK spikes of bloom in late summer when some other perennials are slowing down make this hardy plant (*Physostegia*) welcome at the rear of a border. Growing 2 to 3 ft. high, with flowers in white and shades of purplish pink, it soon forms a big clump. Because it is such a willing grower and spreads so easily, it should not be placed too close to choice plants that could be crowded by it.

Any soil, dry or wet, is good enough. It seems to prefer shade, and for a partly shady

(*Above*) **Birds love the fiery orange-scarlet berries for which the firethorn (described on the opposite page) is famous.**

(*Left*) **A well-grown Laland firethorn is extremely decorative. Give it a prominent location where the whole neighborhood can see it.**

Two varieties of the perennial flax are shown here. (*Left*) Perenne, which bears large, clear blue flowers from early June to August. (*Right*) Flavum, a low-growing, yellow variety.

(*Below*) The annual flax can be grown from seed sown in early spring. It makes a continuous mass of color in a garden.

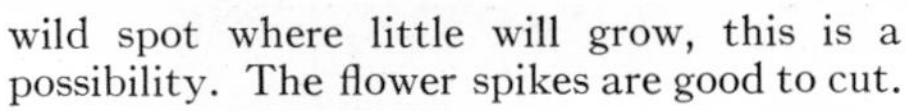

wild spot where little will grow, this is a possibility. The flower spikes are good to cut.

Varieties. *Vivid* is somewhat lower growing (18 to 24 in.) than most. Deep rose to red, it blooms in August and September. Dark pink *Summer Glow* grows 3 ft. tall, as does rose-crimson *Rosy Spire*. *Summer Snow* is ivory-white. Plants cost 75c to 90c.

How and When to Plant. Set out the plants in spring or fall, about a foot apart.

Care and Protection. Every year or two dig up the clump in spring, pull it apart, throw away the center, and replant the outside pieces.

FIRETHORN

(*Illustrations on opposite page*)

FIERY berries and thorny branches have given the firethorn its name. The brilliant fruits, carried in big clusters along the spiny stems of this broad-spreading evergreen shrub, are a spectacle well into winter if the birds spare them. This is a plant that takes plenty of space if allowed to grow naturally. It is sometimes difficult to get started, and at first is irregular and angular in outline. However, it easily stands pruning and can be shaped without any trouble.

A popular way to grow firethorn is against a warm wall or chimney. Here the flexible branches can be trained to produce an eye-catching picture. Pruning to keep them where wanted is done in early spring. Masses of white flowers come in late spring, and by fall have become thick fruit clusters.

Firethorn needs good, well-drained soil and a location in full sun. It does best in mild climates, and there it is sometimes grown as a hedge because of its dense thorny growth and ability to stand clipping.

Varieties. *Laland* is the most popular kind because it is the hardiest. South of Washington, D. C., it grows to huge size, and northward to Boston it reaches 6 or 8 ft. or more in height and width. The berries are orange-red. Semi-upright *Chinese* has large red berries and glossy leaves. Potted plants 12 to 15 in. tall cost about $1.50.

How and When to Plant. Buy potted plants and set them out in spring or fall. Mix leaf mold or peat moss with the soil before planting. Set the pot in a hole of adequate size, and then carefully break it away without disturbing the roots. Firm the soil well around the plant, and water thoroughly.

Care and Protection. No pruning is necessary if the plant is grown naturally.

FLAX

YOU can't make linen or linseed oil from the flax grown in gardens, but you will find this a pleasant little plant with delicate flowers over a long season. It is easily grown in a rock garden and in a sunny spot at the edge of a border. Flowers drop their petals after only a day, but are promptly replaced by others the next morning. For this reason they are not used in bouquets, but they provide a lovely carefree mass of color in summer gardens. Give them an open space in the sun, in light, well-drained soil.

Besides the perennial kinds there is annual flax, about 15 in. tall, which is showy from June on.

Varieties. The common blue flax is *Linum perenne*. Its large, clear sky-blue flowers are produced freely from early June to August. *Heavenly Blue*, 2 ft. tall, has feathery blue-green foliage and luminous blue flowers. The waxy yellow flowers of *Flavum* come on a short, stocky plant in June and July. The price is 50c to 90c.

How and When to Plant. Set out the perennial plants in spring. Sow seed of annual flax in early spring where bloom is wanted, and thin the plants to 6 in. apart.

Care and Protection. To encourage thick new growth, cut back the stems when they have finished flowering. A light winter covering is good insurance in very cold regions.

Fleabane (described on the next page) is not a very descriptive name for this pretty blue perennial. The flowers, produced in June and July, are very good for cutting.

FLEABANE

(Illustration on preceding page)

THESE unassuming flowers look somewhat like hardy asters but they bloom in early summer. In a sunny place in the border where the soil is not very rich, fleabane provides 2-in. flowers usually in shades of lavender and purple. They are very free blooming and are good cutting material. There are dwarfer varieties, too, for rock gardens where good drainage is assured but the soil is only average. Many forms of this hardy perennial grow wild in the Northwest.

Varieties. *Erigeron speciosus*, 2 ft. tall, has good-sized, lavender-blue flowers in June and July. Plants cost a dollar or less. Newer kinds from England are also on the market, priced a little higher.

How and When to Plant. Set out plants in fall or early spring, a foot apart if used in the border.

Care and Protection. Keep the dead flowers picked off. About every third year, dig up the clump, separate it into pieces and replant them.

(*Above*) Flowering almond is an especially good shrub to plant in small gardens, for it keeps its place without heavy pruning. Blooms come early in the spring. (*Right*) The flowering branches, neatly packed with bloom, are lovely for cutting.

FLOWERING ALMOND

NO almonds come from this dwarf, compact shrub, but its profuse early spring bloom is reason enough for growing it. The little double flowers, usually pink but also available in a white form, open ahead of the leaves or with them. The flowering branches, studded with bloom, are very nice for cutting.

Because it grows only 4 to 6 ft. in height, the flowering almond is practical for use in small gardens. The lovely pink color combines well with such early spring flowers as forget-me-nots, pansies, and early bulbs. Its branches grow close to the ground; when planted with other shrubs it should therefore be placed in the foreground where it can be seen easily and not crowded. It is hardy over practically the entire United States.

Varieties. This shrub, listed simply as *Pink* flowering almond, is sold at around $1.50 for a 2 to 3-ft. bush.

How and When to Plant. Plant in early spring or fall in well-drained soil, in full sun or very light shade. Dig a hole big enough to accommodate the roots without crowding. A shovelful of peat moss put in the bottom of the hole and mixed with soil will be a help. Set the plant in place, and half-fill the hole with good soil. Tamp firmly, and water well. When the water has settled, fill the hole with soil, leaving a slight depression to allow for future watering.

Care and Protection. Little if any pruning should be needed, but when done it should be just after the flowers fade. Occasionally borers get into the branches and cause the leaves to wilt. If this happens, cut back the damaged part completely and give the shrub a thorough watering.

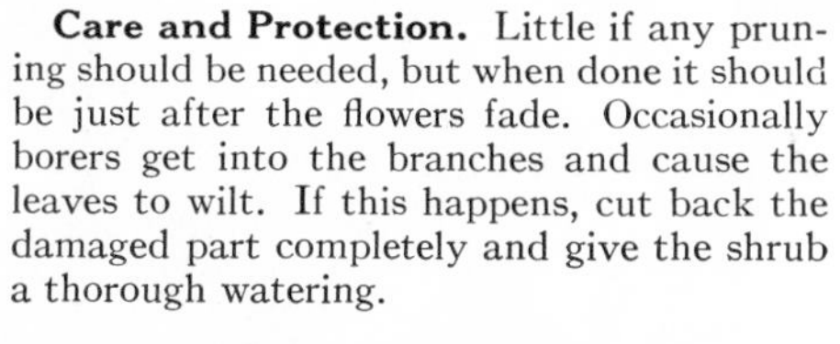

FLOWERING CHERRY

WEST meets East in admiration of the Japanese flowering cherry. These trees have been cultivated in Japan for centuries, and many varieties have been developed. In 1912 the city of Tokyo sent several hundred trees to Washington, D. C., as a good-will gesture, and tourists have for years made pilgrimages there to see them blooming in early spring. Those trees are planted near water, but that is not necessary.

(*Below*) The flowering cherry trees around the Tidal Basin in Washington, D. C., have been a mecca for tourists ever since they came as a gift from the city of Tokyo. (*Right*) White Mt. Fuji and light pink Amanogawa are popular and very satisfactory flowering cherries. Both are fragrant.

(*Right*) A weeping flowering cherry, holding out its slender branches shimmering with pink bloom, is a handsome specimen.

(*Below*) Fugenzo is another fine flowering cherry. The large, double blooms pass from deep pink to a lighter tint. It has been planted in Japan for several centuries.

They grow well all through eastern United States and on the Pacific Coast, but not in the far South or far North. In general, they are considered as hardy as peach trees, or slightly more so. They are among the most colorful and free flowering of all spring-blooming trees and are widely planted around homes.

Some kinds of flowering cherries are of broad spreading growth, while others are more upright. Weeping forms are especially ornamental specimens. They are no higher than 20 or 25 ft. when full grown. The single or double flowers, white or pink, come in profuse masses in mid-spring, just before or with the leaves; some varieties are fragrant. The double-flowered cherries do not bear fruit. They take average, well-drained garden soil; a location in full sun will produce the best bloom. Early-flowering varieties show up best against a background of dark evergreens, and all are among the small flowering trees likely to be the first choice of gardeners for decorating their home gardens. They are an important part of the picture of spring.

Varieties. *Kwanzan*, with 2-in., double or semi-double, rose-pink flowers, is probably the most popular. It is also one of the hardiest. The low, upright tree grows to about 20 ft., and the young foliage is coppery color. Kwanzan and *Yoshino* (or *Yedoensis*) make a great contribution to the Tidal Basin display in Washington. Yoshino is very vigorous and fast growing, producing a profusion of single, white to pink flowers early in spring. This variety is also largely planted in Tokyo. *Amanogawa* is a 20-ft. tree growing in narrow, upright form and bearing fragrant, light pink flowers. It is a good choice for a small garden, as is *Naden*, which is a slow grower of moderate size with rose-pink blooms. *Mt. Fuji* (or *Shirotae*) has large, fragrant, pure white flowers. *Autumnal* blooms profusely in fall as well as spring. It is a bushy grower to about 20 ft. and needs a somewhat sheltered spot. The *Weeping* variety has plentiful rose-pink blooms on slender, graceful branches. It is priced at around $6.00 for a 3 to 4-ft. tree. Other varieties are slightly lower in cost.

How and When to Plant. Trees are planted in very early spring or early fall. Dig a hole large enough to hold the roots without cramping, and place the tree at the same depth as in the nursery. (Note the dark mark around the base of the trunk.) Be careful not to expose the roots to sun or air while planting. Pack good soil around them, without leaving any air pockets. Fill the hole half full of soil, and then fill it to the top with water. When the water has drained away, shovel in the remaining soil. If the planting is done in autumn, spread a layer of leaves or peat moss over the ground.

Care and Protection. If suckers come up from the roots, cut them off at once. The only pruning needed may be the removal of young shoots that would interfere with each other. Cut them off in winter.

FLOWERING CRAB

CONTRIBUTING greatly to the glory of May-time gardens are such trees as the flowering crabs. They are able to stand low winter temperatures and are among the most desirable of all small ornamental trees, living for many years and being of interest at all seasons. Some are large shrubs, some grow to a height of 20 or 25 ft., and others have a weeping habit of growth. Some varieties have reddish or bronzy foliage, and some have leaves that change color in the fall.

It is chiefly for their great masses of pink, white or red, single, double or semi-double flowers when spring gardens are at their peak

(*Left*) Almey flowering crab is extremely showy. The crimson flowers come on a 12 to 15-ft. tree and are followed by bright red fruit.

(*Above*) Katherine is a double, light pink to white flowering crab with dull red fruit.

(*Above*) **Japanese flowering crab does well in practically any soil. Its blooms are produced in profusion, starting when the tree is quite small.** (*Right*) **Its yellowish apples make the tree ornamental in autumn too.**

Hardy and disease-free Hopa crab is an upright grower with good foliage and a fine display of spring bloom.

that flowering crabs are grown. Most kinds are fragrant, like other apple blossoms, and are especially pretty in the bud. By early fall these flowers have become little apples—green, yellow, scarlet or crimson, depending on the variety—varying from the size of a cherry to a fruit 2 or 2½ in. in diameter. Larger kinds are good for making jelly, and all are favorite food for wild birds.

Flowering crabapples do well in full sun or light shade and are not particular about having a sheltered location. They grow in a wide range of soils, and they can stand the fumes and grime of cities. Because they are so hardy and adaptable they are in great demand, and new kinds are continually being offered. A 3 to 4-ft. tree may be bought at nurseries and garden stores for around $2.50 (more, if the roots are wrapped in burlap).

Varieties. The *Japanese* crab, a dense, vigorous tree about 25 ft. tall when full grown, starts to bloom when quite young. The fragrant, deep pink flowers fade to white and are followed by small yellow fruits. *Hopa* also has profuse, deep pink blooms on a rugged tree; its large, orange and red fruits make fine jelly. The double pink flowers of *Bechtel* make it a favorite, plus the fact that the tree is small enough for moderate-sized gardens. *Sargent* is even more dense and shrub-like in growth, with pure white flowers and dark red fruit. *Dolgo* is white also, with early fruits good for jelly making. The tree is sturdy and very

(*Above*) **Eley crab is a mass of red bloom in spring against purplish branches. Foliage is reddish bronze, turning crimson in fall, accompanied by shining dark red fruit the size of a cherry.**

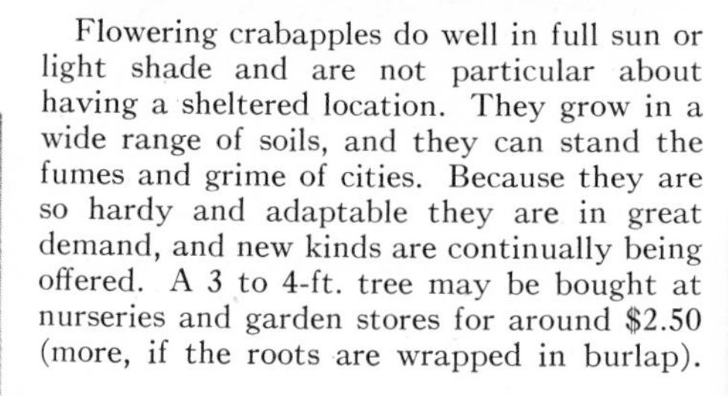

(*Below*) **Flowering crabapples combine dainty appearance with rugged health. They behave well in ordinary garden soil—in fact, they tolerate conditions that would mean death to many flowering trees. They are hardy over most of the United States.**

(*Above*) **Bechtel is a sturdy small tree with double pink, fragrant flowers. This is a rather late-blooming variety.**

hardy. *Carmine* has non-fading, rich pink flowers and good dark foliage, while *Almey* bears masses of bright crimson bloom and scarlet fruit on a 12 to 15-ft. tree.

How and When to Plant. Planting is done in early spring or in the fall. Dig a hole wide enough to hold the roots well spread out, without cramping, and deep enough so that the tree will be at the same depth as in the nursery. (A dark mark around the base of the trunk will show what that depth was.) Be careful never to expose the roots to sun or air, and if any have become broken in moving, cut them off. Pack good soil around the roots, being particular **not** to leave any air pockets. Fill the hole half full of soil, and then pour in water. When that has drained away, finish filling the hole with soil. Wait till it is fairly dry before tamping it down well, and leave the surface raked fine. Water frequently until the tree gets a good start.

Care and Protection. For the first summer, it is well to keep the ground around the tree covered with leaves or peat moss. It is not necessary to fertilize flowering crabs. They may need occasional pruning if they grow too thick. The time to prune is just after the flowers fade, or in the fall after the fruit is gone, or in late winter before growth starts. These trees are generally free of pests.

FLOWERING PEACH

THIS is another small ornamental that has come to us from the Orient. Although not so important as the flowering cherry, it is a lovely little tree of dense, rounded growth with bountiful flowers in early spring. They may be single or double, pink, white or red. There is also a weeping form. This tree presents a pleasing appearance from spring to fall at the edge of a shrub border where its blooms may be enjoyed. It grows perhaps 15 to 25 ft. tall, in any average soil. This ornamental peach does not bear fruit and is not so hardy as the flowering crab.

Varieties. This tree is generally offered as *Double-flowering*, in pink, white or crimson. The long-lasting, rosette-like flowers appear about two weeks before dogwood. The 3 to 4-ft. size costs about $2.00.

How and When to Plant. Spring planting is best in northern areas; in the South, spring or fall. Dig a hole large enough to hold the roots without crowding. Set the tree at the same depth as in the nursery (indicated by a dark mark around the base of the trunk).

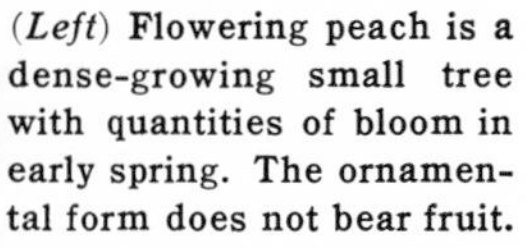

(*Left*) **Flowering peach is a dense-growing small tree with quantities of bloom in early spring. The ornamental form does not bear fruit.**

Take care not to let the roots dry out while planting. Pack good soil all around them, without leaving any air pockets. Fill the hole half full of soil, and then with water. When the water has drained off, finish filling the hole with soil.

Care and Protection. Immediately after the blooms have faded, cut the flowering branches back to about 8 in. This will promote new shoots that will bloom the following year. Do not do any pruning in autumn.

FLOWERING PLUM

THE purple foliage of some varieties of flowering plum is the chief reason for growing this small, compact tree, although the flowers also are showy in spring. They are borne ahead of the leaves. Sometimes there are small fruits, but they are not very noticeable. As an accent point for a special location and as contrast, this is a good choice, particularly for small properties. It can endure hot dry summers and city growing conditions. The tree is hardier than the flowering peach and stands pruning well.

Varieties. *Thundercloud*, a 12 to 15-ft. tree with pink flowers and rich purple foliage, is a popular variety. *Newport* is also good. It has small single white flowers followed by pinkish purple leaves that get darker as the summer progresses. Bronze-leaved *Blireiana* has pink flowers when forsythia is in bloom.

(*Below*) **The foliage of Thundercloud flowering plum holds its bronzy purple color throughout the season. Delicate pink flowers are borne before the leaves appear. This tree is a very upright grower.**

A 4 to 5-ft. tree costs around $3.00 to $3.50.

How and When to Plant. Plant in spring or fall in full sun so that the foliage will be bright. Dig a hole big enough to hold the roots easily, and set the tree at the same depth as in the nursery. Be careful not to allow the roots to get dried out while planting. Pack good soil about them, not leaving any air pockets. Half-fill the hole with soil, and then with water. When the water has drained away, finish filling in the soil.

Care and Protection. If a branch rubs against another, cut it away in late winter.

Japanese flowering quince, a very thorny and dense-growing shrub with scarlet flowers early in the spring.

FLOWERING QUINCE

SPINY branches and a very dense growing habit, with colorful, waxy flowers in early spring before the leaves, distinguish this shrub. Single red flowers are most familiar, but there are also varieties with double blooms, from scarlet to pink to white in color.

(*Below*) **Here Snowstorm flowering tobacco, a dwarf form with white flowers that remain open all day, is combined with bright scarlet zinnias with telling effect.**

(*Left*) **The snowy white, star-shaped flowers of White Bedder flowering tobacco are very sweet scented. This 12 to 15-in. plant blooms from July to frost.**

(*Below*) **Sensation Hybrids bring a fine color range to flowering tobacco. Plants grow 1½ to 2 ft. tall. Sow the seed in light, rich soil and allow 18 in. between plants.**

Foliage is dark and glossy; and while the greenish yellow fruit that comes in the fall is not beautiful, it can be used for making jelly. This shrub is widely planted as a specimen and in borders. It is hardy except in the hardest winters.

Varieties. The common flowering quince, averaging 6 to 8 ft. when full size, may be had in a number of varieties, among them shell-pink *Pink Lady* and coral-pink *Juliet.* The very large flowers of *Stanford Red* make this variety nice for cutting. They are orange-red, turning blood-red. The 12 to 15-in. size costs $2.00 to $2.50. *Japanese* quince is somewhat lower in growth, with masses of single, bright red flowers and round, shiny leaves. A plant 18 to 24 in. tall may be purchased for only $1.25.

How and When to Plant. Plant in spring or fall in full sun, in any good garden soil. Dig a hole large enough to hold the roots without cramping. A shovelful of peat moss put in the bottom of the hole and mixed with soil will be a help. Set the plant in place, and half-fill the hole with good soil. Tamp firmly, and fill with water. When the water has settled, finish filling the hole with soil.

Care and Protection. Pruning may be necessary just after the blooms have faded, to improve the shape of this shrub.

FLOWERING TOBACCO

FRAGRANCE is the main virtue of flowering tobacco, although the clustered, long-tubed flowers are attractive in border groups. Blooming freely from midsummer to frost, they may also be used for cutting. The plant grows almost anywhere, making a 3-ft. spreading mass in full sun or part shade.

Older varieties drooped during the day and didn't open their five-pointed flowers until late afternoon, when the sweet fragrance began to be noticeable. Now there are greatly improved kinds that not only stay open all day but come in many other colors than the original white.

Varieties. *Nicotiana affinis* is the older, 2 to 3-ft., evening-blooming kind. *Daylight,* also white, 1½ ft. tall, remains open all day even in bright sunshine, as do the *Sensation Hybrids* that are offered in mixed colors including mauve, wine, crimson, violet, yellow and coral. *Crimson Bedder* and *White Bedder,* with neat, compact, 15-in. plants, are especially good with petunias.

How and When to Plant. Sow the seed in early spring in fairly light, rich soil, and space the young plants 18 in. apart. Or buy plants (about $1.00 per dozen). Seed is so small that it is not easily handled.

Care and Protection. Pinching back the plants is not advisable.

FORGET-ME-NOTS

THE modest and dainty blue forget-me-not is familiar in springtime gardens, where it serves as a good ground cover for yellow and white daffodils and other early bulbs. This annual kind, 6 to 10 in. high, may also be had in pink and white. It likes sun and well-drained soil, and it flowers best while the weather is still cool. When the ground is moist enough, it spreads quickly, and very often keeps springing up all over the garden from seed dropped the previous year.

There are also perennial forms growing a foot tall or more, which bloom from June on. These are good for massing in borders where they will have cool moist soil and at least part shade. Both kinds are very free blooming.

Varieties. *Royal Blue* and *Victoria* are annual varieties, fine in rock gardens. Rich blue *Myosotis palustris semperflorens,* bright *Pinkie,* and *Sapphire* are perennial. Plants cost around 75c.

How and When to Plant. Seed of annual forget-me-not sown in early spring will bloom in a few weeks. Plants are set out in fall or early spring, 6 in. apart.

Care and Protection. Don't let seed form if you want bloom to continue.

Annual forget-me-nots self-sow easily and spread quickly to form a blue ground cover for spring bulbs.

(*Above*) **Lynwood Gold forsythia is an upright grower with bright golden blooms that never seem to mind bad weather.**

(*Left*) **A study in yellow is presented by Showy Border forsythia and yellow trumpet daffodils.** (*Corner, Above*) **A closer view of a flowering branch.**

FORSYTHIA

PRACTICALLY everyone knows the forsythia, one of the earliest of shrubs to bloom in the spring. Its bright yellow, scentless, bell-shaped flowers, which have inspired the name golden bells, are borne all along the arching branches in April before the leaves come. Its earliness, hardiness, and compliance with almost any growing conditions place forsythia among the most popular of all flowering shrubs. It is hardy as far north as New York state.

Any reasonably good soil and full sun will please it. Heavy fertilizing is not necessary, but each plant should be allowed enough space to grow unhampered. Specimens should not be set closer to walks than 8 ft., for their greatest beauty is realized when they are permitted to grow naturally, with practically no pruning.

Forsythia is useful in creating many early spring garden pictures. It blooms with the spring bulbs and flowering trees, and may be used in countless combinations with them. In the border after its blooms are gone it makes a mass of green all summer. Sprays of forsythia are easily forced into bloom indoors from January on, by merely placing them in water.

Varieties. *Showy Border* forsythia is a fine upright sort with deep yellow flowers. It grows to a height of 8 ft. Slender, very arching branches that bend to the ground make *Weeping* especially good for steep banks. *Spring Glory* has very large flowers of pale yellow. *Lynwood Gold* is a symmetrical bush with erect branches smothered in golden yellow. It reaches 6 to 8 ft. in height at maturity. A 2 to 3-ft. forsythia bush costs $1.00 to $2.00.

How and When to Plant. Either spring or fall planting is successful. Dig a hole of good size for the roots, pack the soil hard around them, and water thoroughly.

Care and Protection. When forsythia gets straggly, some of the older stems may be cut back to the ground immediately after the blooming season, to encourage new shoots to grow and replace the older ones. Forsythia is practically never attacked by either disease or insects.

FOUR O'CLOCKS

THIS quick-growing plant, also known as marvel of Peru, is a perennial in its native home in the tropics but is commonly grown from seed, as an annual. It reaches 2½ to 3 ft. in height and as much in diameter, making a strong bushy mass of growth like a shrub. Because it is such a fast and strong grower, it is very good as a low hedge or temporary foundation planting. The very fragrant, single flowers open late in the afternoon, or earlier if the day is cloudy. They are freely produced from July to fall. Four o'clocks need the sun but almost any soil is good enough, and they even endure a smoky environment without complaint.

Varieties. A packet of mixed seed will give red, salmon, yellow, white and variegated flowers.

How and When to Plant. Sow in the open ground in early spring. The seeds are large and need not be planted close. Plants should be 15 to 20 in. apart. They form large, fleshy roots that can be dug up in autumn, stored over winter in a frostproof place, and planted out again the next spring.

Care and Protection. Japanese beetles are attracted to these flowers, so be prepared to ward them off with DDT or lead arsenate if you live in a beetle district.

FOXGLOVE

(*Illustrations on following page*)

THE long, tapering spires of foxglove are obvious contenders for a place at the rear of a hardy border. Here they bloom in early summer with Canterbury bells and early lilies. Their striking stalks, encircled with speckle-throated white, yellow, salmon or rose flowers, are good accent points. A group of them, 3 to 6 ft. tall, can also be combined with shrubs if given a shady location. They like a cool, damp climate and reasonably good soil that is moist in summer but well drained in winter.

This is a charming flower with an old-fashioned air, contrasting well with daisy-shaped and more airy blooms. Its common

Four o'clocks grow about 3 ft. tall and often that wide, to make a strong shrubby plant that is good as a low temporary hedge.

(*Left and Above*) **Perhaps you will want to try foxgloves on your fingers as well as in your garden! They come in a variety of colors, as shown here, and wherever they are planted they lend a sweet, old-fashioned tone to a garden.**

(*Right*) **Foxtail lilies grow to the impressive height of 6 to 8 ft. The roots need a winter covering of ashes or leaves, which should be removed very slowly so as to protect the early spring shoots from frost injury.**

name conjures up amusing pictures of a wily fox dressed in Sunday best, right down to his gloves.

Varieties. The *Giant Shirley* strain, with flowers in mixed colors, grows 3 ft. tall. A plant costs about 65c. Newer is the *Excelsior* strain, with flowers better distributed all around the stalk.

How and When to Plant. Fall or early spring is the time to plant. In a group, the plants should be 8 to 10 in. apart.

Care and Protection. In regions where severe winters are usual, a light cover of evergreen branches is good protection. The plants are not likely to be long lived.

FOXTAIL LILY

SUCH a commanding plant as the foxtail lily or desert candle will hardly find a place in a small garden, for it grows into a large, imposing clump of sword-like leaves and the flower spike is 6 to 8 ft. tall. But it always arouses great interest, and to raise it successfully is something of a feat. The large, fleshy roots are easily broken and must be handled carefully. Because the spikes grow so tall, the plant must have a location sheltered from the wind. It is hardy about as far north as New Jersey but is safer with some protection, not only in winter but also in the spring as the new growth is appearing. Its requirements include full sun and moist but well-drained soil to which peat moss and sand have been added. The bloom spikes appear in late May or early June.

Varieties. *Shelford Hybrids* offer white, yellow, pink and coppery colors. A root costs about $2.00.

How and When to Plant. Plant the root 6 in. deep, in autumn, but first prepare the soil carefully. Cover with sand over winter.

Care and Protection. Keep well watered in hot spells. Give the plant winter protection but do not try to move it.

FRAGRANCE IN THE GARDEN

OF all the characteristics of a flower, fragrance is the most elusive and the most difficult to describe. In some instances fragrance is the most dominant feature and has inspired the name given to the plant. Examples that come to mind are sweet pea, sweet shrub, sweet alyssum and sweet sultan. Probably perfume is the first association also with such names as lily of the valley, mignonette, heliotrope, gardenia, tuberose, freesia and honeysuckle.

The fleeting and changing quality of fragrance is tantalizing. Many factors have an influence on the amount noticeable at any given time. Some of these, such as light, moisture and temperature, have to do with the physical environment of the plant. The same variety may be sweeter at certain periods of the day than at others. Some kinds are more fragrant after the sun has been shining on them several hours. Many roses are more fragrant after being cut and brought indoors. Some flowers are scented at night; boxwood leaves are especially so after a rain.

Because fragrance cannot be measured or easily defined, it is hard to say whether a flower smells the same to all who sniff it.

(*Above*) **Flowering tobacco is often used near a porch or terrace where its fragrance can be appreciated.**

(*Left*) **The fragrance of stocks helps to make them popular for cutting as well as for garden use.**

(*Left*) The delightfully sweet perfume of Burkwood viburnum is one of the main assets of this hardy shrub.

(*Right*) Carnations have been loved for their scent ever since olden days. *Dianthus,* the family name, which means *flower of Jove,* was given in honor of their fine qualities.

Words used in an attempt to describe various scents are not exact. "Apple pie" fragrance, for example, would not be precisely the same in every kitchen. And a perfume pleasing to one person is not necessarily agreeable to another. Boxwood, marigolds and chrysanthemums have fragrance that delights many persons, but not everybody.

Flowering tobacco and moonflower are frequently planted near patios and windows for their evening fragrance. Petunias and stocks also give off fragrance at night. Lilacs, mock orange bushes, various viburnums and daphne are among the familiar shrubs scenting the spring air. Some newer roses have only slight fragrance, but many are rich with it.

Peonies, irises, lilies and the carnation and pink family furnish satisfying fragrance in perennial gardens. Hyacinths are outstanding in early spring, as well as some pansies and violets. Scented geraniums and bee balm have fragrant leaves, as do the old-time herbs like thyme and lavender. Fringe tree, silk tree, some of the magnolias and flowering crabs are notable for their sweet perfume. (All of the flowers and plants mentioned are described in more detail under their respective headings.)

FREESIA

THESE sweetly fragrant flowers, in white, orange, yellow, lavender and rose, are carried at right angles from the wiry stems. They are best raised in pots because the bulbs are very tender. They may be placed in a sunny window and brought into bloom in about three months. Use good potting soil plus sand and a little bonemeal.

Varieties. Pink *Appleblossom,* white *Purity* and *Snowstorm,* and light blue *Maryon* are among the varieties offered. Bulbs cost 15c to 20c apiece.

How and When to Plant. In early fall place several bulbs in a 5-in. pot of good soil, and barely cover them. Keep on the cool side. As they grow, give them water and some liquid fertilizer.

Care and Protection. After the bulbs have bloomed, keep them growing as long as possible. When the foliage dies off, let the bulbs dry out until the next fall and then repot them in fresh soil.

FRINGE TREE

(*Illustrations on next page*)

AGAINST the blue sky of early summer, this tree's fleecy white clouds of feathery, fragrant flowers are a star attraction in a garden. This lovely native of eastern United States has large, glossy leaves that turn golden in autumn. They are rather late appearing in the spring. The tree may reach 12 to 15 ft. or more in height and should be given adequate space. Hardy as far north as Michigan and New England, it is a slow grower. Moist, acid soil suits it, like that found in its native haunts. Give it full sun and a spot that is well drained.

Varieties. The scientific name is *Chionanthus virginica.* A specimen costs $3.00 up, depending on size. Another kind native in eastern Asia is a rarity.

(*Above*) The snowy white flowers of Purity freesia, large and profuse, are borne on 2-ft. stems.

(*Left*) As with other bulbous plants, freesias must be allowed to ripen their foliage after they bloom if the bulbs are to be used again the next year. Let it grow until it turns yellow.

(*Left*) **Fringe tree, with its feathery white blooms and large, dark green leaves, is a lovely ornamental large shrub or small tree. It blooms after the lilacs and is hardy over practically all of the United States.**

(*Below*) **A close-up of a flowering spray of the fringe tree.**

How and When to Plant. This tree or shrub is easy to move in either spring or fall. Dig leaf mold into the soil, and set the plant in a hole large enough to hold the roots comfortably. Pack good soil around them, and water thoroughly.

Care and Protection. Very little trimming is necessary.

FUCHSIA

IN California this tender shrub is grown outdoors, sometimes on walls or as a hedge. In other sections it is treated as a pot plant, for use on porches and terraces and especially in hanging baskets and window boxes. Flowering in the summer, it may be plunged in the ground with other summer bedding plants. The drooping blooms, single and double, are very graceful and profuse. They cover all the delightful Victorian combinations of color—purple and rose, violet and crimson, magenta and cream.

Although tender, fuchsia (few'shuh) plants live over from year to year if given the treatment they require. They need cool growing conditions, rich soil holding plenty of peat moss, adequate moisture, and some shade.

Varieties. Popular varieties for hanging baskets include *Red Spider*, crimson and white *Mrs. Victor Reiter*, and magenta and rose *Cascade*. Double red and white *Catalina* and single two-tone rose-pink *Black Prince* are bushy types. Plants cost about $1.25. *Magellanica* is a trailer that can be grown on walls. It blooms in late summer. Although considered hardy, it needs a winter covering in most northern areas.

How and When to Plant. Tender kinds are generally grown in pots. If transferred to a bed or porch box, they should not be put out until all danger of frost is past. They need part shade and plenty of water.

Care and Protection. Bring the plants indoors in the fall and gradually give them less water. The leaves will drop as the plants go into their resting season. Store them over winter in a cool place, and in the spring cut them back halfway and start watering again. Give them some liquid fertilizer, and pinch some of the tips of the branches to encourage bushy growth.

(*Above*) **Magellanica is a trailing fuchsia blooming in late summer. A winter cover is safest in northern areas.**

GAILLARDIA

DASHING color combinations make this native American daisy a bold addition to a hardy border. There it looks best in a massed planting, near blue or white flowers. Baby's breath softens its strong colors, which are mainly reds, orange and yellow. A name sometimes applied to it is blanket flower. Plants grow 2 or 2½ ft. high and are profuse bloomers from June to September. They do

(*Above*) **Annual gaillardias are often flecked and tipped with a variety of colors.**

(*Left*) **Ruby and Mr. Sherbrook are large-flowered gaillardias furnishing plenty of material for cutting over a period of many weeks. Their bright colors, suggestive of hand-woven Indian blankets, account for the name blanket flower, which is occasionally given to gaillardias.**

(*Left*) **Pure golden yellow Sun God is a perennial gaillardia of very large size, with a prominent golden center. Stems average 2 ft. tall or more.**

(*Above*) **There seems no end to the showy color combinations in annual gaillardias.**

(*Left*) **Bronzy red Indian Chief gaillardia has a dark brown center. The bushy plants are about a foot tall, bearing great numbers of the 2-in., single blooms all summer.**

well even in heat and drought, providing plenty of flowers to cut.

Full sun is necessary for gaillardia (gay-lard'ee-uh); otherwise the plants are likely to sprawl. Soil should be light and well drained.

There are also annual varieties in showy colors, both single and double flowered.

Varieties. *Goblin*, yellow zoned wine-red, grows only 12 to 15 in. tall. *The Warrior* has big ruby-red blooms on 3-ft. stems. *Burgundy*, too, is ruby-red, with a mahogany zone. *The Dazzler* has a crimson center and golden-tipped petals. Soft yellow *Mr. Sherbrook* and dark red *Ruby* are other good varieties. Plants cost 60c to 90c.

Indian Chief is an annual kind blooming steadily all summer.

How and When to Plant. Spring is the best time to plant. Allow 15 in. between plants. Seed of annual varieties may be sown outdoors in early spring.

Care and Protection. Pick the flowers freely. The plants may need replacing after a year or two.

GARDEN FURNITURE

ANY furnishings placed in a garden must either serve a useful purpose or add beauty—preferably both. Furniture for family use, whether the picnic table and benches near a backyard fireplace or the chaise longue on a terrace, should be practical and comfortable. It must be able to withstand sun, rain and wind; it must be movable and as good looking as possible. Designs and materials are being improved so fast, in response to the demand, that a trip to the furniture or garden store will reveal many attractive pieces.

Folding aluminum chairs and tables are easily carried and easily stored when not needed. Plastic chair coverings are cool and lightweight. Wicker and rattan look well, and so does redwood. Those who enjoy do-it-yourself projects will find many ways of employing their skill to build benches, seats and tables for use outdoors. Magazines and garden pages offer novel and practical suggestions. All wood so used should be treated with a preservative before being painted. The best reason of all for a seat or bench is that it provides the chance to relax and drink in at leisure the beauty and restfulness of the garden.

Stone and iron are suitable for benches, urns and vases of a decorative nature, which are not moved about. Often a piece of sculpture gives a pleasing touch to a garden when in harmony with the mood of its surroundings and in scale with them. It must not be either too large or so small as to look insignificant. It should be as critically selected as any ornament for a home and should be carefully

Put yourself in the picture . . . sun-kissed, leaf-cooled, quiet and relaxed, you can forget everything but the restful scene spread out before you.

(*Left*) "As you like it" is the yardstick for selecting the furniture and ornaments for your home outdoors. All chairs, tables and other pieces should be chosen with their ultimate use in mind.

(*Below*) A bird bath is both useful and decorative. It is indispensable in any garden hoping to have birds as residents.

placed as an accent or focal point in the garden picture. Sundials and bird baths are attractive features that combine usefulness and beauty. A simple bench or love seat, of wood painted white, if properly placed and kept in repair, will not only relieve the solid mass of green presented by the average garden but will add charm to the entire picture.

If you yearn for a living-room outdoors where you can entertain your friends, or a picnic terrace where you can display your skill as a barbecue chef, or a secluded spot where you can relax or do your work undisturbed—any or all of these—you will choose your furnishings accordingly. (See also *Planning Before Planting.*)

GARDENIA

IN the far South gardenias are grown outdoors like other evergreen shrubs. They reach 4 to 6 ft. in height and bloom through the summer. The glossy, dark green leaves and sculptured, waxy white, sweetly scented flowers are equally attractive. Gardenias need a somewhat acid soil and a generally sunny location where they can nevertheless have some shade in hot weather. Always they must be well watered.

The flowers are among the most popular of all for use in corsages, and potted plants are commonly offered in early spring. To grow a gardenia successfully indoors it is necessary to keep the plant in a sunny place away from drafts, at a temperature of about 60 degrees day and night, to supply it with liquid fertilizer, and to spray the foliage often as well as to water regularly.

Varieties. *Veitchi* is the form forced by florists for winter bloom. *Florida* is grown far South as a summer-flowering shrub. *Radicans* is a small-flowered, low-growing variety.

How and When to Plant. Buy a potted plant ($3.00 up) and place it in a sunny room where a 60-degree temperature can be maintained. Do not let the plant stand in water, but keep the soil moist. Spray the foliage often to humidify the air.

Care and Protection. Set the pot outdoors for the summer. Before cold weather bring it indoors, and let the plant rest for several months in a cool light room. Give it less water than in the summer.

GAS PLANT

A HARDY perennial of the highest order, gas plant is a bold and vigorous grower. It makes a bushy specimen more or less like a shrub in appearance, about 3 ft. in height

(*Left*) Very fragrant, waxy white flowers and dark shiny foliage have made the gardenia a favorite garden shrub in the South, where it is also called cape jasmine.

(*Above*) Hold a lighted match under one of these flowers on a warm, quiet summer evening and you will discover how the gas plant earned its name.

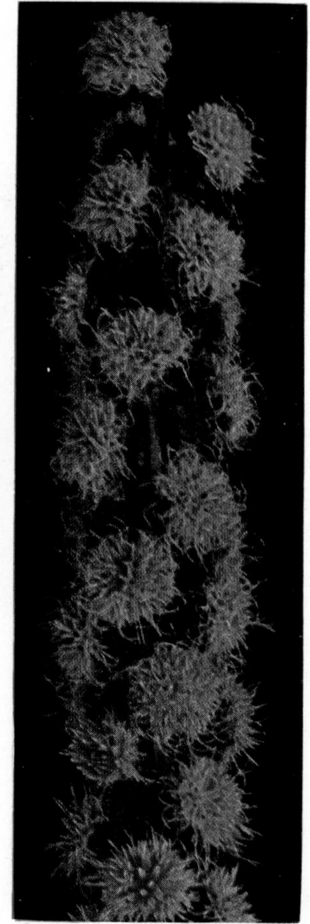

(*Right*) Gay-feather (described on the next page) has very long, slender spikes of bloom late in the summer. The variety shown is September Glory.

(*Left*) **White Spire gayfeather has feathery little white buttons marching up the long flower stalk. Both in the garden and for cutting it is very effective.**

(*Right*) **Hardy geranium or cranesbill, growing in borders and rock gardens, is a good compact plant with pleasing foliage. It prefers full sun.**

and width. The glossy dark foliage with a lemony scent is attractive all season, and in early summer the flower spikes provide a good accent in the garden and in bouquets. On still, hot evenings it is possible to ignite the vapor from the flowers if you hold a lighted match under them. Dittany, fraxinella and burning bush are other names sometimes given to this plant, although burning bush (which see) is best applied elsewhere.

Given good, well-drained soil and a location in full sun or light shade, gas plant will become established and live for many years.

Varieties. *Dictamnus albus*, with white flowers rising above the foliage, and rosy red *Ruber* are most widely grown. The average cost of a plant is $1.00.

How and When to Plant. Allowing a plant 2 to 3 ft. of space, set it out in spring or fall. Do not choose a continuously damp location.

Care and Protection. It is best not to disturb an established plant.

GAYFEATHER

LATE summer finds this striking border plant in all its glory. The long spires of bloom, purplish or white, attract bees; unlike most flowers of this form, they start opening at the top of the spike. Because of its extreme height—3 to 5 ft.—and very straight habit of growth, gayfeather is best used as an accent at the rear of any planting. The lavender tones combine well with hardy asters and late marigolds. When cut, the bloom spikes are long lasting. The narrow, grassy leaves grow in a thick tuft.

Gayfeather or blazing star (*Liatris* is the botanical name) requires little care and does quite well even in hot dry places. Full sun is preferable, and a sandy, well-drained, but fairly rich soil. At least three plants are needed for a good showing.

Varieties. *September Glory*, with long pinkish purple spikes, is especially good to cut because the whole spike opens at once. *White Spire* is a fine companion for it. *Silver Tips*, 3 ft. tall, has a lovely silvery cast to the lavender spike. Plants may be had for around 75c.

How and When to Plant. A little fertilizer added to the soil before planting is helpful. Set out the plants preferably in early spring, allowing 12 in. between them.

Care and Protection. In cutting, leave some of the stem on the plant. Dig up, divide and replant after about three years.

GERANIUM

WHITE window curtains and a singing teakettle are somehow associated with this familiar house plant. The clusters of scarlet, crimson, pink and white blossoms come in steady succession on a sunny window sill through winter and early spring. In outdoor beds and porch boxes they are equally colorful in summer, and in warm climates the plants may be left in the ground all year long. In that case they need pruning from time to time.

Besides the usual geranium that everyone knows, there are many kinds grown by hobbyists who make a specialty of collecting their favorites. There are those with fragrant leaves, grown primarily for their rose or lemon or other scent rather than their flowers. Others have leaves zoned and variegated and frilled in many combinations. Ivy-leaved geraniums are graceful trailers for baskets and the front of window boxes. Martha Washington geraniums, for indoor bloom only, boast large ruffled flowers with dark blotches. Dwarf varieties are very popular, with their fancy colored leaves.

(*Above*) **Can you remember the first geranium plant you ever saw? Besides this sturdy old favorite, there are many fancy-leaved forms that are extremely decorative.**

(*Left*) **Gerbera (described on the next page) is a plant for those able to lavish extra care upon it. The beautiful, long-stemmed blooms are perfect for flower arrangements.**

An entirely different plant is the hardy geranium grown in rock gardens or borders rather than indoors. Cranesbill is another name for it. These plants grow in average soil, preferably in complete sun, and bloom from May through July. Many have foliage that is attractive in itself. Some are 6 in. tall, while others reach 18 in. Plants are available at about 60c each, and should be set outdoors in the spring, a foot apart.

Varieties. Tender geraniums in pots may be bought from any florist at any season. Choose the colors you like. There is always a fine selection for Memorial Day, for planting outdoors.

How and When to Plant. Keep the plant in a sunny window. It doesn't need a particularly humid atmosphere nor a great deal of fertilizer. Don't let it dry out, but don't let the soil get waterlogged either. Outdoors geraniums require full sun and only average garden soil; if too rich it will produce more leaves than flowers, but if too poor it will result in pale leaves and stunted blooms. A little bonemeal is a good fertilizer.

Care and Protection. Plants may be moved to the open ground after all danger of frost is over. Pinching back the tops will make them branch more. They should be given a good soaking in dry spells, but not frequent sprinklings. In late summer, instead of trying to move large plants indoors for winter bloom, take slips and start new plants. Cut off a 5-in. section from a strong branch, strip off the leaves from the end, and plunge 2 in. deep in a box of moist sand. In about a month it may be potted up and brought indoors. It is better not to use a very large pot, for geraniums bloom better when slightly root-bound.

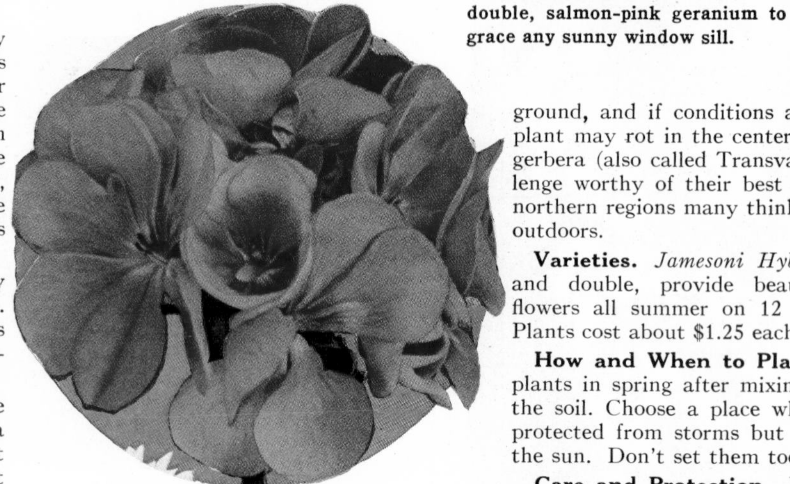

Beaute Poitevine is a lovely semi-double, salmon-pink geranium to grace any sunny window sill.

GERBERA

(Illustration on preceding page)

HARDLY for the beginner, gerbera (gur'-bur-uh) is nevertheless such a graceful and lady-like member of the daisy family that it is especially treasured for indoor arrangements and worth the painstaking care it demands. Either on the plant or when cut, the single or double flowers on long, slim stems are very lasting. They close at night and open again the next morning. Colors of the varieties that have been developed are soft pastels.

This tender perennial from South Africa is a specialty plant grown outdoors in warm climates south of Virginia but mostly in greenhouses in the North. It needs warm sun and a moist but well-drained soil, with plenty of leaf mold added. The hairy leaves grow in a big rosette-shaped cluster on the ground, and if conditions are not right the plant may rot in the center. Gardeners find gerbera (also called Transvaal daisy) a challenge worthy of their best efforts. Even in northern regions many think it merits a trial outdoors.

Varieties. *Jamesoni Hybrids,* both single and double, provide beautiful soft-toned flowers all summer on 12 to 18-in. stems. Plants cost about $1.25 each.

How and When to Plant. Set out the plants in spring after mixing leaf mold into the soil. Choose a place where they can be protected from storms but fully exposed to the sun. Don't set them too deep.

Care and Protection. In the fall, after the ground freezes, give these plants a thick cover of straw, or in September transfer them to pots and bring them indoors for the winter. There they need good air circulation, sunshine, and regular watering and fertilizing.

GERMANDER

HARDIER than boxwood, this little plant may be used as a substitute for it in low edgings, borders and hedges. The small, glossy green foliage is sometimes evergreen, and it can be trimmed to any height desirable up to 8 or 10 in. For small formal beds it makes a neat and pleasing edge. Full sun gives best results, and any well-drained soil of moderate fertility is acceptable.

Varieties. *Teucrium chamaedrys* is the botanical name. Plants cost about 75c.

How and When to Plant. For a hedge, set out the plants in early spring, 6 in. apart.

Care and Protection. Prune in early spring and again later in the summer if necessary. In coldest climates some winter covering is advisable.

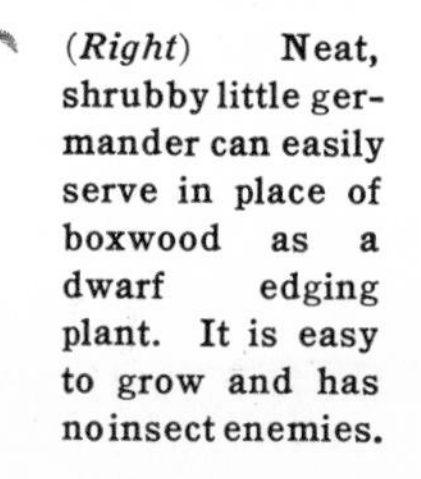

(*Right*) Neat, shrubby little germander can easily serve in place of boxwood as a dwarf edging plant. It is easy to grow and has no insect enemies.

(*Above*) Bright red Wilton Ruby geum has an orange center.

(*Right*) A trio of good geums: light orange Princess Juliana, slightly deeper orange Dolly North and orange-scarlet Fire Opal. All are hardy and useful as cut flowers.

GEUM

THESE gay, open-faced blooms are carried on sturdy but graceful stems well above the foliage. Their color range is limited to yellow through orange to red, but with white flowers or those in blue to purple tones they combine beautifully. Growing 18 to 24 in. high, they belong in the middle area of a hardy border, where they will bloom from late May through the first half of summer. The almost evergreen foliage, growing in a low tuft, is good all season.

Geum (jee'um) prefers the sun and average, well-drained soil that is of light texture. It is perfectly hardy, and the flowers are good to cut.

Varieties. The older varieties *Lady Strathe-den* (golden yellow) and *Mrs. Bradshaw* (scarlet) are still popular. Newer kinds are orange-scarlet *Fire Opal*, with excellent foliage, and bright scarlet *Wilton Ruby*. *Princess Juliana* is a strong-growing, free-blooming orange. *Borisi*, only 8 to 10 in. tall, with orange-scarlet flowers, is especially recommended for rock gardens. Geum plants cost around 75c.

How and When to Plant. If the soil is heavy clay, mix sand with it before planting. Set out the plants in spring or fall. For the best effect, use them in groups of three or more, planted 10 to 12 in. apart.

Care and Protection. Water well in dry seasons. Dig up, divide and replant the clumps every third or fourth spring.

GLADIOLUS

GLADIOLUS (glad-ee-oh'lus) growers describe themselves as "bugs" and "fiends," and the continuing production of new varieties with fresh colors, markings and ruffles leads them on year after year. As with irises, roses and other leading flowers, hybridists from many countries use all the skill and experience they possess to supply the demand for novelties. In summer gardens these are the most widely planted of flowering bulbs, for they afford a colorful display outdoors and are unsurpassed for cutting.

All tints and shades are available, in spikes up to 5 ft. long, with individual florets sometimes as much as 6 or 7 in. across. At the other extreme are dainty miniatures with 1 to 2-in. blooms on 3-ft. spikes. Florets begin opening from the bottom of the stalk. If the spike is cut as the first blooms show color, the remaining ones will open in water. Older florets should be removed as they fade and the water should be changed daily. In cutting, at least four leaves should be allowed to remain on the plant.

Florists rely on "glads" the year round. Blooms are raised both under glass and in huge fields in the South for shipment to the North, and there is not a month in the year when they are missing from the cut-flower market. They are easy to produce, they ship well, and they are long lasting. Special gladiolus shows are a feature of many areas in late summer.

In home gardens glads are generally planted in rows by themselves. They may also be used in groups in a flower border if they are not crowded. Average good garden soil will grow them (neither too sandy nor wet and heavy); full sun is important, as well as good drainage. Plenty of water is more necessary than fertilizer. It is practical to make several plantings, beginning when frost is over, at intervals over a considerable period, so that the blooms may be enjoyed over a longer time. In California and the South, bulbs (called corms) that have been held in cold storage may be planted in the fall for bloom in May and June. It is not possible to dig up the bulbs in the fall and replant them later the same season; they must have a resting period.

Varieties. Among the hundreds of varieties on sale, the All-America Gladiolus Selections winners attract special attention. These include *China Blue*, scarlet-orange *Gypsy Dancer*, smoky-colored *Rusty*, cream

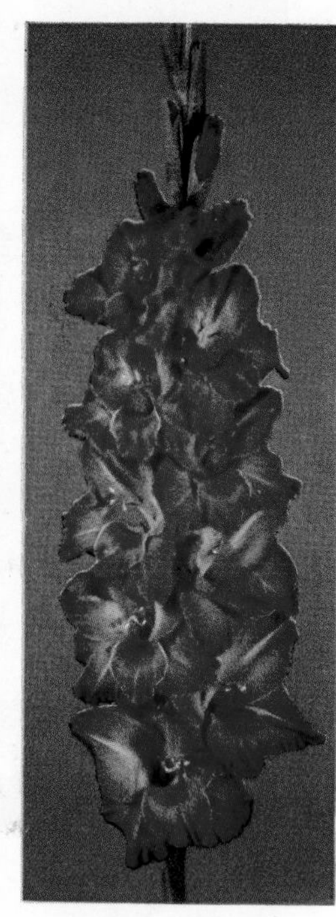

(*Above*) Sparkler, which blends soft yellow tones around the bright red lip of each floret, and deep rose-colored Joyous are recent winners of the All-America award. Both are ruffled and have long, straight spikes.

All the gladiolus shown here are proud All-America award winners. (*Above*) Creamy yellow Landmark and petite Little Pansy, which has deep blue blotches on its light violet florets. (*Left*) White-throated reddish purple Emperor, pink and white Appleblossom, clear red Royal Stewart, white-throated pink Maytime and blue and violet Caribbean.

(*Left*) Elizabeth the Queen, a standard variety of great beauty, has a reddish feather in the throat of the fresh lavender blooms. It is especially lovely under artificial light.

(*Right*) Spic and Span has perfectly formed flowers on long spikes. The color is clear pink with a creamy throat.

Landmark, pink and white *Appleblossom*, blue *Caribbean*, white-throated pink *Maytime*, red *Royal Stewart*, purplish *Emperor*, velvety rose *Joyous*, yellow and red *Sparkler*, and dwarf violet and blue *Little Pansy*. Older choice kinds are shrimp-pink *Picardy*, lavender *Elizabeth the Queen*, deep pink *Spic and Span*, *Blue Beauty*, creamy white *Leading Lady*, and blood-red *Rewi Fallu*. Charming miniatures are gold and red *Frolic*, rose-colored *Atom*, *Snow Baby*, and *Little Gold*. About $1.50 to $2.00 will buy a dozen bulbs of the older varieties; novelties are more expensive.

How and When to Plant. Make the first planting about mid-May, or whenever warm weather is certain; repeat as desired until two months before frost is to be expected in your area. Dig a trench 6 in. deep, and in it set the bulbs 6 to 10 in. apart. Rows should be 18 to 24 in. apart. Cover with 2 to 3 in. of soil, and fill in the remainder after the leaves show.

(*Below*) Picardy is an older shrimp-colored variety that remains popular. Others shown are deep yellow Gate of Heaven, white Star of Bethlehem, rich blood-red Commander Koehl and deep violet-blue Pelegrina.

Heavenly Blue

King George

E. I. Farrington

Richard Diener

Persia

The Orchid

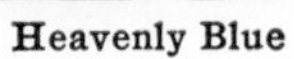

(*Above*). Several tried and true varieties are illustrated here, to indicate additional choice colors through which this amazing flower can roam. Combinations in bouquets can demonstrate great artistry.

Care and Protection. Keep down weeds by very shallow cultivation. Water copiously, especially in dry weather. A small amount of fertilizer may be scattered 6 in. away from the plants when five leaves show; be sure to water it in. Spraying every two weeks with 5% DDT is a precaution against thrips, a tiny insect that breeds on the bulbs.

When the leaves turn yellow, carefully dig up the plants and cut off the tops. Dust the bulbs with DDT, and lay them out to dry for several weeks in an airy place. Then clean them and put them in paper bags (one variety to a bag) where DDT can again be shaken well over them. Store the bulbs in trays at a temperature of 40 to 45 degrees.

Three miniature glads in striking floral arrangements. (*Left*) Bright yellow Frolic with brilliant scarlet blotch on the neatly frilled florets. (*Above*) Yellow-throated salmon-orange Toytown. (*Right*) Little Gold matches its richly glowing color with that of golden marguerite.

More gladiolus varieties are shown on the following page.

The florets at the bottom of a gladiolus spike open first. If you cut the spike just as the lower florets begin to show color, the remaining buds will open easily in water. Pinch off the flowers at the base of the stalk as they fade, and change the water every day. The very last of the flowers, from the tip of the spike, are nice to float in a bowl.

(*Left*) The large, burnt-orange blooms of Golden Queen globe flower show up for many weeks in the early part of summer. Both this variety and lemon-yellow Europaeus (*below*) are very pleasing with blue flowers, especially spikes like delphinium.

(*Right*) Globe thistle furnishes globular heads of metallic blue that are easily dried for winter bouquets, like strawflowers.

GLOBE FLOWER

ORANGE and yellow globe flowers are like big waxy buttercups. This is a shade-loving hardy perennial that succeeds in soil too heavy and damp for many other flowers. In low spots near water it does especially well, where the soil is rich and moist. Sunny locations are acceptable also if the ground is not dry. Because the 18 to 24-in. plant is slow to spread, it is a good choice for small gardens where every foot of space is precious. Flowers are produced in May, June and into July, and are long lasting when cut.

Varieties. *Lemon Queen*, *Golden Queen* and *Orange Globe* are self-descriptive names. *Trollius ledebouri* grows 2 to 2½ ft. high and bears large, rather open, orange-colored flowers in June and July. Lemon-yellow *Europaeus* blooms in late spring. Plants cost 75c to $1.00.

How and When to Plant. Sow seed in early spring and space the plants 2 ft. apart.

Care and Protection. Pick off the dead flower heads, and supply water when needed in dry spells.

GLOBE THISTLE

WHERE "something different" is wanted for a hardy border, globe thistle may be worth considering. This is a coarse plant with grayish, prickly leaves and sturdy stems. The globe-shaped, blue flowers stand out in a group planting and are very long lasting when cut. They appear from midsummer on. This bold perennial (*Echinops*, botanically) may be used in the mid-section or rear of a border, to furnish special interest. Full sun or a little light shade is suitable, and light but fairly rich soil.

Varieties. Silvery deep blue *Taplow Blue* is the variety most used. It is a long-lived plant growing 3½ to 4 ft. tall and costing $1.00 to $1.25.

How and When to Plant. Spring or fall is the time to set out the plant, allowing it 12 to 15 in. of space.

Care and Protection. This sturdy perennial may be left alone for many years without any special care.

GLORIOSA DAISY

THIS newly developed form of coneflower is a very vigorous, free-blooming plant for growing in masses in the garden and also for cutting. Reaching 3 ft. or more in height, it belongs in the mid-section of a border. It likes full sun, but any garden soil suits it. Flowers are long-lasting big daisies with broad petals, carried on sturdy stems. The erect, bushy plant will bloom from late summer into fall if seed is sown early, and for many years afterward it will come up again and bloom from early summer on. Hot dry summers are no drawback.

Varieties. The *Single* variety has huge blooms 5 in. and more in diameter. Flowers are yellow, mahogany and bicolored, with dark centers. *Double* has rich golden yellow blooms, both double and semi-double, averaging 4 in. across; some are dark centered.

How and When to Plant. Sow seed in early spring and space the plants 2 ft. apart.

Care and Protection. Keep the dead flowers picked.

GLORIOSA LILY

THIS low climber with exotic bicolor flowers of red and yellow is not hardy but may be grown outdoors even in the North if treated like other summer-flowering bulbs. It grows 6 to 10 ft. high if given support, and blooms through summer and fall. The curling leaves have tendrils that cling to wire or trellis. Flowers with petals sharply reflexed are carried on long stems; colors are brightest in full sun. They last well when cut and may be used for corsages. Sandy, well-drained soil

(*Above*) Gloriosa lily is a tender climber with gracefully shaped blooms of bright red and yellow. In the North the tubers require a sheltered spot and must be stored over winter indoors.

(*Left*) Double gloriosa daisies are quite newly developed flowers that can stand extremes of both heat and cold. They make excellent cut flowers.

(*Left*) Starry-flowered glory of the snow (Luciliae is the variety pictured) often begins to bloom before snow has taken its final leave. What a joyous farewell to winter!

(*Right*) Glory of the sun, a bulb for warm climates or for growing indoors in a pot. The blue and white flowers are sweetly scented.

and a protected location outdoors are advisable, in either sun or light shade. In the South it is easily grown outdoors.

Varieties. *Superba* has flowers of scarlet and yellow, while *Rothschildiana* is darker red and yellow. The colors are sharply contrasted. Tubers average $1.25 each.

How and When to Plant. For a long season of bloom, start the tubers indoors in good potting soil and move to the open ground when the weather gets warm. Or plant outdoors, 4 to 5 in. deep.

Care and Protection. When frost comes, dig up the tubers, dry them and store over winter in a frostproof place.

GLORY OF THE SNOW

DRIFTS of these sky-blue flowers make a lovely picture with snowdrops and crocuses at the first breath of spring. These hardy bulbs, related to lilies, bloom sometimes just as the snow is leaving. Flowers and leaves appear at the same time, with the blooms in little spikes of a dozen or so. They grow 6 or 7 in. tall in well-drained soil that is not too heavy. In the rock garden, among shrubs or in masses at the edge of a wooded area, they are at home in either full sun or semi-shade.

Varieties. Besides bright blue and white *Chionodoxa luciliae*, lavender-blue *Gigantea*, and gentian-blue *Sardensis*, there is a *Pink* variety and a *White* one. The average cost of a dozen bulbs is 70c.

How and When to Plant. Plant the bulbs in early September, 3 in. deep and 3 in. apart, in groups of at least five.

Care and Protection. Don't cut the foliage before it dies down, and don't disturb the bulbs. They will live for years and spread into a fine colony.

GLORY OF THE SUN

THIS spring-flowering bulb may be grown outdoors only in warm climates, for it is not hardy. Elsewhere it is raised in pots indoors for bloom in March and April. Several of the soft blue and white flowers are borne on the wiry, 18-in. stems. Sweet fragrance reminiscent of heliotrope is noticeable.

Varieties. *Leucocoryne ixioides* is the botanical name. Bulbs may be had for about $2.50 per dozen.

How and When to Plant. Outdoor planting is done in the fall, in well-drained soil. Autumn is also the time to plant indoors. Place several bulbs in a pot of good soil, and barely cover them. Keep in a cool place until growth starts. Then bring the pot to a sunny window and give the bulbs some water and liquid fertilizer.

Care and Protection. Continue to water after the flowers have faded. When the foliage has died down, let the bulbs dry off until the next fall.

GLOXINIA

HUGE velvety flowers, several inches across at the mouth, and velvety leaves as well, combine to make this a handsome house plant. It belongs to the same plant family as the African violet but is a native of Brazil. It grows from a tuber, like a tuberous begonia, and blooms in the summer. While it is usually grown in a pot, it may also be used as a summer bedding plant. The long-lasting flowers are white to rose and purple, sometimes two-tone or with spotted throat.

Gloxinias need good light but must be protected from strong sun and from drafts. They must have potting soil to which sand and peat moss or leaf mold have been added. A warm, moist atmosphere and adequate but not too much soil moisture are also required. A minimum temperature of 65 degrees is recommended.

Varieties. Standard varieties include *Blanche de Meru*, rose with white throat; *Emperor William*, violet with white band; *Mont Blanc*, white; and *Emperor Frederick*, scarlet banded white. Tubers cost 50c to $1.50, depending on size (more for newer

Gloxinias have a proud way of holding their velvety blooms, either when potted like the variety Blanche de Meru (*above*) or when grown in the open ground in summer (*left*). Emperor Frederick and Mont Blanc are here combined to make a fine showing.

Golden chain tree is a delightful ornamental with long, graceful flower clusters in bloom about tulip time. Generally the tree enjoys a long, healthy life. (*Above*) A close view of the pea-shaped flowers.

varieties). Or the potted plants may be purchased, at $1.50 up.

How and When to Plant. In late winter, plant the tuber in a 5-in. pot filled with potting soil. Set it only an inch deep, give it some water and a place in a sunny window. When growth starts, water frequently, and apply liquid fertilizer as the buds form. It takes about four months from planting to blooming time.

Care and Protection. Water freely but do not allow the soil to become soggy, and do not sprinkle the leaves. When the plant stops blooming, give it less water and store it dry over winter. It need not be repotted every year.

A new plant may be started from a leaf with a short piece of the stem attached. Insert the stem in damp sand or peat moss, and when the new little plant is well rooted move it to a pot.

GOLDEN CHAIN TREE

As a companion for tall shrubs in a border or as a specimen on the lawn, especially where space is limited, the golden chain tree is an excellent choice. Its 12 to 18-in. long clusters of deep yellow flowers appear in late spring, hanging like great golden chains of wisteria all through the foliage. When they have gone, it is still an attractive upright tree, growing 15 to 20 ft. tall, with smooth bark and leaves shaped like clover. It gives light shade all summer. Hardy through Missouri, southern Illinois and Indiana, and most of Ohio and Pennsylvania, it is long lived and of easy culture, with no troublesome pests.

Varieties. *Laburnum vossi* is the variety sold by nurseries. A 4 to 5-ft. tree costs around $4.50.

How and When to Plant. Planting is done in spring or fall, in full sun or semi-shade, in well-drained garden soil. Dig a hole wide enough to hold the roots well spread out, without crowding, and deep enough so that the tree will be at the same depth as in the nursery (indicated by a dark mark around the base of the trunk). Be careful not to expose the roots to sun or air while planting. After setting the tree in position, pack good soil around the roots, being particular not to leave any air pockets. Fill the hole half full of soil, and then pour in water. When the water has drained away, finish filling the hole with soil, and leave the surface raked fine.

Care and Protection. Drive in a stake and keep the tree tied to it until well established. If you have young children likely to put any part of this tree in their mouths, choose another ornamental. This one is poisonous.

GOLDEN MARGUERITE

This is one of the most charming of daisy-shaped flowers, and is worthy of a place in any perennial border. It grows freely, it blooms freely, and is hardy anywhere. The ivory to golden-colored flowers on wiry stems are perfect for cutting; their color and form look well with roses, columbine, and a host of other cut flowers. The daisies are profuse from June to September. The 2-ft. plants, with fern-like, aromatic foliage, belong in groups near the edge of a border.

Not the least of this plant's good points is the fact that it resists drought. It takes well to light, sandy, well-drained soil, where it will continue to bloom even through the heat of summer. Full sun is preferable to shade.

Varieties. *Moonlight* is a well-named, very popular variety with pale yellow flowers over 2 in. across, excellent to cut. *Grallagh Gold* has large golden flowers. Plants average 75c each.

Golden marguerite, Moonlight variety, is an erect-growing perennial bearing these charming, soft yellow daisies for many weeks. They look especially well with blues.

A package of mixed gourd seed scattered where the vines can clamber over a fence produces fruits of many interesting shapes. Full sun is necessary.

How and When to Plant. Plant in spring or fall, about 2 ft. apart.

Care and Protection. Dig up, divide and replant about every other spring. Cut the flowers freely.

GOURDS

CURIOUSLY formed gourds are popular as indoor decorations, especially in the fall and winter. Some are shaped like apples, others like a pear, an egg, a turban or a club. Smaller kinds may be heaped up in a bowl; larger ones are sometimes used as a bird-house or dipper. The plant is a trailer growing 20 to 30 ft. long, like a cucumber or squash vine, with white or yellow flowers. It makes a quick screen in summer on a trellis or fence or may be allowed to trail along the ground.

Fruits are picked when they reach a good color. Set them in a warm dry place and rub them clean. If you wish, shellac them or polish with floor wax.

Varieties. Seeds of both *Large* and *Small-fruited* kinds may be bought, in assorted or separate shapes.

How and When to Plant. Make a mound of soil a few inches high and about a foot in diameter. In it scatter six to eight seeds, and cover them lightly. Allow 4 to 6 ft. between mounds. Planting should not be done until the ground is thoroughly warm. Gourds need a warm sunny spot and light, fertile soil.

Care and Protection. The chewing insects that attack squash and cucumbers sometimes find the gourds, too. Spray or dust with a good insecticide.

GRAPE HYACINTHS

PURE deep blue is a pleasing accompaniment for the yellows of daffodils and the pink and white of spring-flowering trees, and grape hyacinth is a fine source of that color. The little upright spikes of bells that never open wide appear in April. There is a white form, as well as the more common blue. Very hardy and easy to please in any soil, this little bulb (*Muscari*) asks only to be allowed to multiply and spread freely. In the filtered shade under shrubs or trees where it can form a blue ground carpet it is contented, as well as in a rock garden where it gets full sun. Its height is 6 to 10 in.

Varieties. Bulbs of *Heavenly Blue* and *White* may be had for about 60c per dozen.

How and When to Plant. Bulbs should be planted just as soon as they can be bought in the fall. Set them in clusters, 2 to 3 in. deep and 3 to 4 in. apart.

Care and Protection. Don't cut off the foliage and don't disturb the bulbs.

(*Below*) When you get acquainted with grape hyacinths and discover how easy they are to grow, you will find many places for these hardy little bulbs. Here they are in close company with trumpet daffodils. Such a beautiful picture as this is easily and inexpensively within reach of every home owner.

GROUND COVERS

IN practically every home garden there are problem spots where, for one reason or another, many plants cannot be coaxed to grow. Most plants, especially those that bear flowers, need sun at least part of the day; if they are in shady places under large trees and dense shrubs, they are denied the sunshine they must have. Even grass requires sun, and efforts to extend the lawn into shady corners are apt to be extremely disappointing. Often tree roots take so much food and moisture from the soil that this is another handicap for grass or any other plants trying to gain a foothold in the same area. Steep banks present another problem. Soil is likely to be washed down, leaving ruts and gravelly sections, sometimes baked in the sun for much of the day. And there are frequently small areas—perhaps between a walk and the house or the street—where it is not practical to plant grass because it would be too troublesome to mow.

All these difficult places can be made into beauty spots if the right plant is found for them. The same plant, of course, will not answer for all of them. A sharp slope needs a sturdy low shrub or trailer that is vigorous and will root deeply, while a narrow space along a walk or under a shrub can take a small-leaved, decorative plant. To be most desirable, a ground cover should be able to establish itself and spread without difficulty, and it should require little care from year to year. When a suitable plant is found, it will add enormously to the looks of the whole property and will cut down the cost of maintenance. Ground covers are a great convenience and improvement for any garden.

A distinction should be made between a ground cover and a mulch. Such materials as dried grass clippings, peat moss, pine needles and buckwheat hulls are often spread on the ground over the roots of plants as protection against drying of the soil. This summer mulch is strongly recommended as an aid in keeping the ground moist, cool and weed-free. A mulch is also placed around plants in late autumn after the ground has frozen, in areas where hard winters are apt to cause alternate freezing and thawing of the soil. The purpose of a winter mulch is to keep the ground at a uniform low temperature so that the plant roots will not be heaved out by a quick thaw.

But the term ground cover is applied to a living, growing vine or perennial or low shrub planted for the special purpose of filling in bare spots. It is a graceful "go-between" that not only improves the looks of many areas but also reduces garden work.

(*Above*) Myrtle, or periwinkle as it is sometimes called, is one of the ground covers most commonly used because it does so well in both sun and shade. (Illustrations of the other ground covers mentioned in this article appear under their respective headings.)

Among the most popular ground covers are English ivy, pachysandra and myrtle. All are very sturdy and dependable, with evergreen foliage attractive all year round. English ivy needs fairly moist soil and grows well in the shade under trees. If it gets an overdose of winter sun it may die back, but generally it puts out new growth again in the spring. Pachysandra spreads easily and quickly even in the heavy shade of Norway maples, but does not do well in complete sun. Myrtle succeeds just as well in the sun as in the shade, and it has the advantage of producing flowers as well as small dark shiny leaves.

Both English ivy and myrtle are useful to keep soil from eroding on banks. Honeysuckle is widely used for the same purpose, especially in half-wild sections of a garden. It roots very quickly. The memorial rose, with white flowers in midsummer, is also a strong grower adapted to planting on banks. It likes either full sun or a little shade. Coralberry is another shrub that prevents soil erosion. Where the ground is poor, this is an especially good choice. On a steep bank, plants should be set rather close together, in horizontal rows so as to catch and hold the soil. A mulch of straw or hay is good protection while they are getting started.

Other Favorites. Besides pachysandra and English ivy, barrenwort makes a fine ground cover in semi-shade. It is particularly good under evergreens where the soil is cool and damp. The foliage is attractive most of the winter. St. Johnswort blooms in half-shady places over a long period, and where it is hardy it is a very good ground cover. Many violas are useful for color in moist shade, and lily of the valley furnishes both fragrance and good coverage of the ground until late summer. All through summer, plantain lily grows well in the shade. Its large leaves are decorative in themselves and also a good background for lower plants.

Where full sun is encountered, the soil may also be quite dry. Among the ground-cover plants able to stand these conditions are yarrow and rock cress. Moss pink is a fine ground cover for full sun, and so are the low-growing speedwells.

Liriope forms a mass of grass-like foliage that remains through the winter. Evergreen bittersweet or wintercreeper is another very vigorous ground cover that is popular and serviceable in many places. Bugle quickly forms a thick, practically evergreen mat in either shade or sun.

Tamarix juniper is used here as a low spreading ground cover. It is successful in many difficult situations and requires very little care. Shrubby in growth, it has short creeping stems and sharp evergreen foliage.

Poor, acid soil is the preference of heath and heather, and these plants will thrive in some seemingly impossible spots. In a small space where the soil is quite moist, coral bells makes a charming ground cover. It bears quantities of dainty flowers through the summer, with tufts of reddish foliage all winter.

Extremely adaptable to seashore conditions is bearberry, an evergreen trailer that likes sandy soil. Sea pink grows fast and also does well at the seashore. St. Johnswort is another plant that likes the sand. Dusty miller grows in poor soil anywhere, and it too may be used as a ground cover at the shore.

Not many plants can survive when they are walked on constantly. Grass is the first choice. Thyme is a tiny-leaved creeper that may be used between stepping-stones. Some sandworts and stonecrops are other possibilities. Thyme is also a good ground cover to use with small bulbs like crocus. Taller bulbs such as daffodils may be underplanted with bugle, myrtle or pachysandra.

Since ground covers are expected to live for many years and to thrive and spread into a fine carpet, it is wise to prepare the soil well before setting out the plants. Whatever the type of soil, it should be thoroughly loosened to a depth of several inches. If the ground-cover plant needs a fairly rich soil, dig in 20 to 40 pounds of a complete fertilizer per 1000 square feet. Until the plants get a good start, they must be kept well watered.

HARDY AMARYLLIS

BECAUSE of its strange growing and blooming habits, this bulb (which incidentally is not a true amaryllis) always arouses curiosity. In early spring long strap-shaped leaves appear and keep growing until the end of June, when they die down and disappear completely. Then in August the thick, 2 to 3-ft. flower stalk comes along, with six to eight fragrant, lilac-pink blooms. Magic lily is another name for this astonishing bulb. It is hardy as far north as southern New England and will grow in sun or semi-shade, in light, well-drained soil. Since the flower stalks are entirely bare, it needs a ground cover at its base, such as anchusa. A group in a border supplies lovely color in late summer when a garden may need a pick-up.

Varieties. *Lycoris squamigera* is the scientific name; a bulb costs about 50c.

How and When to Plant. Bulbs are planted 4 to 6 in. apart and about 4 in. deep, either in early spring or in the fall.

(*Above*) The pretty, lily-like blooms of hardy amaryllis are here seen against the foliage of other summer-flowering bulbs. Their own leaves grow and die off before the flowers appear.

Care and Protection. In the colder areas it may be wise to provide a light covering over winter.

(*Left*) Paul's Scarlet hawthorn is bright red in both flower and fruit (*below*). This small tree is appropriate for almost any type of planting, and the berries always please the birds.

HAWTHORN

DENSE bushy growth, plentiful spring bloom, decorative foliage and bright fruits recommend these small, hardy trees. Some are broad and spreading, some more shrub-like, but all have long thorns and are easy to grow. The berries, mostly bright red and often clustered, are a favorite food of wild birds. Flowers of white or pink or sometimes red come late in spring.

Hawthorns are small enough to be very desirable as lawn trees on small properties. They are also good as accents in a shrub border, and because of their thick habit of growth and their thorns they make a protective hedge or informal boundary plant. They will stand hard pruning. Many kinds are native to North America, and others have been brought in from elsewhere. They prefer full sun and rather rich soil.

Varieties. *Paul's Scarlet* is the variety most commonly grown. A 4 to 5-ft. tree costs about $4.00. It has double, rosy red flowers and bright scarlet berries on a spreading, 12-ft. tree with beautiful broad leaves. It

Illustrated here are several kinds of heather: yellow-leaved Aurea, white-flowered Alba, pink Vulgaris and tall red-flowered Alporti. Heather must have damp, acid soil and a starvation diet. The flower spikes dry easily and are a great favorite for indoor arrangements.

does well at the seashore and in exposed locations. There are white and pink forms of it, too. The *Washington* thorn grows somewhat taller, and has flat clusters of white flowers followed by bright red fruit that lasts well into winter. Autumn foliage is red. *Cockspur* is very bushy and thorny, with white flowers and red berries. The glossy dark leaves turn orange and red in the fall.

How and When to Plant. Early spring and fall are the best times to plant. Dig a hole large enough to hold the roots without cramping, and set the tree at the same depth that it grew in the nursery. (Note the dark mark around the base of the trunk.) Do not expose the roots to sun or air while planting. Pack good soil around them until the hole is half full; then fill to the top with water. When the water has disappeared, finish filling the hole with soil. Tamp it down well after a day or two.

Care and Protection. Frequent pruning is necessary in winter, to keep these bushy trees from becoming too overgrown. Cut out the weakest, twiggy branches. Don't try to move old trees.

HEATHER (and HEATH)

POETRY and sentiment are woven around the heather of Scotland. This evergreen shrub—6 to 18 in. tall, according to variety—has foliage like scales, sometimes very colorful, and tiny pink, white, red or lavender flowers in upright spikes. Where it grows wild in Europe these spikes are short, but garden forms have been developed with blooms 6 to 8 in. long, borne in summer.

This plant makes a dense green mat for use in rock gardens, on banks, and as a ground cover. Full sun produces the best bloom. It must have acid soil, fairly moist but not at all rich. It can be grown as far north as New England if given some winter protection, especially when the plants are young. Branches may be used for indoor decoration as dried bouquets.

Heath is a close relative. Often the two are confused, but heath has needle-like foliage and flowers like little bells very early in the spring or even late in the winter. This plant is especially popular in the Northwest, and some varieties can be grown in New England. It spreads fast in poor soils, and has the same growing requirements as heather.

Varieties. A great many varieties of heather (*Calluna*) have been produced, among them dense, bushy, white *Alba*, purple-flowered *Hirsuta* with a grayish, hairy plant, double bright pink *J. H. Hamilton*, and thick-matting *Sister Anne*, with lavender flowers.

Springwood White, a fast spreader with light green foliage, and crimson *Vivelli* are good heath (*Erica*) varieties. Two-year plants of either heather or heath cost about $1.50 to $2.00.

How and When to Plant. Mix peat moss or leaf mold into the soil, but no fertilizer. Set out the plants in spring or fall, allowing 12 in. between them. Pack the soil hard around the roots, and keep well watered through hot weather until established.

Care and Protection. Heather should be cut back to the ground in very early spring to make the plants thicker. The same should be done to heath just after the flowering season. In the North give these plants a loose winter covering of straw or evergreen branches. Keep lime away from them.

HEAVENLY BAMBOO

SOUTHWARD from Virginia and on the West Coast, heavenly bamboo is a very popular evergreen shrub, widely planted in gardens. Those willing to give it a protected spot may grow it as far north as New York City. In such northern areas the roots may live over winter even if the top is killed back. It is an attractive plant reaching 7 or 8 ft. in height, with white flowers in large, upright clusters in late July or August. The small, bright red berries that follow will last well into winter unless the birds eat them. The foliage too makes this a colorful shrub. New leaves are pinkish, turning green as they grow larger, and finally bronze to scarlet in autumn.

Good soil with leaf mold or peat moss added to it is advisable. In the South the shrub thrives in sun or shade. In colder regions it needs a sunny location where wind cannot whip it.

Varieties. *Nandina domestica* is the botanical name. An 18 to 24-in. plant costs about $3.00.

How and When to Plant. Set out the plant in the spring, in a hole large enough to hold the roots without crowding. Firm the soil well around them, and water copiously.

Care and Protection. In dry periods give it water. If it gets too big, cut some of the old shoots back to the ground in early spring.

Bright scarlet berries and foliage that ranges from coppery pink to light green and finally a bronzy wine color make heavenly bamboo a fine ornamental shrub. Actually it is not a bamboo at all, but is related to barberry.

Flowering hedges of floribunda roses can be a thrilling part of a garden for practically a whole growing season. (*Left*) Fashion, a luminous coral-pink bearing big clusters of bloom. (*Below*) White Bouquet, with sparkling white flowers against shining, dark foliage.

HEDGES

A LUSH green hedge is the modern way of saying "Stay out." Instead of a forbidding board fence to keep your children in the yard and your neighbors' dogs out of your flower borders, a hedge can be just as useful and twice as pleasing to look at. It will screen your patio from the street, and cut down the noise and fumes of nearby traffic. A hedge can act as protection from high winds and storms and, in general, serve as your garden's shield against the world outside your gate.

On the positive side, a hedge can be a wonderful asset as well as a means of protection. Some portions of your grounds, such as the section reserved for swings and sandboxes or the family vegetable plot, are not intended for public view. A fine green hedge will come to the rescue by helping to separate the various areas of your outdoor living space. And what is more desirable than a dense, dark green backdrop to set off and display the lovely mosaic of changing color that your flowers offer from spring to frost? A hedge frames all these glowing tones perfectly. It gives dignity and permanence to any garden, large or small.

Hedges may be of any height desired, trimmed to be precisely formal or allowed to grow at will with almost no pruning. They may be evergreen, they may have bright berries or flowers at certain seasons, or they may be made up of dense thorny bushes that will be effective barriers. Whatever the need, it is important to select the plants that will perform the service intended.

Candidates for a Decorative Hedge. Privet is used everywhere as a hedge because it is easy to please and can stand hard trimming. The thick and thorny growth of barberry makes it another popular choice. Although it does not mind being pruned, it needs much less shearing than privet. Yew and boxwood are splendid evergreen hedge plants, forming a beautiful background and adding greatly to the appearance of any planting. A hedge of holly is a handsome, permanent asset for a garden. Floribunda roses have become favorites for producing flowering hedges that are outstanding for weeks. Many other sturdy flowering shrubs will suggest themselves as candidates for a decorative hedge—lilac, deutzia, spirea and rose of Sharon, for instance.

Clipping. The distance at which hedge plants are set out depends upon the size used. Remember that they will grow wider as well as taller, and don't set other plants too close to them. To make a good thick hedge, the plants must grow bushy at the base. In order to encourage this and avoid a top-heavy effect, there are two main points to keep in mind. First, a hedge like barberry, which loses its leaves in autumn, should be cut back to a height of only 6 in. immediately after being planted (this does not apply to an evergreen hedge). Second, when clipping a hedge, always keep it a little broader at the base than across the top so that the sun can reach the lower part of the plants.

The time to trim hedges is late spring or early summer. Those that flower should be pruned right after they bloom. An overgrown hedge may be pruned hard in very early spring so that fresh new growth may come up from the base. Evergreens, however, cannot stand such severe treatment and should be trimmed lightly as they need it, in early summer. Many hedges are most effective when allowed to grow informally, with just enough pruning to keep them at the height desired.

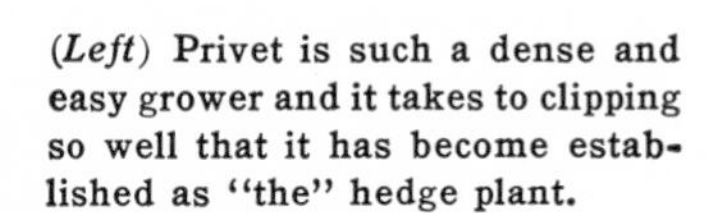

(*Left*) Privet is such a dense and easy grower and it takes to clipping so well that it has become established as "the" hedge plant.

(*Below*) The thick, dark foliage of a yew hedge is beautiful all year round. There is no background more complimentary to flowering plants.

is a natural companion for stonecrop, thriving under the same conditions and furnishing an amusing and fascinating range of low-growing material. White, reddish or yellow flowers come in summer on 5 to 10-in., sometimes grotesque stems.

Planters and dish gardens are often used to display these slow-growing, fleshy-leaved plants. The botanical name, *Sempervivum*, meaning *live forever*, indicates their long span of life. The name houseleek, which is occasionally given them, comes from the European custom of growing them on the roof of a house. These plants belong to the group sometimes referred to as succulents—that is, they are full of juice or sap which helps them to survive under dry growing conditions.

Varieties. Since varieties are so numerous, it is best to choose on sight the ones that appeal most to you. A plant may be had for about 50c.

How and When to Plant. At any time during the growing season a plant may be started in a warm, sunny spot. Soil on the thin, dry side is adequate.

Care and Protection. You can pull off one of the "chickens" and easily start a new cluster by simply pressing the little rosette into the soil.

(*Left*) The bright gold flowers of Incomparabilis heliopsis bloom in late summer and are fine to cut. This bushy plant, very hardy and easy to grow, is a good filler.

(*Right*) The rich deep blue color of heliotrope plus its delightful fragrance have kept this old-fashioned tender plant popular since grandma's day.

HELIOPSIS

BOLD and brassy heliopsis (hee-lee-opp'siss) is a good filler plant in hardy borders, and is useful as a screen in out-of-the-way corners. Growing 3 ft. tall, it may be used near phlox and delphinium, where it will make a showy mass of yellow or orange from July to frost. It is extremely hardy and free blooming. The wiry-stemmed flowers, sometimes called orange sunflower, are excellent for cutting. They are heavy and somewhat coarse looking, but their very boldness is attractive.

Full sun and ordinary, well-drained garden soil satisfy heliopsis. Even in a hot dry location it turns in a good performance, although bigger flowers result from giving it a richer soil. Because it is so easily pleased, this native American plant is "sure-fire" almost anywhere. Just don't try to combine it with anything dainty.

Varieties. *Incomparabilis* is a popular semi-double variety with golden orange, daisy-like flowers on 3-ft. plants. Fully double *Gold Greenheart* has a green center and is fine to cut. Plants cost about 95c.

How and When to Plant. Set out the plants in fall or spring, allowing at least 18 in. for each one.

Care and Protection. Pick the dead flowers, to prolong the blooming season, and keep the plants watered in dry spells. Every third autumn, dig up the plant, divide it into pieces and replant them.

HELIOTROPE

FRAGRANCE and rich violet color are associated with this old-fashioned flower. It is not at all hardy but may be grown outdoors in warm weather and also in pots indoors. Sometimes it is used as a formal bedding plant. (See also *Valerian*, which is known as garden heliotrope.) Full warm sun and rich deep soil will bring best results. Indoors it is very important to give heliotrope plants moist air and as much sun as possible.

Varieties. Seed of *Blue Bonnet* (deep lavender-blue), *First Snow*, and *Mme. Bruant* (dark violet with white eye), as well as *Mixed*, is available.

How and When to Plant. Plants may be raised from seed started indoors in late winter, or florists can furnish potted plants for setting outdoors when frost is over.

Care and Protection. Rather than try to bring plants indoors for the winter, it is easier to buy fresh ones.

HEN AND CHICKENS

IN rock gardens, along walks and in the cracks of a stone wall these interesting rosettes of thick leaves grow into a large solid cluster. There are a great many different kinds, showing a variety of leaf shapes, sizes and colors. The rosettes may be grayish or darker green, sometimes hairy, and often tipped reddish, bronze, purple or bluish. This

Start hen and chickens in a crack between stones or along a walk and you will soon hatch out a whole coop-full!

(*Left*) The large, loosely formed bloom of Crown of Bohemia is bright golden yellow with an overlay of copper and apricot, shading to red at the throat. This is a free bloomer with good foliage.

(*Right*) Brilliantissima, a single form with blazing scarlet flowers that are deep crimson in the center. Average soil will give good results.

HIBISCUS

TROPICAL Asia is the original home of this broad-leaved evergreen shrub, but it has found its way into many warm countries. In Hawaii, in southern California, and in central and southern Florida, hibiscus (hye-bisk'us) is one of the plants that attract most attention and admiration. In the northern part of Florida it may freeze back in winter, but generally it makes a quick recovery. Hibiscus (see also *Rose of Sharon* for a hardy member of this family) is a fast grower reaching a height of 30 ft., with glossy dark leaves and wide trumpet-shaped flowers —single, semi-double or double—of pink, crimson, yellow, orange and white. Summer is its blooming season, although in southern Florida it is in flower practically all year long.

Any garden soil of average richness will grow hibiscus well. It likes complete sun and can endure growing conditions at the seaside. It makes a fine tall hedge.

Varieties. Among the many varieties developed are double copper and apricot *Crown of Bohemia*, pink *Mrs. Johnson*, double ruby-colored *Burgundy*, and *Red Gold*. Plants are available at $2.00 up.

How and When to Plant. Planting may be done any time in the lower South.

Care and Protection. Prune in very early spring to keep this shrub to the size desired. Avoid using lime near it.

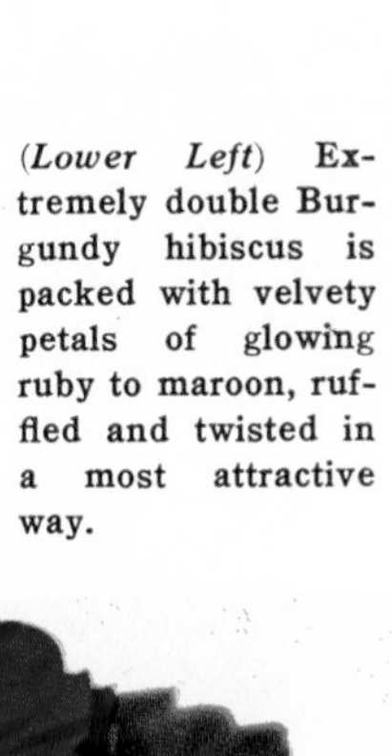

(*Right*) The lovely creamy rose-pink flowers of the variety Mrs. Johnson are spectacular in their beauty. The plant is a fast grower producing great quantities of bloom.

(*Lower Left*) Extremely double Burgundy hibiscus is packed with velvety petals of glowing ruby to maroon, ruffled and twisted in a most attractive way.

(*Right*) The blooms of Red Gold are most dazzling in the shade, but full sun produces more flowers.

HOLLY

HOLLY and Christmas are inseparable, but historians say holly was used in pagan rites long before the Christian era. It grows wild in many widely separated parts of the globe. Native American holly is found from Massachusetts to Florida and from Florida west into Texas. Both this and English holly have been cultivated to such an extent by nurserymen that dozens of different varieties have been developed. In addition to the hollies bearing the familiar red berries and green spiny leaves, there are others with black fruits and smooth, sometimes variegated foliage. Some drop their leaves in the fall, but most kinds are evergreen. Especially in winter their dense, dark foliage and sparkling berries are a valuable asset in any garden.

In foundation plantings, as a hedge, in borders with other shrubs, and as a specimen where a beautiful shrub or small ornamental tree is wanted, holly is unsurpassed. At the doorway of a house it attracts attention all year round, and when it has other evergreens as a background, holly stands out especially well. However, it should not be planted under dense shade trees or where its roots will stand in water. Neither can holly endure strong winter winds. In cold areas it is best to choose a spot with an eastern exposure. It needs soil on the acid side, with plenty of organic matter.

All along the southern Atlantic and Gulf coast and up into Massachusetts and New York state, holly is grown, except in very high elevations. Inland it may be grown in light soil, especially near rivers and lakes, as far as Missouri. The open range country of the West is too dry for it, but the moist, mild atmosphere of the Pacific Northwest is ideal. There English holly is raised in orchards and twigs are harvested for the Christmas trade like any fruit crop.

Some holly trees are male and others are female. To have berries, it is necessary that both male and female trees be grown rather close together. Pollen from the male trees is carried by insects to the flowers of the female trees, and berries are then formed on the female. One male kind will be enough for several of the female if they are growing in fairly close proximity.

It is impossible to tell a male tree from a female until the flowering season. Reliable nurserymen sell the sexes separately, so that you can tell what you are buying. Both kinds have small, inconspicuous white flowers in

(*Above*) American holly is regarded as one of the finest of the broad-leaved evergreens. It can be grown over a large part of the United States. (*Right*) A close view of a spray showing berries and leaves.

(*Left*) A plant of Boxleaf Japanese holly (see it as a hedge on the following page). This is a slow-growing form with very small, glossy leaves like boxwood. In northern areas, particularly, it is a splendid substitute for boxwood.

(*Left*) The very large, showy bright red berries of Burford holly make it a popular variety. It is hardy as far north as Long Island and is beautiful for use as a specimen.

Two hollies especially recommended for the South. (*Right*) Yaupon, which is a loose open grower that takes to shearing well. (*Below*) Dahoon, a good choice for wet soils although it will also grow in normal ones.

late May or early June; male flowers have yellow pollen and female ones have a green center. In small gardens where space is precious, a male and a female tree can be planted together in the same hole to make sure of having berries. (George Washington did this at Mount Vernon.) More fruit is produced in some years than in others. It is relished by birds in late winter.

One of the greatest pleasures of raising holly at home is to be able to snip branches of it for Christmas decoration. When this is done, the tree usually is bushier than ever the next summer. Young trees may be made denser by clipping off the ends of the longest branches in early spring. When holly is grown as a hedge, the shearing is also done in early spring. A 15 to 18-in. plant costs about $4.00.

Varieties. *American* holly (the state tree of Delaware) and its many varieties are very popular. The dense, spiny foliage is not glossy but it is evergreen, and it is hardier than English holly. *Croonenberg*, *East Palatka* and *Old Heavyberry* are among the good kinds of American holly. *English* holly is grown in the Pacific Northwest and shipped for the Christmas trade. Its beautiful shiny foliage and big red berries are in great demand. *Chinese* holly is a shrubby grower with glossy, rectangular leaves and few spines.

Boxleaf Japanese holly is here used as a pleasing low hedge. Its slow rate of growth and naturally low, bushy form are ideal for this use.

Burford is a form of Chinese holly with large smooth leaves and a heavy crop of red berries. It is hardy north to Long Island. *Dahoon* and *Yaupon* are hollies of the South, primarily. The latter shears well and makes a good hedge. *Japanese* holly bears black fruit and small, smooth leaves like boxwood. It is a fine substitute for boxwood in the North, because it is just as easily clipped and is hardier. *Inkberry*, with smooth evergreen leaves and blue-black berries, grows from Massachusetts to Florida and is useful in foundation plantings. The *Winterberry* loses its leaves in the fall. It has red fruits and grows in swampy areas. (The botanical name for holly is *Ilex*.)

How and When to Plant. For a good crop of berries, holly needs sunshine. Deep shade makes it grow open and unshapely. It is best planted in early fall or just as new growth starts to show in the spring. Plants in pots or other containers may be set out at any time when the ground is not frozen. They require good, well-drained soil to which peat or leaf mold has been added. Dig a hole twice as large as the roots, and in the bottom place a mixture of topsoil and peat or leaf mold. Set the tree level with the surface of the ground, being careful not to let air or sun dry out the roots. Fill in good soil around the roots, water well, and spread a layer of the leaf mold over the ground around the tree. Oak leaves or pine needles may be used for this purpose. Cut back the tops of evergreen hollies about half, after planting, if they are bare rooted. Keep the tree well watered until established.

Care and Protection. Never use lime or bonemeal near hollies. In spring, before hot weather, give them some fertilizer especially intended for broad-leaved evergreens, at the rate specified on the label. Rake it lightly into the top of the ground. In cold regions give the trees a thorough soaking each year just before the ground freezes for the winter. In warm sections leaf miner sometimes attacks holly. To combat it, use a malathion or DDT spray in spring just after the new leaves begin to show, as directed on the label.

(*Below*) The very dark maroon flowers of Haile Selassie hollyhock are a rich and glowing color. Plant hollyhocks in full sun, where wind will not easily reach them.

(*Right*) Indian Spring, a hollyhock with fringed petals in shades of rose and pink. It grows 5 to 6 ft. in height.

HOLLYHOCKS

THESE tall sentinels have guarded gates and doorways for many generations, for they are among the old-time flowers most associated with the past. They look well in fairly big groups at the back of a planting, where they are valuable as accents and as a background. Colors range through shades of rose, salmon, pink and maroon to yellow and white. Flowers, both single and double, come into bloom after delphiniums.

A hollyhock should not be expected to live many years, although if the flower stalks are cut off after they fade, it will often survive and bloom again the next year. Plants grow about 6 ft. tall and do well in the warm sun, in fertile, well-drained soil.

Varieties. Annual hollyhocks (*Indian Spring* is a good pink variety with ruffled flowers) will bloom from early August into fall if started early. *Chater's Double* is a perennial strain of varied colors for August and September bloom.

How and When to Plant. Grow hollyhocks from seed, or buy young plants and set them out a foot apart in fall or spring. They cost about 50c apiece. Place them where they will not get the full force of the wind.

Care and Protection. Hollyhocks need staking as protection from summer storms. Annual varieties attract Japanese beetles. People who live where these pests are prevalent should either plan to fight the beetles with lead arsenate or DDT or choose a replacement for hollyhocks.

HONEY LOCUST

MODERN homes, hugging the ground more closely than those of past generations, need shade trees of proportionate height. In the last dozen years the honey locust has been developed and promoted to fill this need.

Older varieties had big thorns that were a drawback, but the new thornless and seedless kinds are a great improvement. They have been suggested as substitutes for the American elm because of their adaptability to many types of soil and their vigorous growth habit. They are easy to move, hardy and long lived. Even in cities where the air is full of smoke and dust, the honey locust proves to be healthy and fast growing. It stands heat and drought as well as cold, and because the foliage is so fine textured and airy, grass can grow easily underneath the branches.

Varieties. A number of fine varieties have been patented and are readily available at nurseries. *Moraine*, growing 40 to 75 ft. tall, is vase shaped when young, becoming wide spreading with age. It has no seed pods or thorns and makes a good street tree, giving filtered shade in a short time. A 5 to 6-ft. specimen costs about $6.00. *Sunburst*, of graceful, symmetrical form, has fern-like foliage with tips that sometimes stay yellow until the leaves drop in the fall, especially on alkaline soils. It reaches 40 to 60 ft. at maturity, and may be bought in the 4 to 5-ft. size for $6.00. *Shademaster*, with fountain-like form, is another good kind.

How and When to Plant. Plant in early fall or spring in an open, sunny spot in fairly moist soil, if possible. Dig a hole wide enough to accommodate the roots easily, and deep enough to hold the tree at the same depth as in the nursery (shown by the dark mark around the base of the trunk). Do not expose the roots to sun or air while planting. Pack good soil around the roots until the hole is half full, and then fill to the top with water. When the water has drained off, finish filling in the soil and leave the surface raked fine.

Care and Protection. These trees are pest-free. Practically the only pruning needed is to cut off any wayward branch that may spoil the shape of the tree.

Sunburst honey locust is a graceful tree giving light shade and growing quickly. Grass can grow right up to the trunk without difficulty.

(*Left*) **In shade or sun, in all types of soil, Hall honeysuckle will root anywhere. It can be a nuisance if not restrained.**

(*Above*) **Its yellow and white flowers, sweetly perfumed, bloom all summer.**

(*Below*) **Goldflame honeysuckle, blooming from late spring to frost, can be grown as a climbing vine or as a ground cover. The two-tone flowers are attractive.**

HONEYSUCKLE

JUST say the word honeysuckle—and can't you smell it? Besides the wild vine running over the countryside in some regions, there are many other kinds, both climbers and shrubs. They are unusually sturdy, willing growers that take to almost any soil and climate. Easy to grow, easy to move, they are hardy over a wide territory, and they don't object to heavy pruning.

The flowers are small but showy because they are borne in such abandon; usually they are yellowish, pink, white or red, followed by small berries, and many are rich with sweet fragrance. This is a sure hit in any shrub planting designed to attract birds, for the fruits are a luscious morsel to them. The berries are formed by summer and generally have been eaten before winter.

Climbing honeysuckle is invaluable not only as a vine but also as a ground cover. It makes such a thick mat that it may overrun a garden, but is especially useful to stop soil from washing away on steep banks. This is a twining vine. When wanted as a climber, it must have a trellis, some wire or other thin support around which it can wind.

Bush types of honeysuckle need a great deal of space, for they are very strong and fast growing. Winter-hardy and sure to bloom, they have no insect enemies. But they do have bird friends in abundance, which devour the red berries. Bush honeysuckle makes an excellent thick screen or hedge. It grows quickly and stands repeated trimming well.

Practically any well-drained soil will grow honeysuckle, often even a rather dry one. Full sun is preferable, but this is one plant that blooms well even when shaded. A dollar or two will buy a plant. (*Lonicera* is the botanical name.)

Varieties. *Hall* has made itself so much at home in some areas that it has become a weed. It is a dense, partly evergreen ground cover and climber that takes hold wherever it touches the ground. The very fragrant, white to yellow flowers are freely produced all summer in sun or shade. *Everblooming* is exactly that, from June to frost. The trumpet-shaped, reddish purple and yellow flowers of this climber are very showy. Another fine climbing type is *Goldflame*, with coral-pink and yellow flowers against blue-green leaves. *Trumpet* is a very hardy native American vine with orange to scarlet flowers that are not fragrant.

Tatarian honeysuckle has been hailed as one of the best hardy garden shrubs in America. It is vigorous, sure to bloom, without disease or insect pests, and is a certain attraction for birds. Pink to white flowers appear in late May on this 9-ft. shrub, followed by red berries. This is a rapid grower that makes a fine screen. The flowers of *Zabel* are red, to match the profuse fruits. This upright, 6 to 8-ft. shrub does well even in an open, windswept location. *Winter* honeysuckle is very early flowering and needs hard pruning after the white flowers have gone. Densely spreading *Morrow*, with cream-white flowers in May and June, stands poor, dry soil well.

How and When to Plant. Plant in fall or spring, in a hole of good size. Pack the soil well, and water freely. For a ground or bank cover, set the plants 18 in. apart (or 3 ft. apart in zigzag rows). For a trimmed hedge of bush honeysuckle, set the plants 12 in. apart; if allowed to grow without pruning, they can be 2 to 3 ft. apart.

Care and Protection. Be careful where you plant honeysuckle as a ground cover. It may go wild and smother choicer plants. To prevent this, cut off the ends of the runners. If you want to control the growth of a climb-

(*Above and Right*) **Trumpet honeysuckle has long tubular flowers carried in clusters at the ends of the branches. This vine is excellent in both the North and the South. In the fall it is covered with bright scarlet berries.**

(*Left*) Tatarian honeysuckle is one of the best of all ornamental shrubs. Perfectly hardy in almost all parts of the United States, it tolerates both wind and shade.

(*Right*) Leaves of Tatarian honeysuckle appear very early, followed by fragrant flowers. Berries are sure to be produced every season.

ing honeysuckle vine, prune it as soon as the flowers have gone, and cut out some of the oldest branches. If bush types get too thick, thin them out when the flowering season is over. A good spray may be needed to get rid of plant lice on climbing honeysuckle.

(*Below*) Wolf's Lilac honeysuckle bears fragrant, lilac-pink blooms in mid-spring, with orange-red berries coming later. This is a rather sprawling plant, to about 8 ft. in height.

(*Above*) Winter honeysuckle has creamy, fragrant flowers in late winter or very early spring. It blooms earlier when planted against a sunny wall where it will have some protection from cold winds.

(*Below*) Zabel is an excellent bush honeysuckle with a sturdy, upright plant and bluish green leaves. The red flowers and red fruits are always profuse.

(*Left*) The pale green foliage of Tellmanniana or Golden Giant honeysuckle forms a pleasing background for the large clusters of golden yellow and orange flowers. This is a strong climber.

(*Below*) Morrow is a bush honeysuckle with wide-spreading, dense branches covered with dark green, gray-backed foliage. Bright red berries follow the creamy white flowers.

HYACINTHS

THAT so much fragrance and pure bright color can be stored in one hyacinth bulb is astonishing. Colors are limited to white, yellow, and shades of blue and pink, but they are very clear and rich. Hyacinths have been garden favorites for several hundred years, and florists force them in quantity for late winter bloom.

The flower spikes are stiff and straight but may be used with fine effect in informal masses and with other spring bulbs at the edge of a shrub border. With an evergreen background the colors are displayed especially well if several bulbs of one color are planted together. Full sun and rich, well-drained soil will produce April blooms. When bulbs have bloomed for several years without being moved, the flower spike gradually gets smaller, with a looser effect, but that is just as pleasing as the original tightly packed spike.

The hyacinth is one of the easiest of all bulbs to grow indoors in winter. This may be done in a pot of soil, in bulb fiber, or in a glass of water. In any case, large-size bulbs or those specially prepared for forcing must be used. French Roman hyacinths are particularly good for this purpose. Instead of one heavy spike of bloom, a bulb will produce several stems of graceful, airy bells.

Cape hyacinth (so-called although not really a hyacinth—the accurate botanical name is *Galtonia*) is an entirely different plant. This blooms in August and is grown in a border like gladiolus. Twenty to thirty creamy white, bell-shaped flowers hang from the top of a 2 to 3-ft. spike. Full sun and well-drained soil are required. It is not hardy in cold climates.

Varieties. Among the varieties best adapted for both garden planting and forcing indoors are white *L'Innocence*, creamy yellow *City of Haarlem*, rose-pink *Lady Derby*, dark blue *King of the Blues*, deep lavender-blue

(*Above*) A stunning spring border of hyacinths and trumpet daffodils. Eight or ten bulbs of the same variety, planted in a group and repeated at intervals, are more effective than a mass of mixed colors.

(*Left*) French Roman hyacinths are especially good to grow in a pot indoors. Plant the bulbs in early fall and keep the pot in a cool dark room for several weeks, until the roots have formed, before bringing it into the light.

(*Right*) A glass of water—a little cup to hold the bulb—a little patience while the roots grow—and soon you will be sniffing a hyacinth like this.

(*Left*) **Lady Derby, a fine bright rose-pink hyacinth that is grown both in garden beds and indoors. For forcing, be sure to buy bulbs specially prepared for that purpose.**

(*Right*) **King of the Blues produces a large, thick spike well packed with deep blue flowers. This is a rather late variety.**

Grand Maitre, deep carmine *La Victoire*, and soft blue *Myosotis*. Bulbs cost 25c to 40c each, depending on size.

French Roman hyacinths are bought by color, at $2.00 to $3.00 per dozen. Bulbs of cape hyacinth cost 15c to 25c each.

How and When to Plant. Plant the bulbs outdoors in September or October, 6 in. deep and 6 in. apart. Be sure the soil is well drained and adequately supplied with peat moss to make it light and crumbly.

For growing the bulbs indoors in water, a special hyacinth glass is convenient. Place a little charcoal in the glass, and add enough water to barely touch the base of the bulb as it rests in the cup at the top of the glass. Keep in a cool dark place until the water is full of roots, and then gradually bring it into the light.

For indoor forcing in a pot, plant one large bulb (or three bulbs of French Roman) in a 5-in. pot (with drainage) filled with good potting soil. This should be done in early fall. Water the bulb, and place the pot in a cool dark room until roots form; this takes about eight weeks. Then gradually bring it into a warm, light window. Or set the bulb in fiber in a bowl without any drainage. This too must be kept in a cool dark corner until rooted, and then moved slowly into the light.

Cape hyacinths are planted in early spring, 7 or 8 in. deep and 15 in. apart.

Care and Protection. Hyacinths grown outdoors are benefited by a light cover of straw over winter. If you want the flower spikes to remain large, the bulbs must be taken up after the leaves die down, dried and stored until planting time in the fall. Bulbs that have been forced in fiber may be planted outdoors afterward; others forced indoors must be discarded.

In the North, cape hyacinths should be stored dry over winter, and in milder areas it is well to give them a light covering.

(*Right*) **The clear, pure colors of hyacinths are a refreshing note in any springtime planting. Bulbs left in the ground after they bloom will produce smaller, looser bloom spikes.**

(*Below*) **L'Innocence has a compact spike of small, flaring flowers of purest white.** (*Below Left*) **Grand Maitre, with violet-striped light blue flowers, gives the effect of deep lavender-blue.**

(*Left*) The Macrophylla type, which is sometimes called French hydrangea. Lime in the soil produces pink flowers, but alum or iron makes them blue. This type is familiar in foundation plantings and is also a favorite pot plant.

HYDRANGEA

THE rugged and trouble-free hydrangea is not a shrub for the connoisseur. It has been planted so freely, far and wide, that it has become commonplace. However, there is much to be said for it, and the climbing form is considered to be a most desirable vine. Hydrangea blooms for weeks, from the middle to the end of summer. Easy to please, it has few if any enemies and is of the simplest culture. It is a big, coarse plant that needs plenty of space and moist garden soil. It will bloom in shade or full sun; if in the shade it can get along with less moisture.

Shrub forms of hydrangea are so vigorous that they are usually planted as specimens rather than in combination with other shrubs. One type (Macrophylla) is grown as a pot plant by florists and is sold in great numbers, especially at Easter. This is hardy over a wide area except when winters are very severe. It is grown in foundation plantings and in tubs and has proved very good for use at the seashore. The large rounded flowers of pink or blue appear in late summer. Lime in the soil makes the flowers pink. Aluminum sulphate (from a garden store or drug store), added to water at the rate of one tablespoonful per gallon and used every few weeks for watering the plants, will turn the flowers to blue. Peat moss at the roots will also help.

Climbing hydrangea, hardy at least as far north as Boston, clings easily to stone, brick or wood walls and to tree bark. It will not

(*Above*) Peegee hydrangea bears large, conical heads of white to pinkish flowers late in the summer. These hardy, vigorous shrubs need plenty of water. They should be pruned hard every spring.

(*Right*) The tree form of Peegee hydrangea used to be a feature of most summer lawns. It is very showy and sturdy.

(*Left*) Hills of Snow is an appropriate name for these large clusters of pure white. They are in evidence from midsummer to October, even in a shady location.

harm a tree, as some vines do. Flowering in shade or sun, it is a handsome vine with glossy, clean dark leaves and large flat white flower heads in early summer.

Varieties. Quick-growing *Peegee* is one of the most familiar of all hardy shrubs. It reaches 6 to 8 ft. in height and is also grown as a small tree. The huge, cone-shaped white flowers come in August; as they get older, instead of wilting and dropping off, they turn pinkish bronze and stay on the bush in a dried state for weeks. *Hills of Snow* bears loose white flowers in 6-in. clusters from early July through September. This 3 to 4-ft. shrub does well in the shade but sometimes the branches get frozen back.

Nikko Blue is a popular variety of the Macrophylla type. It has large heads of rich blue. Another valuable hydrangea is the *Oak-leaved.* This slow-growing, 4 to 5-ft. shrub has large creamy flower clusters in late summer. Its leaves, shaped like those of an oak, account for the name; they turn orange and red in autumn. $1.50 to $2.00 will buy a shrub hydrangea; the climbing variety costs a little more.

How and When to Plant. Set out the plant in early spring or early fall, in a generous-sized hole. Pack good soil about it, and water well.

Care and Protection. Peegee and Hills of Snow should have the old stems cut down almost to the ground in early spring. Macrophylla or florists' hydrangeas, when grown in the open, should have earth mounded about them as winter protection in coldest regions. They must be pruned immediately after they bloom. Cut out the old shoots, so that new ones may grow up from the base and produce buds for the following year.

Climbing hydrangea is a beautiful vine reaching to a considerable height and blooming in early summer. It clings fast to any surface without difficulty.

INDOOR GARDENING (and Home Decorating)

RAISING plants indoors is a fascinating hobby for every age and condition of person. The question is whether the plants do more for the decor of a room or for the happiness and well-being of those who tend them. Surely there is no better way of saying "Welcome" than by having an abundance of growing things in the house. They give the feeling of home to the smallest place and also to the elaborate one where plant stands and brackets can be supplemented by a home greenhouse. For the would-be gardener who must live in an apartment or who is restrained by arthritic joints, window-sill gardening is a perfect outlet.

Green foliage brings a fresh look to the indoors all during the dull winter season. And when a flowering plant comes into bloom—first a bud and then a slowly developing burst of color—it is a triumph for the whole family. Invalids and convalescents are not the only

A home greenhouse at one time was a rich man's hobby, but now low-cost, low-maintenance models bring greenhouse gardening within reach of many home owners. (*Below*) Many of these flowers can be grown indoors even without a greenhouse.

(*Above*) Foliage plants are pleasing all year on shelves indoors. (*In the Top Row*) Philodendron, variegated philodendron, two forms of English ivy, African violet. (*Middle Row*) Three kinds of peperomia. (*Bottom Row*) Kangaroo vine, jade plant, Chinese evergreen, grape ivy.

ones who find a new field of interest here. Every member of the household will take pride in the progress of the plants.

Plastic flowers, no matter how cleverly contrived, will never completely take the place of living plants, any more than a picture on a screen will fully substitute for a live actor on a stage. The end result is not the only aspect to be considered. The joy and satisfaction of the plant grower is even more important.

Foliage Plants—and Flowering Plants. Glossy and hairy, ferny and bold, patterned and slashed and exotic as you please—there is no end to the possibilities of foliage plants. They reach for the ceiling and they hang toward the floor and they are content in a

(*Above*) A dish garden requires much less light than a flowering plant. Don't let dust accumulate on the leaves.

(*Above*) French Roman hyacinths are not hard to bring into bloom in a pot during the winter, in soil or bulb fiber.

(*Left*) Various kinds of narcissus are very popular for indoor forcing in pebbles and water. Shown here is the variety Grand Soleil d'Or.

(*Left*) Their intrinsic beauty and sometimes very capricious temperament have brought African violets to the front rank of flowering house plants.

(*Right*) Petunias are easily arranged as cut flowers. Plants are so free blooming that dozens of flowers can be cut without spoiling the outdoor display.

teacup. They offer so many leaf colors that you never miss having flowers on them too. Any time of year is the time for a foliage plant, and any place is the place for one. Even dark corners and other unlikely spots can be made dramatic by the use of green growing plants. In some cases tropical specimens from far places can find a spot indoors where they can adapt themselves. To learn of their native haunts is in itself an interesting sidelight.

Flowering plants need more light and sun than foliage plants, and over a considerable part of the year some kinds will bloom happily indoors. Forcing them into bloom for a certain holiday season opens up fascinating possibilities for still another hobby, and increases your admiration for the work of commercial growers who can so accurately time their blooms for the flower shows.

(*Left*) Many daisy-shaped flowers like these single chrysanthemums are especially adapted for informal bouquets for any room in the house.

(*Below*) The homey geranium and the exotic gloxinia will provide color indoors for weeks. On porches and terraces the potted plants are also attractive.

(*Left*) Poppy anemones have a delicate air that is charmingly apparent when they are used in floral arrangements. At flower shows they always excite comment.

Illustrations of other flowers that are admirably suited for decorating your home appear under their individual headings.

Other Possibilities. Dried flowers, dish gardening, planters and terrariums are other areas worth exploring. Room dividers and special planting areas built into homes and offices extend the scope of indoor gardening still further. Fluorescent lighting and bonsai growing are capturing the imagination and devoted efforts of many home gardeners. Each offers new delights and challenges. So many books are now to be had, and so many helpful accessories are on the market, that indoor gardeners need never grope for advice. The whole world of plant life is open to them.

Quite as important as using indoor plants for decorating your home is bringing your outdoor garden beauty indoors whenever your flowers are ready for cutting. Often it may mean "robbing Peter to pay Paul," when a choice must be made between allowing the full glory of the outdoor picture to remain undiminished, and borrowing a part of it to add glamor and fragrance to your indoor setting. "Borrowing" may prove to be literally correct in some cases, where the flowers removed may soon be replaced by a new crop of blooms.

The provident gardener, bearing in mind his own hankering for a constant supply of flowers for indoor decoration, will favor certain plants that will meet this desire. (Attention is called to this "good for cutting" feature in the detailed descriptions of the various flowers under their separate headings.)

(*Left*) Dark crimson-red Ranger, a tall bearded iris (like all the others illustrated on this and the opposite page). This is late blooming, with long straight stems.

(*Right*) Ola Kala, with its bright, glistening golden yellow blooms, is a highly rated variety growing about 38 in. tall.

IRIS

THE graceful fleur-de-lis—historic emblem of the royal family of France—and the purple flag so common even in neglected gardens, are members of the large iris family. The very word *iris* refers to the rainbow of colors provided by these beautiful flowers. There are endless contrasts in color and form, and any attempt to describe the combination of shades and markings necessarily ends in a complication of terms that is understood only by examining the variety in question.

Irises have been cherished by gardeners in many countries for many centuries. There

(*Left*) Reddish brown, copper and henna tones compete in Bryce Canyon, a hardy and popular iris that grows 3 ft. tall or more.

(*Left*) Lady Mohr, with its oyster-white standards and prominently veined, greenish yellow falls—an unusual color combination.

(*Right*) Cloud Cap, a large and impressive flower, has broad pink petals and a bright tangerine beard.

(*Left*) Darkly beautiful Sable is a stunning flower of deep blue-black. Blooms are of good size, with very velvety falls.

(*Right*) Solid Gold, a tall bearded iris with wide petals of heavy texture. This is a fine grower with strong stems.

are well over a hundred wild kinds, and plant breeders in many lands have enormously increased the types and varieties available. The names of some of the most planted types —Siberian, Japanese, Dutch, English, Spanish—indicate the world-wide origin and interest in them. A bewildering number are offered by dealers who specialize in iris, and it is not unusual for a new variety to cost $20.00 or $25.00 for a few seasons. However, older sorts of great delicacy and beauty are easily available at a dollar or less, and because there are many irises that grow easily and endure for many years they rank with peonies as basic garden plants.

Most kinds are very hardy and require only ordinary garden soil and good drainage. Practically all parts of the United States can grow some type of iris. There are low growers only a few inches high that bloom with other early spring bulbs, and others that may reach

(*Left*) Silvery overtones soften Blue Rhythm's cornflower - blue color. The large standards are well arched and domed, and the broad falls somewhat flaring.

(*Left*) Gypsy has coppery gold standards and chestnut-brown falls. It blooms late in the spring.

(*Right*) Light violet-blue and deeper violet-purple are combined in Her Grace, and an ermine-white edging sets off the colors.

(*Left*) Japanese irises have broad flowers that are rather shapeless compared to the crisp outlines of other types, but they have an air of distinction that is very appealing.

(*Right*) Perry's Blue, a Siberian iris that does well as a clump at the edge of a pool. Both the flowers and the foliage are graceful in appearance.

over 4 ft. in height and do not flower until midsummer.

By far the most widely planted irises are the tall bearded. They grow 1½ to 3½ ft. high and bloom in late spring with such perennials as poppies and columbine. The upright center petals are called the standards, and the lower petals are the falls; on the falls is the velvety beard for which this type is named. (They used to be called German iris.)

Besides these tall growers there are dwarf and intermediate bearded. The dwarfs grow about 6 to 10 in. tall and are ideal for rock gardens and as clumps at the front of a border. With daffodils and other spring-flowering bulbs they are charming. Intermediates average 18 to 24 in. in height, and furnish bloom between the early dwarfs and the later irises. All these bearded types like a dry, sunny location and a soil that is not too rich.

Japanese irises are beardless. They have wide, flat, very large, soft-looking flowers in midsummer on a 2½ to 4-ft. plant. These are extremely exotic-appearing blooms that must have rich, rather acid soil and plenty of moisture. A low, damp location is good for them, or a place in a border where they can have the moisture they demand.

Siberian irises, also beardless, are valuable with other perennials in a border. Their graceful flowers, although smaller than some types, are very freely produced and their foliage is attractive and lasting. They too like moist soil and look well when massed beside a pool. They bloom a little later than bearded iris.

The Dutch irises so popular with florists may be grown outdoors especially in the South and on the West Coast, where they bloom in May and June. They like well-drained, light soil and a place in the sun. These and the less planted English and Spanish irises are grown from bulbs, as is the very

Wedgwood, a Dutch iris, is extremely popular for early forcing. Florists use it freely in arrangements, where its lovely blue colors look so well with white, yellow and pink.

(*Left*) **Caesar's Brother is an excellent dark blue Siberian iris growing about 30 in. tall. It is a fine addition for any garden.**

(*Below*) **The orchid-like blooms of Dutch iris are borne in May and June. This type requires full sun and light, well-drained soil.**

fragrant, dwarf, early-flowering *Iris reticulata* that is planted in rock gardens.

Varieties. Among recent prizewinners have been these tall bearded varieties: *Swan Ballet* (white), *Blue Sapphire* (powder-blue), *Violet Harmony* (violet), *First Violet* (violet) and *Sable Night* (blackish violet).

Good dwarf bearded varieties are pale blue *Fairy*, cream and yellow *Pam*, bright red *Tampa*, and mauve-pink *Rose Mist*. All are 6 to 8 in. tall.

Among Japanese varieties offered are white *Betty F. Holmes*, *Red Emperor*, mauve *Rose Anna* and *True Blue*.

Caesar's Brother (pansy-violet), *Perry's Blue*, *Snow Queen* and *Eric The Red* are representative of the Siberian group. Bulbous irises that are popular include light blue *Wedgwood*, *White Excelsior* and *Bronze Queen*. Specialists' catalogs should be consulted not only for additional varieties of the groups mentioned here but also for other iris types.

How and When to Plant. All the bearded kinds need very shallow planting. Dig bonemeal and some lime into the soil beforehand. Allow about 12 in. between clumps, and barely cover with moist soil. Foliage should be cut back to 6 in. at planting time. July and August are the best months to plant this type.

Japanese iris may be planted in early spring or in September. The Siberian group is best planted in early spring. Do not use lime where these two kinds are to be grown; instead, mix some fertilizer into the soil.

Bulbous irises are planted in October, like other spring-flowering bulbs. Set them in groups, 4 to 5 in. deep and the same distance apart, in sunny, well-drained soil. They will benefit by a light covering after the ground has frozen.

Care and Protection. When a clump of iris gets too large and crowded, dig it up carefully and divide it. Throw away the center and keep the outer parts. Replant them at once, about a foot apart, either in new soil or in ground newly prepared. Cut back the foliage to 6 in. This should be done in midsummer, immediately following the blooming period, approximately every three or four years.

Lime and bonemeal may occasionally be added to the soil around bearded iris. Dead flowers should be cut off at once, and in the autumn all dead foliage should be removed and burned. Sometimes borers cause the leaves to yellow. If this happens, dig up and destroy the affected root.

(*Left*) **Dwarf irises for rock gardens (reddish Pumila and blue Cristata are shown here) bloom in early spring with the daffodils. They are also valuable as carpeting plants with the spring-flowering shrubs and early perennials.**

(*Left*) Rich dark evergreen English ivy finds many ways of being useful. Here it beautifies a sundial.

(*Right*) Do you need a foliage plant for a room that receives almost no sun? Try a fancy-leaved ivy.

IVY

AS a ground cover for shady banks and for spots under trees where grass will not grow, English ivy is a highly desirable, permanent plant that will give satisfaction for many years. The fact that it is evergreen means that the area it covers will be attractive all year round. It clings to concrete, stucco, brick and wood without any difficulty, and is also used to combine with other plants in window boxes. The thick, dark, leathery leaves reach about 4 in. in length, and small roots along the stems enable the runners to hold fast to any surface and to take root easily in the ground.

English ivy needs a fairly moist soil and some shade. It thrives in locations where it receives almost no sun, and is not to be recommended for hot, dry slopes. In the far South it does best on walls that have a northern exposure. It can stand more severe winters when planted as a ground cover than when grown on walls.

There are many variations, with leaves of different sizes and colorations; many are attractively margined and variegated. These fancy-leaved ivies are often grown as indoor pot plants. For this use they are particularly appreciated because they do not require sun.

Another plant, quite different in many respects, is called Boston ivy. It also clings very tightly to all kinds of masonry and is especially good on stone walls. The large, glossy, dark green leaves are so dense that they overlap like shingles; they turn bronzy red before dropping in the autumn. This is a fast grower standing smoky city conditions well and easily climbing buildings several stories high. Its small black berries are not very conspicuous. It grows in sunny or partly shaded locations, in any fertile soil.

(*Below*) Boston ivy is a fast grower that quickly covers a stone wall. The leaves turn reddish in autumn before they drop.

Related to Boston ivy is the Virginia creeper or woodbine, a vigorous, fast-growing vine for sun or shade, which is a native of eastern North America. Its large, long-stemmed leaves are scarlet and gold in the fall. For trellises, stone walls, rocks and ledges this makes an easy and hardy covering.

Varieties. *Hedera helix* is the English ivy, easily available in pots at about 75c. *Baltic*, smaller leaved and especially hardy, is one of its numerous variations. It is excellent as a ground cover and for use on walls with a northern exposure. Dealers in house plants offer numerous decorative varieties with vari-colored leaves.

Parthenocissus tricuspidata, the Boston ivy, is priced at $1.00 to $1.50 for a potted plant. *Lowi*, with small leaves that color well in the fall, is particularly appropriate for small surfaces like gate posts and low walls.

Engelmanni is a small-leaved form of Virginia creeper that turns scarlet very early in autumn.

How and When to Plant. Set out English ivy plants in early spring, close to the wall they are intended to cover. If wanted as a ground cover, plants should be about a foot apart. It is easy to take a stem and root it by simply inserting it in damp soil where desired. Boston ivy also is planted in early spring.

Care and Protection. Any stems of English ivy that have been winterkilled should be cut back in spring. New growth will follow. Shoots growing out of bounds may be snipped at any time. Some of the runners of Boston ivy may need to be thinned out in spring.

JACOB'S LADDER

THIS is not a very tall grower, as the name suggests, but a foot-high hardy perennial blooming in spring and early summer. This name refers to the way the leaflets grow on the stem. The plant is free flowering and not at all hard to grow. In a rock garden or at the front of a border, it shows a clump of lacy foliage all season. The small cupped blue flowers are carried in loose clusters.

A sunny or partly shaded location is satisfactory, in average, well-drained soil. The plant sows its own seed and so lasts for years.

Blue Pearl, a variety of Jacob's ladder growing 10 to 12 in. high, is good in a wall or rock garden.

Varieties. *Blue Pearl* is the favorite for border planting and wall gardens. Its light blue flowers appear early in spring. *Reptans*, more sprawling in growth, makes a dark mound 2 ft. wide. The bright blue flowers are nice with spring bulbs. Plants cost 65c to 90c.

How and When to Plant. Set out the plants in fall or spring. Allow 8 in. between them (up to 15 in. for the spreading type).

Care and Protection. When a clump gets too large, dig it up in late summer, separate it into pieces and replant.

JASMINE

THESE scrambling shrubs are, for the most part, natives of tropical or semi-tropical regions. Often the yellow or white flowers are very fragrant. The dark green, glossy foliage is evergreen in the South. A number of kinds are grown outdoors as shrubs or climbers where the climate is mild. They need well-drained soil to which leaf mold or peat moss has been added. Trained on walls or trellises, or pruned as a hedge, they are widely used through the South.

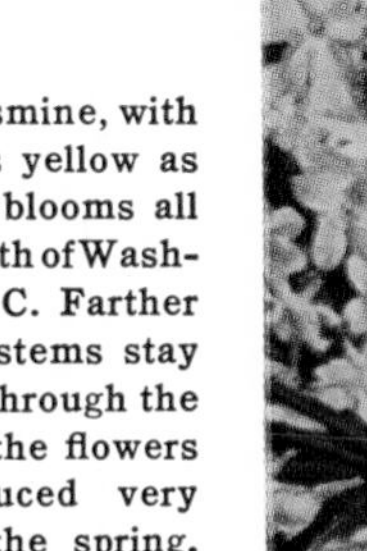

Winter jasmine, with flowers as yellow as forsythia, blooms all winter south of Washington, D. C. Farther north its stems stay green all through the year and the flowers are produced very early in the spring.

One variety may be grown outdoors in protected places as far north as southern New England. Although the yellow flowers are not fragrant, they do appear very early in the spring. This is called winter jasmine because farther south it blooms all winter long. In the North the stems are green throughout the year; the gracefully drooping branches add quite a decorative touch to gardens.

Varieties. Besides the winter jasmine (*Nudiflorum*), available for about $1.50, *Multiflorum* is popular in the South. It has star-shaped white flowers in the fall and may be grown either as a shrub or as a climber. *Grand Duke* and *Maid of Orleans*, with very fragrant white blooms, may also be trained in either form. *Mesnyi*, with yellow flowers, blooms in the spring. *Floridum* is a low-growing shrub with dark yellow flowers in summer.

How and When to Plant. Set out the plant in fall or spring in well-prepared soil. Tamp the ground well, and water thoroughly.

Care and Protection. Cut back hard immediately after the flowering season.

(*Above*) Kafir lily may be grown for years in the same pot. The big cluster of fragrant flowers appears in late winter.

KAFIR LILY

LATE winter or early spring is the blooming season of this magnificent large pot plant. In California it is often grown outdoors, where it forms a big clump, but in other parts of the country it is handled better in a pot. This is a bulbous plant native to South Africa. It has glossy evergreen, strap-like leaves about 18 in. long, and a head of trumpet flowers on a thick stem. The colors are cream to orange and scarlet.

Varieties. *Clivia miniata* is the kind most grown. Plants ready to flower may be bought from florists.

How and When to Plant. Keep this plant where it receives good light and air but not the direct rays of the sun. As it grows, it should be moved to a larger pot.

Care and Protection. The plant should be kept watered while blooming and afterward too. All through summer and fall it should have enough water to prevent the foliage from wilting. Liquid fertilizer should be given it in the summer. After Christmas, when it starts into growth again, it needs more water. It does not require repotting every year.

(*Right*) Kalanchoe endures more dry heat than most flowering house plants. You can start a new plant from a leaf laid on wet sand.

KALANCHOE

THIS is a bushy little plant that does well potted or in a dish garden. It has thick fleshy leaves and clusters of tiny flowers. Indoors it blooms over a long period, from December to April or May, and because it can stand dry heat it is a favorite in homes too warm for many flowering house plants. Kalanchoe (kal-an-koh′ee) needs plenty of sun and should not be given too much water. It is not hardy, but in the South some kinds may be grown outdoors.

(*Left*) **Double kerria has flowers like little golden balls, produced over a long season. This is a clean-looking shrub that will grow in light shade.**

(*Below*) **Kochia resembles a small evergreen but is really an annual grown each year from seed.** (*Right*) **Its fall coloring is very bright. Sometimes kochia is used for quick effects around summer cottages.**

Varieties. Rose or scarlet-flowered plants may be purchased in the fall for less than a dollar.

How and When to Plant. Keep the plant in a sunny window, and don't overwater it.

Care and Protection. Remove the flowers as they fade, to encourage more bloom. Move the pot outdoors to a shady spot for the summer.

KERRIA

GOOD thick growth in summer and decorative twigs that remain green all winter make kerria a pleasing shrub even after the butterball flowers have faded. They start in May and continue to some extent through the summer. This 4 to 6-ft. shrub is hardy to Iowa and through southern New England. Besides the double variety, there is one with single flowers, but the double is a little hardier and taller growing.

Dense sawtooth foliage of bright light green is borne on slender, arching green branches. Kerria finds a place in the foreground of a shrub border and in foundation plantings. The double-flowered type makes a fine hedge. Deep rich soil and light shade are recommended.

Varieties. *Double* is the only variety commonly available. A plant costs around $1.50.

How and When to Plant. Planting is done in fall or spring. Dig a hole large enough to hold the roots without crowding. Pack good soil around them, and water thoroughly.

Care and Protection. Prune immediately after the flowers have gone, cutting the weakest branches all the way to the ground. Older stems should be pruned back to the place where new shoots are starting to grow.

KOCHIA

THE names Mexican firebush and burning bush, sometimes applied to kochia (koh'kee-uh), refer to the bright or purplish red color of its foliage in autumn. Summer cypress is still another name for this easy-to-grow annual foliage plant. Its fine, feathery leaves, light green all summer, make a close, compact bush oval or pyramidal in shape, that could be mistaken for a small evergreen. As a dwarf summer hedge or edging or as a temporary foundation around a new home, this plant is most useful.

Varieties. *Childsi* is the kind usually seen. It is 2½ ft. tall, with feathery green foliage turning crimson in fall.

How and When to Plant. In May sow seed in the open ground, in full sun, and space the plants 18 in. apart when they are large enough to handle.

Care and Protection. Don't fail to keep kochia watered. If growth slows down, the plants may turn color too soon.

LANTANA

IN the far South this shrub is popular because it blooms so freely practically all year round, and because it thrives on the poorest of soil. Flowers of yellow and orange, red, lavender and white are carried in neat little round clusters against the evergreen foliage. In the upper South, lantana (lantay'nuh) blooms from early spring to late autumn; although cold winters cause the tops to freeze back, the plant grows up again the next year. Farther north it is used as a summer bedding plant.

The weeping lantana is especially nice for hanging baskets and window boxes. In the South it is a trailer for sunny locations, and may also be used as a ground cover or as a

Lantana blooms profusely even in poor soil. Gold Rush, the weeping form shown here, also does well in a moss-lined hanging basket.

(*Left*) Regal strain of larkspur has huge, double florets on good sturdy stalks that are superb for cutting. It mixes well with other flowers too.

(*Above*) Lavender (described on the following page) can be grown in your own garden and dried for sachets. Hidcote is the variety illustrated.

(*Below*) Giant Imperial larkspur has long been popular for its sparkling colors and tall flower spikes. For continuous bloom, sow seed in late autumn and again in early spring.

screen if trained against a wire fence. Florists grow lantana in standard or tree form, as well.

Varieties. *Confetti* (yellow, pink and purple), *Pink Frolic* and *Gold Rush* are among the varieties of trailing or weeping lantana. Plants are available at low cost ($1.00 or less). Standard kinds include *Pink Beauty* and *Violet King*, among others.

How and When to Plant. In warm climates the plants may be set out at any season. In the North, bedding lantana is not put outdoors until warm weather arrives.

Care and Protection. Plants grown in baskets need liquid fertilizer periodically through spring and summer.

LARKSPUR

FOR blue masses in the garden and for cutting, larkspur is in great demand. This is the annual form of delphinium (which see), growing every year from seed instead of living over as a plant. Fortunately, it is very easy to grow; indeed, it is likely to spring up year after year because the seed sows itself readily. For tall accents in an annual planting, for the middle section of a border, and for airy spires combined with pink, yellow and white flowers in an arrangement, it is indispensable.

Larkspur grows 3 to 4 ft. tall in sun or light shade, and needs rich soil and plenty of moisture. Seed must be sown either in the fall just before the ground freezes or in very early spring, because plants must have a cool growing season. It is even possible to scatter the seed on top of snow in late winter, in order to get it into the soil at the earliest possible moment. Larkspur may have a rather short blooming season if the weather turns hot.

Varieties. The *Regal* strain is an improvement on the older Giant Imperial. It has huge, double flowers closely set on long strong spikes that come early and are splendid for cutting. The clear bright colors may be bought separately or in mixture. *Giant Imperial* varieties also are offered in blue, pink, rose, salmon, lilac and white, separately or mixed.

How and When to Plant. Broadcast the seed in late fall or very early spring where it is wanted to bloom. Thin the plants to stand 8 or 9 in. apart.

Care and Protection. Don't try to move larkspur plants; that is a hard job because of the long root that grows straight down. Stony soil is to be avoided.

LAVENDER

(*Illustration on preceding page*)

THIS whole plant is fragrant, particularly on warm days—both the erect spikes of lavender-blue flowers and the hoary, gray-green leaves. These flowers are the source of oils used in perfumes, and it is an easy matter to dry them for sachets. If cut as the center buds begin to open and hung in a protected but airy place to cure, they will retain their fragrance for months.

Blooming in midsummer, this neat-growing, shrubby perennial looks well at the front of a border, on a dry bank, or in a rock garden. It makes a very nice low hedge if grown in full sun, in average soil on the dry side. Heavy, damp clay is not advisable.

Varieties. *Officinalis* or *Vera* is the old-time lavender growing 12 to 18 in. tall and blooming in July and August. *Giant Munstead* is more dwarf and compact, with wiry spikes of lavender-blue in June. Deep purple *Hidcote* is very hardy and blooms from July to frost. It grows a foot high and spreads to about 18 in. in width. Plants cost from 75c to $1.00.

How and When to Plant. Plant in early spring, allowing 12 in. per plant. Or do it in autumn, and cover lightly over winter.

Care and Protection. Right after blooming stops, trim back the plants.

Shade presents a special problem in lawn making, but grass and trees are compatible when both are fed regularly. Special grass mixtures for shady conditions are also helpful.

LAWNS

A FINE velvety lawn always wins compliments. It is restful to look at, and it forms a flawless setting for all ornamental plants. It is an essential part of the complete garden picture. If you have a lawn to be proud of, occasional gaps or imperfections in other parts of the garden are more easily overlooked.

Lawns are made of a mixture of grasses, and in order to have first-rate results you must start with top-quality seed. There are no bargains in lawn seed. Over a large part of the United States, Kentucky bluegrass and red fescue form the basis of the most satisfactory mixtures. These are grasses that do best in cool weather, and the time most favorable for getting them started is from mid-August through September. (See also *Planning Before Planting*.)

Like other plants, grass must have food and drink. Good topsoil is necessary, to a depth of at least 5 or 6 in. Work peat into it; but before using lime, have the soil tested by your county agricultural agent or your state agricultural experiment station (or do it yourself with a soil-testing kit). Ground limestone is beneficial if the test indicates a need for lime. Fertilizer high in nitrogen is required by a lawn. A chemical fertilizer containing also phosphorus and potash is effective. Apply it at the rate specified on the bag. A lawn spreader will prove valuable in distributing both the fertilizer and the lawn seed evenly. The seeded area must be kept moist continuously during the ten days to two weeks required for sprouting.

Lawns are renovated in spring by first raking away the debris of winter and then scratching the bare spots, preparatory to sowing seed there. Add fresh new soil to any hollows. If you use a roller, make sure it is very light.

The selection of mowers, edgers and other lawn equipment is continually being increased. The only way to decide which is best for you is to visit a reliable dealer and ask for a demonstration. Mowing must be done more often in the spring while growth is at its peak; sometimes every five days is not too often. Clippings may be left on the lawn if they are not thick enough to mat. They will decay and act as an organic fertilizer. During

Make a hobby of your lawn and you will derive as much pleasure from it as you do from any of your flowering plants. Intelligent, year-round attention is the secret.

hot weather the Kentucky bluegrass-red fescue mixture should not be cut closer than 2 to 3 in. in the North. Close mowing encourages weeds.

What's Good for Your Lawn. Sprinkling the grass is a pleasant occupation on a warm evening, but if you have the interest of your lawn at heart you will cool off under the shower instead. Don't start the watering until a really bad dry spell occurs. Once you start, you must keep it up. When you do water, soak the ground well and do it preferably in the morning.

Lawns benefit from fertilizer given in the fall and again during the winter and early spring. Don't use fertilizer during hot humid weather. Sandy soils and areas under trees need extra applications.

Modern chemistry has worked wonders in developing weed killers. On new lawns of small size it is still advisable to pull weeds by hand just as soon as they are noticeable and before they go to seed. There are a number of preparations to kill crabgrass before it germinates. They must be used very early in spring, strictly according to instructions. Where this weed is a problem, use fertilizer cautiously in spring and summer, don't cut the grass too short, and don't overwater. Broad-leaved weeds like plantain and dandelion may be killed by applying 2,4-D directly to the plants. This chemical does not harm the grass, but it does injure trees, shrubs and other ornamentals and vegetables if it drifts onto them. It should not be used on weeds in a new lawn. Spot weed killers are available also for other weeds. If grubs get in the lawn, the turf should be treated with chlordane and dieldrin in the spring.

In the South. Zoysia grass is especially good for sandy soils and those near the sea. Bermuda, the best-known lawn grass in the lower South, needs rich soil and full sun. St. Augustine grass, which does well in both shade and sun, can be grown all over Florida. In northern Florida lawns are best started from April through July; in the southern part of the state any time is satisfactory, but best growth is made in the summer. About four feedings per year are needed. In the colder parts of the South these grasses are brown all winter but turn green again when warm weather returns. For a green winter lawn, Italian rye grass may be sown on top of them.

The many excellent products now on the market, developed by experts through research and experiment, make it easier to have a thriving green lawn like this one.

A sloping piece of ground where the soil gets more than adequate drainage is a challenge to any lawn maker.

(*Left*) Leopard's bane (Cordifolium is the variety illustrated) is effective in early spring gardens. The foliage dies down when the flowers have stopped blooming, but the plant is hardy and comes up again the next spring.

(*Above*) Leucothoe is not a familiar shrub, in spite of its many superior qualities. Possibly the rather difficult name is responsible (lew-koth'oh-ee).

LEOPARD'S BANE

APPARENTLY this hardy perennial is harmful to leopards, but that need not worry many gardeners! These big yellow daisies, whether cut for bouquets or planted near blue and lavender-colored spring flowers, are very showy. With early bulbs and perennials like alyssum and candytuft, leopard's bane makes an effective picture. The average height is 2 ft.

These are shallow-rooted plants that need plenty of water. Unlike most daisies, they can stand some shade and a somewhat heavy soil that holds the moisture, especially in hot summers. During that time they may die out if left to bake in the sun. After the Maytime bloom is over, the bright green, heart-shaped leaves disappear. It is well, therefore, to have annuals ready to set in among these plants, or a later flowering perennial coming along that will fill their place.

Varieties. *Doronicum caucasicum*, about 2 ft. tall, is good with tulips. The large, bright yellow flowers of *Mme. Mason* last well in water. *Bunch of Gold* also has very large blooms. *Cordifolium* has glossy leaves and somewhat smaller flowers. Plants cost about 75c to $1.00.

How and When to Plant. Very early spring or early fall is the time to set out the plants. Allow 8 to 10 in. between them. Water thoroughly.

Care and Protection. Keep well watered in dry weather. Every second or third year dig up the clump after the blooming period, divide it into sections, and replant.

LEUCOTHOE

WHEN planted with other broad-leaved evergreen shrubs such as rhododendrons and mountain laurel, leucothoe (lew-koth'oh-ee) is especially good because it is lower growing and fills in at their base. It needs the same moist acid soil, and the shade provided by these taller shrubs is just what it likes. As a foundation plant it is useful, too, provided its companions are also lovers of acid soil conditions.

This 3 to 6-ft. plant grows wild from Virginia to Georgia but can be grown north to New England if given a protected location in coldest climates. In May the waxy white flowers are borne in drooping clusters along the lower side of the branches. The leathery, dark leaves, 5 to 6 in. long, are bronze and purple shades all winter. In spite of these recommendations, leucothoe is not well known or generally planted. It deserves better.

Varieties. *Drooping* is the kind most grown in the East. *Dwarf* is smaller and bushier, with leaves that turn cherry-red in the fall. A new *Rainbow* variety is also offered, with leaves of many shades. A bush of planting size costs $2.00 to $2.50.

How and When to Plant. Mix plenty of leaf mold or peat moss with the soil before planting. Set out the plant in spring or fall, in a good-sized hole. Firm the soil well about the roots, and water thoroughly.

Care and Protection. Pruning should be done in the spring. There may be dead wood to get rid of, but in any case some of the older canes should be cut back. A permanent cover of oak leaves, peat moss or pine needles over the ground around the plant will be beneficial, but never allow lime to come near it.

LILAC

THE fragrance of the lilac brings back childhood memories to many people, for a bush in the dooryard has been an accepted feature of American homes for generations. The fact that it is so dependable even when little care is given it, encouraged pioneers to carry slips of it with them when they traveled westward. As a result, lilacs have become widely established and are practically a token of home.

Lilacs are rapid growers reaching 10 or 12 ft. in height, and carrying their single or double flowers in large clusters in late spring. Colors run from deep reddish purple through shades of lavender, blue, pink and white. They are perfectly hardy in northern United

President Grevy lilac has double, soft blue flowers in extra large clusters. Its fragrance is delicious.

(*Left*) At the height of spring when early bulbs, perennials and many other shrubs are vying for attention, lilacs occupy an important place in the landscape picture.

(*Above*) Any number of varieties may be combined with safety, because the tones are always harmonious.

States and into Canada, and may be grown south to the Carolinas and west to the Rocky Mountains. A wide variety of soils will grow lilacs, as is proved by the great range of territory over which they thrive. Extremely acid soil is unsuitable, but in that case some lime dug into the ground after the blooming season will be helpful. Soil that is too rich may produce more leaves than flowers. Full sun and plenty of room are requirements.

For an informal hedge around a garden, for a screen or a specimen plant, there is nothing more enjoyable than lilacs, the state flower of New Hampshire. Blooming with tulips, they are often combined for bouquets.

Because plant breeders in France worked so hard and accomplished so much in the improvement of the common old-fashioned lilac, the varieties they created are called French Hybrids. Most of them carry hard-to-pronounce French names, but that should not stop anyone from growing them. Their heads of bloom are larger, the color range more ex-

(*Above*) The old-fashioned purple lilac has enormous sentimental appeal. Although it blooms for only a short season, it is loved for its fragrance, hardiness and long life. (*Right*) The white form. From these two, the French Hybrids were developed.

(*Left*) About 1870, Victor Lemoine of Nancy, France, began his work with lilacs, resulting in such stunning colors as this glowing deep rose-pink.

(*Left*) **The beautiful crimson-violet bloom of the Charles Joly lilac. The very hardy bush is of moderate size.**

(*Below*) **A tall and imposing plant bears these dazzling white blooms of the variety Mme. Lemoine.**

tensive, and the fragrance pronounced. There are also a number of other lilac types not so widely grown, such as the graceful and profuse-blooming Persian, the Cutleaf, and Late lilac. Considerable work with lilacs has been done in Canada, where the Preston Hybrids have been developed. They are extra hardy and later blooming.

Varieties. Dozens and dozens of varieties are for sale, with new ones added from time to time. One of the French Hybrids may be bought, in the 2 to 3-ft. size, for $1.50 to $2.00. The common purple and white may be a little lower in price. Among the popular French Hybrids are *Ellen Willmott*, *Mme. Lemoine* and *Edith Cavell*, white; *Katharine Havemeyer*, mauve; *Lucie Baltet*, pink; *President Lincoln* and *President Grevy*, blue; *Michel Buchner*, lavender; *Congo*, wine-red; *Ludwig Spaeth* and *President Poincare*, purple.

How and When to Plant. If possible, fertilize with some old stable manure, well dug into the ground. Get own-root plants if they are available, and set them deep into a good-sized hole. Water well. Either spring or fall is the time to plant.

Care and Protection. Cut off all dead flowers so that seed cannot form. In order to keep the bush from growing so tall that you cannot see or reach the flowers, it is necessary also to cut out weak shoots and

(*Above*) **The Persian lilac is a dwarf, compact shrub entirely covered with loose clusters of pale lilac-colored flowers.**

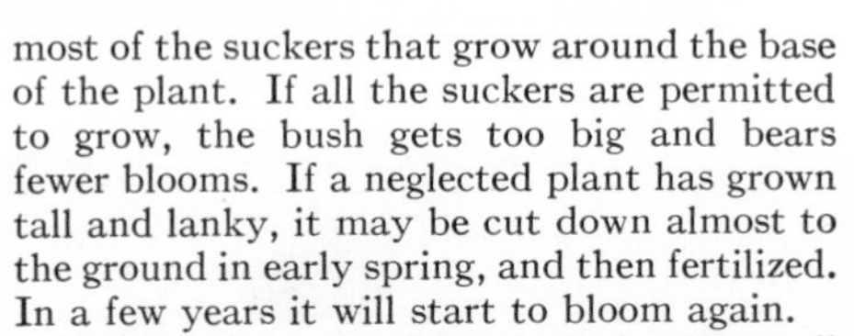

most of the suckers that grow around the base of the plant. If all the suckers are permitted to grow, the bush gets too big and bears fewer blooms. If a neglected plant has grown tall and lanky, it may be cut down almost to the ground in early spring, and then fertilized. In a few years it will start to bloom again.

Scale on the stems is controlled with an oil spray in early spring before growth starts. Borers sometimes make holes in the canes; in this case, cut off the injured branch below the borer hole and burn it.

(*Left*) **Pinkish mauve Katharine Havemeyer and creamy white Mme. Casimir Perier are hybrids introduced by the Lemoine firm of France.**

(*Right*) **Charles X is a very old variety but its vigorous growth and rich reddish purple color keep it in demand.**

(*Left*) **There is nothing demanding about the Regal lily. It is easily managed and is one of the finest of the summer-flowering bulbs.**

(*Below*) **The dainty, bright orange-scarlet Coral lily is lovely in a rock garden. It blooms in June.**

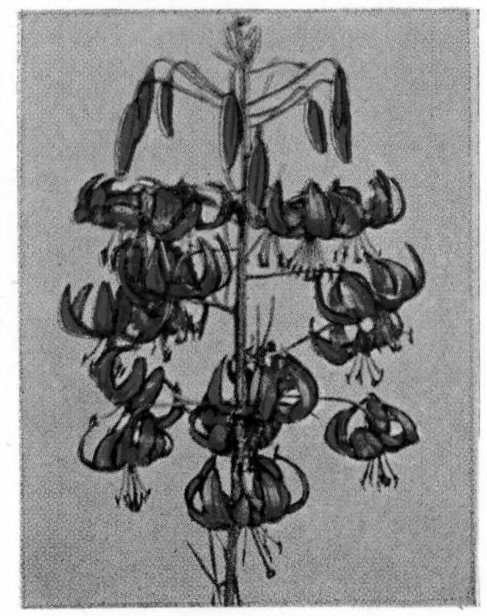

LILIES

FOR centuries the lily has been a symbol of purity and has been vastly admired for its queenly beauty. Many of the most popular garden lilies have been brought to the United States from Japan and China to join those that are native to this continent, and intensive work being done by plant breeders is continually enlarging the long list of desirable varieties. Some kinds are forced by florists, particularly at Easter. With proper choice of varieties, lilies may be had in bloom outdoors from June to October. Heights vary from 18 in. to several feet. Most of them are hardy and need not be disturbed for many years.

Flowers show a delightful variety in both shape and color. They may be big cups facing the sky or at right angles to the stem, they may be trumpet shaped, or may have their petals curled back. Prominent stamens add to the beauty of the bloom. Some varieties are fragrant. Colors range from white to yellow, apricot, orange, pink and crimson.

Garden lilies must have, above all, good drainage. While they tolerate a little shade, better results come from practically full sun; however, the ground must be kept as shaded and moist as possible around them because the roots need a cool space in which to grow. Good garden soil with peat moss or leaf mold added is recommended for most kinds; wood ashes scattered on the surface are also helpful. Delphinium and lilies make a classic picture; other perennials are suitable with lilies also, if not close enough to crowd. It is not good to plant lilies near a brick wall that reflects heat. A shallow-rooted ground cover will help to keep the soil cool. Some lilies send out roots from the bottom of the bulb and also along the lower stem; these require deeper planting than those with bottom roots only.

Easter lilies should be kept watered even after the bloom is gone. Then when frost is over, the plant can be lifted out of the pot and set in the open ground. If it does not bloom again that summer, the next season

(*Left*) **Fragrant Madonna lilies, exquisite in a June border. The bulbs require very shallow planting in late summer. This is said to be one of the oldest varieties in existence.**

(*Right*) **Gold-banded lilies carry their big fragrant flowers on stems 4 ft. tall or more.**

(*Left*) A double form of the Tiger lily, which makes a brilliant showing late in the summer. The stiff stems are about 4 ft. tall.

(*Above*) The Rubrum or Red Speciosum lily is a deeper pink when planted in part shade. The blooms are delightful in August.

(*Left*) The Croft strain of Easter lily. Bulbs that have been forced for indoor bloom may be set outdoors in the open ground when frost is over, with other summer bulbs, but they cannot be forced a second time.

should find it flowering in July and August. It is hardy about as far north as New York.

Varieties. Most popular of garden lilies is *Regal*, with large white trumpets streaked pink on the outside. Blooming in July, it is easy to grow and perfectly hardy. Bulbs should be set 8 to 9 in. deep. *Madonna* is among the earliest and most fragrant. Its snowy blooms march up a 3-ft. stem in June. It looks best in masses, and needs to be planted only 2 in. deep, in early September. Lime is good for this one. *Gold-banded* lilies are huge cups of ivory-white, banded yellow and spotted reddish brown. This kind blooms

(*Right*) Enchantment is a vigorous hybrid lily with huge, glowing nasturtium - red blooms borne upright in large heads.

from July to September and should be set 6 to 8 in. deep. The hardy *Rubrum* is a lovely crimson-spotted pink, with petals curled back. It comes in late summer and is planted 6 to 8 in. deep. *Tiger*, so easy to please that it often escapes from a garden and grows wild, is orange-red spotted purplish. Plant it 6 to 8 in. deep in late fall. The *Coral* lily is a charmer in rock gardens, for it grows only 18 in. high. The small, nodding scarlet flowers have sharply curled petals. About 4 to 5 in. is a good planting depth.

Lily specialists can supply many spectacular strains with flowers of unbelievable size and rich coloring. The very hardy *Mid-Century Hybrids* come in many shades. *Enchantment*, with upright, orange-red flowers

(*Upper Left*) Bellingham Hybrid lilies have been produced from wild kinds growing on the West Coast. They are very desirable for cutting and for informal woodland planting. (*Upper Right*) Golden Clarion, a sturdy strain growing about 5 ft. tall and blooming freely in July.

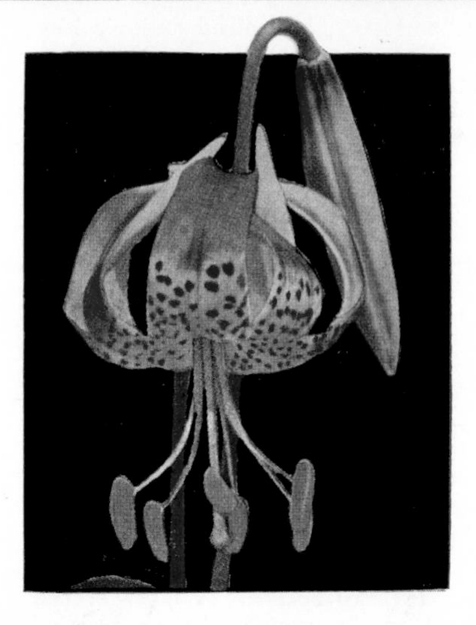

(*Right*) Pardalinum or Leopard lily has spotted orange-yellow flowers. It prefers moist but well-drained soil and a little shade.

(*Left*) Strong but slender stems carry the Formosanum lilies. The exquisite fragrant trumpets appear in September.

(*Right*) Aurelian Hybrids, vigorous and hardy, having trumpet - like flowers in many beautiful colors.

(*Left*) **Henryi retains its deep orange-yellow color best when growing in part shade. It does well in a border and requires no special treatment.**

(*Right*) **Umbellatum lilies are held up to the sun in early summer. Growing only 2 to 2½ ft. high, they are well suited for a spot near the front of a perennial border.**

in June and July, is healthy and vigorous. *Olympic Hybrids* are tall trumpet lilies in delightful colors. You can pay $6.00 or more for a bulb of some of the newest lilies, but about 65c will buy one of the older standard kinds. It is important to buy disease-free bulbs from a reliable dealer.

How and When to Plant. Madonna lilies must be planted in late August or no later than early September, and only 2 in. deep. Other lily bulbs should be obtained as early as possible in the fall and planted immediately. They must not be allowed to dry out. If bulbs are late in arriving, keep a spot ready for them in the garden. If necessary, cover it with straw to prevent the ground from freezing before the bulbs are planted. Put a handful of sand under each bulb when planting. Allow 18 in. between tall lilies, less for low growers.

Care and Protection. A layer of peat moss kept on the ground all summer is advisable unless nearby plants keep the soil shaded. In early spring scatter a little fertilizer on the ground and dig it in very lightly. Do not cut the stems all the way down when flowers fade; let them die naturally. In cold climates spread evergreen branches around the plants after the ground freezes. As long as the lilies grow and bloom well, do not disturb them.

(*Left*) **Flamingo has very large, wide-petaled flowers of firm substance, facing upward. This is a very strong grower.**

(*Left*) **Superbum is a native American lily of great landscape value, especially where it can be given a green background. It likes moist, lime-free soil.**

(*Right*) **Martagon, a robust European species with a long history, is sometimes called the Turks-cap lily. The dull purple petals are spotted with black.**

LILY OF THE VALLEY

WHEN you sniff and admire lily of the valley, you are following the example of artists, poets and just plain gardeners who have long sung its praises. Not only are the dainty, fragrant bells lovely for bouquets, but the plant is a splendid ground cover for shady places. Even under trees it readily forms a good colony and blooms freely in April and May, provided it has soil rich in leaf mold. Thin dry soil will not support lily of the valley.

These plants, 8 to 10 in. high, are entirely hardy. The broad leaves are ornamental even when flowers are absent. Florists raise and use lily of the valley all the year round; they call it "valley lily."

Varieties. Besides the familiar *White* (about 6 for $1.50), there is *Pink* lily of the valley.

How and When to Plant. Plant outdoors in spring or fall, in deeply dug and fertilized soil, setting the roots (called pips) 6 in. apart and 1 in. deep.

To grow indoors, buy pips that have been in cold storage and plant them in special potting soil, 1 in. apart, in a 6-in. pot. Keep them in the dark for two weeks, and gradually bring them into the light as they sprout. About four weeks is required from planting to blooming stage. Potfuls already planted are easily available.

Care and Protection. Give an outdoor bed extra leaf mold over winter and fertilizer in the spring. Otherwise, don't disturb.

(*Above*) If you have a damp, shady spot with plenty of leaf mold in the soil, you can have a flourishing bed of fragrant lily of the valley. (*Right*) Indoors, too, it is an easy matter to bring a potful into bloom when you use pips that have been held in cold storage.

LILY OF THE VALLEY SHRUB

ITS drooping white flowers are responsible for the common name of this excellent evergreen shrub, although they are much

more tightly clustered than those of real lily of the valley. Pieris and andromeda are its more formal names. One kind is a native of southeastern United States and is hardy to southern Illinois and New England. In northern regions it needs a protected location.

Like leucothoe, this is a fine addition to mixed plantings of evergreen shrubs. It reaches a height of about 6 ft. but is slow growing. Moist soil, somewhat acid, is needed, and full sun or light shade. More flowers are produced if the plant is not in deep shade.

Because the flower buds are to be seen all winter long, this is a very interesting shrub that always draws attention. The dark evergreen foliage shows off the tight white buds perfectly. At a doorway or in a place where it may easily be seen from the house, lily of the valley shrub is a valuable accent in the landscape all the year round.

Varieties. *Mountain* andromeda, 4 to 6 ft. tall, is the native kind, blooming in late April. Its flowers grow in rather upright clusters; the small foliage is dull dark green all year. The *Japanese* variety, although less hardy, is more often cultivated in gardens because the flower clusters are larger and the leaves are large, dark and glossy. New foliage in spring is a coppery shade. The handsome buds give the 6 to 10-ft. plant a lacy appearance all winter. Plants sell for $2.00 up.

How and When to Plant. Mix leaf mold or peat moss with the soil before planting. Set out the plant in spring or early fall, and be sure the soil is firmed well around it. Water well. Spread leaf mold or peat moss on top of the ground.

Care and Protection. Keep this layer on the ground permanently, adding to it when necessary. Never use lime nearby. No pruning is needed, but cut off the old flowers before they go to seed.

(*Above*) Lily of the valley shrub is a valuable ornamental all year round. It can stand some shade, although too much of it results in fewer flowers. (*Left*) The clusters of buds are to be seen all winter.

(*Right*) Liriope Muscari (described on the following page) adapts itself easily to a variety of growing conditions in both the North and the South.

Lobelia is a good edging plant that blooms all summer. (*Above*) Cambridge Blue, with masses of light blue flowers on 5 to 6-in. plants. (*Left*) Rosamond, with white-centered, deep carmine-red blooms.

LIRIOPE

(*Illustration on preceding page*)

CLUMPS of liriope (lihr-rye'oh-pee) have grass-like foliage, but this border and edging plant is a member of the lily family. It has a tropical air and is popular all through the southern part of the country, but may also be grown as far north as New York because it stands the cold well. Very dry gravelly soil will grow liriope (also known as lily turf), but moist, richer soil is equally acceptable. Either heavy shade or full sun suits it. In the shade the foliage will be darker green, but in the sun the flower spikes of blue or lilac will be more plentiful. It blooms from late spring all through summer and is a good partner for daylilies. As a ground cover and border plant it finds wide use. When full grown, it reaches about 15 in. in height.

Varieties. *Muscari*, with broad dark leaves and dense spikes of lavender-blue flowers, is a fine edger for walks. *Spicata*, excellent as a ground cover, has narrower foliage. *Bluespire* begins blooming in May; *Lilac Beauty* has flowers from June to August. Some varieties have variegated foliage. Clumps average 50c each.

How and When to Plant. For an edging, set the plants about a foot apart, any time when the ground is not frozen.

Care and Protection. After four or five years, clumps may be divided and replanted.

LOBELIA

THIS popular edger has been developed from a plant that is a native of the Cape of Good Hope. Its masses of blue flowers, borne all summer long, are great favorites for edging beds and borders and for rock gardens. The 4 to 6-in. plant spreads easily and makes a compact mound in either full sun or light shade. A trailing kind is useful for pots and window boxes. The perennial cardinal flower, requiring rich, moist soil and a shady spot and producing stout, 2½-ft. spikes of bloom, is a relative of this little edging plant, although in appearance the two are quite different.

Varieties. *Crystal Palace Compacta*, with masses of dark blue flowers and bronzy foliage, clear light blue *Cambridge Blue*, and *Mrs. Clibran*, with white-eyed, dark blue flowers, are the blue kinds usually planted. Carmine-red *Rosamond*, with white eye, provides variety, as does *White Lady*. *Sapphire* is a deep blue, white-eyed, trailing variety for hanging baskets and porch boxes.

How and When to Plant. Buy plants in small boxes (75c to $1.00 per dozen) or larger plants in pots (about 25c each), and set them out after frost has gone. Space them 6 in. apart in ordinary garden soil.

Care and Protection. Cutting plants back in midseason and feeding them will prolong their blooming season.

LOVE IN A MIST

FOR cutting and for massing in a border of annuals, this is a popular plant even if not a spectacular one. The dainty flowers on 12-in. stems are nestled among the finely cut foliage. When used in bouquets they are long lasting, and they mix well with other flowers. Blooms are produced for several weeks, starting in July. An easy grower, this annual often self-sows.

Varieties. *Miss Jekyll*, with cornflower-blue flowers, is the most popular variety; there is also a white form. *Nigella* is the scientific name.

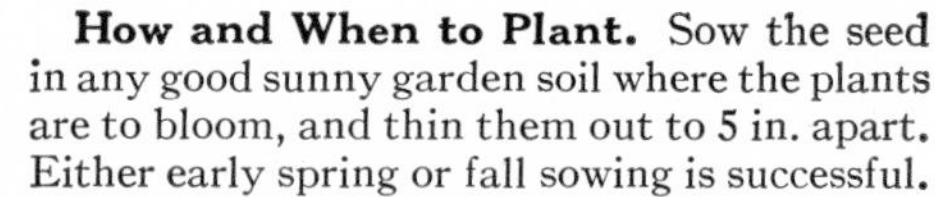

How and When to Plant. Sow the seed in any good sunny garden soil where the plants are to bloom, and thin them out to 5 in. apart. Either early spring or fall sowing is successful.

Care and Protection. These plants are not easy to move. Be sure to thin them out adequately.

LOVE LIES BLEEDING

ORNAMENTAL foliage in many bright colors makes these tender annuals popular for summer beds. They grow 3 to 5 ft. tall and are used as background material. The flowers may be dried for winter bouquets. Full sun and ordinary or even poor garden soil will give best results. Amaranth and summer poinsettia are other names used.

Varieties. *Amaranthus caudatus* has bright red flowers. *Molten Fire* has bronzy crimson leaves with a scarlet tuft at the tip of the stem. *Joseph's Coat* get its name from its mingling of scarlet, yellow and bronze-green.

How and When to Plant. Start the seed indoors or sow it in the open as soon as the soil is warm. Plants should be spaced 12 to 18 in. apart.

Care and Protection. Be careful to place these plants so that the colored foliage does not detract from neighboring flowers.

LOVE seems here to be in a predicament of one kind or another. (*Above*) Love in a mist, an annual especially nice for cutting. (*Left*) Love lies bleeding, grown for its colorful leaves as well as its bright flowers.

(*Above*) Blue and pink forms of perennial lupine. (*Left*) The Russell Strain, with giant spikes in a great variety of colors. (*Upper Right*) Foot-high Texas Bluebonnets, an annual form of lupine.

LUPINE

THE graceful spires of lupine are fine for both cutting and garden decoration. The newest strains bear spikes 3 to 4 ft. tall, in practically all colors, with individual florets shaped like pea blossoms. Foliage of soft green is attractive until after the blooms are gone, when it deteriorates. June sees the plants at the height of their beauty.

Where summers are hot and dry, it is almost impossible to succeed with perennial lupine. It likes the cool damp atmosphere of New England and the Pacific Northwest, but in many other regions it will not survive. Soil must be light and well drained; a location in full sun but protected from hot drying winds is desirable. The stately spires go well with irises, poppies and delphinium in early summer borders. When contented, a lupine plant forms a 2 to 3-ft. clump.

Annual lupines are raised yearly from seed sown in spring. Plants should be thinned to stand 8 to 10 in. apart.

Varieties. The *Russell Strain* is outstanding among perennial lupines. It has thick-set spikes with many color combinations. *Hartwegi,* with blue, white and rose-colored flowers, is the annual kind generally planted. The *Texas Bluebonnet,* with purplish and white flowers on 12-in. plants, is another annual lupine.

How and When to Plant. Set out lupine plants in early spring or fall, about 18 in. apart. Potted plants (at about 75c) are recommended.

Care and Protection. Water well in dry weather. Remove seed pods at once, but let the foliage die of its own accord. Where winters are severe, provide a light ground cover of evergreen boughs or buckwheat hulls.

LYCHNIS

ONE common form of this plant is popularly called Maltese or Jerusalem cross, and another is German catchfly. The botanical name *Lychnis* (lik'niss) covers both. These are hardy perennials with large heads of bright-colored flowers from late May through July. Very undemanding, they have been favorites for summer gardens for many years. Use them in sunny borders where they will have well-drained, sandy soil rather than heavy clay that holds water during the winter.

Varieties. *Maltese* or *Jerusalem Cross,* 3 ft. tall, has flat clusters of bright scarlet flowers in June and July. It does well beside streams, as well as in borders. It is planted all over the United States. The *German Catchfly* gets its name from the sticky stems (German, presumably from its native home). Its rosy pink flowers bloom in early summer. There is also a *Double* variety, hardy anywhere, with rosy red blooms that are excellent for cutting. Plants average 65c each.

How and When to Plant. Early spring planting is preferable, but fall is possible also. Set several plants in a group, with an allowance of 8 to 15 in. apiece.

Care and Protection. Every third year, dig up, divide and replant the clump.

(*Above*) Maltese or Jerusalem Cross is an old-fashioned hardy perennial with brilliant scarlet flowers. It has been grown in gardens of Europe and America for several centuries.

(*Left*) Double lychnis, bearing its large heads of deep rose-pink on stiff stems, is a fine cut flower.

Three varieties of lythrum. (*Above*) Rosalie, with soft rose-pink flowers on 2-ft. spikes. (*Left*) Robert, a newer variety only 18 in. tall. (*Right*) Morden's Pink, a profuse bloomer all summer.

LYTHRUM

IN many parts of the United States this sturdy and self-reliant perennial (also called purple loosestrife) has "gone native" and made itself at home along the banks of streams and in low wet shaded spots. Any garden having similar growing conditions can take advantage of this willingness to endure poorly drained soil. But lythrum (lith'rum) will also grow in sunny locations where the soil is not very good. This ability to thrive almost anywhere makes it a valuable plant. Not only is it easy to please but it blooms over a long span of time.

The rosy purple flowers are carried in long spikes from early summer through September, with July and August finding them at their peak just when garden borders need them. They are used for cutting, too, and may well be combined with delphinium. The vigorous, 3 to 4-ft. plant is perfectly hardy anywhere.

Varieties. The Morden Experiment Station in Manitoba, Canada, has produced some beautiful new varieties. *Morden's Pink* makes a big, showy, deep pink clump, with many spikes to a plant, from June to September. It is a neat grower, 3 to 4 ft. tall, as is *Morden's Gleam*, the nearest red of the family. *Morden's Rose* is a fine newcomer. The older *Dropmore Purple* is fuchsia-purple in color. About 70c will buy a lythrum plant.

How and When to Plant. For best effect, plant in fall or early spring in groups of three, with 2 ft. allowed per plant.

Care and Protection. Cut off the faded flower spikes. Give a neighbor a piece of the root, if you like, simply by taking a section from the edge of the clump without disturbing the remainder.

MADEIRA VINE

IN the South this fast-growing, tropical climber sometimes takes more than its allotted space, for it is a vigorous vine reaching 15 ft. or more in a season. The glossy light green, heart-shaped leaves are about 3 in. long, and in late summer there are small feathery white flowers, profuse and fragrant. The vine, growing from a tender tuberous root, throws out tendrils by which it clings to fences and arbors. It is useful for quick effects. If protected, it may be grown north to New York.

Varieties. *Boussingaultia* is the scientific name, but Madeira vine easily identifies it. A tuber is very inexpensive—25c or less.

How and When to Plant. Plant in the spring after the weather has become warm, setting the tuber 4 in. deep.

Care and Protection. In cold areas give the roots a light cover over winter, or dig and store them in a cool place.

MAGNOLIA

A MAGNOLIA tree in bloom is lord of the garden. How these magnificent flowers manage to appear so soon after a cold winter is one of nature's mysteries. They never fail to attract admiring attention. Several kinds grow into very large trees, but fortunately there are some small enough to be included in gardens of modest size. There they are a point of great interest as the huge, fragrant blooms push their way out of their mossy covering in late April or early May, to be followed by correspondingly large leaves. Some are evergreen trees, but they are not hardy in the North.

Magnolias grow with little care in sunny, well-drained soil. Those commonly planted in gardens are hardy from Missouri northeastward to southern Massachusetts. A 2-ft. tree costs $5.00 to $6.00.

Madeira vine will quickly provide a green curtain from tubers planted as soon as warm weather comes.

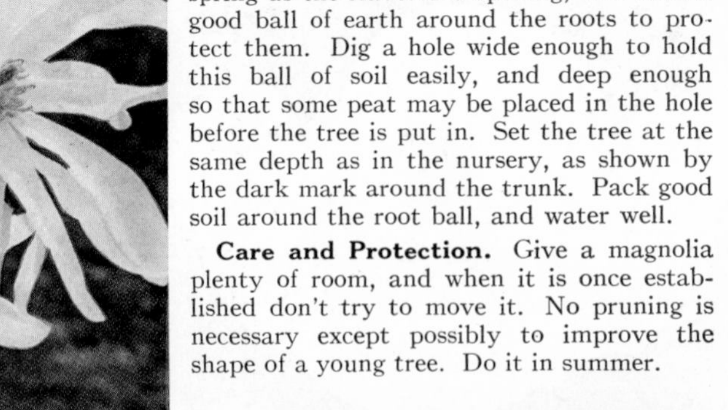

How and When to Plant. Plant in the spring as the leaves are opening, and have a good ball of earth around the roots to protect them. Dig a hole wide enough to hold this ball of soil easily, and deep enough so that some peat may be placed in the hole before the tree is put in. Set the tree at the same depth as in the nursery, as shown by the dark mark around the trunk. Pack good soil around the root ball, and water well.

Care and Protection. Give a magnolia plenty of room, and when it is once established don't try to move it. No pruning is necessary except possibly to improve the shape of a young tree. Do it in summer.

Varieties. Earliest and hardiest is the *Star* magnolia. It has long-petaled, waxy white flowers on a large shrub or small tree growing about 12 ft. tall. In cold sections late frost may nip the flowers, and there this variety is best given a northern exposure. There is also a pink form. *Saucer* magnolia is popular and widely planted. This is a 20 to 25-ft. tree that sometimes has several trunks like a birch clump, and starts to bloom at a very early age. Its 5-in., cupped white flowers, streaked pinkish purple on the outside, come before the leaves. This variety does well in city gardens in the North. Other forms of it have deeper purple markings. *Grandiflora* or *Bull Bay* is a large evergreen tree native in the South, but not reliably hardy north of Washington, D. C. The showy, fragrant blooms of summer are followed by cone-like fruits; foliage is thick and glossy. This is the state tree of Louisiana and Mississippi. (*See illustrations of the Grandiflora blossom and seed pod on the next page.*)

(*Above*) Star magnolia sends out its starry white blooms to greet the early spring.

(*Right*) Saucer magnolia, sturdy and picturesque, is very popular in city gardens in the North.

(*Left*) A close view of the giant blooms of Saucer magnolia.

(*Right*) A dark form of Saucer magnolia, with the reverse of the petals a deep reddish purple.

(*Left*) Magnolia Grandiflora bears these magnificent blooms for several months on a tall, impressive tree native in the South.

(*Right*) The large seed pods of Magnolia Grandiflora stand out strikingly above the thick, polished leaves.

MALVAVISCUS

THE attractive, drooping scarlet flowers of this southern shrub never open wide. They are very showy against the evergreen foliage over a long season—through the winter and more or less all year except in midsummer. Malvaviscus (mal-vuh-viss′kus), or turks' cap, is a fast grower to 6 or 8 ft. in ordinary soil and full sun. It is widely planted from mid-Florida down through the lower South, where it makes a nice specimen or hedge.

Varieties. *Grandiflorus* is the variety commonly used. It is a vigorous and willing grower. There is also a creamy white form.

How and When to Plant. Potted plants (about $1.00) may be set out in the South at any season.

Care and Protection. In spring, cut back the old flowering shoots after the blooms have faded.

(*Left*) Malvaviscus, a fast-growing evergreen shrub for the South, displays these pendent flowers over a long season.

MARIGOLDS

MARIGOLDS, petunias and zinnias constitute the "big three" all-purpose, basic annuals. Marigolds are undemanding, always reliable, and unceasing in their production of bloom from July until frost blackens the stalks. They hold their own in a mixed planting with such perennials as hardy asters and chrysanthemums.

In color, marigolds range from lemon and gold through all the shades of yellow and orange to brown and mahogany. Some have flowers hardly less spectacular than show chrysanthemums; others are looser petaled like carnations, while various kinds have full crested centers surrounded by guard petals. Heights run from 4 ft. down to 6 in. All may be cut with a lavish hand. Indoors they are very long lasting.

The strong scent of the foliage is objectionable to some persons, but several kinds now available are odorless. A search for a pure white marigold has been going on for several seasons; each year finds a new variety that is closer to the goal.

Natives of North America, marigolds are nevertheless classed as African and French, although an attempt is being made to call them American and have them declared the national flower.

Varieties. The tallest marigolds, the African, need a position at the rear of a planting, for they grow to 3 or 4 ft. *Crackerjack* is one of them, with very double flowers

(*Right*) Guinea Gold has broad waved petals of brilliant orange-gold.

(*Below*) Cupid marigolds bear large, very double flowers on a plant only 8 in. tall. The foliage is scentless.

(*Left*) Three tall African marigolds. (*Top*) Dixie Sunshine, a late bloomer. (*Center*) A richly hued specimen of Guinea Gold. (*Bottom*) Yellow Supreme, mildly fragrant.

(*Above*) Crackerjack, among the earliest blooming of the large-flowered marigolds. The always double flowers range through primrose, yellow, gold and orange.

(*Below*) Spun Gold marigold, excellent for low borders and edgings as well as potting, presents a nice color contrast with Blue Mink ageratum.

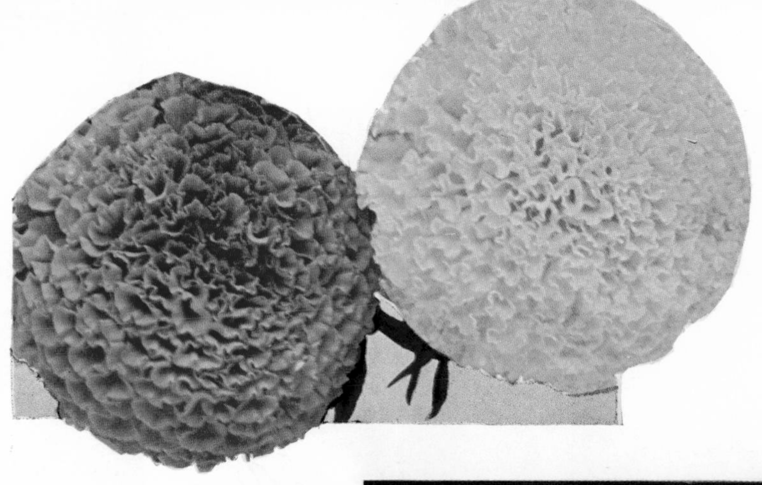

(*Above*) The heavy orange blooms of Toreador and the clear light yellow ones of Yellow Climax are carried on 2½-ft. plants. (*Left*) Glitters could easily serve as a stand-in for a big florist's chrysanthemum.

produced early, on a compact plant. The *Climax* hybrids have huge flowers up to 5 in. across, with ruffled and frilled petals, in both separate and mixed colors. *Toreador* is a popular orange one of the Climax type. *Crown of Gold* is a good chrysanthemum-flowered kind with odorless foliage and golden orange flowers with a broad-petaled collar. *Mammoth Mum* and *Glitters* are big-flowered varieties on stout stems. *Spun Gold*, with early incurved flowers on a plant only a foot high, is fine for low beds and borders.

Among the good carnation-flowered African marigolds are two new ones, *Hawaii* and *Alaska*. Both are 2 ft. tall, the former with odorless foliage and rich orange blooms, the latter light primrose. Others of this type are *Guinea Gold* and *Yellow Supreme*. The *Cupid* series is another with scentless foliage. The large, mum-shaped flowers on an 8-in. plant make a splendid showing.

French marigolds, primarily for borders and massing, are both double and single. The

(*Above*) Butterball, a French marigold of the Harmony type, is a dwarf grower blanketed with these soft butter-yellow blooms for many weeks in summer.

(*Above*) Spry has a pincushion center of bright yellow and a skirt of mahogany-red. Only 9 to 10 in. tall, it grows easily anywhere and is a splendid edging plant.

(*Below*) Flash, a dwarf single marigold that is an early and continuous bloomer. The flowers, less than 2 in. across, are tangerine, red, bronze and yellow.

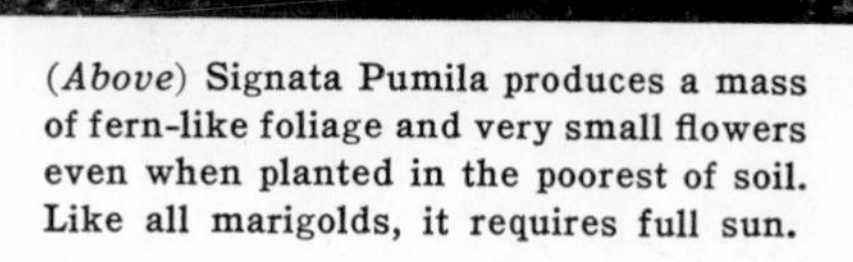

(*Above*) Signata Pumila produces a mass of fern-like foliage and very small flowers even when planted in the poorest of soil. Like all marigolds, it requires full sun.

(*Left*) Red Head becomes bronzy in color as it gets older. The sturdy plants form a compact mound a foot tall and up to 20 in. broad.

(*Right*) Color Magic is a mixture of striped and mottled flowers as well as solid reds and yellows. It grows 8 in. high and blooms very early.

Petite series was bred for uniform low growth, early bloom, and profusion of flowers. The 6-in. plants spread to about 12 in. Fully double *Gypsy* and the older *Spry* with crested center are other recommended 10-in.-high kinds for edging. *Harmony Hybrids*, 12 to 15 in. tall, have 1½-in. crested flowers. Among the singles are *Naughty Marietta*, *Red Head* and *Flash*.

Signata Pumila, only 10 in. tall, with fern-like foliage and tiny single flowers, is a fine edging plant.

How and When to Plant. Sow the seed outdoors in May, either in rows or here and there, as you wish. Or buy the plants by the dozen. Give the plants space; they need it. Tallest kinds should be 18 to 24 in. apart, lower ones 12 in. They require full sun, and they get along well in a hot, dry location.

Care and Protection. Marigolds can pretty well look after themselves. Light-colored kinds may attract Japanese beetles. The tallest varieties will probably need staking. The more you cut the flowers, the better.

(*Left*) Naughty Marietta, another attractive little single marigold. The foot-high plants are very showy in beds and borders.

(*Below*) Uniformly low-growing Petite marigolds have small double crested flowers. Here they are bordering a bed of zinnias.

(*Left*) Mariposa lily received this name from the Spanish word meaning *butterfly,* because the markings on the flowers are similar to those on a butterfly's wings.

(*Right*) Aquilegifolium meadow-rue has fine-cut foliage like that of columbine. It blooms from May into early summer. (*Below*) Lavender Mist bears large, loose heads of lavender and yellow in either full sun or a little shade.

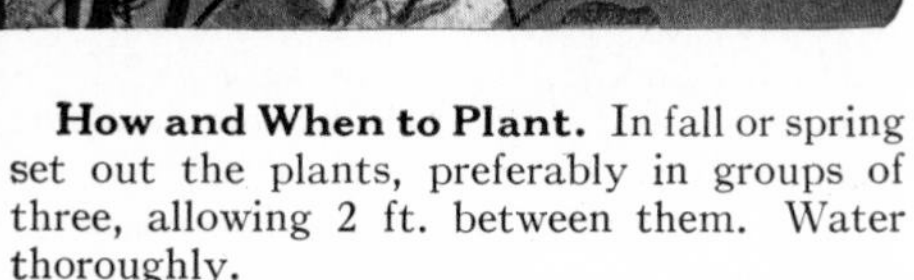

MARIPOSA LILY

IN the West this dainty flower of the lily family grows in light, sandy soil where the bulbs are dry all summer. Often they are planted in raised beds. The cupped blooms are 3 to 5 in. across when fully open, with dots and pencilings of many colors. They are carried on stems about a foot tall in late spring or early summer. Globe tulip, another member of the family, has nodding flowers. Well-drained soil is an absolute necessity; leaf mold and charcoal are helpful additions for most garden soils.

Varieties. *Calochortus venustus* and its several varieties offer many colors with interesting blotches and markings. *Vesta* has white flowers flushed lilac or rose and spotted brown. Bulbs are priced at $2.50 to $3.00 per dozen.

How and When to Plant. Plant the bulbs in the fall, 2 to 3 in. deep, preferably on a slope where drainage is perfect. Give them a thick cover of leaves or straw over winter, to avoid alternate freezing and thawing.

Care and Protection. In the West the bulbs may be left in the ground after they have bloomed. In other areas it is best to dig them up after the foliage has ripened, and store them in a dry place over summer.

MEADOW-RUE

LIGHT and airy in foliage and flower, this hardy plant is good both in the garden and for cutting. Most kinds are quite tall and must be placed at the back of a border. The leaves are fine-cut, and small flowers of white, rose, lilac and yellow are carried in big branching clusters. With heavy flowers like heliopsis, strong spikes like delphinium and bright colors like phlox, meadow-rue (or *Thalictrum*) is extremely attractive because it furnishes such fine contrast in feeling. It does well in fairly moist garden soil where it will receive full sun or a little shade.

Varieties. In late summer *Lavender Mist*, 4 to 5 ft. tall, is most attractive in a perennial border. It bears masses of delicate lavender and yellow flowers. *Aquilegifolium*, not so tall, with gray-green foliage and feathery lavender, pink and white flowers, is nice near tulips in May. *Glaucum* has dusty blue-gray foliage and light yellow blooms in midsummer. Plants cost around 85c each.

How and When to Plant. In fall or spring set out the plants, preferably in groups of three, allowing 2 ft. between them. Water thoroughly.

Care and Protection. Occasionally, but not every year, plants may have to be dug up, divided and replanted in spring.

MEADOW SAFFRON

AMONG horticultural curiosities, this hardy bulb of the lily family ranks with hardy amaryllis. Both produce their flowers after the foliage has matured and disappeared. Meadow saffron (*Colchicum*, botanically) is often confused with autumn-flowering crocus because the flowers are somewhat similar in

Meadow saffron has the surprising habit of leafing in spring and flowering in autumn. Plant the bulbs in groups.

(*Above*) **Mexican tulip poppies (Sunlite is shown) grow and bloom quickly from seed sown in late spring.**

(*Left*) **Mexican sunflowers can get along with little water and fertilizer if they receive lots of sunshine. Pictured here is the popular variety, Torch.**

shape and appear in the fall. Colors are white and shades of lilac and violet.

This bulb is easy to grow in good garden soil. Give it a sunny or partly shaded location in a rock garden or under shrubs. Even in an open tray in a sunny window, without soil or water, it will bloom in the autumn. Outdoors it needs the masking foliage of other plants, such as low creepers, at the time it blooms.

Varieties. White *Album Plenum*, violet-mauve *Autumn Queen*, lilac-mauve *The Giant*, and deep violet *Violet Queen* are among the popular varieties. A bulb costs about 75c.

How and When to Plant. Plant the bulbs in August in groups of at least three. Set them 2 in. deep and 6 to 9 in. apart. They will bloom later that fall, and the foliage will grow the following spring.

Care and Protection. Do not disturb the bulbs or take them up over winter. Let the foliage die naturally without being cut.

MEXICAN SUNFLOWER

QUICK and easy, this is a robust annual with large, coarse leaves and big bold, daisy-like flowers, 3 to 4 in. across. It may very well be a relic of the ancient civilization of the Incas, for it is also known as golden flower of the Incas and it grows wild in Mexico and Central America. Because it is so sturdy and tall it should not be tried in a small garden, but for background planting where a space filler is needed it can be very useful. The flowers, blooming in late summer and early fall, are fine for cutting. They need full sun and a long growing season. *Tithonia* is the botanical name.

Varieties. Fiery orange-red *Torch*, with golden yellow center, is the most popular variety. Its lower growth (4 ft.) and earlier blooming season are improvements over the older kinds. The leaves are velvety gray-green.

How and When to Plant. Sow outdoors as soon as the ground is reasonably warm, in any soil. Thin the plants to 3 to 4 ft. apart.

Care and Protection. If these plants receive too much water or fertilizer, they may produce more foliage than flowers.

MEXICAN TULIP POPPY

THIS isn't a tulip, but a Mexican member of the poppy family. The sturdy, 18 to 24-in. plant with grayish green, fine-cut leaves is nice for midsummer bloom in borders. Its cupped yellow blooms, like a big California poppy, are especially attractive near blue flowers. If picked in the bud, they last very well indoors. Give them full sun and dry sandy soil.

Varieties. *Hunnemannia fumariaefolia* has large, single yellow flowers. A newer one, canary-yellow *Sunlite*, is semi-double.

How and When to Plant. Sow the seed outdoors when settled warm weather has arrived, and thin out the little plants to stand 9 in. apart.

Care and Protection. Don't try to move the plants from the place where seed was sown. Like other poppies, this one resents being disturbed.

MIGNONETTE

HERE's another "grandmother" plant, grown for many years in many countries for its delicate fragrance. Because its soft colors—greenish white to yellow and reddish—are not showy and the plant is sometimes a rather loose grower, it is best kept in a spot by itself, primarily for cutting rather than for garden show. For mixing with other flowers in bouquets, mignonette is a favorite.

This foot-high plant can stand some shade and it prefers cool weather. It needs moderately rich, well-drained, non-acid soil.

Varieties. *Old-fashioned Sweet-scented* is a popular kind, as well as *Machet* with red and yellow flowers over a long season, and *Red Monarch* with deep red flowers in a large truss on a compact plant.

How and When to Plant. The seed is very small. It should be sown sparingly and given a very light covering of soil. Do it in May and again in August if fall bloom is especially wanted. Thin young plants to 6 to 9 in. apart, and pinch them back to make them bushier.

Care and Protection. Don't try to transplant mignonette. If the soil is heavy, mix some sand and a little lime in it.

Three varieties of mignonette. (*Left*) Old-fashioned Sweet-scented. (*Above*) Machet. (*Right*) Red Monarch. Fairly rich, well-drained soil will give quantities of bloom for cutting.

(*Left*) **Virginal mock orange is a strong grower that sometimes continues to bloom more or less through the summer.**

(*Right*) **Minnesota Snowflake mock orange was developed especially for northern regions. It can stand temperatures well below zero.**

MOCK ORANGE

ALTHOUGH mock orange bushes bloom for only a short while in early summer and are leafless all winter, they are loved for their fragrance. These are old-fashioned shrubs grown for many years, but through the work of plant hybridizers newer kinds with larger blooms are also offered. All are white flowered, but some are single and others double or semi-double. Some are much more fragrant than others. There are varieties with dense, compact growth only 5 to 7 ft. high, while others are as much as 12 ft. in both height and width. Some are more graceful than others.

For an easy bush that does not demand much attention, mock orange is a good choice. It is used in a border with other shrubs, where its thick foliage helps to make a fine screen. Any soil and location are acceptable, in either full sun or very light shade. Hardy to New England, the bushes start to bloom while quite young.

Varieties. *Sweet* mock orange is the old-time single-flowered, very sweet-scented kind that blooms profusely in late May and June. It stands dry soil well, and reaches 10 ft. or over in height and breadth. A number of different forms of it are available; one of these is *Golden* mock orange with yellow leaves. It should be used as a contrast plant. *Virginal* has semi-double, white flowers in June, and a wonderful perfume like orange blossoms. An upright grower 6 to 8 ft. tall, this is rather bare at the base and is best planted behind other shrubs and perennials that will hide its lower canes. *Minnesota Snowflake*, with large, very double, sweet flowers, has a well-shaped bush of moderate height, while double *Frosty Morn* is a low grower only 3 to 4 ft. high. A 2 to 3-ft. plant may be had for $1.50 to $2.00.

How and When to Plant. Spring or fall is the time to plant. Dig a hole of good size for the roots, pack the soil hard, and water thoroughly.

Care and Protection. Low-growing kinds bloom better if they are pruned every year just after the flowering season. Branches that have bloomed should be cut back quite hard. Some of the old canes of larger growing varieties may be cut back to the ground when the bush gets out of bounds, but this need not be done every year. All pruning must be carried out immediately after the flowers fade.

MONKSHOOD

THE rich blue spikes of monkshood do much the same for late summer gardens that is accomplished by delphinium earlier in the season. Some varieties grow as high as 4 ft. or more, but others are not so tall. The violet and blue colors are welcome with red, orange and yellow, especially with asters and chrysanthemums in early fall. The dark

(*Left*) **Silver Showers, a fine dwarf mock orange only 3 ft. tall—just a nice size for a small garden.**

(*Right*) **The rich blue color of monkshood is welcome in late summer borders. Napellus, illustrated here, is a well-liked variety.**

Earlham Hybrid montbretias are grown much like gladiolus. They are highly desirable as cut flowers because they last so well.

green, glossy foliage is attractive all season. This is a hardy plant for the rear of a border where it can have rich deep soil and certain shade and moisture. Without them, it is likely to die out. Leaf mold and fertilizer should be mixed with the soil before planting.

Varieties. *Aconitum napellus*, 4 ft. tall, has dark blue flower spikes in late July. *Sparks' Variety* may be a little taller, with violet-blue flowers in July and August. Even more commanding is deep blue *Wilsoni*, which doesn't bloom until September. A lower growing kind is *Fischeri* (2 to 3 ft.), with good glossy foliage and dark blue flowers thickly placed on the spike. About 75c will buy a plant.

How and When to Plant. After preparing the ground well, set out the plants in fall or early spring, allowing them 1½ to 2 ft. of space. Water well.

Care and Protection. Water must be supplied freely in dry spells, and the plants should not be moved or disturbed.

MONTBRETIA

ALTHOUGH the flower stems are branched, montbretia (mont-bree'she-uh) is much like a smaller gladiolus. It too is an extremely long-lasting cut flower that may be planted in rows or in the middle area of a garden border. Attaining a height of 2½ to 3 ft., it has sword-shaped leaves and late-summer blooms in sparkling yellow, gold and orange-red tones. White is a wise choice for neighbors like phlox. Because the stems are so stiff, it is well to have the foliage of other plants nearby to soften the effect.

Montbretia bulbs need full sun and average garden soil that is well drained. They are considered hardy only in regions where mild winters are certain. From Maryland southward it is safe to leave them in the ground over winter if they are planted 6 to 8 in. deep and given light protection.

Varieties. Bulbs in *Mixed* colors average $2.00 per dozen. *Earlham Hybrids* include many bright shades, such as velvety scarlet to gold *His Majesty* and golden *Rheingold.*

How and When to Plant. Plant the bulbs in early spring in groups of at least six, 3 to 4 in. deep and 5 in. apart.

Care and Protection. Keep well watered in dry weather. In cold areas dig up the bulbs in the fall and store in a dry, frostproof place over winter.

MORNING GLORY

THE big trumpets of morning glory, heralding the day, are a far cry from a sweet potato, but actually the plants belong to the same family. These beautiful large flowers—blue, rose, red and white—are produced in greatest freedom on a quick-growing vine with stems that twine readily around wires, fence, trellis or any handy support. In cloudy weather they stay open most of the day, but they soon wilt when the sun strikes them. Next day, along comes a whole new bountiful crop. The vine grows to 15 or 20 ft. and blooms from midsummer to frost. Leaves are heart shaped.

Ordinary soil and a location in full sun or light shade suits morning glories. The best spot is where they will face the morning sun.

Moonflower is an extremely free-growing form that might be called "night glory," for its giant white, very fragrant flowers open at twilight. It makes a dense screen 10 ft. tall.

A recent development is a bush morning glory growing only a foot high. Blooming over a long period, it is fine for beds, edgings and borders.

Varieties. *Heavenly Blue* is said to be the most popular annual vine grown. Its 4-in., silky flowers bring exquisite sky-blue color to the most forlorn fence or post. *Pearly Gates* is a shining white form, and *Scarlett O'Hara* soft rosy red. *Darling* has flowers of wine-red with white throat. New varieties are *Candy Pink* with bright rose-pink flowers that are lovely trailing from a window box, and *Flying Saucers* with blooms delicately striped white and blue. *Royal Ensign* is a bush morning glory with flowers of bright deep blue, centered white.

(*Below*) Scarlett O'Hara morning glory remains open until mid-afternoon. Give the new stems a little help in finding their support.

(*Above*) The blue of the sky comes down within reach when you grow Heavenly Blue morning glory. The vine soon covers a porch or fence.

(*Left*) Candy Pink is the first truly pink morning glory. It is an easily grown variety reaching 15 to 20 ft. in height.

(*Right*) Flying Saucers has many different bright blue and white striped color patterns. Flowers are often 4 in. in diameter.

How and When to Plant. Before planting, soak the seed overnight in warm water to soften its hard coat, or nick it with a file or knife. Wait until the soil is warm to sow it outdoors, beside an arbor or other support. Thin out the plants to 18 in.

Care and Protection. Never give morning glories any fertilizer. If the soil is too rich, they produce leaves but no flowers.

MOUNTAIN ASH

SEVERAL kinds of mountain ash grow wild in North America, but the variety usually cultivated in home gardens is a native of Europe. Since colonial days it has been highly admired for its ornamental foliage and flowers, but especially for the clusters of bright berries that hang from it in late summer.

This is a smallish tree, 18 to 25 ft. in height, with a gracefully spreading top and fern-like, clean dark green foliage. The large, flat clusters of white flowers that cover it in May become brilliant orange-red berries by August. Birds like them so well that they often strip a tree in a short time.

This fine lawn specimen is hardy all over the continent and is even grown in Alaska. Average, well-drained, even somewhat dry soil suits it.

Varieties. *European* mountain ash is the kind generally sold, at about $3.00 to $3.50 for the 4 to 5-ft. size.

How and When to Plant. Trees are planted in spring or fall. Dig a hole of ample size for the roots. Take care not to let them dry out while planting. After setting the tree in position, at the same depth as in the nursery, pack good soil around the roots, being particular not to leave any air pockets. Water thoroughly, and leave the soil surface raked fine.

Care and Protection. Sawdust sometimes appears at the base of the tree, indicating that borers have entered it. Spray 12% DDT on the trunk in the spring, and a second time about three weeks later.

MOUNTAIN LAUREL

BOTH Pennsylvania and Connecticut have chosen the mountain laurel as their state flower, honoring this native evergreen shrub that puts on such a glorious display every spring from New England down through the Appalachians. It grows at the edge of woodlands with azaleas and rhododendrons, in the half shade of large trees. The bushy plant is 10 ft. tall and more, with thick, glossy foliage all year round. In late May and June appear

(*Left*) Mountain ash is a small tree of symmetrical shape, recommended for home planting. The huge clusters of bright berries are attractive.

(*Right*) Mountain laurel likes the same growing conditions as rhododendrons, holly and other broad - leaved evergreens. It is hardy through a wide area.

(*Left*) Mullein grows readily in any warm soil. Both rosy Pink Domino and buff-pink Cotswold Queen are effective in gardens.

(*Right*) Myrtle, Bowles variety, with deep blue flowers on dense-growing plants. Foliage is rich and glossy all the year round.

the large bloom clusters, each flower a little soft pinkish bowl. In their natural setting they gleam against the dark shady background.

Mountain laurel is hardy to the Great Lakes region, and where the growing conditions encountered in the wild can be approximated it can be used with other broad-leaved evergreens in foundation plantings. It is a lovely specimen plant in part shade where there is acid soil, rich and moist. Most garden soils need the addition of plenty of leaf mold or peat moss.

Varieties. The botanical name of mountain laurel—*Kalmia latifolia*—commemorates Peter Kalm, the Swedish botanist and plant scout who explored early America. A 15 to 18-in. plant may cost about $5.00.

How and When to Plant. After putting the soil in good condition by adding leaf mold to it, set out the plant in spring or fall in a hole large enough to hold the roots without crowding. Be careful not to plant too deep.

Care and Protection. A layer of pine needles or peat moss on the ground will help to keep the soil moist. Add to this covering when necessary. Cut off the flower heads as soon as they fade. If the plant grows too tall, it may be cut back hard after it blooms.

MULLEIN

WOOLLY leaves in a big clump at soil level characterize most of this family. Flowers are of shallow saucer shape, borne in early summer on stalks 2 to 3 ft. high. This is a stately plant, easy to grow in almost any sunny soil. At the back of a garden planting it will contribute height and some interest in its foliage as well as its flowers.

Varieties. *Verbascum phoeniceum Hybrids*, in mixed colors, have graceful blooms rising from a rosette of leaves. *Pink Domino* has rose-pink spikes of bloom in June and July. A plant costs 85c to $1.25.

How and When to Plant. Set out in fall or early spring, 8 in. apart. Water well.

Care and Protection. Be sure the soil is well drained.

MYRTLE

IN either sun or shade, myrtle is a very fine evergreen ground cover, good looking all year round. In spring little single blue flowers are sprinkled through the dark glossy leaves. It quickly covers the ground with a neat carpet, for the stems trail along the surface and take root. Myrtle, or periwinkle, is good for keeping a slope from washing away. Like pachysandra, it does an excellent job of covering the bare soil under trees and shrubs, but unlike pachysandra, it will grow equally well in sun or shade.

There is another kind, the Madagascar periwinkle, raised from seed and used in beds and porch boxes. It has pink or white flowers, very freely produced on a 1 to 2-ft. plant.

Varieties. *Vinca minor* is the common ground cover; the variety called *Bowles* has showy dark blue flowers and is not so trailing a plant. Varieties with white and purple flowers are also available. Plants cost around 25c apiece.

How and When to Plant. Set out the plants in fall or spring, about 6 in. apart. Keep well watered.

Care and Protection. No trimming or fertilizing is necessary.

NASTURTIUMS

"STURTIUMS" are old-time flowers, as homey as gingham and pigtails. Very vigorous and dependable, they give big returns on dry, gravelly banks and where a large space needs to be filled. In borders, beds and

(*Above*) Old-fashioned Single nasturtiums, willing to grow and bloom on poor, dry soil. (*Right*) Gleam hybrids, with double and semi-double, sweet-scented flowers in a good color range.

window boxes their red, orange and yellow blooms are always cheery and colorful. Varieties with double and semi-double, fragrant flowers are a new development. They may be cut freely for informal bouquets, garnished with their own round, light green leaves.

Trailing varieties do well when grown on a trellis or allowed to wander down a bank or wall. All nasturtiums need full sun, but hot sticky summers are not to their liking. They bloom until frost.

Varieties. *Old-fashioned Single Mixed* may still be had, but newer kinds have double, sweet-scented flowers. Those of the *Globe* and *Gem* groups come in assorted colors. They have big, double and semi-double, fragrant flowers on a mound-like plant a foot high and 18 in. wide. *Gleam* nasturtiums have giant, fragrant, long-stemmed blooms on 18-in. plants that are fine for beds and cutting. Colors run through mahogany, salmon, gold and orange. A new variety is *Fiery Festival*, with dazzling scarlet blooms and dark green leaves.

How and When to Plant. The seeds are large, and it is easy to space them 10 in. apart when planting. Cover them to a depth of three times their own diameter. Don't plant, however, until frost is over and the ground is warm. Potted plants are also available. They need sun, poor soil, and never any fertilizer. Otherwise, there will be all leaves and no flowers.

Care and Protection. Often nasturtiums get infested with black lice in summer. Use a spray containing nicotine or pyrethrum, putting it on the soil as well as the stems and leaves, early in the morning.

OLEANDER

SOUTH of the Carolinas this is a popular and dependable broad-leaved evergreen shrub that thrives with little care, and keeps looking fresh and attractive even through hot weather. It makes a graceful, informal flowering hedge, and is a fast grower in almost any soil. As a seashore plant it is in demand. Big loose clusters of single or double, pink, white, yellow, salmon or red flowers appear in spring and through the summer. The plant grows about 20 ft. tall unless pruned, and it enjoys full sun.

In the North oleander is grown mostly in pots or tubs. Over the summer it may be used on patio or terrace, or the pot may be sunk in the open ground where it gets the sun. It needs plenty of water and some liquid fertilizer during the growing season.

Oleander, a rapid-growing evergreen shrub that flourishes all through the South with a minimum of attention.

Varieties. Deep red *Cardinal* is one of the hardiest varieties. Other good kinds are shell-pink *Mme. Peyre* and double salmon-colored *Mrs. Roeding.* A 3-ft. size may be had for $2.00 to $3.00. With most nurseries it is sufficient to specify the color.

How and When to Plant. In the South planting is done in winter or at any time, if the plants are potted or dug with a good ball of earth around the roots. Potted plants should not be moved outdoors in the North until settled warm weather has arrived.

Care and Protection. Pruning is done after these shrubs bloom. Slips are very easily rooted in a glass of water or in damp sand. Potted plants should be kept cool and somewhat dry indoors during the winter, then brought to the light and watered in early spring as new growth is ready to start.

ORCHIDS

THE exotic and fragile-looking orchid, the emblem of luxury and glamour, is "simple and easy" to grow in the average home, according to many who have accomplished this feat. This superb corsage flower has long been raised in greenhouses by florists, and it is also a hobby plant attractive especially to anyone who has his own greenhouse. On a sun porch, in a terrarium, under fluorescent lights, and even in an open room, it is possible to raise orchids. General requirements in the home include good ventilation and light, humid atmosphere, proper potting material, perfect drainage, daily spraying, timely watering and regular feeding.

This enormous plant family, with flowers in a bewildering array of shapes and sizes and colors, grows wild all over the earth except in the very coldest areas. Hybridizers have developed innumerable varieties. Some kinds

(*Left*) A yellow form of lady slipper, a wild orchid that grows on the rich damp forest floor.

(*Below*) Two exquisite Cattleya orchids, coveted by teen-agers for that first important corsage.

(*Left*) Oregon holly grape, another broad-leaved evergreen shrub that is extremely useful because it can stand considerable shade.

(*Right*) Oxalis (described on the next page) is a charming house plant with leaves that close at night like an umbrella.

(*Below*) Pachysandra (described on the following page) is a valuable ground cover for shady areas.

grow on trees or rocks, and these need air at their roots. In humid climates they can be grown on bark; pots of osmunda fiber or shredded bark are also used. These tree orchids are called epiphytal. The other big division of the family is called terrestrial because its members grow on the floor of the forest, like the lady slipper.

In southern Florida and southern California some orchids can be raised outdoors—some in beds and others on trees—but for the most part all kinds are grown indoors. Each of the hundreds of types has its own requirements, and enthusiasts who have studied the needs of orchids have written at length about their culture.

Varieties. Practically all of this numerous family have long scientific names not ordinarily translated into common terms. Just a sampling would include *Cattleya*, the best-known florists' orchid; *Phalaenopsis*, said to be the easiest for home culture; and *Cypripedium*, the lady slipper. Plants cost from $5.00 up.

How and When to Plant. Not only plants but equipment of all kinds for raising orchids is offered by specialists. Some types need tropical, others warm, and still others rather cool growing conditions.

Care and Protection. For the beginner it is best to start with just one or two types requiring the same treatment, and to supply their needs according to the instructions that accompany them.

OREGON HOLLY GRAPE

THIS name describes a shrub from Oregon with foliage like holly and berries like grapes. On both the East and the West Coasts it is a fine broad-leaved evergreen for use in foundation plantings with other evergreen shrubs. Because it does well in the shade it may even be planted quite near large trees, and because it spreads naturally it is used as a ground cover on banks. It can stand rather poor soil but appreciates a fairly good one. The 4 to 5-ft. plant is hardy to New York City or southern New England if given a sheltered location.

Painted daisies (described on the following page) are especially nice for cutting. Be sure to trim back the plants after their first blooming so that they will repeat later. (*Left*) The Single form. (*Below*) Rose Mist. (*Right*) Double blooms with crested centers.

In early May this shrub has bright yellow flowers in spikes, and these are succeeded by bluish black berry clusters with a waxy surface. All year round the thick, glossy, spiny-edged leaves are very decorative. Branches may be cut for indoor decoration if desired, for pruning does no harm. In the fall the foliage turns bronzy or purplish.

Varieties. Oregon holly grape has a relative called *Leatherleaf Mahonia*, which is also a fine evergreen shrub. It grows taller (to 10 ft. or more) and has very large, dull, dark bluish green foliage on a stiff, upright plant. A 15 to 18-in. specimen costs $3.00 or more.

How and When to Plant. Plant in spring or fall, in a good-sized hole that will not cramp the roots. Press the soil hard around them, and water well.

Care and Protection. If you want to keep the plant low, prune in spring or summer. In the North it needs protection from winter sun and wind.

(*Left*) Blue Dream, one of the new French Giant pansies. It is very early blooming.

(*Right*) Swiss Giant pansies, a fine strain with flowers of good substance, in many superb colors.

OXALIS

(*Illustration on preceding page*)

THIS modest plant is reliable for winter bloom indoors if it can have a spot in a sunny window. Leaves are shaped like clover, and flowers start to appear about eight to ten weeks after the bulbs are planted. The growth is loose and open, and hanging baskets are therefore especially suitable as containers. Give oxalis (ox'al-iss) light, well-drained soil and all the sun possible.

Varieties. *Bermuda Buttercup*, with bright yellow flowers, and *Grand Duchess*, rose or lavender, are good varieties growing 9 to 10 in. tall. Bulbs cost about 60c per dozen.

How and When to Plant. In early fall place six bulbs in a 5-in. pot and cover them with an inch of soil. Put the pot in a sunny place. Water lightly.

Care and Protection. As growth appears, give more water. When blooming stops and leaves die, dry off the bulbs and let them rest until the next fall. Then repot in fresh soil.

PACHYSANDRA

(*Illustration on preceding page*)

FOR a dependable evergreen ground cover for shady places there is nothing better than pachysandra (pak-iss-sand'ruh). The dark waxy leaves, on stems about 6 in. tall, stand out like fingers on a hand. This is a fast, vigorous grower spreading by underground roots so that in a short time it covers a large space. Wherever grass refuses to grow or is too hard to cut—under big shade or evergreen trees and on steep banks—this is one answer. A location at least partly shaded is better than one in all-day sun. Pachysandra, or Japanese spurge as it is also called, may be grown as far north as the Great Lakes, and it does very well under city conditions.

Varieties. There is a silver-edged variety in addition to the usual dark-leaved form. Plants cost 15c to 20c each (more if potted).

How and When to Plant. Set out in the spring, about a foot apart, and let the plants go their way.

Care and Protection. A clipping over the top of the plants in very early spring will make them bushier.

PAINTED DAISY

(*Illustrations on preceding page*)

BOTH florists and home gardeners prize the painted daisy (or *Pyrethrum*) for cutting. Its long stiff stems are excellent for that purpose, and the white, red or pink flowers are most pleasing either alone or with other perennials in a border. Single, double or with crested centers, they bloom in June and early July. Fine-textured, fern-like foliage adds to the appearance of the 1 to 3-ft. plant. It likes full sun or a little shade.

Varieties. The *Robinson* strain has blooms in bright colors, with long stems to cut. Two feet high, it flowers profusely in early summer. The rose-carmine *Rose Mist* has a double-crested, silvery center and is a prolific bloomer. Plants are 50c to $1.00 each.

How and When to Plant. Spring planting is preferable, although early fall is also possible. Set the plants in groups of at least three, and 15 in. apart. Mix some peat moss into the soil first. Firm the soil well around the plants, and water thoroughly.

Care and Protection. Keep well watered in dry periods. Cut the plants to the ground after they bloom, to encourage new growth and later flowering. Every third or fourth year, dig up the clump in late summer and divide it into smaller pieces. Replant these and cover the ground around them with a layer of peat moss as winter protection.

PANSIES

ANYONE has a heart of stone who can turn his back on the baskets of pansy plants offered for sale at every market in early spring. The lovely velvety-textured flowers, often like charming uplifted faces, come in many rich colors. Fragrant and appealing, they are a reminder of childhood days when one gift plant was a prized treasure.

The smallest garden space has room for half a dozen pansy plants. In the shade of a doorway shrub they give a friendly touch. With early spring bulbs and perennials they contribute colors that blend with anything. In small arrangements, and even in fair-sized ones, pansies are delightful. And the best way to keep plants blooming is to pick the flowers every day. (See also *Viola* and *Violet.*)

(*Left*) Coronation Gold, rich clear yellow without veins or markings. (*Above*) Lake of Thun, deep blue with a large purplish blotch.

Paper-white narcissus blooming on your window sill through the winter will be a foretaste of their hardy relatives, the daffodils, which will be equally welcome outdoors in March and April. Plant several bowlfuls at three-week intervals, starting in September, and you can sniff their delightful fragrance until Easter. (*Left*) The lovely Paper-whites. (*Right*) Chinese Sacred Lilies, with yellow center. (*Below*) Yellow and orange Soleil d'Or.

Cool early spring weather is the best growing time. Pansies love cool moist soil, deeply fertilized, and a somewhat shaded spot. The high protection of nearby shrubs or perennials is ideal. It pays to prepare the bed carefully by adding rotted or dried cow manure or commercial fertilizer before planting. Hot summers are harder on pansies than cold winters. They can stand moderate cold if the ground is well drained.

Varieties. Many excellent strains are available, providing large flowers in a vast array of colors. A few of them are *Swiss Giants*, *Maple Leaf Giants*, and *Engelmann's Giants*. *Masterpiece* has very frilled and ruffled blooms. Newer developments are *Color Carnival*, with many red and wine tones, *Masquerade*, in a rather light color range, and early-flowering *French Giants*.

Separate colors are also to be had, such as garnet-red *Alpenglow*, canary-yellow *Coronation Gold*, deep blue *Lake of Thun*, and yellow and brown *Rheingold*.

How and When to Plant. Buy plants whenever they are available—the earlier the better. Dig the soil well and prepare a good rich spot for the plants. Set them 6 in. apart, and give them a deep watering. Or you can grow your own plants from seed sown in August. Keep the soil moist until the seeds sprout, and cover the young plants with straw after the ground has frozen hard. In the spring transfer them to the place desired.

Care and Protection. It cannot be said too often that pansies must be picked and picked and picked. It is a privilege, not a task, to do this daily. Once allowed to go to seed, blooms stop coming. If plants get leggy in hot weather, they should be cut back. Where winter temperatures go below 15 degrees, a protecting layer of straw should be spread over pansy plants after the ground freezes.

PAPER-WHITE NARCISSUS

A BOWLFUL of paper-white narcissus blooming on a window sill while snow flies on the other side of the pane presents a snug and cheery picture. Both beginners and experienced raisers of house plants find paper-whites easy to grow. They are an inexpensive means of having flowers in the home during the darkest days of winter. By starting bulbs at intervals from September on, you may enjoy the deliciously fragrant blooms until Easter. It takes a bowlful about seven weeks to come into bloom.

Bulbs for forcing should be kept in a cool, dry place until they are planted. In the lower South bulbs may be planted outdoors in September or October, and will then bloom about January. In other regions they are for indoor use only. (See also *Daffodils*.)

Varieties. Besides the starry-flowered paper-whites, dealers offer yellow-centered *Chinese Sacred Lily* and yellow and gold *Soleil d'Or* or *Yellow Paper-whites*. A dozen bulbs cost $1.50 to $2.00.

How and When to Plant. A glass or pottery dish without drainage is used, with pebbles or bulb fiber to hold the bulbs in place. The fiber should be well moistened beforehand. A little charcoal will keep the water sweet. Place the bulbs (three or four to a dish) so that they are half covered with the fiber or pebbles. Add water enough to reach the base of the bulbs. Keep the bowl in a cool dark room until it is filled with roots (about two or three weeks). Then gradually move it to a light, sunny window.

Care and Protection. Turn the bowl occasionally to prevent the leaves from straining toward the light. Throw away the bulbs after they bloom. They cannot be forced a second time.

PASSION FLOWER

IT is said that when early missionaries to South America found this vine growing wild in the mountains, they used it to illustrate the Passion of Christ: the ten petals represented the ten apostles present at the crucifixion, the circle of filaments the crown of thorns, the five stamens the wounds of Christ, the three-parted center the nails, the tendrils the scourges, and the leaves the hands of the persecutors. This vine is hardy only from the Carolinas southward. There it is semi-evergreen and the 4-in. flowers appear from June to late summer. In light, well-drained soil and full sun it reaches 20 to 25 ft. in height. With protection, it may be grown northward to New York.

Passion flower never fails to excite interest, both for its beautiful flowers and for the interpretation put upon them, which prompted their name.

(*Left*) For something different, plant peacock orchids in late spring. This is a tender bulb grown like gladiolus.

(*Right*) Robust-growing pearl bush produces these loose clusters of snowy white flowers in mid-spring.

Varieties. A popular kind is *Passiflora caerulea*, with showy, blue-lavender flowers. Plants cost about a dollar each. Two other varieties, *Edulis* and *Quadrangularis*, are grown in warmer sections of the country for their edible fruits.

How and When to Plant. Spring is the best time to start this tender vine. Plant it where the tendrils will have a support on which to cling.

Care and Protection. After the flowers have gone, thin out the weakest growth. In cold climates plant against a south wall and give the roots some covering over winter.

PEACOCK ORCHID

THIS late summer-flowering bulb (which is not really an orchid but does resemble one) is grown in much the same way as the gladiolus. Five or six of the creamy white flowers with chocolate-brown centers are carried on the arching, 2 or 3-ft. stem. They have a sweet fragrance, especially in the evening, and are fine to cut. The little bulbs require warm soil; they bloom in August and September. Sometimes they are planted in pots in the spring, kept outdoors all summer, and brought in before frost.

Varieties. *Acidanthera bicolor* is the scientific name. Bulbs average $1.50 per dozen.

How and When to Plant. When all danger of frost is over, plant the bulbs 5 in. deep and 4 to 5 in. apart, in rows like gladiolus or in groups along the edge of a border.

Care and Protection. In sections having very mild winters, bulbs may be left in the ground. In colder climates the tops are cut off when they have died down, and the bulbs are taken up and stored over winter in a dry place where they will not freeze.

PEARL BUSH

YOUNG flower buds that look like pearls have given the common name to this vigorous, fast-growing shrub. They come in late April or May, and develop into pure white flowers similar to spirea but larger. The upright, 8 to 10-ft. plant, perfectly hardy in the North, loses its leaves in the fall. It is easy to grow in well-drained soil that gets full sun. As a bushy specimen plant or in combination with other shrubs as a border or screen it is very useful.

Varieties. Nurseries list this shrub simply as pearl bush or *Exochorda*. Two or three similar forms are offered, all with white flowers. A 2-ft. plant costs about $1.50.

How and When to Plant. Set out the bush in fall or spring in good garden soil, at the same depth as in the nursery. Pack good soil around the roots, and water well.

Care and Protection. Pruning away some of the inner branches after the flowers fade will improve the plant. This need not be done every year. A little fertilizer may be dug into the soil about every other spring.

PEONIES

BRIMMING over with the will to live, a peony plant in bloom is a cheering sight in late spring. In Japan this is known as the flower of prosperity; in the United States it has been loved since colonial days. Its hardiness and ability to thrive for forty to fifty years or more has endeared it to home gardeners in all but the warmest parts of the country. In the lower South and in southern California it is not a success, but Canadian winters hold no terrors for peonies.

Decoration Day is usually about the beginning of the peony season in the North. From then on through June the big double, semi-double or single flowers of this vigorous perennial, in shades of red, pink and white, are a dominant part of the garden scene. Plants are used as showy specimens beside steps, at a doorway or garden gate, along a driveway, or in mixed plantings with other perennials such as iris, columbine, phlox and daylilies. The foliage is pleasing long after the flowers have gone. The plant grows 2 to 4 ft. tall, and dies to the ground in late fall.

Full sun and room to reach its eventual width of 3 to 4 ft. are essential for a peony plant. Because it will live for many years in one spot, it deserves to be given good soil, improved with leaf mold, and enriched with bonemeal. Good drainage is very important.

Tree peonies are shrubs, not trees, that have had an honored position in China and Japan for centuries. The Chinese call them the "king of flowers." These are very hardy plants, with graceful light green foliage and striking flowers that are larger and earlier than the better known perennial peonies. The plants grow 3 to 6 ft. high and do not die down in autumn, although they do lose their leaves. They require a somewhat protected location

(*Above*) The globular, compact blooms of the variety Karl Rosenfield are brilliant and striking at the height of the peony season, while those of Edulis Superba (*left*) are very early. Both are reliable older varieties.

(*Left*) L'Etincelante, a handsome single peony bearing cupped, deep pink flowers with a bright golden center.

(*Right*) The high incurved center of the variety Mons. Jules Elie has broad, smooth guard petals.

with high shade from nearby trees. The soil must be well drained, and well fortified with leaf mold and bonemeal.

Whether for home decoration, for graduation platforms, for simple or elaborate weddings, or for any other festivities of early summer, peonies are excellent for cutting. When combined with other flowers they furnish valuable bulk and color. In cutting the flowers, be careful not to remove too much foliage from a plant.

Varieties. Of the perennial type, *Kelway's Glorious* is a very popular midseason variety with fragrant, double white flowers. *Festiva Maxima* and *Le Cygne* are other highly rated whites. Large pink *Mon. Jules Elie*, very fragrant deep pink *Edulis Superba*, dark red *Philippe Rivoire*, and crimson *Karl Rosenfield* are long-standing favorites among the many double kinds. *L'Etincelante* is a fine pink variety with single flowers. *Primevere* is white with a large yellow center; *Ama-no-sode*, rose-pink with yellow center, is a recommended Japanese type. A root may be bought for a dollar or two.

Representative tree peonies are *Gessekai*, double white; *Argosy*, single yellow blotched red; and *Satin Rouge*, double red-orange. A tree peony costs from $5.00 up.

How and When to Plant. In the North the best time to plant perennial peonies is September. In warmer areas a month later is preferable. Be sure to get a freshly dug root (not dried out), with three to five eyes. After preparing the ground well, set the root so that the growing tips will be covered with not more than 2 in. of soil (1 in. in warm regions). Firm the soil well around the root, and water thoroughly. Allow 2 to 3 ft. between plants.

When buying a tree peony, choose a plant of blooming size, at least three years old. Plant in late September or October, at the same depth as in the nursery. Give the roots a covering of straw for the first winter.

Care and Protection. Shallow planting is very important; deep planting is a major

(*Left*) Festiva Maxima, very large and early, has crimson flecks on a few of the white petals. It has been a favorite of generations of peony growers.

Tree peonies originating in Japan have fascinating names. (*Below*) Sakura-Gasane, meaning Drift of the Cherry, has large, salmon-pink flowers with wavy petals.

(*Below*) Hatsu-hinode (Rising Sun of the New Year) is a tree peony with bright scarlet-pink blooms.

(*Left*) Ukaregi-ohi (Golden Center) is named for its central cushion of golden anthers.

Three more tree peonies. (*Left*) A glimpse of the large, semi-double bloom of Iwato-kagami (Sacred Mirror). (*Below*) The salmon-pink Iro-no-seki (Barrier of Gay Color). (*Right*) Souv. de Maxime Cornu, a fragrant, deep yellow hybrid shaded orange-salmon.

reason for failure to bloom. As the shoots appear in the spring, spray or dust them with a good fungicide; repeat every two or three weeks through the summer. A little bonemeal scattered around the roots in spring and fall, and then watered in, will promote good growth. Ants on the buds may spread disease; they are eliminated by dusting with chlordane. Cut off all dead flowers at once, but let the foliage grow as long as possible. In late fall it should be cut off to ground level and burned. In areas where there are low winter temperatures without much snow, a cover of evergreen branches may be necessary, but generally peonies need no winter protection and no dividing in the spring. They are best left alone.

Tree peonies need a feeding of bonemeal in spring and fall. They require little or no pruning. Dusting or spraying with a fungicide is good practice through the summer. Sometimes an extra cold winter kills the top growth back to the ground. In that case, cut the dead wood back in the spring; the plant will then put out new growth.

PEPPERBUSH

SUMMERSWEET is another common name for this fragrant, accommodating shrub (botanically, *Clethra*). Flowering from late July through September, it is welcome at a season when many gardens need a shrub in bloom. It is an upright grower 5 to 8 ft. tall but may easily be kept lower if desired. The glossy, healthy leaves turn soft yellow-gold before dropping in the autumn. The flowers are produced freely for a number of weeks, in narrow spikes 4 to 6 in. long. The black seeds that follow, looking like peppercorns, give it the name pepperbush. This shrub is hardy anywhere in the United States; in fact, it grows wild from Maine to Florida.

A moist, acid soil is needed; even a low, wet location is permissible, with either full sun or part shade. It does well at the seashore, for it is resistant to salt spray.

Varieties. A *White* and a *Pink* form are easy to buy, at $1.50 to $2.00 for the 18 to 24-in. size.

How and When to Plant. Add peat moss or leaf mold to ordinary garden soil to put it in good condition. Set out the plant in fall or spring.

Care and Protection. Keep lime away from this shrub. A 3-in. layer of peat moss is good around the roots. After the bloom fades, cut the old flower stems down to the ground.

Because it thrives in shady, damp locations and blooms so late in the summer, pepperbush is a useful shrub in many gardens. (*Above*) The white form. (*Left*) The pink variety. Both are so sweetly scented that the plant is called sweet pepperbush.

PERENNIALS

IN contrast to the impulsive annuals that grow, bloom and die completely between spring and frost, perennials have roots that live on year after year. Some of the most lordly and best-loved plants in the garden are perennials, such as peonies and iris, columbines and pinks, daylilies, phlox, delphinium and primroses. (All of these and other perennials mentioned in this article are described under their individual headings.) Most can stand considerable cold, and northern gardens in particular would be at a loss without them. Name any color you like, and a perennial can be found to match it. From the violas and bleeding hearts of early spring to the chrysanthemums of latest fall, there is not a week in the season when some perennial does not earn for itself the grateful appreciation of gardeners. The cushions and spires of growth, the daisies and bells and trumpet flowers spell enchantment outdoors, and many are delightful for bouquets as well. A variety of foliage—whether sword-like, heart-shaped, feathery or scalloped—adds to their charm.

Perennials are companionable plants. They like shrubs and hedges as a background if they keep their distance. They don't mind some annuals as neighbors, provided proper space has been allowed. Bulbs, either early or summer blooming, are fine, and the liking is mutual because bulbs appreciate the help of perennials in concealing their foliage as it dies. The mixed border where all these types of plants are living in harmony is the special haven of perennials. Some low growers are perfect for rock gardens, and others are at home beside a pool. Sometimes at the back door or beside the patio or breezeway is the most convenient place for them.

Every perennial cannot be expected to be in flower all summer long. Some kinds bloom over many weeks, however, and these are particularly needed in small gardens. Some, like peonies and iris, are at their peak for only a fraction of the season but at that time they contribute so much that they can hardly be passed by, and when their flowers have faded their foliage remains not only presentable but a real asset. A comprehensive range of color, a satisfying blend of color, a continuing succession of color—these are the aim in a planting of perennials. And yet, if not all are accomplished, there is no reason for disappointment. Often anticipation of the next high point of the season is almost as enjoyable as the display itself.

Caring for perennials is based on common sense and a few general rules. Experience will show which plants prefer a little extra shade or fertilizer (and under the separate headings these preferences are indicated for each plant). The encouraging thing to remember is that

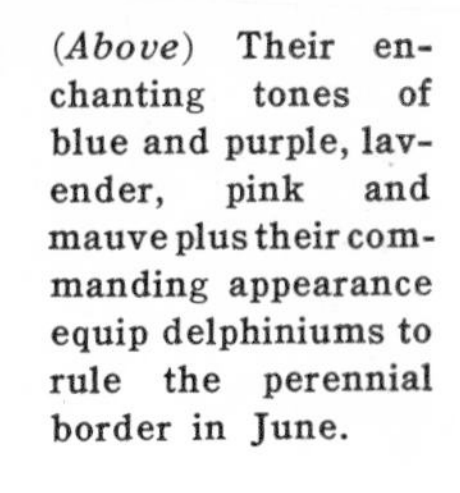

(*Above*) Their enchanting tones of blue and purple, lavender, pink and mauve plus their commanding appearance equip delphiniums to rule the perennial border in June.

(*Left*) When all is said and done, there is nothing more sure to give continuous color through midsummer than daylilies and phlox. The blue in the planting shown here is furnished by balloon flowers.

A boxwood edging, grass paths and leafy trees effectively set off these vari-colored perennials. A green frame or background helps immeasurably in displaying the flowers.

perennials have been grown in ordinary, every-day gardens for centuries, and it is unlikely that they will develop into prima donnas now. The containers in which plants are so widely sold make it easy to get off to a good start. Set out the plant just as soon as you get it home. If the day is cloudy and damp, so much the better. Don't crowd too many plants into a small space, and don't try too big an assortment of varieties. Concentrate at first; diversify later.

A little general fertilizer in early spring is a natural requirement after a long winter of hibernation. Water it in after scattering it at a safe distance from growing shoots. Weeds are a disfigurement that you will want to pull out at once. Hoe, if you want the exercise—but very gently. When you get tired of that you will investigate mulching, the modern way of keeping weeds away and at the same time helping the ground to stay moist and cool. As a rule, perennials are very healthy, but if trouble appears, spray or dust with one of the good preparations stocked by your garden store.

Cut and burn the foliage and stalks in the fall. If you live where winters are severe, some perennials will need a covering of straw or evergreen branches after the ground freezes. When the plant clump gets too big or when it seems to be dying in the middle, it should be dug up and pulled apart. The good sections may then be replanted separately or given to a neighbor. Most plants that bloom in spring may be safely divided in fall, and those that bloom later should be divided in early spring.

PERUVIAN DAFFODIL

THIS is not really a daffodil but a summer-flowering bulb (*Hymenocallis*) belonging to the same plant family. It has long, strap-shaped leaves, and blooms profusely from midsummer on. The very fragrant flowers are like big white lilies, sometimes tinged greenish, with the petal edges cut and fringed. They are carried several together on an 18-in. stem. A group will add interest to any summer garden. Ordinary soil will grow them, in sun or a little shade. Planted outdoors after the soil gets warm, these bulbs will bloom in about six weeks. They are not hardy.

Varieties. Other names for this plant are spider lily and basket flower. A bulb costs 50c to $1.00.

How and When to Plant. About mid-May, or whenever settled weather has arrived, plant the bulbs outdoors, 4 to 6 in. deep and 8 to 10 in. apart.

Care and Protection. Water in dry periods. Where winters are mild, the bulbs need not be disturbed, but in cold climates they must be taken indoors and stored in a warm dry place until the next season.

Peruvian daffodils, natives of the Andes, look best in groups of three or more. They bloom about six weeks after planting.

These Satin petunias are among today's top favorites.

(*Left*) Red Satin, with 2½ to 3-in. flowers on a mound-shaped plant.

(*Right*) Peach Satin—a color with plenty of warmth and appeal.

PETUNIAS

PETUNIAS are extremely versatile annuals that have made a place for themselves in millions of porch boxes and yards. There are no tall kinds to put at the back of a border, but otherwise they can be used almost anywhere—as bedding plants, as low edgers for borders, on banks, in pots, for cutting. They are good as an edging around a paved patio where a softening effect is desirable. The softly perfumed flowers blossom freely until frost, spilling their lovely colors in abandon. Single, double, ruffled and fringed blooms are to be had on plants that may be bushy or sprawling or trailing. Naturally, it is important to choose the right type for the purpose it is intended to fill.

All kinds of petunias can be grown in any soil, but a light, well-drained one is preferable. They like full sun and can endure a dry summer better than most plants. They also do well when planted in part shade, although then the growth is more open.

Varieties. When it comes to petunia varieties, there is an embarrassment of riches. Plant breeders are continually making big improvements, and the newest kinds have more vigorous plants that bloom earlier and more freely than the older varieties.

The hybrid bedding or multiflora class is one of these important new groups. The flowers are large, with plain edges, on plants that average 12 in. in height. All are very showy. Among the varieties are the *Satin* group, which keep their compact growing habit all season, unfading scarlet *Comanche*, and scarlet and white starred *Glitters*. More are offered every season.

The hybrid grandiflora class has 3 to 4-in. blooms that are fringed around the edge. The compact plants grow about a foot high but often spread to twice that much in width. Salmon *Ballerina*, scarlet *Fire Dance*, salmon-pink *Maytime*, rose-pink *Prima Donna*, and the *Lustre* group belong here.

Even larger, 4 to 5-in. flowers are provided by the giant fringed group. These are spectacularly frilled and veined blooms on 18 to 24-in. plants. Soft pink *Apple Blossom* and rose-pink *Theodosia* are examples. The all-doubles, too, have blooms so ruffled and full as to be almost unrecognizable as petunias. *Allegro* (salmon), *Nocturne* (purple), *Minuet* (orchid), and *Colossal Shades of Rose* are fine for window boxes and cutting.

Bedding petunias, 18 to 24 in. tall, are of

(*Right*) Comanche is good for both bedding and cutting. The scarlet color is brilliant and uniform.

(*Below*) Glitters blooms freely all season, spring to fall. Only 8 in. tall, it is fine for edging and potting.

(*Left*) Fire Dance has a pronounced yellow throat. The 3 to 4-in. flowers are fringed and ruffled.

(*Right*) Ballerina, a vigorous and free-blooming petunia of glowing salmon-pink.

more sprawling, branching growth, with medium-sized, single, plain-edged flowers borne in profusion. Popular kinds are cerise-red *Radiance*, white *Snowstorm*, and blackish purple *Elk's Pride*.

The dwarf class, of compact, mound-like growth a foot high, make good bedders and edgers. *Celestial Rose*, *Rosy Morn* and *Fire Chief* are described by their names. They have single flowers of medium size.

Balcony petunias are excellent for trailing from window boxes. They have 2½-in., single flowers available in separate and mixed colors on runners 1 to 2 ft. long.

How and When to Plant. The most practical way is to buy plants, which are easy to find in any market or garden store in May at about 75c per dozen (more for potted plants). Set them about a foot apart.

Care and Protection. Get in the habit of looking over petunias every few days and picking off the shriveled blooms. The bed will look better and produce better. Balcony and bedding petunias should be cut back in midsummer to encourage new growth. Feeding at this time is good practice.

(*Left*) Maytime has clear light salmon-pink blooms veined slightly deeper. It fits well into any garden and holds up through heat and rain.

(*Below*) Blue Lustre, with its large, lightly waved flowers, starts to bloom early and continues to the end of summer. The plants are low and spreading.

(*Left*) In spite of its name, the beautifully fringed Prima Donna is not a bit temperamental.

(*Left*) Apple Blossom has giant double fringed flowers of soft pink on a dwarf plant.

(*Right*) Although developed some years ago, Theodosia is still popular. The golden throat highlights the 3-in. blooms.

(*Left*) Caprice, with deeply fringed, double flowers of bright rose on a low-growing, compact plant.

(*Right*) Flaming Velvet, an excellent bedding petunia of brilliant, satiny blood-red.

(*Left*) Fresh white Snowstorm has 4-in. flowers that make a splendid showing. Pick them off when rain splashes them with mud.

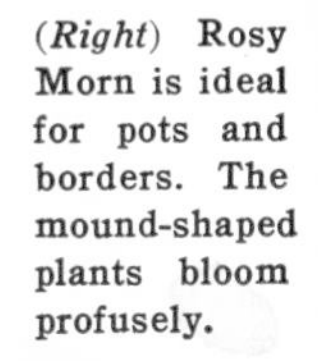

(*Right*) Rosy Morn is ideal for pots and borders. The mound-shaped plants bloom profusely.

(*Left*) Silver Medal petunia really did win a silver medal for its good all-round performance.

(*Above*) The bushy, 9-in. plants of light salmon Linda can withstand bad weather without harm.

(*Left*) Mercury, a non-fading light blue hybrid bedding variety with plenty of vigor. It grows 15 to 18 in. tall.

(*Below*) Carnival is a gay mixture of colors. Some flowers are variegated, starred or edged in various combinations. Most are waved or ruffled. Plants grow about a foot high.

(*Right*) What could be cheerier as a pot plant than clear vibrant pink Loveliness?

Two more of the Lustre group of hybrid grandiflora petunias (see also Blue Lustre on page 184). (*Left*) Lightly ruffled Salmon Lustre. (*Right*) Scarlet Lustre, with its fringed bloom accented by a yellow throat. The plants are a foot high and twice as broad.

(*Below*) Cream Star, a dwarf grower covered with creamy white flowers all season. A bed of white petunias can be a refreshing island in a sea of color.

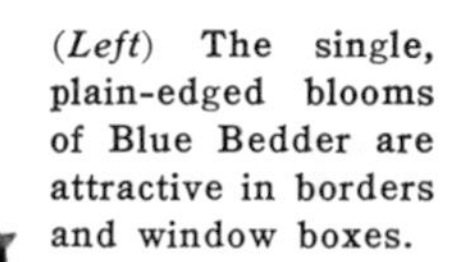

(*Left*) The single, plain-edged blooms of Blue Bedder are attractive in borders and window boxes.

(*Right*) Lipstick is another dwarf bedder bearing a wealth of 2½-in. flowers all summer. The glowing carmine-rose color has an almost fluorescent quality.

(*Above*) A satiny sheen and deeper rose veining in the throat distinguish salmon-pink Cheerful petunia.

(*Left*) Sir John Falstaff, a hardy phlox presenting heads of bloom like big salmon-pink bouquets.

(*Right*) A fine white variety—White Admiral, which grows 2 to 2½ ft. tall and blooms in July and August.

PHLOX

FROM early in the season when rock gardens miraculously spring into color until the dog days of August, there is some kind of phlox ready to contribute a large share of garden color. This is an important family that grows wild in North America, and various sections of the country have their own native kinds of phlox. Some that grow in the West are not adapted to conditions in the East.

The word phlox means *flame* in Greek, and the name is justified by the bright colors of the flowers. The blooms vary in size; some have an eye or star-shaped center of a different color, and some varieties are fragrant. Creeping kinds are extremely showy in rock and wall gardens, but their 3½ to 4-ft. cousins are just as dominant in midsummer borders. Between these extremes are phloxes 12 or 18 in. high, some glorying in full sun, while others prefer part shade.

Tall hardy phlox requires moist soil that has been well fertilized. A place in the sun suits it, and through the hottest weather it can be relied on for a steady succession of bloom. In a border with other perennials it looks best if at least three plants are used together, but they should not be crowded. Varieties should be placed according to their individual height—some at the rear and others toward the front of a planting.

Annual phlox raised from seed makes a fine showing over a long season when used in broad masses. It is good in the border, in rock gardens, and as a ground cover. The newest kinds have very large flowers in big showy clusters.

(*Above*) Glowing red Leo Schlageter has a slightly darker eye zone. This one is early blooming.

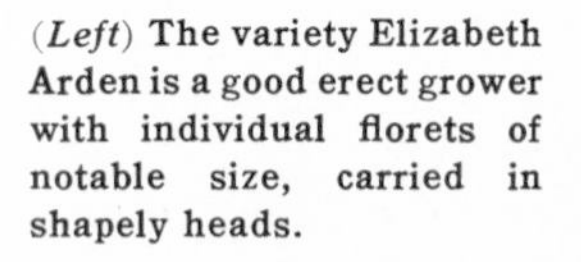

(*Left*) The variety Elizabeth Arden is a good erect grower with individual florets of notable size, carried in shapely heads.

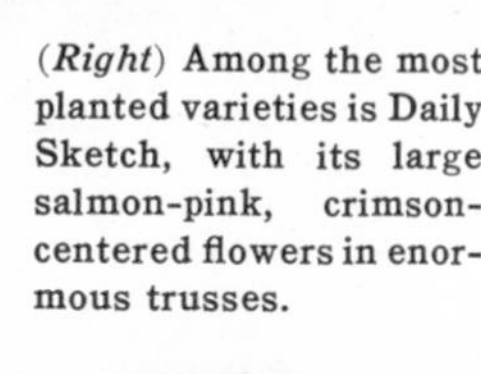

(*Left*) Flash is a reliable hardy phlox with flowers of a bright carmine-crimson. Plants are of medium height.

(*Right*) Among the most planted varieties is Daily Sketch, with its large salmon-pink, crimson-centered flowers in enormous trusses.

(*Left*) Each of the bright salmon florets of Eva Foerster hardy phlox has a large star-shaped white center.

(*Right*) Border Queen is a medium shade of pink. This is an early-flowering variety, moderately tall.

(*Left*) Rich red Charles Curtis holds its color well even in the hottest sun. It is a strong grower with healthy foliage.

Varieties. Hardy phlox has well been called the mainstay of midsummer gardens. It blooms from early summer to frost if not allowed to dry out in the sun. Some of the most popular varieties are salmon-pink *Sir John Falstaff*, fragrant *White Admiral*, scarlet *Leo Schlageter*, watermelon-pink *Border Queen*, *Count Zeppelin* (white with red eye), *Daily Sketch* (pink with crimson eye), and pure white *Mary Louise*. In height they range from 2 to 3½ ft. Plants cost about 75c each.

The rock-garden phlox most commonly grown is known as moss pink. This is a creeping evergreen plant that forms a dense carpet in early spring, so covered with bloom that the foliage is almost invisible. It does well in dry sandy soil in full sun. Good kinds are *Scarlet Flame*, *White Delight*, *Vivid* (bright pink with darker eye), and brilliant salmon-pink *Alexander's Surprise*.

Blue phlox or wild sweet William grows about a foot tall and bears flowers in shades of blue. It does best in part shade, where it spreads fast. Blue *Laphami* and lavender *Canadensis* are representative. They look especially nice with spring bulbs and early perennials like candytuft, for they bloom at the same time.

Glamour is a vigorous new annual phlox about 14 in. tall. The flowers are salmon colored, with a deeper center ring and white eye. *Gigantea Art Shades*, a little lower growing, has large heads of bloom in soft colors. *Twinkle* and *Globe* are about 6 in. high, with blooms in mixed colors. Twinkle has starred flowers; Globe is a mound-shaped plant, excellent as a low edger.

How and When to Plant. Phlox plants may be set out in fall or spring. Tall kinds for the border should have well-prepared soil; an allowance of 2 ft. between plants will assure good air circulation. Lower growing kinds need only 8 or 10 in. of space. Seed of annual phlox is sown outdoors in early spring

(*Above*) Blue phlox (Divaricata), blooming at tulip time, is a perfect neighbor for spring bulbs. It prefers a lightly shaded spot.

(*Right*) Moss pink is a hardy ground-covering phlox for spring rock gardens. Be careful not to allow one variety to completely dominate the picture.

(*Left*) Although Twinkle annual phlox is only 6 in. tall, the flower heads are extremely showy. This is a delightful bedder and edger, covering itself with a mass of color.

(*Below*) Gigantea Art Shades, another annual phlox. The large, pastel-colored flowers have a distinctive white eye. The growth is low and compact.

in full sun. Young plants should be thinned to stand 4 to 5 in. apart.

Care and Protection. Cut off all flowers as soon as they fade. Keep hardy phlox well watered in dry spells. To prevent mildew on the foliage, use the dust or spray recommended for mildew on roses. In late fall cut all the stalks down almost to the ground and burn them. Every third or fourth year, in fall or early spring, dig up the clump and divide it into smaller pieces. Replant the outside portions and discard the center. A little fertilizer may be dug around the plants in early spring.

PINCUSHION FLOWER

BOTH the annual type of this flower in a wide range of colors, and the perennial, mostly in shades of blue and lavender, are grown in garden borders. Both are extremely good for cutting because of their strong, 2-ft. stems and lasting quality. In bouquets they combine well with spikes of larkspur and snapdragon. Their height fits them for an intermediate section of a planting.

Annual kinds are grown in full sun in any good garden soil that is well drained. There they bloom freely in an array of pink, red, lavender, white and yellow as long as the dead flowers are kept cut.

The hardy varieties need rich soil to which a little lime has been added. The ground must not be so heavy that it holds excessive moisture in winter; otherwise the center of the plant may rot. From June to early fall these large blooms—flatter and broader than the annual type—make a fine display.

Varieties. *Imperial Hybrids* (tall, double, mixed colors), deep lavender-blue *Blue Moon*, and salmon-rose *Loveliness* are some of the annual varieties offered. *Isaac House Hybrids* are a fine strain of perennial pincushion flower (or *Scabiosa*), with blue, lavender and silvery blooms. Separate colors are also to be had, at an average of 75c per plant.

How and When to Plant. Sow seed of annual kinds outdoors when the ground is workable, and thin out the young plants to stand 6 to 9 in. apart. Early spring is also the best time to set out plants of the perennial varieties. They need about 15 in. of space and are best in groups of three.

Care and Protection. Always cut off the flowers before they can go to seed. North of New York, or wherever winters are severe, give the plants a covering of straw. If they get straggly after a few years, dig up the clump in the spring, separate it into smaller parts, and replant.

PINKS

COLONIAL ladies and the minuet seem associated with this dainty relative of the carnation (which also see). The single, semi-double and double, often fringed flowers in solid colors or with contrasting center are charming in mixed bouquets. In the garden they make a fine edging or mass planting at the front of a border, and they are also prized in rock gardens. They are easier to raise than

(*Above*) An Imperial Hybrid pincushion flower will bloom freely over a long season if not permitted to go to seed. (More Imperial Hybrids are shown on the facing page).

(*Left*) The gracefully ruffled blooms of perennial varieties appear in soft shades of silvery blue and lavender. Notice the "pincushion" in the center?

(*Left*) Long wiry stems carry the fully double, deep lavender-blue blossoms of Blue Moon pincushion flower.

(*Right*) Three more of the Imperial Hybrid strain of pincushion flower, showing the good color range to be expected from mixed seed.

carnations. All of the family like cool rather than hot dry summers.

Plants grow about 9 to 18 in. tall and like a spot in full sun. Annual pinks are less fragrant than the perennial ones, but even so they are nice bushy plants that often live over winter and bloom again early the next spring. Perennial pinks have a delicious spicy scent and live many years.

Varieties. Annual kinds are called China pinks. Varieties include *Heddewigi*, 8 to 9 in. tall, with fringed flowers from July to fall; *Gaiety*, with deeply cut petals in many bright colors; and *Westwood Beauty* in shades of red. *Sweet Wivelsfield* is especially fragrant and free flowering.

Among the perennial kinds are the *Cheddar* pinks, 10 in. high, the *Clove* pinks with fringed, very fragrant blooms on 18-in. plants, the *Allwood* pinks, and the *Scotch* pinks, in all colors, many two-toned. *Tiny Rubies* is a rose-pink midget for rock gardens.

How and When to Plant. Seed of annual pinks may be sown in late fall or early spring.

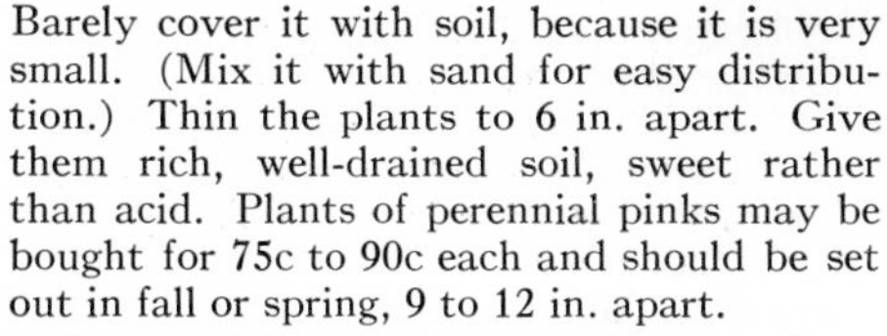

Barely cover it with soil, because it is very small. (Mix it with sand for easy distribution.) Thin the plants to 6 in. apart. Give them rich, well-drained soil, sweet rather than acid. Plants of perennial pinks may be bought for 75c to 90c each and should be set out in fall or spring, 9 to 12 in. apart.

Care and Protection. Cutting the plants back after they bloom will encourage them to repeat later. A light winter covering is advisable in severe climates.

(*Above*) Hardy garden pinks have a delicate charm all their own.

(*Left*) Lacy Lass, one of the old-time laced pinks, blooms in early summer on 12 to 14-in. plants.

EVERYONE is entitled to his own dream of a garden. If you live along the eastern seaboard, you may be able to manage a garden like this, with steps leading to the sea, where you can dream of castles in Spain and a never-never land where flowers bloom forever and weeds die before they sprout.

PLANNING BEFORE PLANTING

(*See illustration on opposite page*)

DEVELOPING a garden, like planning a wardrobe or decorating a room, can be a joyous expression of yourself. Nobody can tell you precisely what you should plant. If you welcome garden planning as an opportunity, you will see that here is a gratifying way of persuading your piece of the earth to say what someone else might express in a verse or a painting. Carrying out your ideas may be accomplished in a season, or you may spread it over a lifetime. If you love plants and working with plants, you will forever be trying some new variety or combination.

Think It Over. Decide, first of all, what you want most from your garden. Take a little while to analyze your living and working and leisure-time habits. If you enjoy reading or writing in the open, consider planning for a sheltered corner with a comfortable seat where you can have a glimpse of your flowers and listen to the birds as you work. On the other hand, if your family enjoys cook-outs you may want an informal area where you can set up a barbecue grill and a picnic table, separate from the rest of the garden. Perhaps a terrace with a more sophisticated air, where you can entertain guests, will serve you better. By examining your needs and picturing the best means of satisfying them, you will go a long way toward a truly personalized garden from which you will derive pleasure in a variety of ways.

Gardening is not an exact science. Although a plant may have a preference for a certain type of soil or location, you may succeed in growing it even when your conditions are not ideal. Plants do not observe certain boundaries, and experimentally inclined gardeners are continually proving that hardiness zones cannot be drawn like state lines. Always there is the possibility that your particular combination of temperature, soil ingredients, rainfall and exposure will prove successful. Plants of doubtful hardiness should be used only on a trial basis at first.

Before making extensive plans, you should consider how much time you can give to your gardening. Don't undertake more maintenance work than you will enjoy doing. If your leisure time or physical ability is limited, you may find evergreen shrubs and ground covers less demanding than flowers that need to be picked daily, perennials that should be divided every spring, and bulbs that must be planted each season. If upkeep will be a chore, it is more important than ever to keep the planting simple. Uncluttered effects are best, in any case.

Just as you would not buy a chair for a room without having a special place for it, so you should never buy any important plant

material without first knowing where it will be used. The need comes first, then the search for the right plant, and finally the purchase. Otherwise you will have a hodgepodge. Think in terms of a group of plants, and always relate one to another. Good landscaping and restful gardens come from thoughtful planning.

First Steps in Wise Planning. A landscape man can give invaluable advice when you plan the grounds around a new home. He can check the slope and drainage, and can help you decide where steps and walks belong for greatest usefulness. A master plan may look very ambitious the first year but in the end will prove sensible, for it will be the blueprint for increased pleasure in your home and for increased property value. Paving should be done first, followed by tree planting. Because a tree requires some time to reach full size, it should be located early and in the right place. Other planting is generally extended over several years.

BUT if, on the other hand, your Shangri-La includes a cottage snuggling in a forest nook—or in a suburban bedlam—you can enjoy a cozy retreat in a magic-filled garden like this. It all depends on how you plan before you plant.

(*Left*) Plantain lilies, with their mass of shiny leaves, are decorative in the shade, even when not in bloom. Caerulea is the variety shown here.

(*Right*) The sweetly fragrant Honeybells, a plantain lily that lives for many years in a rich, shaded spot.

Soil packed down by building operations is a handicap common to most new home sites. In this case sand may be dug deep into the soil to loosen it. Or perhaps the topsoil has been buried during the work of construction. Organic matter such as rotted leaves, peanut hulls or sphagnum peat improves almost any type of soil and is of greater immediate benefit than fertilizer. Whatever is to be planted, the soil must first be put in condition. The best time for the job is before any planting is contemplated.

The shape, color and height of your house must be considered when you plan the planting that will frame it. Low houses need plants with horizontal lines, although some shrubs and trees of moderate height are also desirable. Varying shapes and foliage in different shades of green will create a better picture. Trees of pyramidal form are more appropriate for taller houses. Keep in mind the mature height and width of the trees and shrubs you choose, and don't plant under a window any material that will grow tall. Ground covers are extremely useful in covering awkward spots and sharp corners.

Keep unbroken grass plots in the center of the space, and concentrate plantings at the sides. Don't hesitate to blend various leaf-losing shrubs with the evergreens. Some bare branches in winter are very attractive. For variety, mix bulbs and bright annuals with the shrubs and perennials. Color, form and texture are the elements to consider in blending plants.

Be cautious about using ornaments of any kind in a garden. A bench, sundial or a purely decorative piece of sculpture can be a fine accent when thoughtfully placed; otherwise anything of the kind may seem out of place and a distraction. (See *Garden Furniture.*) Plants with highly colored foliage should be located with great care, or they too can be disturbing.

If the first year's results are not what you imagined, don't be discouraged. Most permanent plants need several seasons to get established. Old-fashioned varieties are good or they would not have survived, but keep an open eye and mind for improvements and try some now and then. Garden planning is never finished.

PLANTAIN LILY

WHEN a plant is wanted for providing a bulk of excellent foliage in moist shade, plantain lily is hard to beat. It needs soil to which leaf mold has been added to help keep it moist. Shade at least most of the time is an advantage. The large leaves make a broad mass; some kinds are dark green, others light or bluish or variegated with white. All are very ornamental and furnish a good solid background for flowers of light texture and color. In addition, there are sturdy spikes of blue or white flowers in midsummer. These vigorous, hardy perennials are long lived and trouble-free. They are also listed as *Hosta*.

Varieties. *Honeybells* has fragrant, soft lavender-blue flowers on 3-ft. spikes in July and August; foliage is olive-green. *Thomas Hogg* has tall lavender flower spikes and rich green leaves edged with silver. Other kinds have harder names: *Glauca* (blue-gray foliage and pale blue flowers), *Lancifolia* (narrow, glossy leaves and lilac-blue flowers in September), *Subcordata Grandiflora* (shiny, light green foliage and flowers like big white lilies), *Caerulea* (large, shining leaves, with purplish flowers), *Variegata* (green and white leaves with wavy edge). Plants cost 75c to $1.25.

How and When to Plant. The plants may be set out in either spring or fall. They need plenty of space to spread—about 2½ to 3 ft. Do not set them too deep.

Care and Protection. Water during long dry spells, and give young plants a winter covering of straw or leaves.

POINSETTIA

THIS traditional flower of Christmas is raised in great quantity by florists and finds ready sale, even though the dry heat of homes in winter often makes the leaves drop quickly. The great showy heads are especially striking when massed; sometimes they are arranged with evergreens to make a most effective display like a flowering Christmas tree. Southward from central Florida, poinsettias are grown outdoors like any other shrub, and visitors from cold northern states are astonished to see how large and handsome they can be.

Varieties. Pink and white-flowered varieties are to be had from florists, as well as the more usual red.

How and When to Plant. Keep the plant away from drafts, and see that it gets good light but no direct sun. It needs moisture in the air as well as in the soil; setting the pot on a tray of wet pebbles will help to keep a moist atmosphere around it. The temperature at night should not go below 65 degrees.

Care and Protection. As the leaves begin to turn yellow and drop off, gradually stop watering the plant. Keep it dry and cool until about the end of April. Then prune it quite hard and give it more light, heat and water. When the weather is warm and settled, sink the pot in the ground outdoors. Supply the plant with liquid fertilizer from time to time through the summer, and bring it indoors in the early fall. Keep it watered, in a sunny window, ready for bloom again by Christmas.

A poinsettia, bravely flying its bright blooms, is a part of every Christmas celebration. Try to coax your plant to live on and bloom again.

POOLS FOR GARDENS

A POOL for waterlilies and other aquatic plants can be a refreshing feature of a garden, for even the sight of water is inviting on a hot midsummer day. It can be the main attraction, either formal or naturalistic, depending upon the mood of the garden as a whole; or it may be only a simple tub in a secluded nook with a bench nearby, where you can absorb the peace and tranquility of the scene. If you are fortunate enough to have a small stream or pond on your ground, a place to be planted is quite easily prepared at the edge. Sometimes a shallow rectangular, circular or semi-circular pool is cemented, with a deeper spot made for holding the tub or box in which the waterlily is planted. A series of small pools arouses special interest. Even plastic pools are on the market.

Like other elements of a garden, a pool needs a becoming setting. Moisture-loving plants like iris, daylilies, caladium and pepperbush are appropriate along the edge. Tall trees and shrubs that would shade the water should not be too close by, because full sun is needed to make waterlilies bloom. The pool should not be overplanted. About a third of the total water area should be open. A few goldfish will keep down mosquitoes.

In small pools it is no problem to siphon out the water when necessary. Larger ones require a drain. When a new pool is lined with concrete, plants and fish are not safely installed in the water for another week or two. During this period the pool should be filled and emptied several times in order to get rid of the free alkali from the concrete.

Where very low winter temperatures are to be expected, it is safest to empty the pool in the fall and cover the concrete with leaves or straw and boards. Hardy waterlilies may be left on the pool bottom and also protected with the straw, or they may be moved indoors for the winter. Each spring the pool needs a good scrubbing, and the soil in the plant boxes needs an application of fertilizer.

As with every special feature in a garden, a pool should be in perfect harmony with its surroundings. (*Above*) Japanese iris enjoy the moist growing conditions beside a pool. (*Right*) A naturalistic water garden in a woodland setting. (*Below*) A pool mirroring the sky is encircled by spring bulbs.

(*Left*) Light pink Helen Elizabeth, darkred Wurtembergia and free-blooming Barr's White are standard varieties of Oriental poppy.

(*Right*) Salmon Glow, an extra large, double variety of beautiful salmon-orange.

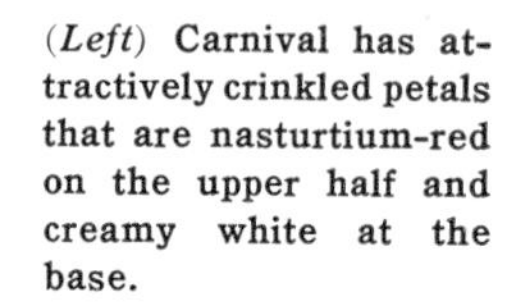

(*Left*) Carnival has attractively crinkled petals that are nasturtium-red on the upper half and creamy white at the base.

POPPIES

CAREFREE poppies flaunt their bright flowers on the breeze of early summer. They are a sure source of dancing color, whether the annual or the perennial kind is planted. In the garden they need to be massed for most telling effect; if a solid border of poppies is raised from seed, they can be replaced by later-blooming marigolds or by summer-flowering bulbs. Orange and red are the colors most often associated with poppies, but pink, white and apricot are also seen. Flowers are both single and double.

The huge blooms of Oriental poppies come with the irises and peonies in June. They develop from hairy buds carried on 2 to 3-ft. stems. These are particularly showy because of their immense size, flaming color, and the delicate paper-thin petals. They are long lived and a splendid adornment of the early summer garden. After the flowers are gone, the leaves too disappear for a time, but they start to grow again in the fall. During this resting period the poppies need to be masked by other plants nearby, such as phlox or Shasta daisies, both to cover the bare spot and to protect the poppy roots.

Iceland poppies are 2 to 3 in. in diameter, single and double, on strong slender stems. They are best raised from seed, like the Shirley poppies. (See also *California Poppies.*) Annual kinds grown from seed will bloom over a longer period if the plants are not too close together and if the dead flowers are picked off. They reseed easily and come up again the next year without any help.

All poppies like the sun. None of them like to be moved. They do well in ordinary garden soil that is well drained. Perennial kinds will appreciate having some fertilizer and leaf mold mixed into the ground before planting. If you want to cut the flowers for bouquets, do it while they are still buds. Hold the stems over a flame to char them before plunging them in deep water.

Varieties. Among the most popular Oriental poppies are salmon-pink *Mrs. Perry*, mahogany-red *Indian Chief* and big double

(*Above*) Yellow Wonder Iceland poppy bears buttercup-yellow, cupped flowers on long stems. The blooms last several days when cut.

(*Left*) Shirley poppies are quickly raised from seed sown in earliest spring. Or scatter seed in the fall, for bloom the following year.

(*Left*) A package of mixed portulaca seed will provide many colors. This fast-growing annual is a good ground cover for dry spots.

(*Right*) Potentilla Gold Drop, a healthy, hardy low shrub that is densely clothed with fine foliage and covered with little golden flowers from June to frost.

salmon-orange *Salmon Glow*. *Helen Elizabeth* has crinkled pink petals, *Barr's White* has purplish black spots, while *Perry's White* is blotched crimson. Plants cost about 85c.

Kelmscott Strain of Iceland poppy has graceful cupped flowers in many soft tints. *Gartford Giant Art Shades* specializes in pastel tints. *Yellow Wonder* is fine for cutting.

Mixed seed of annual Shirley poppies is easily obtainable. Named varieties include *American Legion*, bright orange-scarlet, and *Sweet Briar*, double, deep pink.

How and When to Plant. August or September is the best time to plant Oriental poppies, although potted plants may also be set out in the spring. Cover with 3 in. of soil and then with a layer of straw or peat moss for protection the first winter.

Seed of Iceland and Shirley poppies is sown preferably in early fall, to bloom the next year. Or it may be sown in very early spring. Mix a little sand with this fine seed, and don't be too generous in scattering it. The young plants must be thinned to 10 to 12 in. apart. They cannot be transplanted; throw away the plants you pull out.

Care and Protection. Don't disturb the roots of Oriental poppies. Cut off all dead flowers promptly.

PORTULACA

FOR a quick flowery carpet in any hot, dry, sunny place there is nothing more sure of success than portulaca (port-yew-lak'kuh). It has many uses in a garden—as a ground cover following spring bulbs, in a sunny rock garden, on banks, and even in porch boxes. Any soil will do, preferably on the poor side. The many-colored little flowers, single or double, open every morning when the sun strikes them, and keep right on blooming until frost. Since the plants are easy to move, even in full bloom, they are handy for filling in dry bare spots. They grow 6 to 8 in. high and often self-sow. This annual enjoys a variety of names, such as rose moss, sun plant, moss rose, rock rose and Mexican rose.

Varieties. *Mixed Colors*, single and double, are generally used, although it is possible to buy separate colors. *Single Jewels* has large, deep crimson flowers.

How and When to Plant. Scatter the seed broadcast after all danger of frost is over. Seed is very fine, so mix it with dry sand and press it into the soil lightly.

Care and Protection. The only care portulaca may need is weeding.

POTENTILLA

SOME of this family are dwarf perennials with white, crimson or orange-yellow flowers for sunny rock gardens or borders. The shrubby kinds are especially useful in small gardens in the North because they bloom freely all summer long, are neat and slow growing, and are unusually hardy. These are particularly recommended for regions having below-zero winter temperatures. They are easily grown in well-drained, somewhat sandy soil, where they form a compact, 2 to 3-ft. bush covered with single yellow flowers like buttercups from early June to October. The small, dense, fern-like leaves are not kept through the winter.

At the front of a sunny border, potentilla (poh-ten-till'uh) or cinquefoil is a pleasant, dependable bloomer all through the growing season. It also makes a fine low informal flowering hedge.

Varieties. *Gold Drop* has small, golden yellow flowers on a compact, 2 to 2½-ft. plant. It likes either moist or dry soil. *Katherine Dykes*, also low growing, has arching branches and lighter yellow flowers. There are a number of other good varieties. An 18 to 24-in. plant costs around $1.75.

How and When to Plant. If the soil is very wet and heavy, mix some sand into it. Plant in fall or spring. For a hedge, allow 12 in. between plants.

Care and Protection. If the hedge needs a little pruning, take care of it in early spring.

PRIMROSES

LACKING damp, rich soil in the shade, you will not have much success with primroses. The cool moist atmosphere of the Pacific Coast and New England is well suited for their culture, and in these sections they are grown easily, as they have been in England for a long, long time. Wherever their needs can be met, they are of prime importance in spring. This is a large family of perennials, with some kinds only for greenhouse use. Their very name comes from the Latin for *first*, indicating their extra early blooming season.

Some primroses are so eager to greet spring that they start to open before the snow has gone. Others come in April and May, but by early summer most of them have stopped blooming. They have all the charm of wild flowers and come in a splendid array of colors, from yellow, orange and lavender to mahogany, cream, rose and apricot. In some varieties the flowers are carried one to a stem,

(*Above*) English primroses are dainty spring-blooming perennials with flowers borne singly on the stems. Give them a cool, damp location.

(*Left*) Polyanthus or Bunch-flowered primroses, averaging 10 in. in height, are appropriate with daffodils in early spring borders where they receive adequate moisture.

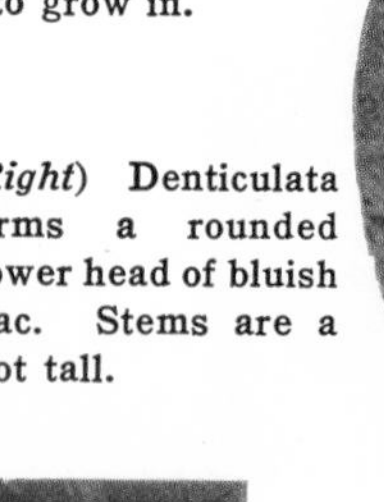

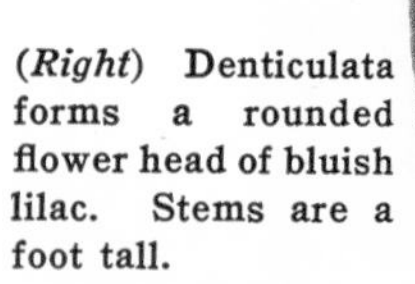

(*Left*) **Japanese primroses often have three tiers of florets on one stem. They like a bog to grow in.**

(*Right*) **Denticulata forms a rounded flower head of bluish lilac. Stems are a foot tall.**

while in others they are in clusters, globular heads, or in tiered effect on the stem. Leaves grow in a big rosette close to the ground.

Usually primroses have to be planted in a fair-sized group to make a showing. Those that especially like bog conditions are perfect beside a shady stream or spring where the soil is cool and moist all the year round. Others more adaptable to garden beds also need rich deep soil that does not dry out in the summer. It must, however, be well drained and not heavy with standing water. Shade is necessary, but not from a hedge or shrubs so close that they take all the nourishment from the earth.

With early bulbs in spring borders and in rock gardens, and with flowering trees and shrubs as a backdrop, primroses are the very breath of spring. Always they must have soil full of leaf mold and peat moss to keep it moist and cool.

(*Left*) **Cowslips hold their blooms well above the foliage. Like all primroses they require moist growing conditions.**

Varieties. *Polyanthus* or *Bunch-flowered* primroses are very popular. Growing 6 to 12 in. tall, they have large, fragrant flowers in many colors. This is a fine edging plant that blooms profusely, often with the last of the winter's snow if located near a protecting wall. With daffodils and other bulbs for company, this sturdy plant is quite happy.

The *English* primrose (*Acaulis* or *Vulgaris*) was grown by the Elizabethans. Its friendly, petite flowers, often in soft yellow tints, are borne just one to a stem. This is very easy to grow in cool pockets in a rock garden, where it blooms in April.

Japanese types, on the other hand, have stems up to 18 in. tall, with flowers carried in two or three layers at the top. These are showy blooms of crimson, pink and white, rising from a large clump of leaves in May and June. Beside a pond or in an open wooded area where the roots will be continuously moist, there is no difficulty in raising these primroses.

Another strong grower is *Denticulata*, with white to lavender flowers in round heads. The flower stem reaches 12 in. or more and the leaves too are very long. *Auricula* has leathery, gray-green leaves, powdery looking, and fragrant heads of bloom. This is from the Alps and is good in rock gardens. *Veris*, or cowslip, with nodding, bell-shaped flowers, and *Juliae Hybrids*, a low spreader covered with flowers very early in spring, are other popular and hardy kinds. Primrose plants cost about 75c.

(*Below*) **Auricula has grayish green leaves and fragrant flowers in clusters.**

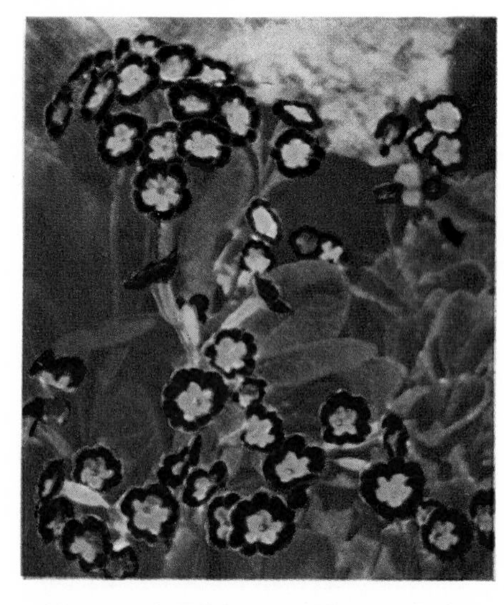

How and When to Plant. Spring or early fall is the time to set out the plants, about 6 in. apart. They must have a naturally damp, shaded location and soil rich with leaf mold.

Care and Protection. Polyanthus kinds grow and multiply so fast that they need to be dug up, divided and replanted every second year. This may be done at any time, even when plants are in bloom. Other types need dividing after about three or four years, following the blooming season.

(*Left*) **A quaint hybrid of the English primrose with double or hose-in-hose flowers. Give it shade and damp but well-drained soil.**

(*Right*) **Wanda, a rich purple Juliae Hybrid with yellow eye. It grows only a few inches high and blooms very early.**

(*Left*) Suwannee River, a newer variety of privet that makes a fine specimen plant or low hedge. It is hardy in the same area as Glossy privet.

(*Right*) In the South, Glossy or Waxleaf privet is considered the best of its family. It can be clipped or allowed to grow into a small tree.

PRIVET

THE word *hedge* immediately brings privet to mind, for there is no plant more widely used for this purpose. These shrubs take to shearing so well and have such small, neat, thick leaves that they invite clipping. However, when untrimmed they are also ornamental not only for their foliage but for their clusters of tiny white flowers and black or blue berries. Vigorous and fast growing, they make fine additions to a foundation planting, and especially in the South they are extremely popular landscape material. Some kinds are hardier than others, and in the South some are evergreen. Any soil will grow this healthy shrub; it does not object to part shade or to the smoke and grime of cities. For hedges the cost is $5.50 to $6.00 for 25 plants; larger specimens are more expensive.

Varieties. For a trim, clipped hedge *California* privet is a popular kind with glossy, rich green foliage, but its hardiness is not dependable in the North. *Ibolium* is similar but more hardy. *Amur* is excellent for a hedge in the North and also in the South, where its small leaves remain on the plants all winter.

Others that are evergreen in the South but not hardy north of Virginia are strong, upright *Japanese* privet, compact-growing *Chinese* with large flower clusters in summer, and the dense, bushy *Glossy* or *Waxleaf* privet. The latter is one of the top broad-leaved evergreens for the South and is greatly valued for foundations and borders. It grows all over Florida.

A very hardy variety doing well in dry soil is *Regel*. This is a low, spreading grower excellent for use in foundation plantings and on banks. A new kind advertised as *Chartreuse Shrub* has foliage that remains bright yellow all season.

(*Left*) Regel privet, a low-growing shrub with spreading branches of neat appearance. (*Below*) Dull bluish black berries cover Regel privet plants in winter.

How and When to Plant. Privet may be planted in spring or fall. For a hedge set the plants 9 to 12 in. apart, and prune them back at once to 6 to 10 in. above the ground.

Care and Protection. To keep a hedge in shape, trim it as soon as the flowers fade. If it is too tall or straggly, cut it back hard—to 6 in. above ground level—in early spring before the leaves come out. The hedge should always be clipped so that it is wider across the base than across the top.

(*Left*) Even where the soil is on the dry side and rather well shaded, privet flourishes. In pruning a hedge, always keep it broader at the base.

(*Above*) California privet, easy to transplant, is a stiff and upright grower widely used as a clipped hedge.

(*Above*) **An evergreen hedge like the yew shown here requires light clipping in very early summer to keep it in trim. Train your children to pick up the papers that blow into your hedge, so that it always looks its best.**

PRUNING

WHEN and how to prune the long-lived, valuable shrubs and trees around a home are important questions. If you want your plants to develop their fullest beauty, you will be interested in knowing at least the basic steps. (Specific pruning advice is given under the separate subject headings, where appropriate.)

To saunter forth on the first fine spring day, pruning shears in hand, gives you a remarkable feeling of importance. You are the champion of the new season, anxious to give it proper assistance. But before taking any action, you should consider not only *what* you will cut but *why*. There is no good reason to prune all plants every year. The natural shape of a shrub is part of its attractiveness, and this should not be spoiled by indiscriminate whacking. On the other hand, a little trimming annually is preferable to letting a plant grow so big and ungainly that it must be rejuvenated by drastic pruning.

First, be sure that your pruning tools are sharp, strong and adequate for the job to be done. Don't try to cut a heavy branch with lightweight shears. That will only ruin the shears and mangle the plant.

Basic Rules. The general rule is that spring-flowering shrubs and vines should be pruned immediately after they bloom, but those that flower in summer and fall should be pruned in early spring. Thin out any branches that are crowded, and cut back the stems that have carried flowers. Shortening a branch forces out new shoots, which are the ones that bear the flowers. Production of fresh young growth is the object of the pruning, not preservation of old wood. Make the cuts sharp and clean, and don't shorten all the branches to the same length. Plants that normally reach large size should not be chosen for spots where they must continually be pruned to be kept within space limits. Low growers should be found instead.

Most berry-bearing shrubs need very little pruning. Only the weakest shoots and branches that overlap should be removed. The time to do it is early spring.

To Renew Overgrown Shrubs. If a shrub has become too bushy and broad for the allotted space, you can bring it back to size by judicious pruning. Cut some of the older canes in the center of the bush all the way down to the ground. Clear out the thin, weak shoots, allowing more light and sun to reach the center, and also cut back all the other branches part way. This work needs to be done in late winter or very early spring before growth starts.

Sometimes rhododendrons and other broad-leaved evergreens grow tall and leggy. To prevent this, pinch back the tips of the shoots now and then, as they grow, and occasionally cut an old cane back to the ground. Too much shade and too little space are the conditions mainly responsible for lanky growth. Sometimes it is advisable to remove some of the shrubs in a crowded planting, in order to give the others more room. When a shrub has gone completely out of hand and you want it bushier at the base, you may cut it back to within a foot of the ground in early spring. Give it fertilizer, a summer mulch of leaf mold and peat moss, and plenty of water, and after a season or two it should bloom again. Although such treatment is rather drastic, many shrubs and broad-leaved evergreens respond to it.

Dead wood on any plant should be cut out as soon as you discover it. The season of the year is immaterial.

Shearing of evergreens is done in late spring and again in late summer. The newest shoots should be shortened, to make the plant bushier. (For hedge pruning, see *Hedges*.)

Ornamental trees need only enough trimming to keep them in shape. Extensive pruning after they bloom is unnecessary. Pruning of large trees is best left to professional tree surgeons who have the necessary equipment.

(*Below*) **This flowering quince needs pruning. Some of the center canes should be cut back to ground level, and weak shoots should be eliminated.**

(*Left*) Bring pussy willow branches indoors where you can watch the furry pussies unfold. They last a long while in water.

(*Right*) Have you marveled at the ranunculus used so freely at the spring flower shows? In the South they may be raised outdoors.

PUSSY WILLOW

WHEN spring feels months away, the puckish pussy willows hold out hope that green things will grow again. Soon after Christmas the branches may be cut and brought into the house. The soft furry catkins will last for several weeks in water. This is a fast-growing, vigorous shrub that deserves a place in many borders, just for the sake of having branches to cut. It needs full sun and fairly moist soil.

Varieties. *French* pussy willows have large, silky catkins of silvery pink. *Rose-Gold*, a new form, is silvery gray at first and then becomes rose and yellow. A plant 18 to 24 in. tall costs about $1.50.

How and When to Plant. Set out the bush in either spring or fall, packing the soil well around the roots and watering afterward.

Care and Protection. Branches that have rooted indoors in water may be planted, to make new bushes. Every third or fourth spring the plant may be pruned hard to induce more catkins to form.

RANUNCULUS

THE showy double and semi-double flowers of ranunculus (ran-nun′kew-lus) are like waxy buttercups. They come in lovely clear colors—yellow, orange, pink and red—and many have a black center. These are tender bulbs forced by florists to bloom in the winter. At the big spring flower shows they make a striking effect with anemones. They are not hardy north of Maryland, but in warm areas they may be grown outdoors in rich soil to which leaf mold and bonemeal have been added. Good drainage is important.

Varieties. *Tecolote Giants* have large, double and semi-double flowers in many colors. They may be bought in mixture or separately for $1.00 to $2.00 per dozen.

How and When to Plant. Plant in late fall, with the claw of the bulb pointing down, 2 to 3 in. deep and 6 in. apart.

Care and Protection. After the bulbs bloom, dig them up and store them in a dry place until the next planting time.

REDBUD

ANYONE who has visited the Gettysburg battlefield in early spring when this little tree casts a purplish haze over the hillsides is not likely to forget the redbud. There it appears to jump in full bloom from the very rocks, and tiny trees only a foot or two in height have the clusters of purplish pink flowers all along their branches. Redbud grows wild through eastern United States and is hardy as far north as Michigan and most of New England. It is the state tree of Oklahoma.

The flowers come before the foliage, at the same time that dogwood blooms. The two trees are therefore often planted near each other, with spring-flowering shrubs and bulbs to complete the picture. Redbud grows to about 25 or 30 ft. tall, though often it is more like a large shrub. Its heart-shaped leaves turn yellow before they fall. Because Judas is said to have hanged himself on one variety of this tree, it is sometimes called Judas tree.

Varieties. *American* redbud is commonly sold in nurseries, at about $2.00 for the 3 to 4-ft. size. There is also a white form. *Chinese* has larger leaves and is more shrub-like.

How and When to Plant. Plant in fall or early spring, in ordinary soil, in sun or light shade. Dig a hole wide enough to hold the roots without being cramped. Set the tree at the same depth as in the nursery (as

Redbud is a charming tree, small enough for use on almost any lawn. Heart-shaped leaves follow the springtime blooms. (*Above*) The little pea-shaped flowers are carried in generous clusters.

(*Left*) The showy spikes of red hot poker are like gleaming beacons in a garden. The plant is not completely hardy.

(*Right*) Galpini is especially good for cutting because it is dwarfer than most other red hot pokers.

shown by the dark mark around the base of the trunk). Be careful not to expose the roots to sun or air while planting. Pack good soil around them, being particular not to leave any air pockets, and water thoroughly. Leave the soil surface raked fine.

Care and Protection. Keep the tree well watered until it gets a good start.

RED HOT POKER

THIS impressive-looking plant is best left to large gardens, for its long grassy leaves grow into a big clump and the flower stalks are as much as 3 to 4 ft. tall. The tubular flowers of red, orange and yellow, glowing like a poker just pulled out of the fire, are good to cut. They bloom mostly late in the summer, although some may start as early as July. Torch lily is another name used for this perennial, which traces its origin to South Africa.

The fleshy-rooted plants need all-day sun and sandy, well-drained soil. They do not like cold wet feet in winter and are not dependably hardy in the North, although newer kinds are likely to be hardier than the older ones.

Varieties. Plants may be bought by color (red, yellow, bicolor), and there are also named varieties like bright scarlet *Empress of India*, *Primrose Beauty*, and *Goldmine. Galpini*, only 2 ft. tall, producing orange-salmon flower spikes from July to frost, is very nice for exotic arrangements. Plants cost 70c to $1.00.

How and When to Plant. Spring is the best planting time. Allow a foot or more of space per plant, and set only 1 to 2 in. deep.

Care and Protection. In coldest latitudes give the roots a winter cover of leaves or straw and a little fertilizer in spring. Or they may be dug up and stored over winter in a frostproof place indoors in a box of dry soil.

RHODODENDRONS

RHODODENDRONS and azaleas belong in the top rank of flowering shrubs, and for permanent plantings to grow in beauty with the years there is nothing more highly valued. These plants are classed together by botanists, but many azaleas lose their foliage in autumn and practically all rhododendrons hold their thick, leathery leaves all year long. Over twenty kinds of rhododendron grow wild in North America, but many others have been brought in from the Himalayas, the Orient, and other far-away places. These shrubs are worldwide in origin and have been honored for centuries for their noble bearing and their handsome foliage and flowers. In this immense family there are some types as large as trees, while others are small enough for rock gardens. A few varieties are fragrant.

Hybridizers, first in Europe and later in the United States, have devoted a great deal of time and labor to rhododendrons, resulting in the addition of many very fine hybrids. Often these are more desirable than the native kinds and are more adaptable to growing conditions in certain areas.

Rhododendrons grow well in the eastern part of the country in areas where the winters are not excessively cold or the summers unduly dry and hot. They do well in mountainous regions in the Southeast, and are very successful in the Pacific Northwest. In the

The pale to deep pinkish lilac clusters of Carolina rhododendron are a familiar sight through the southern Appalachians.

This mixed planting of rhododendrons shows what an extremely pleasing picture can be had by blending colors rather than by planting for startling contrast.

Central States, where both summers and winters are likely to be severe, there is increasing hope that testing will prove the adaptability of certain varieties to that region. Rhododendron specialists and books on the subject should be consulted for the names of varieties recommended for particular locations.

In gardens, rhododendrons are used as specimen plants, in shrub borders, and for screens. With other broad-leaved evergreens they are fine for massing. The heavy, dark green foliage makes a splendid background for lesser plants. These shrubs need a somewhat sheltered location with a northern or eastern exposure rather than a southern one. They cannot endure either sharp winds or strong sun in winter. The distant protection of trees is desirable, furnishing high but not dense or continuous shade in summer.

Soil should have an acid reaction. The surest way to get the desired condition is to mix rotted oak leaves, peat moss, cottonseed meal, and special fertilizer for acid-loving plants into the soil before planting. The ground must be moist but well drained. Since the roots are shallow, it is advisable to cover the top of the ground with pine needles or peat moss to keep the soil cool and damp.

Varieties. Among the most reliable hybrids are pure white *Boule de Neige*, rose-pink *Roseum Elegans*, rose-lavender *President Lincoln*, and rosy red *Mrs. C. S. Sargent.*

Carolina is one of the earliest native rhododendrons to bloom. In May and June its pinkish lavender flowers come in great abundance on the rather low-growing plant. Foliage is small and neat. This is excellent in a foundation planting with other evergreens. From *Catawba* a great many of the best hybrids have been produced. Its lilac-purple flowers are borne in large round clusters on the bushy, spreading plant. In height it may

(*Above*) **The handsome bloom of the variety Mrs. C. S. Sargent.**

(*Left*) **A fine compact cluster of rosy lavender President Lincoln.**

(*Left*) Roseum Elegans, a hybrid rhododendron that is hardy and dependable in northeastern United States.

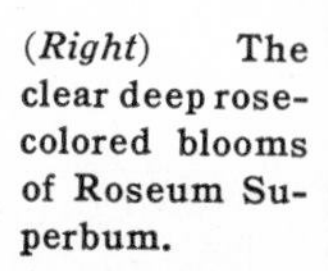

(*Right*) The clear deep rose-colored blooms of Roseum Superbum.

reach 15 ft. or more. This native is hardy as far north as New England, where it blooms following very hard winters. Considered even hardier is *Rosebay*, which blooms in June and July. This is a tall, strong grower to 20 ft. or more, with extremely large heavy foliage which partly hides the purplish pink flowers. Plenty of moisture and some shade are necessary. An 18 to 24-in. rhododendron plant averages $5.00 to $6.00 in price.

How and When to Plant. After getting the soil in proper condition, set out the plant in spring or fall, always with a ball of earth around the roots. Do not set it deep in the ground. Water well, and if necessary shade it from the sun until well established.

Care and Protection. Maintain a 3-in. mulch of pine needles, peat moss or oak leaves on the soil at all times. Never dig around the roots, and never allow lime, bonemeal or wood ashes to come near. Cut off all dead flower clusters so that seed cannot form. No regular pruning is necessary, but any damaged branches may be cut off at the ground in early spring. At this season too, a little fertilizer may be lightly worked into the soil. After a dry summer, give the plant a thorough soaking before winter sets in. A screen of burlap or evergreen branches should be used as winter protection for plants in exposed situations. Leaves rolled up in the winter merely show that the plant is protecting itself from the cold.

(*Above*) Lavender and Old Lace, a hybrid with white stamens and lightly ruffled petals. This is a dwarf grower with very good, heavy foliage.

(*Left*) Rosebay rhododendron produces a big bold mass of foliage, with blooms in late June. It is very hardy.

ROCK CRESS

EVEN neglect and poor soil will not prevent rock cress from growing. This little perennial (*Arabis*, botanically) makes a mat of practically evergreen foliage that is covered with bloom in spring. All it asks is sunshine and well-drained, light soil without any fertilizer. It spreads fast and is useful on banks and dry walls; in low borders it makes a nice edging. The fresh white blooms are good for cutting and look well with spring bulbs. Hardy and free flowering, rock cress grows no more than a foot high.

Rock cress is willing to grow wherever it can have full sunshine. It is a rapidly spreading plant for rock gardens, edgings and banks.

Varieties. *Snowcap*, 6 in. tall, produces gray-green foliage and a mass of white bloom. It is fine for rock gardens and edgings. There is also a pink form and one with double white flowers. Plants cost about 60c.

How and When to Plant. Early spring or early fall is the time to set out the plants, 6 to 8 in. apart.

Care and Protection. Cut back the plants quite hard right after they bloom, to keep them from sprawling. Every third or fourth spring dig up the clump, separate it into sections, and replant them.

ROCK GARDENS

FOR an absorbing hobby, you may want to try your skill at developing a rock garden. At its best, a rock garden is a subtle mingling of plants in a naturalistic setting, far different from the miscellaneous collection of stones sometimes seen, with a few plants scattered between them. The aim is not to produce a quick effect or color all season, but rather a setting for low, compact plants that like the growing conditions provided by rocks. This can be moist and cool, or dry and hot. In a relatively small space a rock garden affords the chance to grow a great variety of perennials, low shrubs, and even some bulbs and annuals.

Any sloping ground offers a charming place for a rock garden. This is a good way to protect a bank from soil erosion. Some plants will thrive in light, shallow soil where they are baked by the sun, while others will want the cool, deep pockets between rocks. The stones will give both moisture and protection. Part shade is desirable. Paths and stepping-stones will give access to the different levels. A pool—even a small one—will prove to be an exquisite addition.

The Rocks. If there is a natural outcropping of rock, you can take advantage of it; or you can bring in rocks and try to place them as they might be in nature. They should be mostly in a horizontal position rather than tipped on end, and the bottom third should

A whole community of plant life can be nourished in a carefully planned rock garden. Early spring will find most plantings of this kind in top form.

taller is good—perhaps a bright annual. Plants with rosettes of foliage are suitable in small crevices. All these different plant forms slowly merge, filling the bare spaces and giving a beautifully mature look to the planting.

A rock garden will be one of the easiest parts of your grounds to take care of. In the spring you will have to clear away the leaves and trash that accumulated during the winter. Push back into the soil any plants that were heaved out by frost. Where necessary, bring in some new soil for washed-out spots. Some perennials will have to be sheared back after they bloom, and occasionally a clump grown too thick will need to be thinned out. In the very coldest regions, the light protection of straw or evergreen branches may be needed over winter.

be buried in the ground. Rocks that are native to your area are by far the best choice, because they must never look like an assortment displayed for their own sake. The rocks are merely the setting; emphasis should be laid on the plants. Don't be satisfied with small stones; some must be heavy rocks. And don't lay them out in a pattern of any kind. Study some natural rocky ledges and try to imitate them.

Make certain that each rock is firm, and when you place a second one near or overlapping it, fill the intervening space with good soil. The cracks between rocks should slope downward and back, so as to catch the rain. Pockets of soil should be deep enough to hold and nourish plant roots. Don't leave air spaces, for they could spell death to any roots that reached them. The higher slopes of the rock garden will have the drier soil, while the low spots will be damper. Choice of location for the various plants should be made accordingly.

The Plants. Who can define a rock plant? It can be almost anything dwarf and compact, hardy in your area and easy to please. Ground covers and low creepers to run over the rocks are fine; so are some of the dwarf evergreen trees and shrubs. Many hardy perennials are at home in a rock garden, and some of the little spring bulbs are delightful in such a setting. Trailers are best when falling gracefully from the top of a rock or bank. Here and there something a little

(*Above*) A rock garden ideally is a mixture of both low creeping plants and some that are taller. Both moisture lovers and dry-soil plants can be suited when properly located.

Often a section of the property that is on sloping ground can profitably be made into a rock garden (*as above*). Water (*left*) contributes a note pleasing all year round.

(*Below*) A dozen candidates for a rock garden—four below and the rest on the next page. All are worthwhile, reliable and long lived.

Candytuft

Bellflower (Campanula Carpatica)

Phlox (Moss Pink)

Hardy Aster

Bellflower (Campanula Garganica)

Rock Cress

Hardy Pinks

Perennial Alyssum

Sun Rose

Barrenwort

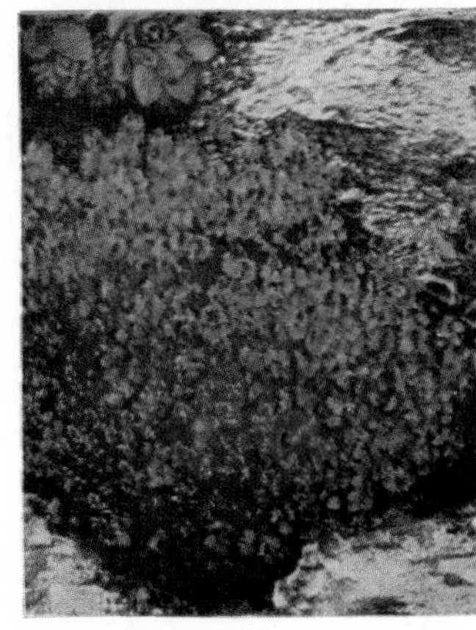

Speedwell (Veronica Rupestris)

Stonecrop

(*Above*) More favorites for the rock garden (see also those on the facing page).

ROSE OF SHARON

As a screen or as a specimen in a border of tall shrubs or perennials, this plant is used mainly because it blooms so late in the summer. It grows erect, as a large shrub or small tree, to 6 to 10 ft. in height. Very vigorous and free flowering from July through September, it is grown over most of the United States. (See *Hibiscus* for warm-climate varieties.) The large, single or double flowers of white, blue or pink and red shades are somewhat like those of a hollyhock, which belongs to the same plant family. Shrub althea is another name for rose of Sharon. It grows fast in any well-drained, fairly moist soil and must have full sun.

Varieties. These shrubs are often sold simply by color, but named varieties are also to be had, among them double violet *Ardens*, single blue *Coelestis*, double white *Jeanne d'Arc*, and double *Banner* (white with red center). *Blue Bird* is a new one with very large flowers over a long period. Plants 18 to 24 in. tall cost $1.00 to $2.50.

How and When to Plant. Set out this shrub in the spring, in a large hole. Press the soil well about the roots, and give it a good watering.

Care and Protection. Cut off the flowers as they fade. No regular pruning is needed, but for larger flowers the canes may be cut back in early spring. If a specimen is spreading too much, it may be given the same treatment.

Rose of Sharon, hardy and serviceable, is a sturdy shrub furnishing bloom late in the summer. (*Above and Left*) Two popular colors.

(*Right*) Blue Bird, a rose of Sharon with 5-in. flowers produced the first year after planting.

A lavish rose garden, whether public or private property, is a source of great pleasure for many months.

ROSES

WHEN florists recently conducted a poll to find the most popular flower, the rose won without any real contest. The artists, poets and songwriters who through the ages have glorified roses have long since been joined by florists, nurserymen and plain dirt gardeners who declare them supreme as cut flowers and garden plants. No flower surpasses the rose for sparkling color, superb form and size, and rich fragrance. Producing the blooms for cutting and the bushes for garden planting occupies a large segment of the florist and nursery industry.

Flowers range from those scarcely an inch wide to exhibition beauties 6 or 7 in. across. Petals vary from five to more than a hundred. Colors span the rainbow (with the solitary exception of true blue). Among the new varieties are some tinted lavender, orchid and

(*Right*) Christian Dior, an All-America hybrid tea like the other roses on this page, glows with health and beauty.

Duet combines a soft salmon-pink face with a contrasting rosy crimson reverse. Flowers are of medium size, beautifully formed.

Garden Party is a luscious pastel ivory tint flushed delicate pink. The plant is a vigorous grower with dark foliage.

(*Left*) King's Ransom, a splendid rich yellow with petals of heavy texture forming a flower that holds its shape well.

(*Above*) Talisman, an old favorite that is still loved. It has now been joined by many other multicolor roses.

tan. Perfume is sometimes very pronounced and varied. Plants may be miniatures less than a foot high, stately bushes 3 to 4 ft. tall or more, or climbers covering the side of a house. Bush roses are best grown by themselves in a garden. Even when space is limited, solid beds will prove most satisfactory. Some kinds make excellent hedges and bank covers.

For practical purposes roses may be reduced to about half a dozen classes. The long-stemmed, large, shapely flowers so admired for cutting are hybrid teas. These plants grow 2 to 6 ft. tall and bloom repeatedly from early summer to late fall. Floribundas are produced both one to a stem and in clusters; they have smaller blooms than hybrid teas, although some are just as well formed. This type, bushy and very free flowering all season, makes beautiful hedges.

(*Below*) Radiance will bloom for anyone, and on this account has won a permanent niche for itself among hybrid teas.

(*Above*) Crimson Glory, another older variety that refuses to step aside for newcomers.

(*Right*) The warm colors of a desert are merged in Mojave. They grow deeper as cool weather advances.

(*Left*) Wonderful buds, good stems and a strong constitution keep the variety Charlotte Armstrong among the leading hybrid tea roses.

©

(*Right*) You can't beat Peace! At least, no variety has yet matched its superb performance in home gardens, local shows and world-wide rose competitions.

©

(*Left*) Flower arrangers love to work with such roses as Sterling Silver. The warm lilac-lavender color inspires originality.

(*Below*) Helen Traubel is still another perfect hybrid tea to cut. Buds are especially lovely.

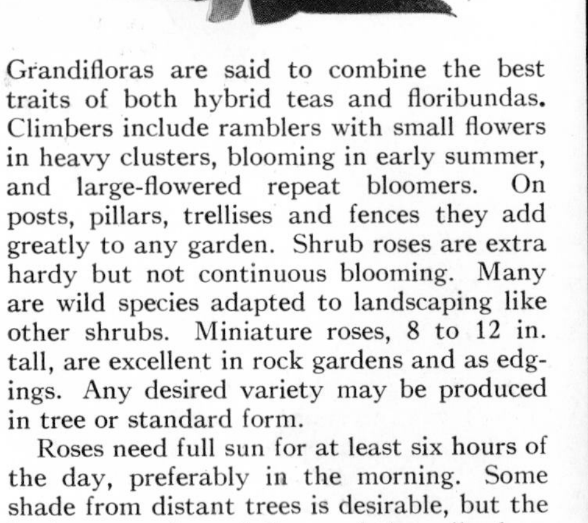

Grandifloras are said to combine the best traits of both hybrid teas and floribundas. Climbers include ramblers with small flowers in heavy clusters, blooming in early summer, and large-flowered repeat bloomers. On posts, pillars, trellises and fences they add greatly to any garden. Shrub roses are extra hardy but not continuous blooming. Many are wild species adapted to landscaping like other shrubs. Miniature roses, 8 to 12 in. tall, are excellent in rock gardens and as edgings. Any desired variety may be produced in tree or standard form.

Roses need full sun for at least six hours of the day, preferably in the morning. Some shade from distant trees is desirable, but the bushes must have full use of the soil where they are planted. There must be no competing shrub or tree roots. Good air circulation is necessary, but exposure to heavy winds should be avoided. As with most plants,

(*Left*) Stamens are prominent in the open heart of Golden Wings, a charming sulphur-yellow hybrid tea with only five petals.

(*Left*) A bowlful of the variety Mary Margaret McBride. The deep coral-pink blooms are shimmering gold at the base.

(*Above*) **Fascinating hybrid tea rose is a fragrant combination of crimson and yellow. The 5-in. flowers are borne continuously until frost.**

drainage is extremely important. Average, fertile garden soil will grow roses, provided it is well dug and pulverized before the bushes are set out. Add peat moss and leaf mold to put it in top condition. A little fertilizer may also be mixed in, but more benefit will come from feeding the plant after it is established.

Any section of the country can enjoy roses when allowance is made for soil and climatic differences. In Florida, planting and pruning are best done in late December or early January. To solve drainage problems, the bushes are sometimes planted in raised beds; special fertilizer to supply elements lacking in the soil is frequently needed. Tender climbers do especially well in the South. In California, early January is the time for planting; pruning is done during the following month. Irrigation and extra fertilizer and mulch are customary.

Varieties. All-America Rose Selections are a reliable guide to the newest varieties. Recent winners of this award are the hybrid teas *Christian Dior* (crimson-red), *King's Ransom* (golden), *Duet* (two-tone pink), and *Garden Party* (cream flushed pink); the grandifloras *John S. Armstrong* (rich red) and *Pink Parfait;* and the floribundas *Golden Slippers* (orange-gold), *Fire King* (scarlet), and *Sarabande* (single orange-red).

(*Below*) **Tiffany, with high-pointed flowers on long stems, is heavily perfumed and admirable for cutting. Petals are of heavy substance.**

(*Above*) **Kordes Perfecta has attracted favorable attention for its unique coloring. Its petals are creamy white, with pink-splashed edges curling outward.**

(*Left*) **Exceptionally tapering buds guarded by long sepals distinguish Eclipse, which first bloomed on Eclipse Day, August 31, 1932. Time has only added to its fame.**

(*Left*) **John S. Armstrong is the newest of the grandiflora roses featured on this page. The blooms are carried both in clusters and one to a stem.**

(*Below*) **The beautiful buds of Pink Parfait contribute enormously to the effect of a plant in bloom. Pastel pink tints are mingled in a winning way.**

Peace, with a very sturdy plant and huge, pink-flushed creamy yellow flowers, is the rose scoring highest for performance. Other top hybrid teas are fragrant, velvety *Crimson Glory*, cerise-red *Charlotte Armstrong*, and crimson *Chrysler Imperial*. For many years two-tone pink *Radiance* has been regarded as the standby for beginners. *Queen Elizabeth*, a tall and handsome pink, was the first of the grandiflora class.

Betty Prior, with single pink flowers, is a fine floribunda. Coral-pink *Fashion*, cherry-coral *Vogue*, and orange-red *Spartan* are other superb representatives of this class. *Paul's Scarlet Climber* is old but still very popular; *Blaze* is an everblooming form. Apple-blossom-pink *New Dawn* is another exquisite climber, as well as white *City of York*, dark red *Don Juan*, and *Golden Showers*.

Flesh-white *Cinderella* and *Red Imp* are popular miniatures. The trailing *Memorial Rose* (*Wichuraiana*) makes a good ground cover for banks. Other notable shrub roses are early yellow *Hugonis* and red *Gruss an Teplitz*. The *Multiflora Rose* promoted as a living fence is best confined to meadows and fields because it is too rank a grower for garden use.

A good rose bush costs from $2.00 to $5.00 ($6.00 or more for a tree rose). Plants offered at cut-rate prices are seldom worthwhile.

(*Left*) **Buds of Starfire are urn shaped. They are rich currant-red, on a plant covered with bronzy, holly-like foliage.**

(*Below*) **Golden Slippers, a floribunda rose like all the varieties shown on the facing page, is a recent All-America winner.**

(*Left*) **Queen Elizabeth is a fittingly majestic grandiflora crowned with luminous pink flowers of good size and form.**

Two All-America floribundas. (*Left*) Sarabande, with brilliant light orange-red, semi-double blooms on a rather low-growing plant. (*Right*) Fire King, darker in color and very double.

How and When to Plant. In coldest regions plant in early spring; in most other areas either spring or fall planting is successful. A bush needs about 2 ft. of space. Buy a dormant, 2-year, No. 1, field-grown plant. Dig a generous hole in well-prepared soil. Be careful never to expose the roots to air while planting. Cut off any roots or twigs that may be damaged; if necessary, prune the top to 9 to 12 in. Spread out the roots, and work soil around them. In coldest areas the swollen part of the stem just above the roots should be 2 in. below soil level, but in milder climates it should be at soil level. Press hard around the roots, water thoroughly, and hill up the soil for several days.

Plants growing and often blooming in containers are widely available. These may be planted at practically any time.

Care and Protection. Prune bush roses as the leaf buds start to burst in early spring. Cut out dead branches and weak twigs; also shorten moderately the main canes and eliminate overlapping ones. On ramblers cut back the older canes after the blooming period. Everblooming climbers need less pruning; cut back the dead flowers to the first leaf bud.

In early spring scatter some rose fertilizer around the bushes and follow with a deep

©

(*Left*) For a continuous-blooming floribunda with shapely, orange-red to coral buds, you can hardly make a better choice than Spartan.

©

(*Right*) Vogue bears quantities of cherry-coral buds that open to nicely formed, fragrant flowers.

©

(*Left*) Well established as a standard floribunda is Fashion, which has won countless awards in many countries.

©

(*Right*) Betty Prior, dubbed the "pink dogwood" rose because of the general shape and size of its many flowers.

(*Left*) Jiminy Cricket, a tangerine-red floribunda with pleasing old rose fragrance. The plants are healthy and up to 4 ft. tall.

(*Right*) Goldilocks, a dependable floribunda like all the others shown on this page, has nicely formed flowers on a 2½-ft. bush.

watering. A second feeding may be given six to eight weeks later. Don't overfeed.

Keep the bushes healthy by spraying or dusting them regularly and thoroughly with a reliable combination insecticide and fungicide. A number of excellent preparations are on sale at garden stores. Follow directions implicitly.

Never let the plants go thirsty, but never sprinkle them lightly. Saturate the ground. Prevent weeds from growing and keep the soil moist by providing it with a layer of buckwheat hulls, peat moss or ground corncobs.

In cold regions mound the soil around the plants after the first hard frost. Add a cover of evergreen branches or straw if temperatures are likely to go lower than 10 degrees below zero. Uncover gradually the next spring.

(*Left*) The long slender buds of Ivory Fashion open to slightly cupped blooms of large size, which last well when cut fcr bouquets.

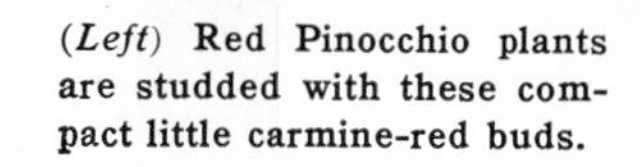

(*Left*) Red Pinocchio plants are studded with these compact little carmine-red buds.

(*Right*) Flowers of Circus proceed from rich gold and red to orange-buff, pink and apricot. The plant is of medium height.

©

(*Above*) Blaze is a smashing scarlet climber making a showplace of the most modest yard. It blooms repeatedly through the season when well established.

(*Right*) Paul's Scarlet Climber, a profuse bloomer in June, is very hardy and long lived. The flowers are practically identical with those of Blaze but do not recur through the summer.

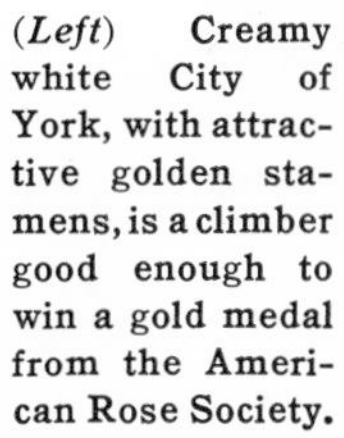

(*Left*) Creamy white City of York, with attractive golden stamens, is a climber good enough to win a gold medal from the American Rose Society.

(*Right*) Train Golden Showers either as a bush or as a low climber—it will do well either way.

(*Left*) New Dawn was the first plant to be patented (in 1931). This is a hardy everblooming climber of softest blush-pink.

(*Right*) The large, velvety dark red blooms of Don Juan climber are produced all summer long on a healthy plant.

©

MINIATURE roses—not over a foot high when full grown—are illustrated here. (*Left*) Red Imp, unfading crimson. (*Above*) Cinderella, dainty flesh color. (*Right*) Pixie, white. All may be grown outdoors or in pots on a window sill.

Red Pinocchio   Katherine T. Marshall   New Yorker   Fashion   Diamond Jubilee

TREE roses (above) are not actually tree size. The head of bloom is near the level of your eyes. In a suitable location they can be a dramatic garden highlight. Plant them in the spring.

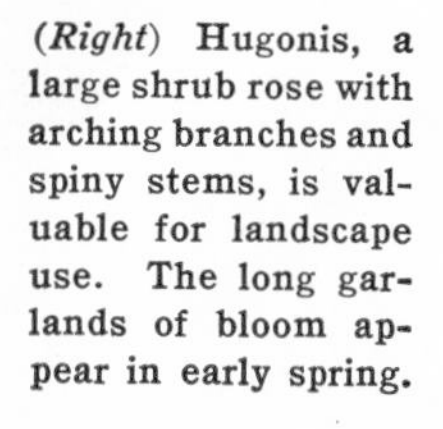

(*Right*) Hugonis, a large shrub rose with arching branches and spiny stems, is valuable for landscape use. The long garlands of bloom appear in early spring.

(*Left*) Mexicali Rose, a floribunda with gay fiesta colors—bright gold and red, changing to rose-pink and cerise.

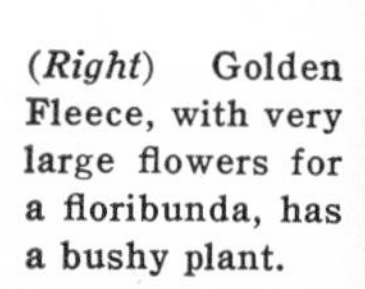

(*Right*) Golden Fleece, with very large flowers for a floribunda, has a bushy plant.

(*Left*) Russian olive, extremely hardy and sturdy, has been grown in the United States since early colonial days. The gray-green leaves are very ornamental.

(*Right*) Salpiglossis has funnel-shaped flowers in a riot of harmonious colors. Give it a sheltered place in full sun.

RUSSIAN OLIVE

SILVERY leaves are the chief feature of this vigorous and fast grower. As a large shrub or small tree reaching a height of about 20 ft. at maturity, it is an excellent choice for northern gardens, being dependably hardy all through southern Canada. Long, narrow leaves make dense growth in summer, and when they drop in autumn the shredding bark is a point of interest. The small, fragrant, yellow flowers are not very showy, and the yellow-orange berries with silvery scales are not even related to edible olives. A sunny spot in average garden soil will grow this drought-resistant ornamental.

Varieties. A 3 to 4-ft. plant costs $3.00 to $4.00. (For other members of this family, see *Elaeagnus*.)

How and When to Plant. Set out in spring or fall, in a hole large enough to hold the roots easily and at the same depth as in the nursery. Pack good soil around the roots, and water thoroughly.

Care and Protection. If pruning becomes necessary, do it in the spring.

SALPIGLOSSIS

CALL it painted tongue if you prefer, but that is not a very dignified name for this dainty cutting flower. Like other annuals such as mignonette, this is largely grown for cutting rather than for the showing it makes in the garden. Salpiglossis (sal-pig-gloss′iss) has narrow, sparse leaves and is not especially pleasing in the way it grows, but the clusters of petunia-shaped flowers are graceful and long lasting when used for indoor decoration. They come in shades of maroon, purple, blue and scarlet, penciled and veined in blended colors, and reach the height of their bloom in July and August. The 2½ to 3-ft. plants like good soil, a location in sun or part shade, and a cool growing season with not too much moisture. A dwarfer form about 20 in. tall is sometimes used in borders.

Varieties. *Emperor* is a 3-ft. strain with beautiful colors and velvety texture. The *Dwarf* strain has large flowers on a more compact plant.

How and When to Plant. Plants may be purchased at about 75c per dozen and set outdoors when frost is over. Or seed may be sown in April in very fine, rich soil. Because the seed is small, it should be mixed with sand and barely pressed into the ground. Thin the plants to 6 to 9 in. apart.

Care and Protection. Young plants need to be pinched back to make them branch better. Tall kinds require staking—or better yet, a place sheltered from summer storms. Feeding pays dividends.

(*Above*) Mountain sandwort, an excellent rock plant, provides a dense mass of foliage and white flowers in a sunny, sandy location.

SANDWORT

BECAUSE it does not mind being walked on, this little creeper (*Arenaria*) is excellent for planting between stepping-stones, around terraces and pools, and along paths. It forms a thick carpet almost like moss, with minute white flowers in May and June. In sunny rock gardens it is also useful, not for show but for a carpet. This hardy perennial likes gritty sand to grow in, enriched with some leaf mold.

Varieties. *Moss* sandwort, only 2 to 3 in. tall, is the kind commonly used as a carpeting plant. *Mountain* sandwort, 4 to 6 in. high, has larger white flowers. A plant may be bought for 60c.

How and When to Plant. Set out the plants in early spring or fall, 6 to 8 in. apart.

Care and Protection. Water in prolonged dry spells. When the plant spreads too far, divide it in early fall and replant the pieces.

(*Right*) Satin flower (described on the following page) is raised from seed sown very early. Plants bloom best before hot dry weather sets in.

Scarlet sage, like St. John's Fire (*left*) is fiery indeed, but there are also perennial members of this salvia family that have extra fine blue flowers. (*Above*) Pitcheri, a tall perennial. (*Right*) Farinacea, with slender flower spikes in summer and fall, is a tender perennial usually treated as an annual.

SATIN FLOWER

(*Illustration on preceding page*)

A NATIVE of the West Coast, this satiny-petaled annual furnishes masses of bloom in gardens where its needs can be met. The showy flowers, both single and double, are fine to cut for bouquets through the summer and fall. A cool moist climate is ideal, and a location in part shade. Hot weather is unbearable for satin flower. In the front ranks of a border, the dwarfer strains are attractive; taller kinds, to 2 ft., are also grown.

Varieties. Seed may be had in separate colors and also mixed. The botanical name is *Godetia*.

How and When to Plant. In early spring sow the seed outdoors in a partly shaded spot, where bloom is wanted. Cover it very lightly with soil. Thin out the young plants to 9 in. apart. In warm climates seed sown in August will provide flowers the following spring.

Care and Protection. These plants resent being moved, and it is therefore advisable to sow seed in the place where the plants are to remain.

SCARLET SAGE

THIS plant is not always scarlet, but the name seems to stick. The old-time scarlet sage that has sometimes been overplanted is available in other colors, and it has a number of relatives in the salvia family that come in shades of blue and lavender. In the garden it should be used in masses. It is a favorite for beds, edgings and borders, with perennials and against evergreens. A 10 to 20-in. tender plant, it needs rich soil and full sun or partial shade. It blooms until frost.

Several worthwhile blue salvias are perennials fine to cut and to combine with other moderate growers in a border. They take ordinary, well-drained soil and full sun.

Varieties. *Fireball* and *Fireworks* are among the newer varieties of scarlet sage. Both are early-blooming, dwarf plants that make good edgers. *St. John's Fire* is another very popular for edging. *America*, *Blaze of Fire* and *Bonfire* are older kinds. The *Welwyn* strain is offered in separate colors such as pink, white, lavender and maroon.

Blue Bedder, with slender spikes of deep Wedgwood-blue, is charming with pink flowers. This perennial grows 2 to 2½ ft. tall and blooms from July to October. The flowers can be dried, if desired. Another perennial salvia is *Patens*, with broad, tubular blooms of clear indigo-blue in late summer and fall. The branching stems of *Pitcheri* have deep blue flowers in autumn.

How and When to Plant. Because scarlet sage must be started early indoors, it is easier to buy plants (at about 25c each; 75c or more for perennial varieties). Set them out in May, 12 to 15 in. apart.

Set out plants of perennial salvia in early spring or fall.

Care and Protection. Spikes of taller kinds need staking. Pinching the early growth will make the plants bushier.

SCILLA

TWO quite different kinds of scilla (sill'uh) are popular for use in gardens. The one with starry white or blue flowers only 4 to 5 in. tall is called squill. Coming from Siberia, this spring-flowering bulb is very cold resistant and long lived. This dainty little flower appears among the first ones of spring, in March and April. It grows in full sun or part shade in good, well-drained soil. At the edge of the grass, in masses with other early bulbs, in rock gardens and in informal groups wherever a bit of early color can be enjoyed, it strikes a cheerful note.

The taller scilla is also known as wood hyacinth or Spanish bluebell. It blooms later, in May, and bears clusters of drooping blue, pink or white bells on 12 to 15-in. stems.

Scilla is a small hardy bulb indispensable in any spring planting. (*Left*) The 4 to 5-in., early-blooming kind sometimes called squill. (*Above and Right*) The taller, May-flowering variety.

It also is hardy and easy to grow. Under shrubs, naturalized in a half-wild area, and even under trees where it receives considerable shade, this proves effective.

Varieties. *Spring Beauty* is a large-flowered squill with rich blue flowers. Among the wood hyacinths offered are *Heavenly Blue*, *Queen of the Pinks*, *White Triumphator*, and blue *Myosotis*. A dozen bulbs cost 75c to $1.00.

How and When to Plant. In early fall scatter the bulbs on the ground where wanted. Plant squills 2 to 3 in. deep and 3 in. apart, and wood hyacinths 4 to 5 in. deep and the same distance apart.

Care and Protection. Leave the bulbs alone so that they may spread to make a nice colony.

SEA PINK

THRIFT is another name for this trim, compact perennial; its botanical name is *Armeria*. The grassy leaves, evergreen in most sections, grow in a neat tuft, and small, globular flowers come in early summer and often continue for several weeks. On wiry stems 6 to 18 in. long, they are nice for cutting. This is a hardy plant that does well at the seashore. It needs a sandy, well-drained soil, never heavy or waterlogged, and a sunny location. In rock gardens and low borders, and as a ground cover, it is a real acquisition.

Bees' Ruby sea pink has flower heads like powder puffs, perfect for cutting. This variety was named for the English firm that introduced it—Bees, Ltd.

Varieties. *Bees' Ruby*, with large, ruby-red flower heads on 18-in. stems, is an excellent variety, especially for cutting. Vigorous-growing *Formosa* has glossy foliage and bright pink flowers about 16 in. tall. Bright rosy-flowered *Laucheana* and white *Maritima Alba* are dwarf, tufted plants with flower stems only 6 in. high. They bloom in late May and are good edgers. About 60c will buy a plant.

How and When to Plant. Early spring or fall is the best time to get plants established. Allow 12 in. between them.

Care and Protection. Sea pink easily spreads into large clumps. Every second or third year, in early fall, separate them into smaller parts and replant.

SHADE PLANTING

A GARDEN of any kind flourishing in full shade is a credit to the person who takes care of it. Few plants will do well in all-day shade because the chlorophyll essential for their growth is dependent on sunlight. The deeper the shade and the more constant it is, the fewer the plants that will be able to survive. Flowering plants, in particular, must have sunshine. For this reason it is well to be content with green color in the shade and not expect many bright flowers.

If you have trouble with shaded areas under large trees, you will do well to investigate ground covers (which see). Sometimes it is possible to thin out part of the tree branches and allow at least more light, if not sunlight, to reach the ground below. When the branches are high, the problem is less serious. The dappled shade of trees with small leaves makes a pleasing design on the ground, and also permits a greater number of plants to grow there.

Avoid setting plants close to large trees. The roots of a tree may extend farther than you might assume, and the competition for water and sustenance may prove too much for plants sharing the same soil. Hemlocks and yews are the needled evergreens most reliable for growing in the shade. (See *Trees* for shade trees.)

There are some compensations for these difficulties. Generally plants growing in the shade need less watering. Colors are deeper and they last longer, even if they are scantier.

This serene picture does not reveal the problems that had to be met. To have both a smooth green lawn and the glorious shade of large trees is a genuine accomplishment.

Shade-loving plants are in evidence here, including ferns and the May-flowering scilla or wood hyacinth. Most flowering plants require more sun than this.

Seed germinates well in cool, shaded, protected spots. White flowers show up beautifully in the semi-darkness, and here they have a special, mysterious appeal.

Most broad-leaved evergreens do well in some shade. Camellias and rhododendrons like the protection of trees at a little distance, but if the shade is intense they will be more open in growth.

Among the perennials that tolerate some shade are coral bells, meadow-rue, leopard's bane, foxglove and Christmas rose. Bleeding heart, bluebells and columbine are early spring bloomers that stand part shade; many small bulbs can be used under trees because they flower and disappear before the leaves come out. Flowering plants that not only like some shade but actually require it to do their best are tuberous begonias, lily of the valley, primroses, plantain lily, snakeroot and monkshood. (See these under their separate headings.) Ferns and caladiums are indispensable in midsummer shade.

Vines such as Dutchman's pipe, honeysuckle and climbing hydrangea do well in part shade. Privet and barberry, English ivy, myrtle and pachysandra are valuable in countless shady places; in fact, they are the first line of defense in more than one garden.

(*Below*) Shasta daisies are hardy perennials that are particularly valued for cutting. They must always have a well-drained location. Shown here is the variety Jenifer Read, which has especially long stems.

SHASTA DAISY

THESE large daisies belong to the chrysanthemum clan. Growing 2 to 3 ft. tall on good sturdy stems, they are valuable for cutting as well as for planting in a group with other hardy perennials. Their white color makes it possible to use them with any other flowers, and they are fine blending material in a mixed bouquet. The plant makes a leafy crown close to the ground, which remains green all winter. It likes good garden soil and blooms freely in midsummer. Full sun is to be preferred, although a little shade does no harm.

Varieties. *Alaska* is a popular single variety, growing 2 ft. tall and blooming in June and July. *Edgebrook Giant*, another single, is 5 to 6 in. in diameter. *Esther Read* has very double blooms, with petals in thick layers, while *Wirral Supreme* boasts an attractive crested center. *Cobham Gold* is deep cream color. Plants cost 75c to $1.00 each.

How and When to Plant. Clumps or potted plants may be bought and set out in spring, allowing a foot of space to each. Dig some peat moss into the ground prior to planting. Press the soil firmly about the roots, and water thoroughly.

Care and Protection. Never let these plants suffer from lack of water in dry spells, but do not locate them where they will stand in water during the winter. They must have good drainage. Give them some peat moss or leaves as a winter covering, but see that whatever material is used does not mat on the crown of the plant and cause rotting. Every second or third year, when the flowering season is past, dig up the plant, divide it into smaller clumps, and set them out separately. Discard the center of the original clump and use only the outside pieces.

Such broad-leaved evergreen shrubs as the rhododendrons and azaleas in bloom here are satisfactory for planting where they receive some high shade part of the day.

SHRUBS

SHRUBS are sometimes taken for granted because they are so long lived and undemanding. Often the word *shrub* is carelessly applied to almost anything that grows, but by definition this is a woody plant with several stems growing from the base. Both the roots and the parts above ground live for many years. It is impossible to draw a hard line between large shrubs and small trees, although a tree has only one trunk while a shrub has several stems or shoots. Some shrubs are deciduous or leaf-losing (like lilacs). Those that do not shed all their foliage at one time may be needled evergreens (like yew) or broad-leaved evergreens (like rhododendrons and holly). Needled evergreens are continually dropping their old needles and replacing them with new ones, and all varieties are not as richly green in winter as in summer. Broad-leaved evergreen shrubs are slow growing, and they improve with age. Some are evergreen in the South and less so in northern regions.

A mixture of leaf-losing and evergreen shrubs is generally more pleasing in a home garden than a large collection of either type alone. Bare winter-time branches are not depressing in moderation, and the pleasure of watching them leaf out again in spring is ample compensation for the months of bareness. Besides, many of them have bright berries or an attractive bark in winter to offset the lack of foliage.

When you plan a border (see article on *Borders*), you will surely want to include shrubs, not only for their own beauty but for the stable air they give to any planting. At every season of the year they are an asset, whether in bloom or furnishing the backdrop for other plants. The bulk of their flowers will come in the first half of the growing season, although some shrubs bloom later. Smaller home grounds should concentrate on shrubs that stay low without pruning and are not rampant growers. Many of the compact ones of horizontal, spreading habit are especially appropriate for modern low rambling houses.

How to Choose the Right Shrubs. There is such an abundant assortment of shrubs available that you will enjoy making a choice. First decide where you will plant some shrubs. Don't count on moving them later; pick the right locations now. Next to the house, at the property line, in the border, at entrances, are some of the general areas that need them. Scattering shrubs around the lawn is an old-fashioned practice that

Where the roof of your house is low, you must be careful to use shrubs that will not grow high and appear to choke the building.

(*Left*) **Shrubs with autumn leaves as bright as those of burning bush may be excused for their winter-time nakedness. In deciding which shrubs to buy, investigate also their pruning requirements.**

(*Below*) **Pfitzer juniper is a needled evergreen shrub with horizontally spreading branches. Because of its hardiness and willingness to endure a smoky atmosphere, it enjoys wide use.**

only gives a spotty effect and makes grass trimming a bother.

Turn these points over in your mind as you try to fit the proposed shrub to the place where you will plant it: is this plant considered hardy in my area, how fast will it grow and how large will it get, will it receive enough sun (or shade) in this location, is my soil of the type it likes, when and for how long will it bloom, will the flowers clash with neighboring ones, what will it look like when not in bloom, is it interesting in winter, has it berries in addition to flowers? Try to visit a nursery and see the shrubs at several seasons, before you buy. Avoid too great a mixture, but also avoid monotony and skimpiness.

For soils that are damper than average, consider sweet shrub, pepperbush, lily of the valley shrub, mountain laurel, rhododendron and leucothoe. Some hollies, viburnums and spireas also can stand wet soil. On the other hand, privet and barberry, chaste tree, tamarix, beauty bush and smoke tree do well in dry soil. (See separate headings for all these shrubs.)

Important Rules for Proper Care. For most shrubs, improvement of the soil through the use of peat moss and leaf mold is more important than fertilizer at planting time. Get the soil in good condition to hold moisture and to allow penetration by plant roots. Deciduous (leaf-losing) shrubs may be planted in early spring before the leaf buds open, or early in the fall. In mild climates any time during the winter is satisfactory. When trying a plant that is not very hardy in your area, you will do best to set it out in spring. Evergreen shrubs can be planted a little later in spring than deciduous ones; just as the new green growth appears is the right time. Early fall planting is also successful for evergreens.

If the shrub is bare rooted when you get it, don't expose the roots to the air while planting. Cut off any bruised roots, and also shorten the branches of deciduous shrubs somewhat when you set them out. (Don't top-prune evergreens.) Plants sold with roots in a ball of earth wrapped in burlap (B&B) need not be removed from the burlap. Set them in the planting hole at the same depth as in the nursery; merely cut the burlap at the top and fold it back from the stem. If the shrub is in a container, it may be planted at practically any season. Don't disturb the ball of earth around the roots, and soak the soil both before and after you set out a container-grown plant.

After a year or so, a feeding of a complete fertilizer in early spring will benefit your shrubs. Broad-leaved evergreens will appreciate the fertilizer especially mixed for them (available at garden stores). A layer of peat moss, pine needles or grass clippings spread on the ground will help to keep it moist.

Cut the seed pods from lilacs, azaleas, weigela and rhododendrons as soon as they form. (For pruning of shrubs, see *Pruning* and separate listings.) Shake snow from all branches before it has a chance to freeze on them. Keep your shrubs in top growing condition and they will not easily become the prey of marauding insects and infections. There are many reliable remedies on the market that will be helpful when needed if you follow instructions faithfully.

SILK TREE

THIS little tree is beautiful in both foliage and flower. Its feathery, fern-like leaves are crowned in midsummer by heads of tassel-like, fragrant blooms of good pink color that last over a period of several weeks. Following the bloom come the long flat seed pods. The tree reaches 30 to 40 ft. in height, with a broad, spreading top. It blooms while quite young, even in poor dry soil. The first frost makes the leaves drop.

In the South, where it is sometimes known as mimosa, this ornamental is used as a street tree. (Botanically, it is *Albizzia.*) It is not considered hardy, although there is one form that is grown as far north as New England in sheltered places.

Varieties. In the North it is important to buy the hardy form. A 4 to 5-ft. specimen costs about $3.50.

How and When to Plant. Set out the

Silk tree, with lacy foliage and dainty pink bloom in midsummer, is sure of admiring comment wherever planted.

tree in spring or fall in a protected location. Provide a planting hole of ample size. Pack the soil hard around the roots, and water well.

Care and Protection. Early spring is the time to prune, but this graceful tree is best left alone.

SILVER LACE VINE

IN summer and early fall this vigorous, fast-growing vine is a mass of foamy, greenish white flowers. Also known as China fleece vine, it has dense bright green foliage untroubled by insects. It is a native of China, hardy over most of the United States. Growth the first year is as much as 15 or 20 ft. This is a twining vine for fence, trellis, post or lattice. It needs a warm, sunny location. Soil should be fairly rich and can be slightly on the dry side.

Varieties. *Polygonum auberti* is the scientific name of this sturdy vine, which is priced at about $1.50.

How and When to Plant. Plant in spring or fall beside the support it is to climb.

Care and Protection. Hard pruning in early spring is necessary to keep this exuberant grower within limits.

Quick-growing silver lace vine is hardy and healthy. It bears great clouds of feathery white bloom from midsummer on. This is a strong twiner.

SMOKE TREE

A VERY old garden favorite is the smoke tree or purple fringe, which gets its name from the misty appearance of the silky flower stalks covered with hairs. They come in summer and last over a long period. In the ordinary variety they are pinkish, turning gray, and the foliage, dense green in summer, becomes red and yellow in autumn.

This is a bushy, wide-spreading shrub to about 15 ft. in height, making a fine specimen on the lawn. It is easy to grow in well-drained, even rather poor, dry soil and is hardy as far north as southern Massachusetts. A shrub 2 to 3 ft. tall costs around $2.00.

(*Above*) Smoke tree is a dense, fast grower that does best in full sun. Once established, it can stand a somewhat dry soil.

(*Right*) Snakeroot is not an especially pleasing name for this perennial, and neither is bugbane, but plant it anyway if you have the place for it.

Varieties. The common smoke tree also has a form offered as *Royal Purple.* This is purple both in foliage and in its cloudy mass of "smoke." Growing 8 to 10 ft. tall, it has proved hardy in southern Iowa and western New York state. There is also a *Bronze-leaved* variety. These improvements are somewhat more expensive.

How and When to Plant. Give smoke tree a sunny location if possible, and plant in spring or fall. Dig a generous-sized hole, pack soil hard around the roots, and water well. Leave a slight depression around the base to allow for future watering.

Care and Protection. In planting, be extra careful not to disturb the roots or to let them get dried out by air or sun. Water well in dry spells during the first summer after planting. A layer of leaves and peat moss helps to keep the ground from drying out.

SNAKEROOT

IF you like bugbane better as a name for this hardy and very vigorous perennial, you may use it. A tall, upright grower, it makes a striking accent at the back of a border. It has large shiny leaves, and from midsummer on, the long, slim white flower spikes are outstanding. In moist rich soil they reach as much as 5 or 6 ft. in height. Part shade is a distinct advantage, as well as soil composed of leaf mold that will not dry out in hot summer weather. A shady location close to water is a good place for this plant.

Varieties. *Cimicifuga racemosa*, with graceful spikes of creamy white flowers in July and August, is especially nice near the edge of woods. It grows to 5 ft. *Simplex* is later, with plumy white spires plentifully produced in the shade in September and October. The spikes of *Davurica*, 3 to 4 ft. tall, are much branched. Plants cost 75c to $1.00.

How and When to Plant. Groups of plants, set 12 to 18 in. apart in early spring or fall, are good exclamation points in any garden.

Care and Protection. Don't let the soil get dry in hot spells (mulching is advisable), and don't disturb the planting.

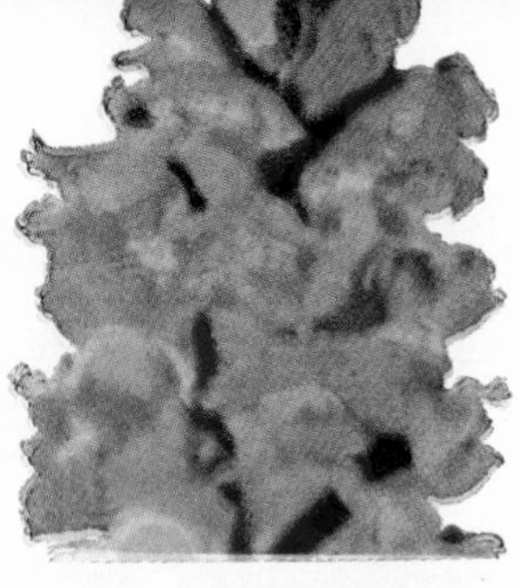

Snapdragons are easy to raise in the average garden, especially if you get improved rustproof strains. (*Left*) Rocket, which bears several crops per season. (*Above*) Extra large-flowered Tetra. (*Right*) A thriving bed of Mardi Gras.

SNAPDRAGONS

MANY admirable qualities have made snapdragons popular. They are an important greenhouse crop for the florist because they are so good for cutting and come in such a wide assortment of colors. Dozens of varieties are available to florists, who carefully time their flowering periods. The name snapdragon is an attempt to describe the shape of the individual flowers with their "jaws" that open wide when pressed at the base. The botanical name, *Antirrhinum*, meaning *like a nose*, is another reference to the form of the flower.

Outdoors snapdragons are fine for several uses. They appear in dwarf, medium and tall strains, and therefore can be used as edging plants, in borders, and as stately accent spots with other summer-flowering annuals. They bloom from about the middle of July to frost, and are a welcome highlight for bouquets. Often the seed sows itself, and new plants come up the next year. Plant breeders have greatly improved the varieties on sale.

Varieties. *Tetraploid* (or shortened to *Tetra*) snapdragons have particularly heavy stems and big ruffled flowers. They grow about 2 ft. tall. Hybridists produced them by treating older varieties with the drug colchicine. *Rocket* snapdragons have been bred especially to resist the heat of midsummer. Their 3-ft. spikes are set with large flowers, evenly spaced. *Mardi Gras* is another vigorous, early-flowering hybrid. Double-flowered *Vanguard*, 3 ft. tall, is an award winner. *Magic Carpet*, only 6 in. high, may be used as an edger, in rock gardens and even in porch boxes.

How and When to Plant. Sow seed (be sure it is rustproof) outdoors in April, or indoors in February. Mix it with dry sand, cover with very little soil, and transplant the seedlings as soon as you can handle them. Tallest varieties should be set outdoors about 18 in. apart, medium tall kinds 10 in. apart, and the low ones 6 in. apart. Perhaps the easiest way is to buy the plants locally in May. They need quite rich soil and a spot in full sun.

Care and Protection. About twice in early summer, pinch out the center of the little plants to make them bushier, and give them some fertilizer. Tallest kinds require staking. Be sure to use nothing but rust-resistant strains.

SNEEZEWEED

IN late summer and early autumn the big flower clusters of this sturdy perennial (*Helenium* is the scientific name) make a mass of color. They bloom with hardy asters, before chrysanthemums take over the garden. The daisy-petaled flowers come in shades of yellow, brown and orange, with a prominent center. Older kinds were very rank and coarse growing, but the new varieties are more restrained and also excellent to cut. This is a native American plant, hardy and easy to grow in average soil and full sun. It needs a fair amount of moisture and may be planted in the background for mass effect. Height varies from 2½ to 5 ft.

Varieties. *Moerheim Beauty*, a very fine plant for any border, grows 2½ to 3 ft. tall and bears glowing crimson flowers from July through September. *Crimson Beauty* and *The Bishop*, with yellow blooms, are 2 to 3 ft. high. Copper and gold *Chippersfield Orange* and *Riverton Beauty* (bright yellow tinted orange) reach 4 to 5 ft. in height. Another good deep yellow is *Bigelovi*. Plants average 75c in price.

How and When to Plant. Plant in fall or spring, and allow plenty of room—about 2 ft. Water well.

Care and Protection. Stake the plant, and pinch back the tips of early growth to encourage bushiness. Every spring dig up the clump, throw away the center, and replant the outer pieces.

(*Left*) The lively, glowing colors of sneezeweed combine well with other flowers of autumn.

SNOWBALL

LOGICALLY, this shrub belongs with others of its family (see *Viburnum*), but such a household name as snowball deserves separate listing. The flowers, exactly like big round white snowballs, are a familiar sight as summer comes in. This is perhaps not a very choice plant, but sentiment keeps it for the sake of old-time associations. It is very free blooming and grows to 6 or 8 ft. in height. The vigorous bush prospers in full sun or part shade, in any garden soil that is not too dry.

Varieties. *Japanese* snowball is preferable to the *Common* or *European* because it is not attacked by plant lice. It is not quite so hardy, but can usually stand the winters in New England. In the South, *Chinese* snowball is used. A 2-ft. plant costs about $2.00.

How and When to Plant. Set out in spring or fall, in a good-sized planting hole. Press the soil well around the roots, and water thoroughly.

Care and Protection. Any pruning necessary should be done immediately after the blooming season. To renew an old bush, cut some of the old canes back to the ground.

(*Above*) Japanese snowball is a hardy and familiar shrub grown in the United States for a hundred years or more.

(*Left*) Snowberry is laden with these fat white berries even if grown in only moderately good soil.

(*Right*) Snowdrops will tell you spring is on its way, even if they have to push through the snow to do it.

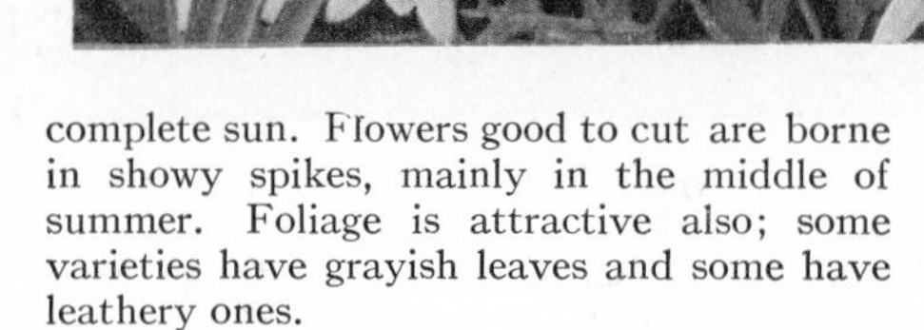

(*Below*) Snow on the mountain is a vigorous grower with green and white leaves that are very showy.

SNOWBERRY

THESE waxy white berries come in such big, heavy clusters that the arching branches of this shrub bend to the ground. They are formed by September, and they last through the fall. Dense clusters of small pink flowers bloom in June and July. Practically any soil suits this 3 to 4-ft. shrub, and semi-shade is just as acceptable as full sun. It grows wild all across the northern part of North America and is easily raised from there southward. Its leaves drop in the fall. (See also *Coralberry*, of the same family.)

Varieties. Waxberry is a less-used name. An 18 to 24-in. plant costs about $1.00.

How and When to Plant. Set it out in spring or fall, in a hole big enough to hold the roots comfortably. Firm the soil around them, and water well.

Care and Protection. Yearly pruning is not necessary. If desirable, some of the older shoots may be thinned out occasionally in the spring.

SNOWDROP

FOR planting in the lawn, snowdrops are preferable to crocuses because the foliage dies faster. But a better place for this dainty forerunner of spring is under trees, at the edge of an evergreen hedge, in rock gardens, or at a doorstep where it will attract instant attention. Wherever used, it must be in a sizable mass to be effective. Delicate stems hold the drooping bells among narrow, dark green leaves. This hardy small bulb grows 6 to 8 in. high in almost any soil, in sun or cool damp shade.

Varieties. *Single* snowdrops cost about 75c for a dozen bulbs; *Double* a little more. *Elwesi* has especially large bells.

How and When to Plant. Set out the bulbs in very early autumn, 3 in. deep and 3 in. apart or closer.

Care and Protection. Left alone, snowdrops form a colony that will be enjoyed for many years.

SNOW ON THE MOUNTAIN

EVEN poor soil will satisfy this familiar, old-fashioned annual. The white-edged light green foliage is a showy highlight through the growing season. Reaching 2 to 2½ ft. in height, the strong, well-branched plants are attractive in borders. They grow easily from seed and often self-sow; in many parts of the United States they grow wild. Snow on the mountain is often used as a filler in mixed bouquets. It will flourish either in part shade or in full sun.

Varieties. *Euphorbia marginata* is the botanical name of this relative of the Christmas poinsettia.

How and When to Plant. Sow the seed in the open ground in early spring, and thin out the young plants to 9 to 12 in.

Care and Protection. Be sure to sow seed where the plants are wanted, for transplanting is not very successful. The stems produce a milky juice poisonous to some persons.

SPEEDWELL

BOTH mixed perennial plantings and rock and wall gardens enjoy the excellent blue color supplied by most types of this hardy plant. Pink and white varieties are also to be had, but blue is the predominant color. Speedwells are not difficult to grow and will give a fine account of themselves in any reasonably fertile garden soil. They do like complete sun. Flowers good to cut are borne in showy spikes, mainly in the middle of summer. Foliage is attractive also; some varieties have grayish leaves and some have leathery ones.

In rock gardens, low-growing kinds are very useful, with flowers in neat little spires that give a bit of height. Excellent also as a ground cover, these drought-resistant plants need good drainage. Plants average 75c each. Their scientific name, *Veronica*, is prettier than the common one.

Varieties. Among the pleasing blue-flowered varieties for border planting are *Blue Champion*, *Blue Spire* and *Sunny Border Blue*. Flower stalks are 18 to 24 in. tall. *Minuet* and *Barcarolle* are rose-pink, the former with gray-green foliage. Gleaming white *Icicle* also has soft gray leaves. Its 15 to 18-in. flower spikes are excellent for cutting from June to September. *Holophylla*, with glossy leathery leaves and dark indigo-blue flowers in late summer, is not so tall—only 12 in.

For sunny rock gardens *Incana* is recommended. This one is a low grower with narrow silvery leaves and 6-in., violet-blue spires in early summer. Another splendid kind for wall and rock gardens and for the edge of a

Speedwell varieties suitable for garden borders are shown here. (*Above*) Sunny Border Blue and darker Blue Spire. (*Left*) See how graceful the spikes are when cut?

(*Left*) **Spider flower, variety Pink Queen, is a fresh salmon-pink that turns to white, giving a soft blending of colors.**

(*Right*) **A clump of spiderwort like this can be relied on for a long life, even if neglected.**

paved terrace is *Rupestris*, a creeper that makes a solid evergreen mat. It is covered with little deep blue flower spikes in June. This plant is strong growing and persistent, and it stands hot weather well.

How and When to Plant. Plant in groups of three for a nice effect, in early fall or spring, leaving 12 to 15 in. between plants.

Care and Protection. Cut back the flower stalks after the color fades. Every third or fourth spring the tall kinds should be dug up, divided into smaller clumps, and replanted.

SPIDER FLOWER

IF you don't like spiders, think of these flowers as big airy clusters of butterflies. (Botanically, they are *Cleome.*) They grow on a tall spike, as much as 3 or 4 ft. high, which puts them at the back of the border, grouped with cosmos and hollyhocks or with perennials and shrubs. Because spider flower is a quick grower it is particularly valuable for temporary effects. Free flowering through the summer, this annual is nevertheless not good for cutting because the spikes wilt so quickly. It takes to a hot dry spot and can endure considerable shade.

Varieties. *Pink Queen*, with big heads of salmon-pink, stands the heat well and blooms until late fall. A white one is named *Helen Campbell.*

How and When to Plant. Sow seed outdoors in spring, in either poor or rich soil. When plants are large enough to handle, set them 12 to 18 in. apart, or closer if among shrubs. Best effects are produced when lower plants are set in front; blue would be a good color choice. Spider flower often self-sows.

Care and Protection. No insects or diseases seem to affect this plant.

SPIDERWORT

THIS absolutely dependable perennial enjoys a long, carefree life no matter where it is planted. Even when forgotten, it will make the best of things and continue to grow and bloom for years. If given a choice, it likes a fairly moist soil and slight shade part of the day. The plant forms a large grassy clump with foliage to 15 in. in length and blue, rosy or white flowers snuggled at the base of the leaf. A steady succession of fresh flowers is produced from midsummer on. Where growing in the wild, spiderwort (or *Tradescantia*) reaches a height of 2 or 3 ft., but newer kinds 15 to 18 in. tall are more usual for the front of a border.

Varieties. *Iris Pritchard* (white tinted blue), *Pauline* (orchid-pink), *James C. Weguelin* (pale blue) and *Purple Dome* (clear bright purple) are among the kinds offered by nurserymen. A plant costs around 90c.

How and When to Plant. Either fall or spring is the time to set out the plants. Three of them spaced a foot apart will make a fine bushy clump.

Care and Protection. Every few years dig up and divide the clump in spring.

SPIREA

THE only trouble with spirea is that everybody plants it. If it were less accommodating, it would be seen more rarely. These sturdy shrubs fall in the medium-height class and are of the easiest culture, lasting many years. They are hardy and have attractive foliage even when not in bloom. The flowering season of some is May and June, of others a month or two later. Full sun is best for them, or very light shade. Bushes are easy to move. A dollar or less will buy a plant of the common kinds.

The name spirea is sometimes applied to astilbe, but that is an entirely different plant, as is blue mist shrub which is often called blue spirea. (See also *Bridal Wreath.*)

Varieties. *Anthony Waterer*, with flat heads of rosy crimson, comes in midsummer. Its compact, 2 to 3-ft. plant looks well in front of taller shrubs. Rose-colored *Froebel* has a 3-ft., spreading plant that is drought resistant. *Arguta* and *Thunberg* are two good white kinds, the former with slender branches and the latter very early blooming.

How and When to Plant. Spring or fall is the time to plant, in any kind of soil, preferably in full sun.

Care and Protection. Cut away any dead branches in early spring. If the plants start to get out of bounds, trim them after the blooming period. Try to retain the natural shape of the plant, and allow new shoots to grow up to replace the older ones.

STAR OF BETHLEHEM

(*Illustration on next page*)

THE star-shaped white flowers of this hardy bulb are greenish underneath and are borne in clusters on 6-in. stems in late spring. The plant soon spreads to form a large mass and should be used only where there is plenty of space, as in a shrub border, under trees, or naturalized in a semi-wild area. Sun or light shade and ordinary, well-drained garden soil will grow it. The grassy foliage dies away in midsummer.

There are also tender kinds which are grown outdoors in the lower South and indoors in other regions. Chincherinchee, with long-lasting flowers imported from South Africa, is one of this family.

Spirea is always hardy and easy to grow, but don't restrict yourself to it. (*Left*) Thunberg, a graceful, 4 to 5-ft. variety. (*Above*) Anthony Waterer, attractive and free blooming.

(*Left*) **Star of Bethlehem multiplies very rapidly and should be allowed ample room to spread.**

(*Right*) **St. Johnswort, an extremely useful little shrub even if not completely hardy. It can endure rather dry soil.**

Varieties. *Ornithogalum umbellatum* is the hardy star of Bethlehem. A dozen bulbs may be bought for about 50c. *Arabicum,* with fragrant white flowers, is popular for growing indoors.

How and When to Plant. Plant bulbs outdoors in early fall, 2 in. deep and 2 to 3 in. apart. To grow tender varieties indoors, plant several bulbs in a 6-in. pot and barely cover with soil. Keep in a cool place until well rooted, and then move to a sunny window.

Care and Protection. When the planting gets too crowded, dig up and divide the bulbs.

ST. JOHNSWORT

BLOOMING through most of the summer when shrubs in flower are not too plentiful, this plant is useful at the front of a border and as a low hedge. There are a number of varieties, all yellow flowered; one is good as a ground cover. Hardy to about the Philadelphia area, their bright yellow, cupped blooms are produced in profusion for many weeks. Practically any soil is satisfactory, and a location in sun or part shade.

Varieties. *Hypericum calycinum*—sometimes called Aaron's beard—is the kind that makes an excellent ground cover, especially on banks, but it is not hardy in the North. Growing 12 to 18 in. tall, it does well in light shade. *Hidcote* has 2 or 3-in., fragrant, bright yellow flowers on an 18 to 24-in. plant. In the North it freezes to the ground in winter but easily re-establishes itself the next spring. *Sungold* is perhaps hardier, with attractive foliage and golden flowers all summer. A 2 to 3-ft. plant costs about $2.50; smaller sizes of the ground-cover variety are less expensive.

How and When to Plant. Set out the plants in spring or fall, in generous holes that will not crowd the roots. Pack the soil well, and water thoroughly. For a hedge or ground carpet, allow 18 in. between plants.

Care and Protection. Unless winter kills back these shrubs, they should be pruned hard in spring. Also when used as a ground cover, they need a spring clipping.

STOCKS

BLOSSOM-PACKED columns of stock are familiar in florists' arrangements, and it is possible to grow this flower in the home garden—but not easy. But because of its sweet scent, fine tall spikes and excellence for cutting, it is highly prized in the border with other annuals. The rosette-shaped flowers come in such colors as pink, rose, red, blue, purple and yellow, but if the buds are not formed before hot weather sets in, the plants are not likely to bloom. They want rich soil, full sun and cool, moist conditions. For garden use, it is necessary to get early-blooming strains.

Varieties. *Trysomic Seven Weeks* is the earliest-blooming stock yet produced. The branching, bushy plants, 12 to 15 in. high, have many double flowers. *Ten Weeks,* 15 to 18 in. tall, is an older attempt to get plants into bloom early. It too may be had in separate or mixed colors. Many are double and all are richly perfumed. *Giant Imperial* (*Bismarck*) grows tall (2½ ft.) and has very long-stemmed, double flowers. *Beauty of Nice* has pyramidal-shaped, 18-in. plants. *Night-scented* stock opens its purplish white, deliciously fragrant flowers in the evening.

How and When to Plant. It is safer to buy plants (about 75c to $1.00 per dozen) and set them out in May than to try growing stock from seed. Give each plant 9 to 12 in. of space.

Care and Protection. Keep well watered in dry weather. The plants must be kept growing and not allowed to get stunted. Frequent feeding pays.

STOKES ASTER

IN areas where winter weather is not too severe or variable, this fine perennial (*Stokesia*) is a valuable addition to late summer borders, where it provides pink and white flowers as well as those in shades of blue. It is a native plant growing from South Carolina to Louisiana, and in those latitudes it is a vigorous grower with glossy foliage, flowering from July through September or later. With care, it may even be grown in New England. The blooms, 3 to 4 in. across,

(*Above*) **In both form and color, Blue Moon is a most desirable variety of Stokes aster.**

(*Left*) **When you find marigolds and nasturtiums "too easy," you will want to try a more difficult annual like these Ten Weeks stocks.**

Stonecrop likes warm, sandy soil. (*Left*) Golden Carpet, a fine ground cover blooming from June to frost. (*Above*) Spectabile, a taller kind that is good looking for many weeks. (*Right*) Sieboldi, with pink-tinged leaves that grow in whorls of three around the stem.

are good to cut. Late-flowering annuals make good companion plants. Full sun and well-drained, sandy soil are essential.

Varieties. *Blue Moon*, with giant, light lavender-blue flowers on 12 to 18-in. stems, is a choice variety, as is *Silver Moon*, with white flowers. *Blue Danube*, of about the same height, bears large blue flowers. Plants cost 75c to $1.00.

How and When to Plant. Spring is the best planting time. Set plants 12 to 15 in. apart, and water well.

Care and Protection. Where winters are likely to bring alternate freezing and thawing, provide a protecting cover of straw or evergreen branches.

STONECROP

A CROP from stones does not appear possible, and yet this plant literally runs away over the stones and clothes them with soft color. Both its leaves and its flowers are pleasing. The very large family also includes taller plants excellent for flower borders all summer long, and especially late in the season when they bloom.

Foliage is thick, smooth and fleshy; in some varieties it is decidedly gray or bluish, often tinted pink or purple or edged with lighter green. Many kinds are evergreen trailers, or they form carpets of delightful thick leaves covered with bloom in their season. Leaves may be in rosettes or on longer arching stems. These plants are very hardy, and probably nothing is easier to establish in a garden. In fact, some members of the tribe are a nuisance because they crowd out everything else. The low growers offered by nurserymen make a fine carpet in sunny rock gardens, and are easily grown between paving blocks and in pockets in a stone wall. Full sun, perfect drainage and poor soil suit its needs. It can stand dry conditions better than most plants.

Varieties. *Sedum acre* forms a thick light evergreen carpet of flat leaves, with bright yellow flowers in May and June. It is a very useful rock-garden plant and ground cover, as is *Kamtschaticum*, which has broad prostrate green leaves and wide heads of orange-yellow flowers in midsummer. *Golden Carpet* is a form with variegated foliage and golden yellow flowers on a 6 to 8-in. plant. *Spurium* is another low grower for dry banks, but it also can be used as an edging for a flower border. It has pink or red to white flowers. The rounded, bluish gray leaves of *Sieboldi* are sometimes edged with pink. It has curved stems and pink flowers from August to early fall. This one is attractive when grown in crocks on a terrace or patio.

A tall variety for perennial borders is *Spectabile*. It is an 18-in., showy plant with thick stems and leaves of light gray-green. The large, flat heads of rose-pink flowers, produced in August and September, are an attraction for butterflies and are also good for cutting. This plant likes fairly rich soil. *Brilliant* is a red-flowered variation. Plants of stonecrop cost 50c to $1.00.

How and When to Plant. Very easy to grow, these plants may be started at practically any season. Taller kinds are best set out in spring.

Care and Protection. Tall varieties may require dividing and replanting if they grow too large.

STRAWFLOWERS

XERANTHEMUM, *Ammobium*, *Gomphrena*, *Helipterum*, *Acroclinium*, *Helichrysum*, *Statice*—shake them together and you will be calling them strawflowers or everlastings. Their flowers are of varied form and size, whether daisy-like or ball-shaped or like a little cat-tail, but all are good for drying and using for home decoration in winter. When the job is done properly, the flowers retain their color for dried bouquets, arrangements and holiday decoration. Plants of these various kinds are sturdy and not fussy about soil. Flowers range through pink, rose, red, purple, violet, yellow and white.

Varieties. Seed of strawflowers or everlastings may be bought under any of the names listed above, or as a mixture.

How and When to Plant. Sow the seed in spring in any average garden soil, in full sun. Thin the plants to about 8 in. apart.

To Dry the Flowers. Cut the flowers just as they reach the peak of bloom, taking as much stem as possible. Strip off the leaves, and tie the flowers in small bunches. Hang up to dry in a warm, dark place (never in the sun or in artificial heat) where there is free circulation of air. In two or three weeks they will be dried.

(*Above*) Strawflower is a term applied to several annuals easy to dry for winter. Shown above is Acroclinium.

(*Left*) Sunflowers (described on the next page) are used for bold effects. Coronation, illustrated here, has blooms about 4 in. wide.

SUNFLOWERS

(*Illustration on preceding page*)

THE name proclaims this to be a flower for the sun. Extremely vigorous in growth, the old-time black-centered variety reaching huge proportions was once an accepted part of a family vegetable garden, where its seeds were devoured by birds. There are also more refined kinds for flower gardens. They are very sturdy growers—some annual, some perennial—for background use and for screens. They need just ordinary soil and all the sun they can get.

Varieties. Annual kinds grown from seed include *Sun Gold* and *Chrysanthemum-flowered* (very double, golden yellow), *Stella* (single, yellow with black center), and *Excelsior Hybrids* (wine-red, brown and gold). Plants are 3 to 4 ft. tall or more.

Coronation, 4 ft. tall (broad-petaled flowers with a cushion center) and *Loddon Gold* (double, deep yellow) are good perennial kinds that are suitable for cutting. Plants cost about 95c.

How and When to Plant. Sow seed of annual kinds outdoors in early spring where wanted. Set out perennial plants, 12 in. apart, in fall or spring.

Care and Protection. To keep perennial plants from spreading too much, dig up the clump every other fall, divide it into smaller parts, and replant.

SWEET PEAS

FRAGRANT, fragile, pastel sweet peas are grown to be cut. By the handful or in an elaborate arrangement from the florist, they are loved for their sweet perfume and delicate beauty. Commercial growers find them an important crop, and large numbers of varieties are available for winter cultivation in greenhouses.

To raise sweet peas in home gardens requires careful attention to their needs. They must have cool soil and cool weather, rich, well-drained soil, and wire or brush to which they can attach their tendrils. They grow 4 to 7 ft. high, although there is also a bush form.

Varieties. *Giant Spencer* sweet peas were developed for their huge, frilled flowers, but newer strains stand warm weather better. *Cuthbertson* kinds bloom early and were bred to resist the heat. They are richly fragrant and come in all colors. *Cuthbertson Floribunda* is an improvement, with five or more flowers on a stem. *Zvolanek Multiflora* is vigorous and fragrant, also with many blooms per stem. *Early Flowering* kinds are for winter culture indoors or for planting in the fall in warm areas. The bush form, only 8 in. high and requiring no staking, is *Little Sweetheart*. The large, fragrant, ruffled flowers in all colors are produced early and over a long season. This is more adaptable to a place in a bed or border than any other sweet pea. *Hardy* sweet peas, blooming from July to September, make a good bank cover but are not fragrant.

How and When to Plant. Just as early as the ground can be worked in spring, sweet peas must be planted. Soak the seed in water overnight. Dig a trench a foot wide and deep, and in the bottom put a 6-in. layer of organic fertilizer (dried manure) and rich loam. Press this down well and on it place the seeds 1 to 2 in. apart. Cover with 2 in. of soil. As they grow, gradually fill up the trench with soil. When the plants are 6 in. high, they need a support of chicken wire, brush or strings. Don't try to transplant them, and never let the soil dry out. Grass clippings spread on the ground around them will help keep it cool and moist.

Care and Protection. Green lice on the stems must be sprayed with a solution containing nicotine, malathion or lindane. Keep the flowers cut, to make them bloom longer.

Even a few stems of fragrant sweet peas make a pleasant little offering. Cut them freely to keep the plants blooming. (*Left*) Little Sweetheart retains this mound-like form through the season.

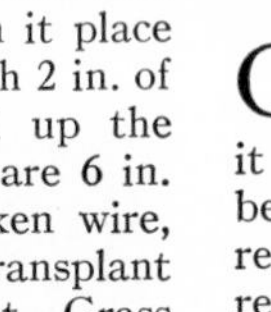

SWEET SHRUB

CAROLINA allspice is another name for this old-time native American shrub, but it is hardy far beyond the Carolinas. It may be grown as far north as the Great Lakes region. When crushed in the hand, the reddish brown flowers have a delightful and lingering, spicy scent. They bloom from May to July. The symmetrical, 4 to 5-ft. plant has an open habit of growth and glossy green leaves that are attractive until they drop in autumn. The shrub grows vigorously in almost any well-drained soil.

Varieties. The scientific name is *Calycanthus floridus*. A plant 18 to 24 in. tall costs $1.50 to $2.00.

How and When to Plant. Set out the plant in fall or spring, in a hole of generous size. Pack good soil around the roots, and water thoroughly.

Care and Protection. Pruning and fertilizing are unnecessary.

Sweet shrub, an old-fashioned plant with flowers that children—and grown-ups too—like to squeeze in their hands for their fragrance.

(*Left*) The fluffy flowers of sweet sultan last well both on the plant and in water. They bloom quickly from seed.

(*Right*) Sweet William won its place in gardens centuries ago, and it is still loved for its masses of bright blooms.

SWEET SULTAN

THE silky, fringed flowers of this easy annual are related to bachelor's button. Feathery and light, they are very sweet scented and come in delicate tints of white and pink, lavender and yellow. Plants grow 2 to 3 ft. tall, and the slender stems are good for cutting during many weeks in summer if the flowers are not allowed to go to seed. Ordinary garden soil and full sun fill its needs.

Varieties. Generally *Giant Mixed* seed is sold, providing large fringed flowers on 3-ft. plants.

How and When to Plant. Sow seed outdoors as early as possible in spring, and thin the little plants to 9 in. apart.

Care and Protection. Be generous in cutting the flowers so that they cannot form seed.

SWEET WILLIAM

OLD-FASHIONED flowers are always in fashion when they are as pretty as this one. The colorful and fragrant flower clusters of ruby and pink, crimson and white—often zoned or starred—are long lasting when cut. They are good massed in a garden border where they bloom in early summer. Varieties 12 to 18 in. tall are excellent with spires like delphinium and foxglove; dwarf ones are much used for edging. In full sun and ordinary garden soil the plants are very easily handled. While not long lived, they often live over from year to year where winters are not too severe, and it is easy to raise fresh plants from seed. Often the plants self-sow. They are of the same family as pinks and carnations (which see).

Varieties. *Crimson Beauty*, *Scarlet Beauty*, *Giant White* and *Newport Pink* (pure salmon-pink) are popular varieties. Both seeds and plants are easily available. *Wee Willie*, a dwarf one only 5 to 6 in. tall, is a fine edger. The single flowers of many colors are at their peak seven or eight weeks after the seed is sown. *Sweet Wivelsfield*, a cross between sweet William and Allwood pinks, is a bushy, 12-in. plant that blooms profusely. It has large flowers with dark centers.

How and When to Plant. Plants may be set out in fall or spring, 10 in. apart. Or seed may be sown in June or July and the plants moved that fall or early next spring to the place where bloom is wanted. Seed sown early in the spring will sometimes produce flowering plants later that year.

Care and Protection. With a little winter covering in very cold areas, plants will often live through to the next season.

TAMARIX

SUCH a feathery-looking shrub might appear tender and hard to grow, but that is not true of tamarix (tam'uh-rix). It does well even at the seashore, where it is subjected to wind and salt spray. Inland it also grows into a 6 to 15-ft. plant of very open, graceful habit, losing its tiny silvery leaves in the fall. Several kinds are hardy as far as southern New England. The thin branches carry their very small, usually pink flowers in late spring or early summer. This shrub

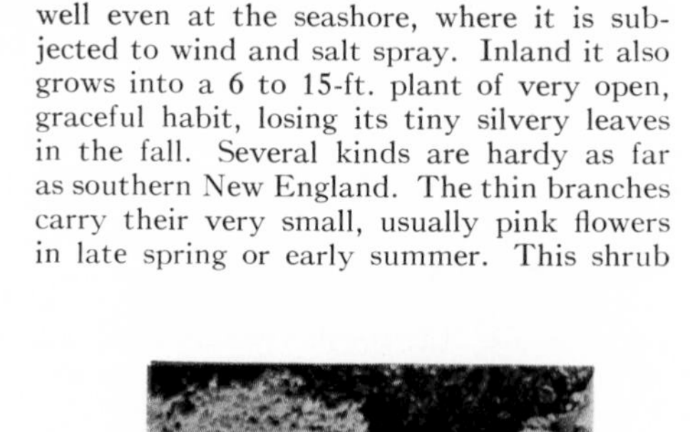

(*Above*) Woolly thyme (described on the facing page) is here growing in a crack between the stones, where it forms a thick mat.

(*Left*) Pink Cascade tamarix, a fleecy pink cloud. Prune it early in the spring.

Tiger flowers are treated like gladiolus. Try some for their novelty value, both as cut flowers and in groups with white phlox.

may be grown either as a specimen or as an informal hedge.

Varieties. *Odessana* is a good choice where space is limited because it reaches a height of only 5 or 6 ft. It bears feathery pink flowers in June or July and is hardy to the Great Lakes. *Hispida* is recommended for midwestern and southern areas. *Summer Glow*, with silvery blue-green foliage and airy rose-pink flowers, grows 8 ft. tall unless pruned, as does rose-flowered *Pink Cascade*. A 2 to 3-ft. plant costs around $2.00.

How and When to Plant. Set out in fall or spring, in good garden soil. (In the North, however, it would be safer to plant in the spring.)

Care and Protection. Prune hard in early spring to keep the plants low and bushy.

THYME

(*Illustration on preceding page*)

BETWEEN flagstones, as a ground cover, on walls and in rock gardens, thyme (time) finds many ways to make itself indispensable. In general, the flowers are less noteworthy than the dense evergreen foliage and the thick creeping way it grows. At all seasons of the year it is fresh and attractive, doing well in sunny locations where the soil is light and not too rich. It stands dry weather well. Some kinds hug the ground, and none are more than a few inches high. The blooming season is June and July.

Varieties. *Creeping* thyme is a tiny-leaved evergreen creeper that can be walked on. Pink flowers appear in June. At the edge of walks and between stepping-stones its value is appreciated. An excellent ground cover for sunny areas is *Lemon-scented*. It grows about 6 in. tall, with fragrant foliage and lavender-pink flowers. *Common* thyme has gray leaves used for seasoning, which can be dried for winter. The tiny soft gray leaves of *Woolly* thyme make a thick curtain when this plant is set in the crack of a stone wall. It likes the sun and well-drained soil. Thyme plants cost about 60c each.

How and When to Plant. Set out the plants in early fall or spring, about 6 in. apart. Even the smallest roots will grow.

Care and Protection. A little winter protection in northern sections is desirable.

TIGER FLOWER

CALLED tiger flower for its spotted flowers, or Mexican shell flower because of its origin, this tender bulb is grown like gladiolus. The huge blooms are sometimes 6 in. across, on stiff stems 2 to 2½ ft. tall. They have three large petals of yellow, orange, pink or white, with three smaller spotted ones at the center. This unusual combination is pleasing and distinctive. The slender stem has several buds in a tight cluster. Each flower lasts only one day but is immediately replaced by another over a period of several weeks from mid-July on.

These bulbs are best planted in groups in light, well-drained garden soil. They need full sun. A ground cover will help to mask the lower part of the stems.

Varieties. Bulbs in mixed colors are popularly sold at around $2.00 per dozen.

How and When to Plant. In late spring when frost is over, plant in groups of at least five, 4 in. deep and 6 in. apart. Put a little sand under each bulb.

Care and Protection. Water in dry weather. When the foliage dies down, dig up the bulbs and store them in a dry, frost-free place over winter.

TOADFLAX

DAINTY in every way, this annual (*Linaria*) is also called baby snapdragon because of the shape of the individual flowers. Blooms in many colors—crimson and gold, pink, rose and blue—are borne on thin stems. Some kinds are only 8 or 10 in. tall, while others about 18 in. high are especially fine for beds and borders. The erect plants are very free flowering and are often grown in masses in rock gardens. The delicate little blooms are nice for miniature flower arrangements. Light, well-drained soil and either full sun or slight shade are needed.

Varieties. *Fairy Bouquet* makes a dwarf mound of color only 8 to 10 in. high. *Northern Lights* is a taller grower, in mixed colors.

How and When to Plant. Seed sown in the open in spring should bloom in about eight weeks. Thin out the young plants, allowing 4 to 6 in. between them.

Care and Protection. This seed often sows itself; pull up the new plants if they appear where they are not wanted.

The delicate little toadflax is a joy to cut for toy-like flower arrangements, and it also is an excellent rock-garden subject.

A treeless neighborhood cries for help. Regardless of how smart the houses may be, streets and lawns are incomplete without the priceless benefit of trees. Shade trees, evergreens and small ornamentals may be mixed very effectively.

TREES

WITHOUT trees, your home will look and feel unfinished. Trees will contribute so much to your contentment and well-being, as well as to the beauty of your grounds, that they deserve first consideration. By locating them in the proper place and planting them first of all, you will have shade sooner and will avoid tearing up the lawn later on. You can depend on them to frame your home in beauty and dignity for many years. They will shield you from winter storms and act as air conditioners in hot weather. In short, trees are a priceless asset to a home in many ways.

To distinguish between ornamental and shade trees is impossible; obviously, the terms overlap. But for the purposes of this book, only small trees with especially noteworthy flowers or other decorative features are treated individually. (See *Birch*, *Dogwood*, *Flowering Cherry*, *Crab*, *Peach and Plum*, *Fringe Tree*, *Golden Chain Tree*, *Hawthorn*, *Holly*, *Honey Locust*, *Magnolia*, *Mountain Ash*, *Redbud* and *Silk Tree*.)

Wide-spreading maples, elms and sycamores are just as desirable for shade now as they have been for many generations, but in addition to these large trees owners of small properties should be well informed about evergreen and shade trees of smaller dimensions. Like all other plant material used around a home, the trees should be in proportion to the height and width of the house and the size of the lot. A blend of leaf-losing trees and evergreens is pleasing; when flowering shrubs and ground covers are chosen to complete the scene, a harmonious picture results.

Picking the Right Trees and the Right Location. In deciding where to plant, remember that a tree set on the west side of a house will shade it best during the heat of the day. Place a tree near a terrace or patio so that the shade will fall where you want it at the time you want it there. Don't plant too near drains and sewers, and don't plant close to the property line if your neighbor will object to the shade. Good-sized trees look better somewhat to the side instead of directly in front of the house. Consider how the tree will look at different seasons, and whether the shade will be heavy enough to prevent grass and flowers from growing underneath. Naturally, you will not want trees so large or so numerous that in a few years the house will be crouching behind them, practically hidden.

In addition to the ornamental trees mentioned above, which will furnish shade as they grow larger, there are other trees of medium size to be recommended. A number of maples with bronze or purplish foliage

(*Above*) Pin oak is a rapid grower, easy to move. Plant it where the lower branches may be allowed to follow their natural habit of sweeping toward the ground.

(*Left*) A wide-spreading Moraine® honey locust, thornless and seedless, valuable for both lawn and street planting. Grass can grow under its branches because the shade is not heavy.

are fine when carefully placed. Trees with other than green foliage should be used with restraint. Golden rain tree, with yellow flowers in summer, grows only 25 or 30 ft. tall and is strong enough to resist storms well. Another good small tree is American hornbeam. Its gray bark and orange-red fall color are of special interest. Among larger trees that do well under suburban conditions are the pin oak, ginkgo, Japanese pagoda tree and green ash.

(*Above*) An upright Japanese yew, a splendid ornamental evergreen with rich dark green foliage that is particularly beautiful when covered with the lighter green tips of new growth in spring.

(*Left*) Schwedler maple has leaves that are red when they first appear but turn green by early summer. It casts dense shade.

Yews are the most widely planted of the needled evergreens. They make splendid hedges, screens and specimen plants, and their many forms—dwarf and compact, columnar, pyramidal, vase shaped and spreading—are useful in practically every garden. Robust, long lived, hardy and healthy, they seem to answer every need. Evergreens are invaluable at every season, but foundation plantings composed entirely of them can be uninteresting. Avoid setting out an assortment of sizes and shapes; instead, mix in some leaf-losing shrubs and spring bulbs.

In Florida and California, palms of many kinds contribute graceful tropical effects. Temperature and rainfall largely determine which kinds can be grown in any given location. In general, they need plenty of water, plant food and good drainage.

Planting, Care and Protection. Trees of small size and not in full leaf are easiest to establish in a new location, although professionals can move even large trees at any season. Evergreens can be moved a little later in spring and earlier in fall than leaf-losing trees; just as new growth starts or after the hottest summer weather are the two best times. Smaller trees—with a trunk diameter of not more than 2 in.—may be moved with bare roots, but larger specimens and trees in leaf should have a ball of soil around their roots. All should be set at the same depth as in the nursery. Bare roots must always be protected from drying out, and broken ones should be trimmed away before planting. Generally the branches of deciduous trees must be pruned to compensate for the roots lost in moving. Adequate soil preparation, large planting holes and thorough watering are as essential for trees as for other plants. Wrapping the trunk with burlap or tree wrapping paper, and bracing the newly set tree for a season or longer, are good insurance against harm.

You can keep your trees in thriving condition by giving them tree food occasionally and seeing that they are never thirsty. In spring or late summer, punch holes in the ground around the tree, pour tree fertilizer into the holes (at the rate specified on the package), and replace the soil or turf. Holes should be about 15 in. deep and 2 ft. apart. Cottonseed meal is an especially good fertilizer for evergreens. When necessary, soak the soil deeply, or keep it covered with a 2 or 3-in. layer of ground corncobs, peat moss or straw to conserve the moisture. Always give your evergreens a thorough watering just before the ground freezes.

Late spring is the usual time for pruning leaf-losing trees. Dead branches should be removed as soon as they are discovered. Use sharp tools, don't leave any stubs, and cover the cuts with tree wound paint. Evergreens may be trimmed in early spring or fall. A little clipping annually is better than allowing them to become overgrown before doing any pruning.

Don't allow salty water to seep down to tree roots. Shake snow off your evergreens before it freezes and breaks branches. Evergreens in exposed locations may need a burlap screen in winter to protect them from wind

A white clump birch is not only extremely pleasing in itself but it also offers grateful relief from the mass of green prevailing on many suburban streets. (*Right*) The stage is set by a fine lawn and flowering trees.

Most palms grow where heat and rainfall are high. (*Right*) Needle palm, a low shrubby plant that likes semi-shade. (*Below*) A palm especially good for the Gulf Coast and hardy as far north as South Carolina, *Butia capitata* (or *Cocos australis*).

and burning by the sun. Plastic sprays are also available that will prevent winter damage to evergreens. Premature dropping of leaves, change of foliage color, dying branches, fungi and insects, are signs that trees are in precarious health. If you detect any of these signals, consult a reliable nurseryman. For cavity repairs and major surgery you will need a tree expert.

TRUMPET VINE

THIS vine grows wild from Pennsylvania southward and is quite hardy in most of the United States. It is a fast climber to about 30 ft. high and is grown in gardens for the showy display of trumpet-shaped, orange to scarlet flowers in midsummer. It fastens itself easily to a rough surface of any kind—brick, stone or wood—and will quickly cover a post. Trumpet vine needs full sun and can stand either dry or wet soil.

Varieties. *Campsis radicans* is the native plant with orange-scarlet flowers from July to September. *Mme. Galen*, with larger blooms of apricot-orange, is a fine variety; *Yellow Trumpet* has apricot-yellow flower clusters all summer. Plants cost $1.50 to $3.00.

How and When to Plant. Set out in early spring, where the rootlets on the stems can have a support on which they can cling.

Care and Protection. Prune in late fall or very early spring to keep this vine to the height desired and to promote blooming. Cut back some of the longest shoots.

TUBEROSES

THOSE who like the strong, sweet scent of the tuberose can grow this summer-flowering bulb outdoors without any trouble, even though it is not hardy. It is a native of Mexico, like tiger flower. The waxy white flowers, borne in 2 to 3-ft. spikes from July to frost, are particularly fragrant at night. Light, sandy soil and warm sun are essential. Planting in groups produces the best effect in the garden, preferably where perennials with decorative foliage can help to cover the rather bare stems of the tuberose.

Varieties. Both the double *Excelsior Dwarf Pearl* and the single *Mexican* are popular. A dozen bulbs cost $2.00 or $2.50.

(*Right*) Trumpet vine is not particular about soil, so long as it receives plenty of sunshine. The variety Mme. Galen, illustrated here, bears its heavy clusters of bloom for many weeks.

How and When to Plant. Set the bulbs in the open ground in late spring when all frost is over. Plant them in groups of at least three, 2 in. deep and 6 in. apart.

Care and Protection. Take up the bulbs in autumn and store them in a warm room over winter.

(*Left*) Tuberoses require well-drained soil and full sun. The double flowers of Excelsior Dwarf Pearl have waxy petals and a fragrance that is more penetrating at night.

TULIPS—in all their glory!

TULIPS—described and pictured on the following pages—are shown here in full panoply, at the crest of their beauty. This planting is dominated by the peony-flowered type, skillfully arranged in harmonious groups. In addition to having a glorious range of color, tulips are among the easiest flowers to grow.

(*Right*) Clara Butt—a Darwin tulip, like all others illustrated on these two pages—has a lovely transparent texture.

(*Left*) Rich violet The Bishop has a grayish bloom on the outside, with a blue and white base and black anthers.

TULIPS

(*See illustration, preceding page*)

WHEN Shakespeare was a young man, tulips were introduced into England. They had been brought from Turkey to Austria and other European countries, but it was in Holland that the business of growing the bulbs was developed. A national crisis resulted when wild speculation in tulip bulbs sent them to fantastically high prices. Now Holland exports millions of them every year, and in turn welcomes millions of tourists who come to see the tulip fields in bloom.

The sensation created when these bold-colored, rugged flowers were first cultivated is repeated each spring wherever they are grown. Every color imaginable is to be found. Tulips of some kind may be had over a period of about five or six weeks in the spring, from late April through May. They are the most colorful of all the spring-flowering bulbs, and fortunately they are extremely easy to bring into bloom. Full sun and well-drained soil are their two basic requirements.

Large beds of tulips are often planted in parks and near public buildings. When massed in this way, the best results come from using a large number of the same variety together. In home gardens smaller

(*Above*) Look deep inside every tulip to realize its full beauty. Eclipse has a steel-blue center edged white.

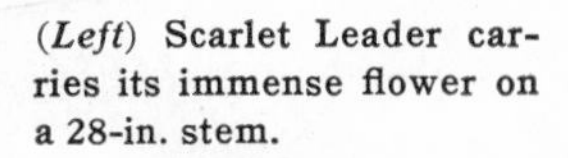

(*Left*) Scarlet Leader carries its immense flower on a 28-in. stem.

(*Right*) The deep buttercup-yellow of Golden Age is suffused with soft orange tints. Stiff stems hold the flowers upright.

(*Left*) White City is considered to be one of the finest white Darwins. It is very long lasting.

(*Right*) The Peach is all the prettier for its large white base and black anthers. It stands 28 or 30 in. high.

beds are very effective, with the colors in bands. Also in front of evergreens or against a hedge or fence where their dramatic color and form are clearly seen, groups of tulips look well. In a border they combine perfectly with pansies, primroses and forget-me-nots; shrubs and trees that bloom early complete the picture. In a stiff straight row or with too many varieties mixed in a planting, they are least pleasing. Even if only a dozen bulbs are used, it is better to concentrate than scatter them.

Tulips are choice flowers for cutting, but no more foliage than necessary should be cut from the plant. Dead flowers should be removed at once. If the stems of cut blooms are flabby, they may be wrapped in paper for their entire length and plunged in cold water for a few hours before being arranged in a bouquet.

(*Left*) La Tulipe Noire, the Black Tulip, has been grown for about seventy years. Its silky sheen and dusky color are equally admired.

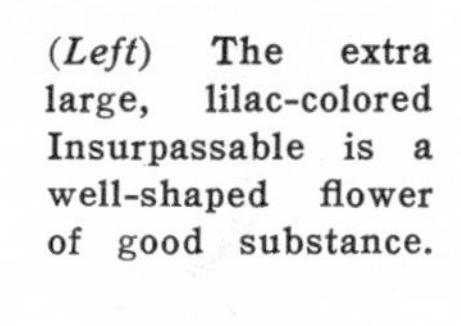

(*Left*) The extra large, lilac-colored Insurpassable is a well-shaped flower of good substance.

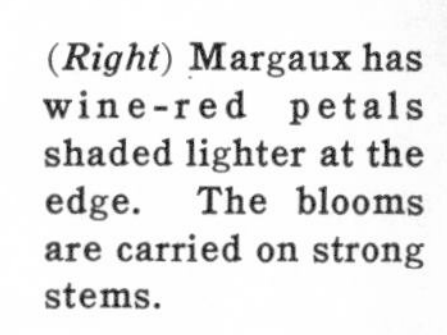

(*Right*) Margaux has wine-red petals shaded lighter at the edge. The blooms are carried on strong stems.

BREEDER tulips are shown in this group. (*Left*) Indian Chief, mahogany with yellow center. (*Above*) Lilac-flushed yellow Coridion and violet and bronze Louis XIV. (*Right*) Morocco Beauty, reddish brown with yellow base.

There are more than a dozen classes of tulips, some more distinctive than others. Best known are the Darwins with their large cups, 2 to 3-ft. stems, and dazzling solid colors at the peak of the tulip season. Breeders are more egg shaped and originally were of more subdued colors. Triumph tulips also come in midseason but are not so tall as the Darwins. Cottage varieties have more slender, light-colored blooms, and lily-flowered have flared, pointed petals. Often these classes are catalogued simply as May-flowering tulips.

Parrot tulips are probably most easily recognized of all because of their twisted,

(*Above*) Bronze Queen, a tall and graceful flower of bronzy buff shaded rose.

(*Left*) Tantalus, fawn color flushed violet, with yellow center and violet anthers.

(*Right*) Elmus is of the triumph class. The warm cherry-red flowers are deeply edged with white.

COTTAGE tulips are illustrated on this page. (*Left*) Mrs. Moon, golden yellow with reflexed petals, is always a favorite. (*Above*) Carrara has faint gray-blue lines at the base of its broad petals.

slashed petals flecked green on the outside. Double late tulips are also called peony-flowered because of their shape. Single early and double early varieties are especially good for forcing indoors and for mass planting. Rembrandts, bizarres and bybloemens are the "broken" tulips with striped and streaked flowers that were so popular in the early days in Holland. It is known now that a virus disease is responsible for the breakdown of the colors. Earliest to bloom are the species or botanical varieties. These last for many years and are much used in rock gardens. Peacock and multi-flowered tulips are among the interesting developments.

To force tulips indoors, the bulbs are planted in September or October in a potful of good garden soil to which some leaf mold and bonemeal have been added. Broken crockery is needed for drainage. Cover with an inch of soil, water, and bury outdoors in sand or peat moss where the pot will be cool and moist for eight to ten weeks. Then bring indoors to a cool place for ten days before gradually moving the pot to a sunny window.

(*Above*) Summer Glow has a large, oval flower of carmine-rose shading to orange at the petal edges. The base is bright yellow.

(*Left*) Forget-me-nots are charming companions for globular, rose-colored Inglescombe Pink tulips.

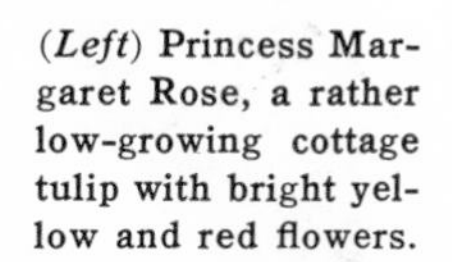

(*Left*) Princess Margaret Rose, a rather low-growing cottage tulip with bright yellow and red flowers.

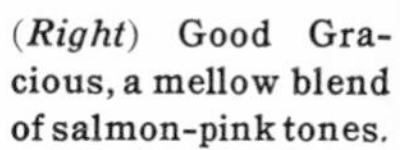

(*Right*) Good Gracious, a mellow blend of salmon-pink tones.

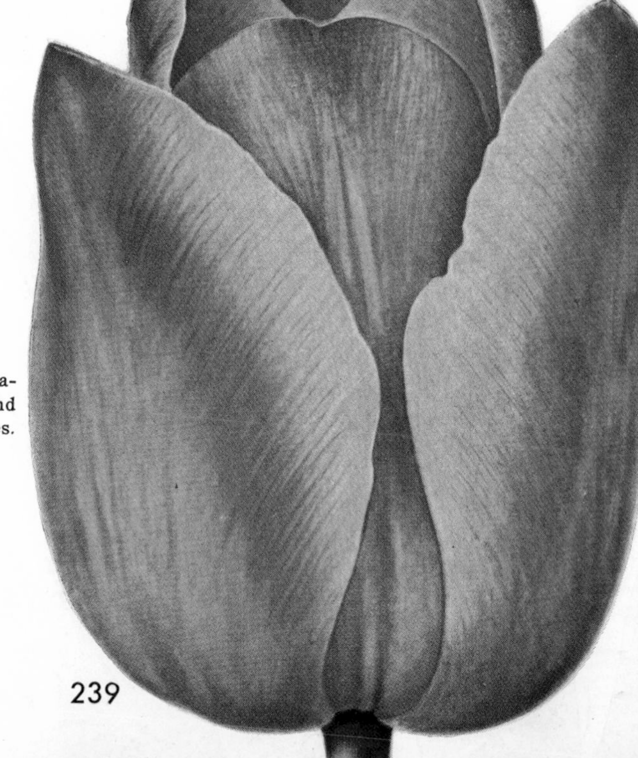

Two LILY-FLOWERED tulips are pictured here. (*Left*) Sirene has sharply pointed, curving petals of great delicacy, with a white base. (*Right*) Picotee is distinctive enough to deserve planting by itself.

Varieties. Hundreds of varieties are available. Except for the newest ones, the average price is $1.50 per dozen bulbs.

Scarlet *William Pitt* and salmon-pink *Clara Butt* are old standbys among the Darwins. Also very fine are rosy lilac *Insurpassable*, *Golden Age*, *Scarlet Leader*, and clear violet *The Bishop*. *Indian Chief* (mahogany flushed purple), bluish violet *Louis XIV*, and red-brown *Morocco Beauty* are representative of the breeders. Triumph tulips include creamy white *Blizzard* and scarlet-orange *Princess Beatrix*.

Yellow *Mrs. Moon*, white *Carrara*, and *Rosy Wings* are standard cottage varieties,

(*Right*) Multi-flowered or bunch-flowered tulips produce several blooms on one stem. Shiny red Wallflower, softest pink Rose Mist, and creamy white Mons. Mottet form the trio shown.

REMBRANDT tulips were presumably named for the great Dutch painter because they combine colors so artistically. (*Left*) Some of the colors long popular. (*Below*) American Flag, brilliant red with marbled white lines.

while *White Triumphator*, *Golden Duchess* and *Red Shine* are lily-flowered. *Fantasy* has long been a popular parrot; other good ones in this class are *Sunshine*, *Blue Parrot* and *Black Parrot*.

Among the peony-flowered or double late kinds are glossy maroon *Uncle Tom*, old-rose *Eros*, and pure white *Mount Tacoma*. Red and yellow *Keizerskroon*, golden orange *De Wet* and *Pink Beauty* among the single earlies, and *Orange Nassau* and soft rose *Murillo* among the double earlies, are fine for forcing. *Kaufmanniana* (cream marked carmine) and *Clusiana* (white and rose) are low-

PARROT tulips, as demonstrated so strikingly here, are the show-offs of the family. (*Upper Left*) Fantasy, still the best-known parrot tulip. (*Upper Right*) Black Parrot—or more accurately, maroon. (*Right*) Blue Parrot, a skillful display of heliotrope and steel-blue. (*Below Left*) Sunshine, bright and attractive. (*Lower Right*) Rosy red Therese.

PEONY-FLOWERED or double late tulips are pictured on this page. (*Left*) Orange Triumph, soft orange tipped with gold. (*Above*) Eros, a large, old-rose flower. (*Below*) Mount Tacoma, with very full blooms like peonies, is an excellent bedder.

growing botanical kinds. *Red Emperor*, of immense size, blooms with the daffodils in April.

How and When to Plant. Fertilizer is not necessary if the soil is of average richness. If the bulbs are to remain in the same spot for several years, it pays to work bonemeal into the ground before planting. Very heavy, damp soil should be lightened by the addition of sand, because good drainage is essential. In cold areas the best planting time is early October; southward the bulbs may go into the ground from late October through November. Average planting depth is 6 in. (in very light soil, 8 in. is better), and about 6 in. should be allowed between bulbs. Damage from rodents is avoided by placing the bulbs in a wire enclosure before planting them.

In the upper South, tulips are planted at least 7 in. deep, in November or December. In the lower South, bulbs must be kept in

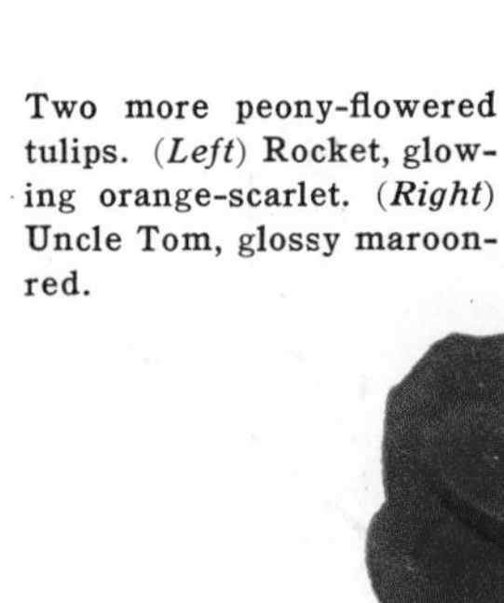

Two more peony-flowered tulips. (*Left*) Rocket, glowing orange-scarlet. (*Right*) Uncle Tom, glossy maroon-red.

SINGLE EARLY tulips, about 15 in. tall. (*Left*) De Wet, a fiery golden orange flower with sweet scent, beautiful with lavender hyacinths. (*Right*) Keizerskroon, scarlet and rich bright yellow.

cold storage for several weeks and not planted before December. As cool a location as possible should be chosen for them outdoors.

Care and Protection. Tulip bulbs may be left in the ground for several years before being taken up and replanted. Whether lifted or not, they must be allowed to ripen their leaves completely; the foliage must never be cut off before it has died down. Usually after three to five years the flowers grow smaller, and it is then necessary to dig up the bulbs after the foliage has turned yellow, dry them in the shade, and then store them in a cool dry room until fall planting time. Tulips should not be planted repeatedly in the same soil. In the very coldest climates a winter covering of leaves is advisable.

DOUBLE EARLY varieties. (*Left*) Willemsoord, carmine-red with a white edge, growing a foot tall. (*Above*) Electra, extremely double, deep carmine flowers with a satiny luster, carried on sturdy, 11-in. stems.

BOTANICAL tulips, low growing and very early blooming, for rock gardens. (*Left*) Kaufmanniana, also called the Waterlily tulip. (*Right*) Clusiana, the Lady tulip, which likes a sheltered spot.

More botanical tulips (see also the preceding page). (*Left*) Scarlet Elegance in the foreground, and Red Emperor, which is shown below in larger detail. (*Right*) Eichleri, a fine early tulip with **sharply pointed petals.**

(*Right*) Marjoletti, a very pretty creamy yellow flaked deep pink. About 15 in. tall, it makes a beautiful cut flower.

(*Left*) An intimate view of Red Emperor. Although this is the last tulip pictured here, it is generally the first to bloom. The flowers are of dazzling color and unbelievably large size.

(*Left*) In damp shady borders valerian can often be used as a background plant. Its delicious fragrance is always appreciated.

VALERIAN

THIS rangy perennial may be planted in informal parts of a property, especially where the soil is inclined to be damp. Its fragrance has earned it the name garden heliotrope. The big heads of little lavender to pink and white flowers appear in midsummer. Plants may grow 3 or 4 ft. tall, with rich green foliage. At the rear of a border of perennials, where it gets mixed sun and shade—also beside a stream—it makes a good impression.

Varieties. Besides this common tall kind (*Valeriana officinalis*), there are lower growing valerians. *Coccinea*, with fragrant, showy rose-colored flowers, is 18 to 24 in. high. Plants cost around 70c.

How and When to Plant. Spring or fall is the season to set out the plants, spacing them 2 ft. apart.

Care and Protection. The plants are inclined to spread; cut them back after they bloom, if necessary.

(*Right*) Rainbow-hued verbenas—trailing, mound shaped or taller—are anxious to go to work in any garden, even one likely to suffer from summer drought.

VERBENAS

GARDEN verbena is a plant for problem areas, giving a profuse, continuous, colorful display of bloom from June to frost even in hot, dry places. The flat heads of bloom, 2 to 3 in. in diameter, run from white through rose to scarlet, lavender and deep violet, some with a white eye. They are as nice for home decoration as outdoors. This very adaptable annual needs full sun and will even stand drought conditions. It is good for holding a bank, for covering bare spots after spring bulbs have bloomed, for massing in the front of a border, for planting in a sunny porch box or in a rock garden.

Varieties. Giant types, available in mixed or separate colors, grow about a foot high and bear large trusses of bloom. *Beauty of Oxford Hybrids*, with 3-in. flower clusters in shades of rose, *Floradale Beauty* (rosy pink), and *Lavender Glory* with creamy eye, are among the giant varieties. *Sparkle* is a newer dwarf type with white-eyed scarlet flowers. The plant is a compact mound 9 in. tall. *Crystal* is a white companion for it. These are fine for a massed effect in edgings and rock gardens. *Salmon Queen*, *Snow White*, and scarlet *Firelight* belong to the bush type growing 8 to 10 in. tall and 12 in. across. Their blooms are borne in big showy heads. There are also some perennial verbenas for cutting and bedding.

How and When to Plant. Sow seed in the open in April or May, in any well-drained soil. Or you can buy plants at small cost and set them out, 12 in. apart.

Care and Protection. Cut the plants back after they bloom the first time, to prolong their flowers until October. Don't let the flowers go to seed; keep picking them. If the foliage turns whitish, use a dust containing sulphur.

VIBURNUM

THE viburnums are one of the most important of all shrub groups. They are among the basic plants depended on for permanent garden beauty throughout the year, season after season. There are many fine members of the family, each offering something special in the way of plant growth, flowers, foliage or fruit—and most often a combination of several attractive features.

Some are almost tree-like in growth, while others are rather low, compact shrubs. Some have foliage that colors brilliantly before it falls; the kinds that lose their leaves are hardy as far north as New England. Others are semi-evergreen, or completely evergreen in the South. All are sturdy and dense growing. Many are planted especially for their red or blue or black berries, which are borne in great abundance. Flowers are white or creamy white to pinkish, in clusters of varying size and shape but always very decorative in May and early June; some are fragrant.

Viburnums give rich returns for a small outlay of labor and expense. They are not at all hard to grow in average garden soil, in the sun or in light shade. They will give satisfaction wherever used. A plant 2 to 3 ft. tall averages $2.50 to $3.50 in price. (See also *Snowball*.)

Varieties. The most fragrant kinds for the North are *Burkwood* and *Fragrant* viburnum. Both have pinkish white, very sweet-scented flowers in rounded clusters. Fragrant is a well-shaped, bushy plant, 5 to 6 ft. tall and

(*Above*) The sweet-scented, waxy blush-white flowers of Fragrant viburnum. (*Right*) The Burkwood variety. Both are lavish with their blooms at tulip time.

(*Left*) Cranberry-bush or High-bush Cranberry is the common name given this sturdy viburnum because of the cranberry-like fruits that it produces in late summer.

(*Below*) Linden viburnum, a densely rounded bush with great clusters of small red berries that remain conspicuous for many weeks in the fall.

wide, with rounded leaves and blue-black berries. Burkwood is a little taller and more vigorous, with red berries turning black. It is semi-evergreen in warm climates.

A splendid all-round viburnum is the *Cranberry-bush* or *High-bush Cranberry*. Actually, there is a European and an American form, but they are very similar. They have flat heads of white flowers, big clusters of red berries, and red fall foliage. The large, spreading plants grow to about 10 ft. tall and do well in sun or part shade. The American form is the hardier of the two.

Siebold viburnum has handsome large, dark, wrinkled leaves on a tall, vigorous, almost tree-like bush. The big, flat, creamy white flower clusters become red to blue-black fruits relished by birds. For a more dense, compact plant reaching 6 to 8 ft. in height, *Linden* viburnum is a good one to choose. Its coarsely toothed foliage turns russet-red in autumn. It has large, feathery flower clusters and small red berries. The loose bunches of orange-red fruits produced by *Tea* viburnum are very attractive. It is a slow, stately grower to 8 or 10 ft.

The horizontal branches of *Doublefile* viburnum are distinctive, with their exquisite flat bloom clusters lying spread out on top. Red fruits follow in early summer, and the foliage turns crimson in the fall. A very fine kind to plant for the birds is the *Wayfaring-tree*. Fruits are red, changing to black. The gray-green leaves become red before they drop. This is a tall grower doing well in dry soil. The blue berries of *Arrowwood* are food for the birds too, but this 15-ft., fast-growing shrub prefers wet soil. Its foliage is glossy red in the fall.

Leather-leaf viburnum has large, dark, crinkled leaves that are evergreen in the South. Growing 6 or 8 ft. tall or more, with red berries, it does well in part shade. Two other valuable evergreen kinds for the South are *Sweet* viburnum, with fragrant flowers and red to black fruits, and *Laurestinus* with creamy white flowers opening from winter through early spring, followed by blue berries. It makes a fine hedge.

How and Where to Plant. Either spring or fall is a good season to set out viburnum. Such long-lasting, decorative shrubs are especially deserving of careful planting. Be sure the soil is well prepared and the hole of generous size. Give the soil a good soaking after it is packed hard around the roots.

Care and Protection. Pruning young plants just after they bloom will encourage them to grow bushy. Older specimens need not be pruned every year, but if they get too large some of the old canes may be cut back to the ground following the blooming season.

(*Above*) Tea viburnum has especially noteworthy berries. It is an excellent shrub for any garden. (*Left*) Wright viburnum is another abundant producer of scarlet berries. The prominently veined leaves turn brilliant purplish red in autumn.

(*Left*) Boston ivy asks no help in clinging fast to any surface. In the fall the shiny foliage becomes orange and scarlet shades.

(*Right*) Give clematis a rack or trellis to climb, and keep its growing area cool. Either plant a ground cover over its feet or spread out a layer of peat moss.

VINES

VINES will do for your garden what draperies do for your windows. You can get along without them, but they add so much softness and charm that they contribute greatly to your pleasure and your comfort. Vines can be used to frame a doorway, to give shade and privacy on a porch or terrace, and to relieve sharp building lines. Sometimes a distant view that is unsightly can be blocked out by a well-placed vine. Or you may have a tree stump or a fence that you would like to hide or at least partly cover. An uninteresting blank wall, such as the side of a garage, can be turned into a beauty spot by a climbing rose.

If you want only a temporary vine, you probably will think at once of morning glories. These and other annuals like cardinal climber and cypress vine are fast growers, very satisfactory for one season. A woody vine like wisteria, on the other hand, often lives for many years and becomes as gnarled as an old tree. Some vines have extremely delicate and beautiful flowers, like clematis, while others such as Dutchman's pipe are grown primarily for their leaves. Slender sweet-pea vines need only some twine to support them, while heavier kinds may require a post or a pipe.

Vines grow in different ways, and in choosing the climber for the special place you have in view you must make certain that your support will be of the kind needed. For example, Boston ivy, Virginia creeper, trumpet vine, English ivy and evergreen bittersweet have little aerial roots or discs that act like suction cups and allow these vines to cling tightly to any surface—wood, stone or brick. But it is not advisable to use them against a wooden building because they make the wood damp and may damage it. On stone walls they are fine. Climbing hydrangea can be allowed to run up a tree trunk, but bittersweet and wisteria twine so fast that they can harm a tree.

Tendrils like little wires are used for clinging purposes by other types of vines. Madeira vine, clematis, coral vine, and cup and saucer vine are in this class. Any of them would be a possibility for a trellis or fence.

Still other vines completely twine around their support. Wisteria, one of these, is often planted where it can wrap itself around a porch pillar. Honeysuckle, silver lace vine, clock vine and Dutchman's pipe are twiners. Notice how some of them twine from left to right, and others from right to left.

In the South bougainvillea, jasmine and allamanda can be trained with handsome effect on fences and walls. (See separate listings for all the vines mentioned above.)

A vine allowed to grow unrestricted may become a tangled mass. Thin out some of the shoots, and train the runners to go where you want them. Help new shoots to find support at once, before they start to run on the ground. Tie them up, if necessary. Leave about a foot of space between a wall and the vine planted near it. If building rubble remains in the ground, dig it out and fill in with good soil before planting.

The clean dark green foliage of climbing hydrangea is set off by large white flower clusters in the summer. This is a fine hardy vine that will bloom even in the shade.

VIOLA

THESE little sisters of the pansy (which see) are extremely cheerful and informal. They are very hardy and so easy to grow that they may be used in many places. As a ground cover under shrubs, as an edging along a path, in sun or shade, and as clumps in a rock garden, violas are always welcome. One kind reseeds so freely that it is called Johnny-jump-up, for it is likely to pop up almost anywhere once it is started in a garden.

Like pansies, violas need rich moist soil. Although long hot dry summers are not to their liking, they bloom better in warm weather than pansies do.

Varieties. Some favorites are royal blue *Eileen*, creamy yellow *Vixen*, ruby-crimson *Arkwright Ruby*, *Blue Perfection*, apricot *Chantreyland*, soft lavender *John Wallmark*, and violet-blue *Jersey Gem*. Both seeds and plants are available.

How and When to Plant. Set out the plants in early spring, about 4 in. apart, and water well. Or sow seed in early spring or late summer.

Care and Protection. Pick off the flowers as they fade, so that seed does not form and stop bloom production. Cut back the plants lightly in summer, and water thoroughly in hot dry weather.

Violas give a happy-go-lucky spirit to any planting. (*Above*) John Wallmark has good-sized, lavender flowers veined deeper. (*Upper Left*) Rich violet Jersey Gem. (*Lower Left*) Apricot Queen, a fascinating shade of golden orange.

More violas. (*Above*) Normandie, a handsome burgundy-red, which with the soft yellow (*Left*) and others shown on this page forms a hardy and long-lasting ground cover.

(*Above*) **Dainty, deliciously fragrant Rosina may be grown in a rock garden or a shady border.**

VIOLETS

VIOLETS are said to be shy and shrinking, but that does not describe them at all. Individual blossoms of wild violets may appear modest; however, the plants are so durable and hardy that one type or another grows wild on every continent except South America, from the Middle East to Japan and Australia. Many of them may be cultivated successfully in semi-wild gardens and in shady spots under trees and shrubs.

The large, fragrant violets raised in greenhouses by florists have been developed from one kind of viola. They may also be grown outdoors by home gardeners willing to give them a protected place where they can be coaxed to bloom in April and May. They must have moist, well-fertilized ground and some shade, with a protective cover of leaves or straw over winter.

Varieties. Dark purple *Royal Robe*, richly scented, is a good ground cover in semi-shade; stems are up to 8 in. long. *Double Russian*, with lighter purple flowers, prefers almost full shade. *Rosina* is a lovely rose-pink variety, very sweetly fragrant, that blooms in early spring and again in the fall.

How and When to Plant. Set out the plants (available at about 75c) in early spring in well-prepared soil, and water deeply.

Care and Protection. Never let violets suffer from lack of water in summer. Pick the flowers freely.

(*Above*) **A bunch of Royal Robe violets. Impossible ever to have too many of such glossy deep violet-blue beauties!**

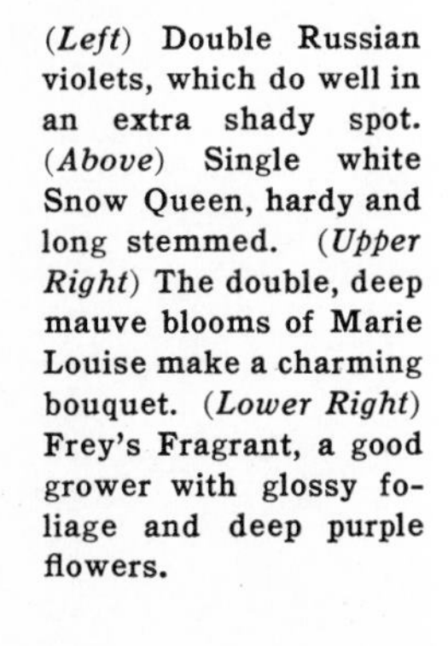

(*Left*) **Double Russian violets, which do well in an extra shady spot.** (*Above*) **Single white Snow Queen, hardy and long stemmed.** (*Upper Right*) **The double, deep mauve blooms of Marie Louise make a charming bouquet.** (*Lower Right*) **Frey's Fragrant, a good grower with glossy foliage and deep purple flowers.**

(*Left*) **Waterlilies may not be possible for you in such quantities as this, but in a smaller pool they can also give great pleasure.** (*Above*) **A close-up of a flower supported by its large flat leaves.**

WATERLILIES

A LARGE pool is not necessary for all waterlilies, nor must a large assortment be grown in order to enjoy these delightful flowers of midsummer. Even one or two in a pond or at the edge of a quiet stream contribute unusual charm to a garden during the hottest part of the summer. The pink, yellow, white or blue flowers are shown against big flat leaves resting on the surface of the water. Blooms last for many weeks. Hardy waterlilies carry their flowers directly on top of the leaves, but tropical kinds bear theirs on upright stems above the water.

Waterlilies need a sunny area in which to grow. Hardy varieties require a pool about 2 ft. deep, but tender ones need only 10 in. of water over the root of the plant.

Varieties. Among the lovely hardy varieties are yellow *Chromatella*, *Marliac White* and *Gloriosa* (early, fragrant, red). Tropical varieties that are open only in the daytime include blue *Henry Shaw*, pink *Mrs. C. W. Ward*, and large white *Mrs. George H. Pring*. *Panama-Pacific*, purple, is recommended especially for small pools. Some fine tropicals blooming at night are bright red *H. C. Haarstick*, white *Juno*, and pink *Mrs. George C. Hitchcock*. Roots cost from $3.00 up.

How and When to Plant. Secure a wooden box or tub 2 ft. square and 1 ft. deep. Fill it with good garden soil enriched with fertilizer and bonemeal. Set one waterlily root in it, cover with soil and then with an inch of gravel or sand; sink the box in the pond. Hardy waterlilies can be put out from May through August, but tender ones not until the temperature of the water is 70 degrees.

Care and Protection. Hardy waterlilies may be left in the pool all year where winters are not severe. In cold regions the box containing the plant must be stored indoors over winter in a frostproof room; the soil should be covered with peat moss to keep it moist. Or if the pool is drained for the winter, the box may be left on the bottom of the pool, but the plant should be protected by a layer of leaves or straw. Tropical waterlilies are usually replaced each season.

WEIGELA

WIDELY grown in home gardens, this shrub is considered practically foolproof. The bright, profuse flowers are its chief recommendation. Some kinds bloom in May and some a little later. The blooms come along the branches, which sweep to the ground to make a vigorous, wide-spreading specimen. Foliage remains attractive until it drops in the fall. A sunny location in any good garden soil that is not too dry will suit weigela (wye-jeel′ uh).

Varieties. *Pink* weigela, a 6 to 10-ft. plant, is popular; it has a form with variegated leaves. *Eva Rathke*, a favorite for years, has crimson flowers on a 4 to 6-ft. bush; *Bristol Ruby*, with bright ruby-red blooms in June and intermittently through the summer, is a little hardier. *Cardinal Shrub*, also a hardy kind, bears red flowers the first year planted. It can take a little shade. An 18 to 24-in. plant costs $1.00 to $2.00.

How and When to Plant. Plant in either spring or fall, in a good-sized hole. Firm the soil well about the roots, and water copiously.

Care and Protection. A layer of peat moss spread on the ground will keep it cool and damp during hot weather. Sometimes northern winters kill back the canes; if so, cut them away in early spring and let new growth come up. After the blooming season, cut back some of the older branches and any that are thin and twiggy.

(*Above*) **Bristol Ruby is a superior variety of weigela with a shapely plant that never fails to bloom.** (*Left*) **Cardinal Shrub, another excellent weigela that is extra hardy.**

WILD GARDENS

If the natural grace of many wild flowers attracts you, you will be well repaid if you devote part of your efforts to a wild garden. A woodsy area, particularly near a brook, makes a perfect setting. Here you will have a great deal of enjoyment if you provide the same growing conditions that the plants have in the wild. Your aim will be to imitate nature as nearly as possible.

Most native plants need more leaf mold and moisture and less hot sun than garden flowers. Some of the rarer kinds are rather fussy about their soil requirements. Some can be grown on the north side of a house in part shade if they are away from the drip of the eaves. Ferns are perhaps first choice for shady corners, where they provide a cool, refreshing look.

Native shrubs like pussy willow, dogwood, hemlock and mountain laurel belong in a wild garden; partridge berry makes a fine ground cover. Whatever wild flowers grow in your locality—jack in the pulpit, bluets, trillium, violets, Dutchman's breeches, hepatica, bloodroot, marsh marigold, trout lily, and many more—should succeed if you can duplicate their wild environment.

(*Above*) **This little wild plant has many common names, such as dogs-tooth violet, adders tongue and trout lily.** (*Right*) **Trillium, or wake robin. The trick in establishing all wild plants in your garden is to make them feel they have never been moved from the woods.**

If you gather native plants yourself, be sure to pick only those you are permitted by law to take, and don't be careless in digging them. Plants bought from dealers in wild flowers are more likely to succeed because they have stronger root systems.

WINDOW-BOX GARDENING

Window boxes bring gardening within reach of everyone with a window sill. If you are confined to a small apartment where your green fingers haven't a square yard of ground to work with, you can still have some flowering plants tapping at your window all during the summer. And in cold weather too the box will continue to be attractive with dwarf evergreens. Any house in the country, town or city has a more neighborly look when decorated with window boxes filled with gaily colored flowers.

Boxes may be made of metal or stone, but wood is more usual. Cypress, cedar and redwood are long lasting. They should be at least 8 in. deep and about a foot wide. Under a broad window two boxes are more easily managed than an extra-long box. Several holes in the bottom are necessary for drainage. Lay some gravel or cinders over these holes, and then an inch layer of pebbles or coarse leaves. Soil consisting of good garden loam, leaf mold and sand, with a little bonemeal added, comes next.

In selecting the plants for your window box, think of them as part of the outside decoration of your house. If yours is a red brick, you will hardly want orange or scarlet-flowered plants. But if you live in a white clapboard house, you will want to choose something bright and cheerful. When the box is shaded most of the time, foliage plants are the best choice. They need not be drab and uninteresting, for many of them, such as coleus, caladium and fancy-leaved ivy (see separate headings), have leaves that are just as colorful as flowers.

Geraniums are perhaps the most popular among flowering plants suitable for window boxes, with petunias and sweet alyssum close seconds. Others good in full sun are

(*Right*) **For a window or porch box that will receive sun for most of the day, geraniums prove a satisfactory choice. They thrive in only average soil. Salmon-colored geraniums and ageratum are a pleasing combination, or scarlet geraniums with candytuft.**

(*Left*) **Portulaca is a useful filler for sunny window boxes where a low dense carpet is wanted. Never try to combine these or other sun-loving plants with those that do best in part shade.**

(*Left*) **A window box filled with petunias is a common sight. But choose beautiful colors like this and pinch off the flowers as they wilt, so that the box is always picture-perfect, and you will truly have something special.**

(*Right*) **This Chinese wisteria vine is a patriarch that has withstood many hard winters. In late spring the long flower clusters are a spectacle.**

dwarf marigolds, portulaca, heliotrope, candytuft, periwinkle, verbena and ageratum. Cactus is another possibility for sunny window boxes. Nasturtium, morning glory, trailing lantana and English ivy are good at the edge. Pansies, wax and tuberous begonias and fuchsias will bloom in part shade. (See separate listings for all.)

Markets, garden stores and florists offer plenty of little plants in late spring that are ideal for window boxes. Be generous in using them. The plants will look better and bloom better if they are set close together. Water them every day, and occasionally give them some liquid fertilizer. If they start to get lanky, pinch them back a little.

WISTERIA

THIS long-lived, hardy vine is just as sturdy as it is decorative. In some varieties the beautiful blue, purple, pink or white flower clusters grow to an astonishing length; they are an outstanding sight in any home grounds where they are in bloom. Wisteria grows so vigorously that it must be given plenty of space. The vines are so heavy that they need the support of a strong fence, wall or arbor. Often they are planted where they can climb over a porch roof. They are twining rather than clinging. They may also be trained in tree form to make lawn specimens. The seeds are reported to be poisonous if eaten.

The kinds most often cultivated are natives of the Orient. They have been widely planted and have proved hardy in all but the northernmost states. Big old specimens with thick, twisted trunks and branches often survive even when neglected. Average garden soil will produce good results; it should not be too rich. Like other flowering plants, wisteria needs practically all-day sun for best flower production. A southern or western exposure is preferable.

Varieties. *Japanese* wisteria has extremely long flower clusters; there are pink, white and reddish varieties as well as purple and blue. *Chinese* kinds are somewhat less hardy; the bloom clusters are shorter and more compact. *Frutescens*, a native American wisteria, has still smaller clusters.

How and When to Plant. Prepare the planting hole carefully by adding some peat moss to the soil. Buy a grafted plant (at about $2.50) and set it out in early spring, at the same depth at which it was previously growing (as shown by the mark at the base). Firm the soil well, and water thoroughly.

Care and Protection. A balanced fertilizer or bonemeal is beneficial if given in very late autumn after the leaves have dropped. Pruning time is early summer. Cut back the newest shoots as they grow, leaving only three or four buds. If wisteria does not bloom well, harder pruning is necessary. In addition, in very early spring a trench may be dug around the base of the plant, several feet away from the trunk, the roots being cut with the spade in the process. A feeding of bonemeal should follow.

YARROW

LIKE rock cress, yarrow is a plant for thankless spots with dry, sandy soil full of stones. It does best without fertilizer, in a location where it receives all-day sun. It can stand both drought and neglect. This is a hardy perennial (*Achillea*, botanically) with soft foliage, fine and fern-like, and heads of small flowers carried upright in summer. There are kinds as much as 3 or 4 ft. tall, which are good at the back of a border, as well as low ones for the rock garden. They cost 50c to $1.00.

Varieties. *The Pearl* has been commonly planted for years. It has clusters of dainty white flowers from June to September on a 15 to 20-in. plant. *Crimson Beauty* is a fine rosy crimson blooming all summer. *Gold Plate* has 6-in. heads of bright yellow flowers on sturdy stems. It grows 3 to 4 ft. tall. With *Coronation Gold* (smaller yellow clusters and grayish foliage), it is a good cut flower. *Parker's Variety*, about 2 ft. high, is still another golden yellow with flower heads that are easily dried for winter decoration. Especially successful in hot dry locations is *Taygetea*. It has flat heads of pale yellow bloom from June to August on 18-in. stems. In a rock garden *Tomentosa* makes a compact mat of woolly gray-green, with yellow flowers.

How and When to Plant. Add lime if necessary, to make the soil sweet. Plant in fall or early spring, allowing 10 in. of space to a plant.

Care and Protection. Cut back the stems after they bloom. In spring dig up the tall-growing kinds, divide into smaller sections, and replant.

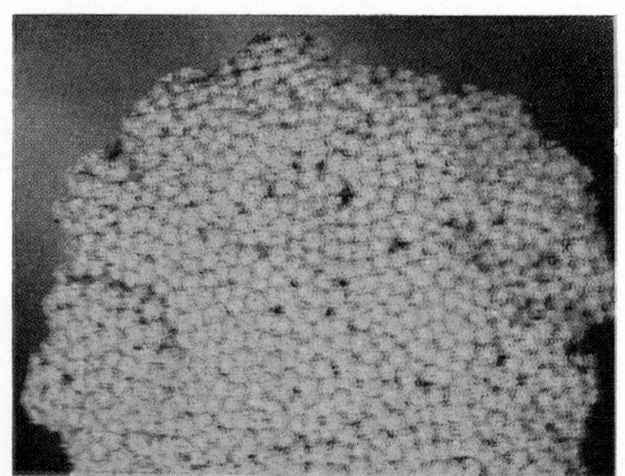

(*Above*) **The Pearl is an old-time variety of yarrow bearing a profusion of little double white flowers on strong stems.** (*Left*) **Gold Plate has flower clusters 6 in. broad, which are easily dried if desired.**

(*Left*) Here zinnias are used like a dense-growing shrub, to form a border along a curving driveway. In the latter half of summer they make a cheerful display.

(*Below*) Pink Lady, of the California Giant type. This soft bicolor has a warm pink center merging into buff at the petal edges.

ZINNIAS

IT is safe to say that everyone knows zinnias. Like bread and milk, they are a staple item, and just as indispensable. Nothing beats them for a dependable riot of color in the garden all through hot weather and for countless, effortless bowlfuls for indoors. Easy to grow from seed, these are the beginning gardener's standby. And with new varieties being introduced every year, it is impossible for anyone to become bored with the possibilities they offer.

Zinnias grow quickly and bloom from midsummer to frost. When many other plants are listless in the heat of summer, zinnias do their best. They are coarse plants—many of them massive—with tough foliage and stiff stems. Some grow as high as 3 ft., but others are much lower. Flowers, too, vary from immense 5 or 6-in. heads to dainty little buttons. Whatever your need, there's a zinnia to fill it. Both in the garden and in bouquets it is important to combine zinnias with other self-reliant, bolder flowers rather than fragile ones.

Varieties. Seedsmen put out so many varieties of zinnia that it is hard to keep up with them. New types and new colors within the older types are a continuing source of

Dahlia-flowered zinnias are shown here in three separate colors. (*Left*) Lavender. (*Upper Right*) Purple. (*Right*) Rose. The huge, showy blooms, so symmetrical and lasting, are long-time favorites in large beds and borders.

Cactus-flowered zinnias are tall growers with blooms 4 or 5 in. broad. The tousled petals have an attractively informal air. (*Left*) Blaze, a combination of flaming red and orange, is a striking sight both in a border and in a bouquet. Plants grow 2½ ft. high. (*Right*) Merry-Go-Round is a razzle-dazzle of sharply contrasting colors. Each flower is tipped or edged in a different shade. This is lower in growth—to about 2 ft.—but very full and bushy.

interest. *Dahlia-flowered* and *California Giant* zinnias are two of the oldest, tallest and largest flowered kinds. They grow 3 ft. high and have huge blooms up to 5 or 6 in. across. California Giants are flatter and looser in form than the thick Dahlia-flowered. A newer type among the tall zinnias is the *Cactus-flowered.* Reaching 3 ft. high, this has informal flowers with petals curled, fluted, quilled and interlaced in a bewildering way. *New Century* is another novelty, with 6-in. flowers on a 2½-ft. plant. *Ortho Polka* and *Peppermint Stick* have variegated and striped blooms.

Pumila or *Cut-and-Come-Again* is a medium-sized plant with medium-sized flowers. It blooms early and is a long-time favorite.

For gardens too restricted or for tastes running to smaller flowers, there are the dwarf zinnias, all of them wonderful for edgings and borders and small arrangements. These include the *Lilliput* or *Pompon* with

(*Right*) A most harmonious arrangement of cactus-flowered zinnias in a pottery jug that is appropriately sturdy. The thick, stiff stems and bold colors of zinnias look best in simple, undecorated containers.

(*Below*) Cupid zinnias, with inch-wide button flowers on a foot-high plant, are useful for edging borders.

The new Ortho Polka zinnia produces very broad flowers. All are fully double, and about three-fourths of them are arrayed in striped or dotted colors. Even on one plant the blooms will be varied. The height is about 3 ft.

compact, 1½-in. flowers, *Cupid* with button flowers on a 12-in. plant, *Persian Carpet* with double and semi-double, variegated blooms on a mound-like plant, and *Linearis* with single flowers.

How and When to Plant. Just sow the seed outdoors when settled warm weather has come to stay. Thin out the plants to 12 to 15 in. apart for the tallest kinds and 8 to 10 in. for the lower ones. They are very easy to grow from seed, but are also readily available as little plants at your local store. Zinnias deserve a fairly good soil, although they are not demanding. Give them full sun, and don't let them go thirsty.

Care and Protection. No troubles to speak of. Possibly a little mildew, in which case dusting with sulphur should help. Cut the flowers freely.

(*Left*) Poly-Pink has a compact, very vigorous plant continuously covered with these 4-in. flowers of clear pink suffused salmon. It starts to bloom early.

(*Below*) For a novelty, plant Peppermint Stick. Both plants and flowers are of moderate size. Bloom continues until frost if the flowers are cut off as they fade.

(*Left*) Treasure Island is a good mixture of bold, bright colors. The cactus - flowered blooms, 6 to 7 in. in diameter, are borne all summer long on 3-ft. plants.

(*Above*) Pumila or Cut-and-Come-Again zinnias are dome-shaped flowers midway in size between giant and dwarf types.

The Lilliput zinnias, growing 12 to 18 in. tall, are perfect edgers and cut flowers. (*Left*) A mixture of colors. (*Below*) Salmon Glow, a lovely shade, popular for cutting.

(*Left*) Persian Carpet zinnias are reminiscent of little dahlias, with their neat, miniature blooms. The pointed petals are bordered with a pleasing contrasting color. Plants are 12 to 15 in. high. They are easy to grow and eager to bloom.

(*Above*) The unassuming but hard-working Linearis zinnias are healthy, 10-in. plants with long, narrow foliage and daisy-like flowers from early summer on.